Voices in American Archaeology

Edited by Wendy Ashmore, Dorothy T. Lippert, and Barbara J. Mills

SOCIETY FOR AMERICAN ARCHAEOLOGY
The SAA Press

The Society for American Archaeology, Washington, D.C. 20002
Copyright © 2010 by the Society for American Archaeology
All rights reserved. Published 2010
Printed in the United States of America

Printed on acid-free paper

Library of Congress Cataloging-in-Publication Data

Voices in American archaeology / edited by Wendy Ashmore, Dorothy Lippert, and Barbara J. Mills.
   p. cm.
 Includes bibliographical references and index.
 ISBN 978-0-932839-39-8 (alk. paper)
 1. Archaeology--Research--United States. 2. Archaeology--Social aspects--United States. 3. Archaeologists--United States. I. Ashmore, Wendy, 1948- II. Lippert, Dorothy Thompson, 1967- III. Mills, Barbara J., 1955-
 CC95.V65 2010
 930.1072--dc22   2010002516

Contents

1. Introduction — 1
   Wendy Ashmore, Dorothy T. Lippert, and Barbara J. Mills

2. Re-Visioning Archaeology, or, the Future Matters as Much as the Past — 8
   Margaret W. Conkey

3. Professional Societies and the Lives of American Archaeologists — 27
   James E. Snead and Jeremy A. Sabloff

4. Consultation and Collaboration with Descendant Communities — 48
   Stephen W. Silliman and T. J. Ferguson

5. Crossing Boundaries and Academic Fair Trade — 73
   José Luis Lanata and Robert D. Drennan

6. Inequality and Archaeology — 94
   Maria Franklin and Robert Paynter

7. In the Public Interest: Creating a More Activist, Civically Engaged Archaeology — 131
   Barbara J. Little and Larry J. Zimmerman

CONTENTS

8. Archaeology and Historic Preservation Law:
   Twenty-Five Years of Interesting Times 160
   Lynne Sebastian

9. NAGPRA and Indigenous Peoples: The Social Context and
   Controversies, and the Transformation of American
   Archaeology 178
   Michael Wilcox

10. Changing Theoretical Directions in American Archaeology 193
    Timothy R. Pauketat and Lynn Meskell

11. Interdisciplinary Studies in Archaeology 220
    Melinda Zeder, Jane Buikstra, and Sander van der Leeuw

12. Communicating Archaeology in the 21st Century 270
    Mitchell Allen and Rosemary A. Joyce

13. Trends in Employment and Training in American
    Archaeology 291
    Jeffrey H. Altschul and Thomas C. Patterson

14. *Politicae et Publicae*: Aspects of Influence 317
    Joe E. Watkins

About the Contributors 324

Index 330

1
Introduction

WENDY ASHMORE, DOROTHY T. LIPPERT, *and* BARBARA J. MILLS

By its 50th anniversary, the Society for American Archaeology had grown to become one of the world's premier professional archaeological bodies (Meltzer et al. 1986:7). As enduring ways to celebrate American archaeology and the Society at its half-century,[1] nearly 40 prominent archaeologists contributed critical assessments of the Society's history, accomplishments, future prospects, and the status of understanding on key research issues. Many essays were commissioned for a theme issue of *American Antiquity* (Watson 1985). Others were presented at the SAA meeting in Denver marking the 50th anniversary; papers from sessions there, on "The History and State of the Art of American Archaeology" and "Views of the Development of American Archaeology," were the nucleus for the volume *American Archaeology, Past and Future* (Meltzer et al. 1986:8). These works offer invaluable insights into the Society and American archaeology at that point in their development. Much had been accomplished and the many authors celebrated the different achievements of the Society at the same time that they observed how much was yet to be done. Copies of both the volume and the journal issue are appropriately dog-eared from continuing consultation.

Not surprisingly, as the Society's 75th Anniversary approached, the task force charged with marking this juncture agreed that a new volume was warranted. Task force members also agreed unanimously that it would not be a reprise of that for the 50th Anniversary. Too much had changed, in American archaeology and in the Society, and acknowledging that change—as well as pointing out prospects for the future—required different kinds of topics with a new range of authors. While research continues to be a central focus of the Society and its members, sometimes subtle, sometimes dramatic, and many times significant shifts in theoretical, ethical, and legal environments have shaped how that research is conducted today—by whom, for whom, and about what. The volume before you was commissioned to consider such changes, the factors behind them, and their implications for the future of American archaeology and the SAA.

The volume's title, *Voices in American Archaeology,* expresses the sense that much in the aforementioned shifts has involved the changing nature of participants in the research, and the diversity of views those participants hold about how and why we undertake archaeology. We editors identified ten topics as domains in which these changes are especially evident. Certainly those choices are far from exhausting the possibilities. The selections focus on the proactive *practices* of the Society and its members, and particularly on developments within the last quarter century. Further, recognizing the diverse standpoints of participants in American archaeology, we proposed that multiple voices partner in writing about each of those select topics. We invited collaboration among authors who had not previously written together, and whose vantages we anticipated would be mutually complementary. We also invited a statement of vision about the Society from Margaret Conkey, its President in its 75th year, and a closing commentary by Joe Watkins. As editors, we have found the result electrifying. New articulations have been forged, different vantage points acknowledged. Individual readers will find agreement with some chapters, and doubtless, disagreement with others. We trust that the range of voices discussing these and other issues will continue to grow.

Voices in American Archaeology

Labeling the current volume a snapshot of archaeology and the SAA at 75 would be a cliché. We nonetheless believe it important to recall that the topics and views highlighted here are historically contingent choices, emblematic of the times. As a reminder, in 1985 processual archaeology was the strongly prevailing theoretical framework in American archaeology. The Native American Graves Protection and Repatriation Act (NAGPRA) was under heated consideration, but not yet legal fact. Cultural Resource Management (CRM) was firmly established as archaeological employment outside of the academy, but still new to many archaeologists, and few colleges and universities incorporated it into their curriculum. Concern for the role of archeology in issues of social justice was on the rise.

Archaeological matters commonplace or mainstream at the SAA's 50th Anniversary have seen challenges and experienced transformative change in the last quarter century. Reflections on the discipline appear regularly, in journals, symposia, books, and web exchanges (e.g., Fagan 1989; Feinman and Price 2001; Kehoe 1998; Little 2002; Meskell and Preucel 2004; Patterson 2003; Sabloff 2008; Watkins 2000). But rarely is their focus the particular nexus of American archaeology and the SAA. Taking that context as their key, authors in this volume attend to some of today's most noteworthy issues, continuing or new. Their charge was situating the specific topics within social, intellectual, and other contexts from which their significance arises, critically assessing pertinent accomplishments (and problems), and offering programmatic remarks for the future.

One theme that emerges strongly is the opening up of possibilities, in theory and practices of archaeology. Perhaps not surprisingly, in light of our invitation, authors refer most often to research and research participants within the New World, and particularly to contexts within the United States. The overall scope, however, is decidedly worldwide: not only do chapter contents repeatedly demonstrate that *American archaeology* extends from the Arctic south to Tierra del Fuego, but authors also frequently acknowledge as well the shared benefits from many *American archaeologists'* engagements with and contributions in the Old World. Indeed, many chapters substantiate the importance of articulating local and global experiences. In making these and other arguments, authors draw from cases that reflect dramatic shifts in research bases during the last quarter century, from predominantly academic to increasingly CRM and heritage milieus. Let us now introduce briefly the chapters that follow.

Conkey opens discussion by asking what might be envisioned for archaeology and the SAA at this juncture—and why. Situating our collective reflections within recent such endeavors in other fields, she urges strongly that no one view of archaeology suffices. Rather, multivocality and distributed practices strengthen the discipline while promoting constant re-evaluation and reflection. More specifically, while expressing continued concerns about conservation and preservation of archaeological heritage, Conkey finds strong encouragement from archaeologists' increasingly shared commitment, both to that material heritage and to its diverse stakeholder heirs.

In their historical overview of the Society, Snead and Sabloff critically discuss the contexts out of which the SAA emerged, outlining key shifts in the Society's professional focus, constituency, and mission statement since the 1980s. They highlight tensions among social and professional responsibilities, intellectual goals, and policy roles as ongoing challenges where the Society will continue to seek balance.

In discussing collaboration between archaeologists and descendant communities, Silliman and Ferguson examine ethical, theoretical, and methodological dimensions of archaeological collaboration. They remind us that collaboration takes quite divergent forms, and urge continued exploration of the possibilities and ramifications.

Asked to consider "erasing boundaries" in American archaeology, Lanata and Drennan review thoughtfully a multiplicity of boundaries affecting communication and collaboration. Drawing from experience across the Americas and in China, they focus on boundaries that affect academic fair trade. By offering specific programmatic suggestions for crossing those boundaries, they outline avenues for enhancing academic fair trade in the twenty-first century.

Franklin and Paynter remark that, while explicit concern with social inequalities in archaeology was evident in the 1980s, its expression at that time was at best seen as incipient. Although attention to how race, class, ethnicity, and gender shape archaeological questions—and archaeological practice—has both expanded and grown more critical, the issues raised are far from resolved.

Considering archaeology in the public interest, Little and Zimmerman trace historical articulations of American archaeologists with varied publics. They argue that archaeology's value lies precisely in its potential for engaging varied publics, with capacities to address questions with specific local reference, as well as global issues of justice and human rights.

In mutually complementary chapters, Sebastian and Wilcox review key legislative changes and their impact on archaeology in the U.S. Both remark that no one envisioned the magnitude or changes the legislation has brought to pass.

Sebastian examines a quarter-century of developments related to the National Historic Preservation Act (NHPA), especially Section 106 and its regulation. With insightful expertise, she discusses how the Section 106 process has been (and continues to be) pushed and pulled in new directions.

INTRODUCTION

She remarks, as well, on the impact of NAGPRA on CRM as distinct from academic (non-CRM) archaeology.

Wilcox reviews NAGPRA in depth. Observing the centrality of recognizing Native Americans as stakeholders in the archaeological record in the last quarter century, Wilcox analyzes intently how NAGPRA's passage and implementation have both affected and refracted changing relations between archaeology and indigenous peoples.

Critically assessing trends of theory informing American archaeology, Pauketat and Meskell argue that divisive epistemic debates of recent decades increasingly give way to productive rapprochement, offering case applications from across the Americas and beyond. Prominent in their view are approaches that foreground history and landscapes, materialilty, agency, and identities. Like many other volume contributors, Pauketat and Meskell stress how articulation with global-historical issues, descendant communities, and indigenous concerns shape archaeological theory and practice.

Zeder, Buikstra, and van der Leeuw demonstrate the interpretive strength of interdisciplinary research in which American archaeologists are involved. Dramatic growth in interdisciplinary alliances is undeniable, and as they argue, promises expanding interpretive reward, with insights about the human past—and future. Moreover, while much interdisciplinary research addresses long-standing "big questions" about the human past with increasing precision, many applications simultaneously contribute to social, economic, political, medical, and other issues affecting people today.

Communicating archaeological ideas clearly to multiple publics has bedeviled archaeologists schooled in technical language and traditional publishing outlets. With prose infused with wit and zest, Allen and Joyce both critique current practices and offer thoughtful solutions for enhancing our abilities.

Writing about the contours of employment opportunities in American archaeology (especially those that are U.S.-based), Altschul and Patterson discuss complex structural and economic realities and prospects. They emphasize, concretely, the changes needed in training for those pursuing archaeological careers in light of the dramatic needs for applied archaeologists in the U.S. and abroad.

In his concluding commentary, Watkins considers select, intersecting dimensions of archaeology and archaeological issues. Echoing themes in preceding chapters, his perceptive remarks center on archaeologists' effectively "coming to grips" with politics and the public—and the increasing diversity of what is understood by each of those terms.

American Archaeology and the SAA at 100?

If any kind of consensus can be recognized among the contributors to this volume, it would combine two themes. One is a sense of how deeply archaeology and its practice articulate with social, economic, and political milieus, and from the local to global scales. The other theme is a conviction that much is to be done in the years ahead. Indeed, the scope of this volume includes only a selection of core matters on archaeologists' minds today, let alone all possible topics of concern. Authors herein note areas requiring consideration, from critical conservation to curriculum development. Like the authors writing at the 50th anniversary, those here express concerns for the future, most commonly tempered by optimism about the collective potentials for American archaeology and the SAA. Just as those writing 25 years ago might not have foreseen that more than half of the Society's members would be employed outside of academia, or that there would be dozens of Tribal Historic Preservation Officers, we may not be able to foresee exactly where and how our members will be situated 25 years hence. What we do know is that archaeology continues to hold the imagination of our many publics, that there will be exciting new developments in methods of recovery and analysis, and that the preservation and protection of archaeological sites is no longer mandated at just the federal level. We also know that the newest cohorts of professional archaeologists are becoming well versed in the ethical and intellectual challenges of our discipline. We look forward to what they will write at the time of the Society's 100th anniversary.

Acknowledgments. We thank the SAA for commissioning an anniversary volume, and people on both the Task Force and the SAA Press for encouraging the approach taken. From the book's inception, Task Force members offered helpful critique as well as encouragement: David Browman, Don Fowler, Lisa LeCount, Linda Manzanilla, Bruce Smith, and co-chairs, James Snead and Jeremy Sabloff. Paul Minnis and The SAA Press Editorial Board not only officially accepted the manuscript but also provided critical counsel. We are grateful to the two anonymous reviewers for the insights in their discerning assessments.

We are deeply grateful to the volume's contributors for having crafted such thoughtful remarks. They took on not only the topics we requested of them, but also our collaborative arrangements, and the schedule for completion in time for the 75th Anniversary.

At the SAA, Tobi Brimsek and John Neikirk expertly shepherded the project through to publication. They exhorted (and supported!) us all with an extraordinary mix of enthusiasm and patient calm. Kieran Daly graciously designed the cover.

References Cited

Fagan, Brian (editor)
   1989 Archaeology in the 21st Century. *Archaeology* 42(1)(whole issue).

Feinman, Gary M., and T. Douglas Price (editors)
   2001 *Archaeology at the Millennium: A Sourcebook*. Kluwer Academic/Plenum Publishers, New York.

Kehoe, Alice Beck
   1998 *The Land of Prehistory: A Critical History of American Archaeology*. Routledge, New York.

Little, Barbara J. (editor)
   2002 *Public Benefits of Archaeology*. University Press of Florida, Gainesville.

Meltzer, David J., Don D. Fowler, and Jeremy A. Sabloff (editors)
   1986 Editors' Introduction. In *American Archaeology Past and Future: A Celebration of the Society for American Archaeology, 1935–1985*, edited by David J. Meltzer, Don D. Fowler, and Jeremy A. Sabloff, pp. 7–19. Smithsonian Institution Press, Washington, D.C.

Meskell, Lynn M., and Robert W. Preucel (editors)
   2004 *A Companion to Social Archaeology*. Blackwell, Malden, Massachusetts.

Patterson, Thomas C.
   2003 *Marx's Ghost: Conversations with Archaeologists*. Berg, Oxford.

Sabloff, Jeremy A.
   2008 *Archaeology Matters: Action Archaeology in the Modern World*. Left Coast Press, Walnut Creek, California.

Watkins, Joe
   2000 *Indigenous Archaeology: American Indian Values and Scientific Practice*. AltaMira Press, Walnut Creek, California.

Watson, Patty Jo (editor)
   1985 *American Antiquity* 50(2)(whole issue).

Note

1. The SAA was founded in December of 1934, but the Society celebrates the anniversary of the first meeting and the first publication of *American Antiquity*, which were both in 1935.

2

Re-Visioning Archaeology, Or, The Future Matters As Much As the Past

MARGARET W. CONKEY

It's much easier to speculate about the future than to truly understand the past [Anonymous].

We are responsible for the world in which we live not because it is an arbitrary construction of our choosing, but because it is sedimented out of particular practices that we have a role in shaping [Barad 1998:102].

In this chapter, I intend to explore what it might mean to re-vision archaeology at this moment of the 75th anniversary of the Society for American Archaeology. Are we at a real moment of reflection or one constructed by the anniversary? Does archaeology need to sit down and take stock of itself or are we "on track"? Or, rather, as I believe, should we always be charting our futures, thinking ahead, being reflexive, adjusting, and reshaping? While I do not intend to answer these questions systematically, I am sure that historians of science are interested in why certain moments bring forth explicit engagements, and engagements of a specific kind and nature, with the state of affairs or the discipline of the discipline. In this chapter, then, I would like to do the following: first, some thoughts on the "vision thing" and its many dimensions; then some specifics—what the voices in this volume say to us, and what we might want to foreground in our sights; and lastly, some thoughts on how to sustain shared sensibilities and social belonging as a key to our professional future.

On "Visioning"

When I first thought about a consideration not just of our vision for the future, but for a re-visioning of archaeology, I was not too surprised to find that we would not be alone, given the calls for re-visioning that are extant in the literature: for *Revisioning Psychology* (Hillman 1975); for *Revisioning History: Film and the Construction of a New Past* (Rosenstone 1994); for *Revisioning Women, Health and Healing: Feminist, Cultural and Technoscientific Perspectives* (Clarke and Olesen 1999); for Revisioning Art History through the book series *A Ver: Revisioning Art History* (UCLA Chicano Studies Research Center n.d.); or for *Revisioning Gender* (Ferree et al. 1999). Some of these are attempts at revising a field or a subject (e.g., *Revisioning Gender*) and others are about developing a new vision of practice, one that may or may not involve or rest upon a re-visioning and rewriting of the assumptions and subject matter at hand.

But the "vision" metaphor is itself interesting, since it has many possible variants and a singular role in Western epistemologies and ontologies (e.g., Jay and Brennan 1996 among others). Many of us, especially as we pass the age of 45, need glasses, and indeed most such programmatic "visions" are often like a pair of glasses that structure and focus what we "see." But there are also impaired visions, blind spots, and optical illusions. In one of my own fields of interest, feminist theory, there is the very interesting suggestion by Burton (2000) that in much scholarship that attempts to envision and "see" what has been left out, ignored, or suppressed (and there is much exciting work in archaeology on this, and not just with the women of the past), we sometimes "see" things in specific historical terms of our own, and our visions are more optical illusions than more approximated realities of the historical situations at hand. Burton's critique of both "voice" and "visibility" (in feminist historiography) suggests indeed that visions and making visible often reproduce hegemonic norms. So as we tread into the domain of re-visioning our discipline and our professional organizations, we must do so with caution and a critical stance so as to guard against such optical illusions. And, in retrospect, we can surely recognize now some of the more obvious "blind spots" of an archaeology that many of us practiced without realizing them (e.g., Franklin and Paynter, this volume, and references therein), and that are often still with us.

Another dimension to "vision" is disciplinary vision, or what Goodwin (1994) calls "professional vision": how do practitioners learn to see those phenomena that constitute the objects of their profession? His ethnomethodological work focuses on those social and material interactions through which this can happen. The phenomena that are our objects (e.g., subsistence systems, peer-polity relations, trade networks, ritual acts) are not pre-existing but, as Suchman would suggest (e.g., 2005:3), "have been constituted as disciplinarily relevant through occasioned performances of competent seeing—not 'seeing' as a narrow or merely 'scopic' or 'perceptual' event, but multi-sensory embodiments." How many of what we take for granted as things or processes that we come to "see" are themselves "optical illusions"? Why might any one archaeologist insist that we can "see" a subsistence system, but not "see" gender relations?

Intriguingly, Goodwin actually uses archaeology as a prime example for his broader discussion of professional visions. To him, archaeological knowledge is generated from and by relations between particular culturally and historically constituted practices and their associated materials and tools: "it is out of those relations, quite literally, that the objects of archaeological knowledge and the identity of the competent archaeologist are co-constructed" (Franklin and Paynter, this volume; Goodwin 1994; Suchman 2005:30). His specific example is nowhere near as lofty as features/characteristics of sociocultural systems (such as peer-polity relations); it is the uses of the Munsell soil color chart—but nonetheless his points and insights are applicable to other phenomena that we have co-constructed as see-able, and as part of our archaeological vision. What is striking here is that the topics for our 2010 voices in this volume are things not widely "seen" 25 years ago and therefore not widely spoken of or heard. What our archaeological realities are, or may be, are, after all, "sedimented out of the process of making the world intelligible through certain practices and not others" (Barad 1998:105).

Twenty and Twenty-five Years Ago, and Moving Forward...

For archaeologists who are perhaps more often looking in the rearview window of history, just how well might we be able to look forward, to not only "see" what might lie ahead but also ask explicitly what do we *want* to lie ahead and then seek out how to get us there? That the chapters in this volume are as much about what we *want* to lie before us and are doing about it than about some imagined outgrowth of the current state of things is a real testimony to the editors who conceptualized this and to the authors, often working with partners of different perspectives and positions. Usually predictive scenarios for the discipline or for our areas of inquiry are often more "wishful thinking" exercises, but a systematic attempt to engage various archaeologists in just such an exercise was carried out in the 1989 publication of a special edition of the journal *Archaeology* in which ten articles were commissioned to predict the issues of certain topics or fields in the year 2050. This was a somewhat different enterprise than the publications commissioned for the 50th anniversary of the SAA (e.g., Meltzer et al. 1986; Watson 1985), which are discussed in several chapters in this volume (Franklin and Paynter; Snead and Sabloff). Since we are now 20 years from that 1989 *Archaeology* publication (but 40+ years from their target date of 2050), it is interesting to look at a few aspects of what was said and predicted. Not surprisingly, the table of contents of that special issue bears little similarity to the table of contents of this SAA volume, which is explicitly more about "voices" than "visions." Understandably, that 1989 issue is more international/global in scope (e.g., including classical archaeology) and on the "grand themes" of world archaeology—early "man," peopling the globe by modern humans, the transitions from hunter to farmer, the rise of civilizations. Here it is relevant to note that many of these same themes characterized the volume honoring the 50th anniversary of the SAA (Meltzer et al. 1986).

But several of the chapters in the special issue of *Archaeology* in 1989 attest broader disciplinary-wide issues that engage us more today and into the future: for example, preservation, ecotourism, and the "archaeologies of people without history." The editor of that special edition of *Archaeology*, Brian Fagan, predicted that the twenty-first century would be "the century of the small object"; "minutiae is the word" (1989:24). Most articles spoke enthusiastically of the technologies that would be available. Archaeology comes across as being propelled forward by all sorts of technological advances that would render actual excavations less frequent or central, with increasing use of sub-surface imaging technologies, as well as becoming ever more deeply forensic, with archaeo-chemistry and material science methods and techniques doing most of the analytical work. Most articles envision archaeology as an increasingly humanistic science, while only one expresses concern that if archaeology "continues along its humanistic course," it will "be reduced to an arcane academic endeavor" (Dunnell 1989:105).

Remember, of course, that in 1988 when these articles were written, NAGPRA was not yet enacted, the new SAA Ethical Principles had not been developed, computer use in the field or analysis was only emergent, feminist and other politically engaged archaeologies were also only emergent, following key "wake up" articles such as those by Trigger (1984), Conkey and Spector (1984), and others. But it is no coincidence that in the 1989 *Archaeology* and in the 1986 SAA 50th anniversary publication, only one or two articles address broader topics related not to the "human career" and its archaeological manifestations, but to conservation and preservation (Fowler 1986; Knudson 1986, 1989) and relationships with communities and indigenous peoples (McIntosh et al. 1989). In fact, Knudson's prediction for what we need to foreground to reach 2050 as an intact discipline has already come to pass in many ways:

> We scholars have the responsibility to halt the destruction of our public archaeological heritage, and we must make our archaeological research and results available in lay language and relevant to our ever-changing society. We also have to take ethical positions about the cultures whose sites we are disturbing and studying [1989:106].

I think Knudson will be greatly relieved to read today's archaeological voices on some of these issues, in this volume. That there is even wider interest in making public and socially engaged scholarship more central, rewarded, and validated (e.g., Cantor and Lavine 2006) reminds us that archaeology is not outside wider cultural contexts from which we should both take and give.

And yet, what might the predicted (hoped for?) invention and application of all sorts of new technique and technologies "do" to the archaeological process and practice? What might they do to the kinds of phenomena that archaeologists might "see" and to an understanding of the ways in which the sociomaterial relations of archaeological practice and subsequent interpretation might be reconfigured? Many studies of medical practices and technologies have suggested that these innovations and technologies often show how the capacity for action is relational, dynamic, and collective, rather than inherent in specific (new) elements or tools (e.g., Aanestad 2003). These studies, as reported by Suchman (2005:4), "re-specify agency from a capacity intrinsic to singular actors to *an effect* of practices that are multiply distributed and contingently enacted across humans and things."

We should be just as ambivalent about new technoscientific developments and applications in and for archaeology: there are always possibilities for new and expansive insights and thus reconfigurations of "what we know," but at the same time, these can threaten the reassuring ground of familiar categories on which our experiences of relationship, knowing and being known, depend—and perhaps have done so, in the history of archaeology (see Pauketat and Meskell, this volume, on all sorts of new and reconfigured topics of archaeological interest that are understandably obscure or befuddling to some archaeologists). Furthermore, are we not somewhat susceptible to having our work and our inquiries be driven, motivated, and directed (even mis-directed?) by new methods and technologies? Almost every contributing article in the 1989 special issue of *Archaeology* mentioned the new technologies that we would be using in the mid-twenty-first century, technologies that perhaps would be determining the work we do because they are available, they are "there." While such techniques/methods as remote sensing were cast as integral to most future archaeological work, no matter what time period or part of the world, they were presented primarily as the latest new method in the archaeological toolkit to maximize recovery at less cost, or to help determine the best way to proceed, with the ultimate goal, nonetheless, being excavation. No one noted that these non-invasive techniques are just as important an addition to our repertoire because they are more congruent with the beliefs and worldviews of some indigenous groups as a means to evaluate archaeological potential—groups who find excavation to be invasive and even unacceptable. We must ask how any and all new technologies are embedded not just in the economics of archaeological practice or the novelties of technologies, but also in the relations and contingencies of local settings (e.g., Lightfoot 2008).

When one is asked to do something very special and challenging, such as be a candidate for a leadership position in the SAA, one is asked for a statement, a set of goals or that "vision thing." To say I was apprehensive about doing just that, in the face of the honor of being a candidate for the Presidency of this organization, is to underestimate the enormity of the task. Of course, there are even word limits, which is probably a good thing! I had to ask myself, then and there, "what is it that matters to me?" "What is it that I want to see accomplished during my term, if elected?" And how in the world does that happen in light of unforeseen exigencies (such as the current global economic crisis) or when realizing that there is no way one can ride on a unified constituency (see Snead and Sabloff, this volume, for reminders of what a professional society has to balance and what impressive accomplishments past presidents have brought about). In reviewing my candidacy statement, I stick by it.

I noted in it (with no space to discuss or elaborate!) several issues that, as it turns out, are taken up in this volume with clarity, conviction, and needed elaboration. In fact, it was one of those wonderful convergences to see the already planned and developed proposal for this commemorative volume for the 75th anniversary that I would be privileged to be a part of, because it is a volume that I can endorse as appropriate and tailored precisely to the voices and visions of contemporary, and of future, archaeology, as I conceptualize it. Simply put, the three core issues I suggested that we need to see continue and flourish are those of diversity, collaboration, and communication. I see these as including a diversity of practitioners, of theoretical perspectives, of research problems and topics, and of practices; expanded collaborations and more visibility of the collaborative actions, arrangements, and engagements; communication to wider publics, both more proactively and in more diverse media, contexts, and among ourselves in more varied venues (see Allen and Joyce, this volume).

Lastly, one trend we need much more discussion about is the increasing engagement with and varying structural "moves" in regard to "archaeology" as an academic discipline in relation to anthropology, to other social and human sciences, and to other "disciplines" (e.g., two recent well-attended SAA symposia; Gillespie and Nichols 2003). New kinds of schools and departments are being created, new cross-disciplinary centers, new bridging grant programs, and new intellectual alliances are in the making, such as at Stanford or at Arizona State University. Often in our academic departments and in the wider worlds of development, CRM, and heritage/preservation we have viewed ourselves—or been treated—as somewhat marginal. And of course, we believe we are deserving of a more central place, more respect and attention. But rather than spending too much time asking "How do we situate ourselves? How do we find a viable space on the margins we think we occupy?" we might benefit from asking instead, "What can we see from where we are, from the various 'here and nows' of our situations?" These may not be so marginal once we look. In fact, I do not overstate the case by saying that many of our current graduate students and recent Ph.D.s (as well as numerous more senior scholars) are among the most broadly trained among anthropologists. Pauketat and Meskell (this volume) draw this out even more with specific examples and topics of inquiry. In order to "do" the archaeology of the twenty-first century, we are drawing on literatures, issues, skills, methods, and theories that suggest that many so-called archaeologists have been "erasing boundaries" between the classic four-fields of Americanist anthropology. Furthermore, our archaeological colleagues in related fields and departments, such as Classics and Near Eastern Studies, are themselves often engaged with the same literatures, problem-orientations, and research as so-called anthropological archaeologists; some *are* anthropologists. This suggests a more vibrant complementarity of archaeological practices. This suggests that the boundary erasures discussed by Lanata and Drennan (this volume)—and how we might make them more porous, especially across membranes of language, nationality, and regional research foci—may be even more numerous than they can consider here.

So, where do we stand in relation to the recent discussions of and challenges to the "unity of science" (e.g., Galison and Stump 1996), and, by extension, to the unity of archaeology? And, thus, what's at stake in adhering to a unity of archaeology as a discipline? If we recognize and accept the varieties (but how can one not do so?), how do we not become the "arcane academic endeavor" predicted by Dunnell (1989) or reconcile ourselves to an "uncertain future" (Clark 2003)? "Who gains and [who] loses," asks Galison (1996:3), "if our representation of science [read, archaeology] has its standards varying from place to place, field to field, and practitioner to practitioner?" These are weighty issues, but to me, the pathway is clear: there are and must be many routes "in" toward understanding past human experiences. We need them all. We learn something different from them all, and they all are to be, nonetheless, measured up against our much-discussed, often varying standards of evidence, argument, evaluation, and reflexivity. As Wylie suggests (1999), when she takes on this gnarly issue in relation to historical archaeologies, there is a tension and yet balance between the recognized disunities, on the one hand, and the inter-field and inter-theory connections that must exist, on the other.

> However much the weight of critical argument tells against old–style global unity theses, it is important to not lose sight of the fact that

ideals of epistemic and methodological unity remain a powerful force in many sciences, and that local and contingent unifying strategies are crucial to scientific inquiry [Wylie 1999:294].

While we may want to contest the ways in which we may gain authority and respect in relation to other sciences and among ourselves with a representation of homogeneity and unity, precisely because such a representation cannot hold (e.g., Gero 2007), at the same time, it is those "local and contingent strategies" that are the key to communication, efficacy, respect, and the production of useable knowledge. My vision sees the future of archaeology as "more like a quilt than a pyramid" (after Galison 1996:3).

Shared Sensibility and a Sense of Social Belonging

I find it useful to pivot here from a provocative and timely one-page symposium proposal by Tamara Bray for the 2009 meetings of the Society for American Archaeology, "Of Crystal Balls and Possible Pathways: Visions of (Co) Futures in Archaeology." On the one hand, Bray suggests a certain stagnation of Americanist archaeology—"adrift and disconnected"—a proposition with which I would take strong exception, as would Pauketat and Meskell (among others in this volume). But at the same time, she invites contributors to "consider how we might envision creating 'co-futures' with others who also have vested interests in the past." I like the concept of co-futures, but as with any such proposition, it would be in how this might be further operationalized and put-into-practice that is the challenge and the promise (see Silliman and Ferguson, this volume). Already there are such co-futures being mapped out and enacted, and which have been reported on (e.g., Atalay 2006; Colwell-Chanthaphonh and Ferguson 2008; Crow Canyon 2008; Dongoske et al. 2000; Killion 2008; Ludlow Collective 2001; among many; see more references in Silliman and Ferguson, this volume), but her vision is also ampliative. Bray suggests that it will be in the context of developing "co-futures" that "significant paradigmatic shifts" would ensue, if not be required. From her own perspective, which has been "shaped by interactions with empowered native peoples," she suggests some such shifts, such as more engagement with "cultural continuity" rather than the core mantra of archaeology in which what we primarily focus on and contribute to is understanding culture change. What Bray's symposium generates and what follows from that remain to be seen, but there is much to be explored and considered with a concept of co-futures. Indeed, many of the dimensions of Bray's concerns and interests are explicitly attended to in the chapters that follow here (albeit not in response to her challenge). In her symposium proposal, Bray notes that "while marching in step to an archaeological pied piper or ratifying a unified paradigm may not be desirable," and I would strongly agree, it is a "shared sense of purpose," or purposes, that will "hold much benefit for the future of the discipline" (Bray 2009).

Perhaps there are some insights to be gained from Daston's (1998) historical analysis of the three major European Academies in the late nineteenth century—the Royal Society of London, the Académie Royale des Sciences (Paris), and the Akademie der Wissenschaft (Berlin)—in which she shows how each grappled with the tension between specialization and professionalization. Many archaeologists today complain about the specialization they perceive in the discipline, which they feel fraction the field. In the cases that Daston analyzes, specialization refers to "the degree to which scientific work is concentrated narrowly in one or a few areas" while professionalization refers to "the possibility of making a career out of scientific work, both in the sense of making a living and achieving a collective identity with other practitioners in the field" (1998:69–70). Each of the three academies that she discusses seems to have arrived at different solutions to the tensions, and she concentrates on the Akademie Wissenschaft that, she suggests, became professionalized but not specialized. How this happened, she argues, can be traced to the overarching shared practices, the seminar training formats and other factors that contributed to an "academic togetherness," a "social unity that gave them a sense of place in the world map of knowledge" (1998:83).

Although such organizations as the SAA have as their goal to promote scholarly togetherness and, for sure, to help provide us a sense of place in the world map of knowledge (see Snead and Sabloff, this volume), I am among those who suggest that there must be more to it than having certain effective supra-organizations. Indeed, as Daston (1998) showed for the Akademie Wissenschaft, it was not only what the Akademie promoted but how the members themselves participated and what they took upon themselves, as in the very formalized and enthusiastically endorsed training seminars. In her always provocative assessments of the practice of science, feminist scholar Lucy Suchman proposes that a more honest practice (of any discipline) will involve the "de-centering of sites of innovation or discovery from singular persons, places and things to multiple acts of everyday activity," including de-centering those "actions through which only certain actors and associated achievements [have] come into public view" (Suchman 2005:1; see also Suchman 2000, 2006). And while it is predictable that "tensions and contradictions arise when we de-center and distribute practices previously identified exclusively with certain locales across a wider landscape," it is by "distributing those practices more widely, [that] they are given correspondingly greater presence" (Suchman 2005:2). Elsewhere, Suchman has advocated generating innovations through the "artful integration" that shifts attention "from the figure of the heroic designer and associated next new thing, to ongoing, collective practices of sociomaterial configuration" (Suchman 1999, quoted in Suchman 2005:13).

Archaeology is indeed a perfect example of a field in which we gain not only a shared sense of purpose and being, but new insights and new ways of working and doing through "ongoing collective practices of sociomaterial configuration"—practices that need greater recognition and instantiation. That we draw on most disciplines and fields that are today housed in many different university departments, from business and law, to the physical and chemical sciences, along with the social sciences and humanities, is often not widely recognized nor heralded (but see Zeder et al., this volume). I have been known to say to our University administrators that if they have to close down most of the campus, they could retain much of it by supporting a vibrant archaeology program. To simplify Suchman's point, we need to parade and proclaim more widely and publicly all that goes into the doing of archaeology, all the contributors, the labor, the veritable encyclopedia of conceptual frameworks that are brought into play. With this publicizing of our distributed practices, greater presence accrues.

While we often stand in quite striking contrast to colleagues in related fields, what with our teamwork mentality and requisite collaborative mandates, we may still erect more than erase boundaries, perpetuate more than eliminate inequalities (see Franklin and Paynter, this volume), need greater and a differently understood tolerance and respect for theoretical diversity, and need a wider vision of what we do, who does it, and how. In stressing the scholarly benefits and expansions of knowledge through our more traditional interdisciplinary collaborations (see Zeder et al., this volume), but through increasingly important community archaeologies, and varied collaborations with all sorts of stakeholders and descendant groups (see Silliman and Ferguson, this volume), archaeology is not impeded, slowed down, or diluted. *Au contraire*. There is an enrichment of questions, possible answers, methods, and the co-engagement with exploring and comprehending human experiences. As Shanks and McGuire (1996) made clear some time ago, archaeology is a craft coproduced with and for communities. The fact that who some of the communities are has expanded, way beyond the readers of *American Antiquity* or our professional colleagues, is one key source of our shared sensibilities and sense of social belonging. I would venture to say that one factor that has contributed to what Pauketat and Meskell (this volume) and many others would say is a vibrancy to contemporary American archeology is this widening of the circle, this attention to and rewards from an explicit political awareness, concern for social justice, enhanced reflexivity about all aspects of archaeological practice, and a realization of the benefits—intellectual as well as social—of multivocality (see Silliman and Ferguson, this volume).

Thus, we need not mourn the absence of an "archaeological pied piper" (Bray 2009) nor some unified theoretical mandates. Rather, there is much more—not less—to make of the practice of archaeology and of the knowledge that is being produced, knowledge that is itself ever changing and evolving, but primarily through the distributed practices and actions of archaeologists and their ever-present collaborators—from students, field and lab laborers, and various other stakeholders, to dating laboratories and material scientists, among others. In this sense, then, Hegmon (2005) has perhaps missed a deeper issue in her call for "no more theory wars." Although she recognizes that one cannot (ontologically nor practically) separate theory from practice, she does not engage with such linkages in her original article (Hegmon 2003; see critique by Moss 2005 and reply by Hegmon 2005). By calling for theoretical consensus and even doubting the role of tensions as being productive, Hegmon (and she is not alone, just a convenient and widely read example) has not punctured the outer skin of a discipline that would derive from scrutinizing more deeply the socio-materialities of how archaeology gets done, and how to reconfigure them for ever-changing circumstances.

Furthermore, it is not a closing down of theoretical options that must engage us; it is an opening up and learning how to deal with them, how to make the most of them. This is explicitly the case as we increasingly involve multiple stakeholders and erase or at least make more porous many boundaries as to "who a knower can be" (a long-standing concern of feminists, e.g., Code 1991). In perhaps the most prescient article in the 1989 special edition of *Archaeology* magazine, dedicated to predictions about archaeology in the year 2050, McIntosh, McIntosh, and Togola write that "no single paradigm or interpretive tradition can do justice to the real complexity of the human prehistoric experience. The archaeology of the twenty-first century must probe that complexity with new research strategies grounded in methodological and interpretive pluralism" (McIntosh et al. 1989:80). Much like Bray's proposition that "co-futures" will engender, if not require, new conceptual foci and different research questions, McIntosh and colleagues would argue that from a truly collaborative dialogue, archaeology will enter new interpretive fields (see also Silliman and Ferguson, this volume).

We still have a problem of not coming to grips with what has been described as "who shows up and who disappears" (Suchman and Jordan 1989; see also Carroll 1990; Conkey 2007; Star 1991; Watkins 2003) in our prevailing discourses and literature, about all the underlying webs of labor and sources of support for the production of archaeological knowledge, as well as all the "missing voices" that could render our understandings more complex and complicated, and yet much richer. It is Gero's call (2007) for "honoring ambiguity and problematizing certitude" more so than Hegmon's for "no more theory wars" that should be heeded most as we head into the next quarter century of archaeology; an honoring of ambiguity/problematizing of certitude that is firmly tied to an across-the-board reflexivity—about our goals, where our questions and project ideas come from, how we are going about addressing them, and how the webs of social and material relations are developed, refined, revised, and put into practices and by which parties. Maybe what Hegmon might accept is a proposal by McGuire (2004, see also 2008): "Effective praxis is only possible if archaeologists abandon the opposition between subjectivity and objectivity and give equal weight to knowing the world and to critiquing it" (2004:19, see also 2008). Maybe regularized and widely communicated reflexivity in contemporary archaeology could serve one of the same functions as the Akademie Wissenschaft's formal seminar training programs in the nineteenth century, as a core practice that contributes to a shared sensibility and a social sense of belonging.

Some Concluding Thoughts

There is no single vision that can or should be packaged and handed out. We each bring hopes and aspirations to our archaeology, and each project is as much embedded in the contingencies of geopolitics and local opportunities as in an idealistic objective programmatic. No archaeologist stands alone, nor who would want to? The past 25 years have played out in unanticipated ways that have had high and low points. We are learning many things: archaeological tourism is an "unreliable ally" (Herscher 1989), site destruction proceeds apace, but our consciousnesses have been raised in many ways (and everyone should be required to read Wylie 2005); new and articulate voices have come into the dialogues, and old voices have changed their tunes—we see much of that in this volume. Some are still somewhat pessimistic of what we are doing, but from different vantage points (e.g., Clark 2003; Conkey and Gero 1997; Meskell 2002), others are trying to sort out our goals and our theories (e.g., Baines and Brophy 2006; Johnson et al. 2006), and yet others are articulating the transformative possibilities (and accomplishments) of politically engaged, and empirically rigorous, archaeologies (e.g., McGuire 2008). We have asked our Berkeley graduate students to try to rewrite the narrative of the history of Americanist archaeology given the ways in which such histories are, of course, themselves neither neutral nor "given" (White 1975)—the culture history to processual to post-processual story. Most wrote about trends that cross-cut these "standard" periods. Among the many creative suggestions, one student (Sapienza 2008) wrote about how one can think of the changes in archaeology over the decades in terms of the introduction and subsequent changes in television and associated media. Color TV—which Sapienza associates with the changes in archaeology since the 1980s—is objectively blurrier than black-and-white; "color," he notes, " is *only* gained," ironically enough, "by the sacrifice of clarity" (see http://www.colorado.edu/physics/2000/TOC.html for the physics that support this). Yet, as Sapienza suggests, "our perception of the blurry past is much more colorful" despite the loss of a black-and-white way of seeing. In the end, then, the voices and the many visions in the pages that follow are part of the increasingly colorful field of archaeology as we make our way into the twenty-first century: charting co-futures, celebrating the coproduction of knowledges and involving more actors. Despite the predictions of more and more technologies in our service, "the most significant remedies will come from human agencies"

(McIntosh et al. 1989:79) and from attention to reflexivity, ambiguity, social justice, evidence-based multivocality, and a shared commitment to the gains from a deeper and wider understanding of the knowledge-making enterprise known as archaeology—it produces insights into the past but as embedded in the realities of the many situations of the present. Who could ask for anything more rewarding?

References Cited

Aanestad, M.
   2003 The Camera as an Actor: Design-in-use of Telemedicine Infrastructure in Surgery. *Computer-Supported Cooperative Work (CSCW)* 12:1–20.
Atalay, Sonya (editor)
   2006 Decolonizing Archaeology. Special issue, *American Indian Quarterly* 30(3–4).
Baines, Andrew, and Kenneth Brophy
   2006 Archaeology without –isms. *Archaeological Dialogues* 13:69–91.
Barad, Karen
   1998 Getting Real: Technoscientific Practices and the Materialization of Reality. *differences: A Journal of Feminist Cultural Studies* 10:88–128.
Bray, Tamara
   2009 Of Crystal Balls and Possible Pathways: Visions of (Co) Futures in Archaeology. Symposium abstract for the 74th Annual Meeting of the Society for American Archaeology, Atlanta.
Burton, Antoinette
   2000 Optical Illusions. *Women's Review of Books* Vol. XVII (5):21–22.
Cantor, Nancy, and Stephen Lavine
   2006 Taking Public Scholarship Seriously. *The Chronicle of Higher Education* 52 (issue 40):B 20ff.
Carroll, Bernice A.
   1990 The Politics of 'Originality': Women and the Class System of the Intellect. *Journal of Women's History* 2(2):136–163.
Clark, Geoffrey A.
   2003 American Archaeology's Uncertain Future. In *Archaeology Is Anthropology*, edited by Susan D. Gillespie and Deborah L. Nichols, pp. 51–67. Archeological Papers of the American Anthropological Association, No.13, American Anthropological Association, Arlington, Virginia.
Clarke, Adele E., and Virginia Olesen
   1999 *Revisioning Women's Health and Healing: Feminist, Cultural and Technoscientific perspectives.* Routledge, London.
Code, Lorraine
   1991 *What Can She Know? Feminist Theory and the Construction of Knowledge.* Cornell University Press, Ithaca, New York.

Colwell-Chanthaphonh, Chip, and T. J. Ferguson (editors)
   2008   *Collaboration in Archaeological Practice: Engaging Descendant Communities.* AltaMira Press, Lanham, Maryland.
Conkey, Margaret W.
   2007   Questioning Theory: Is There a Gender of Theory in Archaeology? Special Issue: Doing Archaeology as a Feminist, edited by Margaret Conkey and Alison Wylie. *Journal of Archaeological Method and Theory* 14:285–310.
Conkey, Margaret W., and Joan Gero
   1997   Programme to Practice: Gender and Feminism in Archaeology. *Annual Review of Anthropology* 26:411–437.
Conkey, Margaret W., and Janet Spector
   1984   Archaeology and the Study of Gender. In *Advances in Archaeological Method and Theory*, vol. 7, edited by Michael B. Schiffer, pp. 1–38. Academic Press, New York.
Crow Canyon
   2008   *A Vision for the Future of the Crow Canyon Archaeological Center.* Crow Canyon Archaeological Center, Cortez, Colorado.
Daston, Lorraine
   1998   The Academies and the Unity of Knowledge. Disciplining the Disciplines. *differences: A Journal of Feminist Cultural Studies* 10(2):67–86.
Dongoske, Kurt, Mark Aldenderfer, and Karen Doehner (editors)
   2000   *Working Together: Native Americans and Archaeologists.* Society for American Archaeology. Washington, D.C.
Dunnell, Robert
   1989   Hope for an Endangered Science. Special Issue: Archaeology in the 21st Century, edited by Brian Fagan. *Archaeology* 42(1):63–65, 104–105.
Fagan, Brian
   1989   A.D. 2050: The Science of Humankind Comes of Age. Special Issue: Archaeology in the 21st Century, edited by Brian Fagan. *Archaeology* 42(1):22–23.
Ferree, Myra Marx, Judith Lorber, and Beth Hess (editors)
   1999   *Revisioning Gender.* Sage Publications. Thousand Oaks, California.
Fowler, Don D.
   1986   Conserving American Archaeological Resources. In *American Archaeology Past and Future: A Celebration of the Society for American Archaeology, 1935-1985,* edited by David J. Meltzer, Don D. Fowler, and Jeremy A. Sabloff, pp 135–162. Smithsonian Institution Press, Washington, D.C.
Galison, Peter
   1996   Introduction: The Context of Disunity. In *The Disunity of Science: Boundaries, Contexts, Powers,* edited by Peter Galison and David J. Stump, pp.1–36. Stanford University Press, Stanford.
Galison, Peter, and David J. Stump (editors)
   1996   *The Disunity of Science: Boundaries, Contexts, Powers.* Stanford University Press, Stanford.
Gero, Joan
   2007   Honoring Ambiguity/Problematizing Certitude. Special Issue: Doing Archae-

ology as a Feminist, edited by Margaret Conkey and Alison Wylie. *Journal of Archaeological Method and Theory* 14:311–327.

Gillespie, Susan D., and Deborah L. Nichols (editors)
  2003 *Archaeology Is Anthropology* Archeological Papers of the American Anthropological Association, No. 13. American Anthropological Association, Arlington, Virginia.

Goodwin, Charles
  1994 Professional Vision. *American Anthropologist* 96:606–633.

Hegmon, Michelle
  2003 Setting Theoretical Egos Aside: Issues and Theory in North American Archaeology. *American Antiquity* 68:213–243.
  2005 No More Theory Wars: A Response to Moss. *American Antiquity* 70:588–590.

Herscher, Ellen
  2003 The Future is in Ruins. Special Issue: Archaeology in the 21st century, edited by Brian Fagan. *Archaeology* 42(1):67–70.

Hillman, James
  1975 *Revisioning Psychology.* Harper Collins, New York.

Jay, Martin, and Teresa Brennan (editors)
  1996 *Vision in Context: Historical and Contemporary Perspectives on Sight.* Routledge, New York.

Johnson, Matthew, and contributors
  2006 On the Nature of Theoretical Archaeology and Archaeological Theory. *Archaeological Dialogues* 13:117–132.

Killion, Thomas (editor)
  2008 *Opening Archaeology: Repatriation's Impact on Contemporary Research and Practice.* SAR Press, Santa Fe, New Mexico.

Knudson, Ruthann
  1986 Contemporary Cultural Resource Management. In *American Archaeology Past and Future: A Celebration of the Society for American Archaeology, 1935–1985,* edited by David J. Meltzer, Don D. Fowler, and Jeremy A. Sabloff, pp. 395–413. Smithsonian Institution Press, Washington, D.C.
  1989 North America's Threatened Heritage. Special Issue: Archaeology in the 21st Century, edited by Brian Fagan. *Archaeology* 42(1):71–73,106.

Lightfoot, Kent G.
  2008 Collaborative Research Programs: Implications for the Practice of North American Archaeology. In *Collaboration at the Trowel's Edge: Teaching and Learning in Indigenous Archaeology,* edited by Stephen W. Silliman, pp. 211–227. Amerind Studies in Archaeology No. 2, University of Arizona Press, Tucson.

Ludlow Collective
  2001 Archaeology of the Colorado Coal Field War, 1913–1914. In *Archaeologies of the Recent Past,* edited by Victor Buchli and Gavin Lucas, pp. 94–107. Routledge, London and New York.

McGuire, Randall H.
  2004 Knowledge Claims in a Politically Committed Archaeology. Paper presented at

the 103rd Annual Meeting of the American Anthropological Association, Washington, D.C.

2008 *Archaeology as Political Action.* University of California Press, Berkeley.

McIntosh, Roderick, Susan McIntosh, and Téréba Togola

1989 People without History. Special Issue: Archaeology in the 21st Century, edited by Brian Fagan. *Archaeology* 42(1):74–80,107.

Meltzer, David J., Don D. Fowler, and Jeremy A. Sabloff (editors)

1986 *American Archaeology Past and Future: A Celebration of the Society for American Archaeology, 1935–1985.* Smithsonian Institution Press, Washington, D.C.

Meskell, Lynn

2002 The Intersections of Identity and Politics in Archaeology. *Annual Review of Anthropology* 31:279–301.

Moss, Madonna

2005 Rifts in the Theoretical Landscape of Archaeology in the United States: A Comment on Hegmon and Watkins. *American Antiquity* 70:581–587.

Rosenstone, Robert

1994 *Revisioning History: Film and the Construction of a New Past.* Princeton University Press, Princeton.

Sapienza, John Thomas

2008 Rewriting the Narrative of Americanist Archaeology's History. Manuscript on file with the author, Department of Anthropology, University of California, Berkeley.

Shanks, Michael, and Randall H. McGuire

1996 Craft of Archaeology. *American Antiquity* 61:75–88.

Star, Susan Leigh

1991 Invisible Work and Silenced Dialogues in Knowledge Representation. In *Women, Work and Computerization*, edited by I. Eriksson, B. Kitchenham, and K. Tijdens, pp. 81–92. North Holland Press, Amsterdam.

Suchman, Lucy

1999 Working Relations of Technology Production and Use. In *The Social Shaping of Technology,* edited by Donald Mackenzie and Judy Wajcman, pp 258–268. 2nd edition. Open University Press, Buckingham and Philadelphia.

2000 Embodied Practices of Engineering Work. *Mind, Culture, Activity* 7:4–18.

2005 Agencies in Technology Design: Feminist Reconfigurations. Paper presented at Gendered Innovations in Science and Engineering, Stanford University, April 2005.

2006 *Plans and Situated Actions, II: Human-Machine Reconfigurations.* Cambridge University Press, Cambridge and New York.

Suchman, Lucy, and Brigitte Jordan

1989 Computerization and Women's Knowledge. In *Women, Work and Computerization,* edited by I. Eriksson, B. Kitchenham, and K. Tijdens, pp. 153–160. North Holland Press, Amsterdam.

Trigger, Bruce

1984 Alternative Archaeologies: Nationalist, Colonialist, Imperialist. *Man* 19: 255–370.

UCLA Chicano Studies Research Center

n.d. *A Ver: Revsioning Art History.* CSRC Press, Los Angeles.

Watkins, Joe
> 2003 Beyond the Margin: American Indians, First Nations and Archaeology in North America. *American Antiquity* 68:273–285.

Watson, Patty Jo (editor)
> 1985 *American Antiquity* 50(2) (whole issue).

White, Hayden
> 1975 *Metahistory: The Historical Imagination in Nineteenth Century Europe.* Johns Hopkins University Press, Baltimore.

Wylie, M. Alison
> 1999 Rethinking Unity as a "Working Hypothesis" for Philosophy of Science: How Archaeologists Exploit the Disunities of Science. *Perspectives in Science* 7(3):293–317.
>
> 2005 The Promise and Perils of an Ethic of Stewardship. In *Embedding Ethics*, edited by Lynn Meskell and Peter Pels, pp. 47–68. Berg Publishers, Oxford and New York.

3

Professional Societies and the Lives of American Archaeologists

JAMES E. SNEAD *and* JEREMY A. SABLOFF

Learned societies are an essential element of professions. They provide a range of opportunities and services for practitioners, representing them "as a whole" when such representation is needed. Perhaps most importantly they are a standard of legitimacy: thriving associations are symbolic of the importance of the activity that they oversee, both in the eyes of the membership and those beyond (Haber 1991). They are also complex systems in their own right, embodying the diverse interests and ambitions of their constituents. Not all of these can coexist in harmony, so the common ground provided by professional associations is contested, with the identity of the group itself often in play.

Competition is inherent within and between these societies. Since there are often multiple associations within disciplines, defining the "mission" is significant to practitioners, who have the option of seceding to other organizations with which they perceive more common interest, or even convening like-minded associates to establish their own. Professional needs and scholarly interests are not necessarily aligned, and in an organization oriented toward work in an intellectual field that is also a career to many, there can be tensions between goals in these areas. Thus what many perceive as a benign forum for the presentation of papers and reunions among colleagues is actually a core component of their profession, one that deserves critical thought.

These dynamics are particularly interesting in the case of archaeology, which has long been perceived as peripheral to central intellectual traditions (Levine 1986). The earliest learned societies in the United States represented communities of interest, serving as forums for the discussion and dissemination of knowledge. In the pre-professional era of the late eighteenth and early nineteenth centuries the membership of such groups consisted of like-minded individuals who had sufficient leisure time to keep abreast of scholarly opinion through discussion and correspondence with their fellows. They closely emulated the structure of organizations such as the Royal Society (Hunter 1971) and the Society of Antiquaries (Evans 1956), which dominated British scholarly circles in the eighteenth century. Thus the American Philosophical Society (APS), founded in 1743, was seen both as a vehicle for advancing knowledge and a hallmark of American advancement. Its membership was drawn from the colonial elite, and subject matter ranged widely (Carter 1993). Antiquarian activity, however, was limited, perhaps reflecting the ambiguous perceptions of the New World past on the part of the colonists.

Interest in the topic of American antiquities grew in the early republic, particularly as settlement beyond the Appalachians brought people into contact with the archaeological remains of the Ohio Valley (Willey and Sabloff 1993). New associations sprang up in response to this interest, such as the American Antiquarian Society (AAS) of Worcester, Massachusetts, founded in 1812. The AAS was the product of local ambitions, but the limited integration of intellectual life in the United States provided opportunities for such small-scale institutions to succeed. Through a network of correspondents and a program of acquisition of antiquities, the AAS actively gathered information about the North American past for several decades.

Funding and continuity are the principal challenges facing professional associations, and these factors played a critical role in the early American archaeological societies. The Linnaean Society of Boston competed with the AAS in the antiquities market but dissolved in the 1820s. The American Ethnological Society, founded in 1842, is considered the first true "anthropological" organization in America. Despite the prestige of its founder, Albert Gallatin, however, after his death it languished for decades before its revival under Franz Boas (Bieder 1986:43; Bieder and Tax 1974). While the APS and AAS were more successful in the long run, the interests of their members shifted away from antiquarian research by the mid-nineteenth century. In all these cases support for scholarship was interrupted, dispersing collections and breaking the continuity of what had been productive debates and discussions about the American past.

It is also evident that, while these early organizations supported archaeology as an endeavor, they did little to sustain archaeologists themselves. The handful of "practicing" fieldworkers of the era, such as Caleb Atwater, Henry Schoolcraft, and Ephraim Squier, corresponded with all of these groups and others in search of financial support and publication opportunities, but very little was forthcoming (Barnhart 2005; Meltzer 1998:14). Prior to the 1880s, federal funding was essentially the only way that active research could be sustained, and the small number of patrons willing to support the field were largely focused on bricks-and-mortar projects. Even the most famous of these early institutions, the Peabody Museum of Archaeology and Ethnology at Harvard, was a relatively marginal entity within its university context, with curator Frederic Ward Putnam working for 11 years before achieving professorial rank (Browman 2002; Hinsley 1985:61). The scale of patronage increased toward the end of the nineteenth century and became a significant force in shaping research priorities, although it was often idiosyncratic and subject to the whims of fashion (Snead 1999).

There were important complementarities between the small number of scholars working for the eastern institutions and the much larger but comparatively marginal avocational community scattered throughout the United States. It was difficult for public officials to engage in field research, and they were thus heavily reliant on extensive networks of correspondents (e.g., Goldstein 1994). In return, engagement with the institutions of federal science, in particular the emergent Smithsonian, legitimated the intellectual ambitions of schoolteachers and others in remote corners of the United States. Competition was also inherent in this relationship, however, since funding was unequally distributed and the results of fieldwork, both the artifacts themselves and the intellectual capital with which they were associated, were in the end accessible largely to elite audiences in the eastern cities. These conditions were exacerbated over time, as American archaeology achieved greater public visibility and enhanced intellectual standing.

Indeed, the successful promotion of archaeology after the Civil War was led by both the federal government and more humble local organizations. The collecting expeditions and data gathering of the Bureau of American Ethnology (Hinsley 1994; Judd 1967) concentrated authority in the field, but the florescence of smaller groups was essential to the character of anthropology in that era. Avocational organizations made up almost entirely of local residents supported fieldwork, held meetings, established exhibits, and playing profound roles in the organization of American archaeology in the late 1800s.

Local societies were often ardent advocates of preservation and frequently lobbied legislative bodies for funds in support of local work, and the success of early antiquities legislation in the United States is due almost entirely to their efforts (Harmon et al. 2006). The State Archaeological Association of Ohio began with a convention of 49 members in 1875 with the explicit purpose of promoting archaeological fieldwork in the state (Barnhart 1998:130). Some local groups gained notoriety for promoting tangential research agendas, such as the Davenport Academy's championing of fraudulent carvings of mammoths on precolumbian artifacts (McKusick 1970).

Communication was central to the mission of local archaeological societies and some achieved success in the creation of journals. These included Stephen Peet's *The American Antiquarian*, which was published from 1878 through 1911, and *The Archaeologist* (also known as *The American Archaeologist*) beginning in 1893 (Barnhart 1998:140; Milanich 2001). These periodicals included reports on research written by regionally based scholars as well as national figures. The precarious finances of some of these groups are suggested by the fact that some, including *The Archaeologist*, were intended to make a profit (W. K. Moorehead Journals, OHS, MSS 106. Box 20, Diary v. XXII. 19 October 1893).

The role of women in archaeological and anthropological societies differed significantly on national and local levels. Men dominated the early national organizations at all levels. Challenges to this exclusivity were made, and the Women's Anthropological Society of the United States led by Matilda Cox Stevenson and Alice Fletcher had a healthy membership in the 1880s and 1890s (Lamb 1906). Despite this, and Alice Fletcher's eventual prominence in some of the national organizations, very few women played a role in their leadership councils until well into the twentieth century.

In contrast, women played a central role in many of the local societies. This was not only because the avocational membership of the local groups was less structured than the national societies but because women took the lead in creating a range of cultural and educational opportunities in civic settings, categories that included archaeology. One of these local organizations, the Colorado Cliff Dwellings Association (CCDA) led by Virginia McClurg, had emerged at the end of the nineteenth century out of the federation of Colorado Women's clubs and took as its motto "Dux Femina

Facti" (roughly translated, "the women shall lead") (BL MS 549). The CCDA played an entrepreneurial role in the preservation of Mesa Verde (Smith 1988:17–18; Snead 2001). Ultimately there were branches of the CCDA in several major cities, and the southern California chapter persisted for nearly 50 years (BL MS 549).

In effect, local groups in the late nineteenth century served most of the functions of professional societies despite the fact that none of their members were truly "professional." They also suffered from the same difficulties to which the national organizations were exposed, including maintaining continuity, funding, and factionalism. The CCDA was not immune to these pressures, and a schism between McClurg and another leader, Lucy Peabody, had a significant impact on the activities of the organization (e.g., Lucy E. Peabody to Edgar Lee Hewett, 12 August 1907. Box 21, ELH). In this complex era several attempts to overcome the structural liabilities of archaeological associations in the United States were made, ultimately leading to the establishment of the Society for American Archaeology (SAA).

Models for Organization

The interplay between "national" scholarship and local activity is embodied in the structure of the first truly professional archaeological organization in the United States, the Archaeological Institute of America (AIA) (Dyson 1998; Sheftel 1979). Founded in 1879, the AIA was established by members of the New England elite to promote American engagement with Classical archaeology. This mission required substantial funding, however, and following a financial crisis an 1884 reorganization created a network of local chapters that supplied dues and donations to the national body (Snead 2002). In return a lecture circuit was established, so that scholars affiliated with the AIA were soon addressing audiences throughout the country. Americanist archaeologists and anthropologists such as Frederic Ward Putnam and John Wesley Powell were closely involved with the AIA from the outset. Powell persuaded the organization to fund Adolph Bandelier's southwestern expedition in 1879 (Lange and Riley 1996), and the AIA leadership was closely involved with the passage of the Antiquities Act of 1906. The *American Journal of Archaeology* provided a venue for formal publication, with *Art and Archaeology* (published 1914–1934) aimed at the broader market of the local affiliates.

The AIA thus synthesized national ambition with local interest, providing one model for a professional archaeological association in the United States. At the top it was an academic organization, since its professional membership consisted of classical scholars in a small number of universities and institutes, supported by the hundreds of avocational members of the local chapters. Despite the preferences of the AIA leadership (Hinsley 1986), these affiliates were not passive and often sought to influence policy. One source of conflict was the national organization's tight focus on Mediterranean fieldwork, since members of the local affiliates were more regularly exposed to American antiquities than the leadership. One of these groups was the AIA's St. Louis Chapter, which found itself in competition with the Missouri Historical Society over "local" archaeology after the turn of the century (F. W. Shipley to F. W. Kelsey, 6 November 1905. AIA Papers 12.5, SSL). The St. Louis affiliate also supported fieldwork at Quirigua in Guatemala, with the expectation that a museum would be established to display Maya artifacts brought back from the field alongside more local finds (D. I. Bushnell to Edgar Lee Hewett, 12 April 1912. Box 23, ELH). At the same time dues were apparently being forwarded to the national organization to support its various endeavors in Classical scholarship.

Tension between the support of local and classical work was reflected in the AIA's leadership at the turn of the last century, with different regional "cliques" seeking dominance. AIA meetings in the 1910s provided the arena for complex negotiations between these subgroups that, by the end of the decade, led to the withdrawal of the AIA from nearly all American activities. The affiliate system was retained and persists today, in many communities amicably coexisting with other archaeological interest groups.

The American Anthropological Association (AAA) was produced by the same professionalizing forces that created the AIA, sharing some aspects of its organization and some of its inherent tensions. It was, in effect, an effort to create a single umbrella organization out of three smaller anthropological societies created in the late nineteenth century; Section H of the American Association for the Advancement of Science, The Anthropological Society of Washington (ASW) and the revived American Ethnological Society (AES) (Bieder and Tax 1974). The latter two organizations also represented the power centers of American anthropology, the "academic" center in New York, Cambridge, and Philadelphia in effect represented by the AES and the federal, "museum" center embodied by the WAS (Darnell and Gleach

2002). Following the launching of the new series of *American Anthropologist* and the inauguration of annual meetings in Pittsburgh in 1902, the new organization quickly transcended its parent groups.

The professional and avocational constituencies within the anthropological community were not necessarily reconciled, however, and forceful debates on the organization of the membership characterized the early years of the AAA. Tensions between the emergent subfields of anthropology also manifested themselves, given additional weight by personal animosity within the leadership, particularly between Franz Boas and W. H. Holmes (see Meltzer and Dunnell 1992). A certain degree of intellectual coherence was maintained by the placement of Boas-trained anthropologists in universities throughout the United States, but contrasting perspectives persisted. Some of these differences were regional, since the proliferation of institutions of higher learning encouraged the growth of locally based scholarship in the Midwest and West. In effect this transformation replicated the east-west divide of earlier decades, in this case creating a division between the urban graduate schools and the smaller institutions where students were, increasingly, employed.

The diminishing influence of federal science in the early decades of the twentieth century also had the effect of making anthropology an increasingly academic discipline, exacerbating the divide with the avocational community. Boas in particular led the push toward greater professionalization of the field, which in practice meant that AAA became more exclusive. These pressures were felt throughout American archaeology. There was a considerable struggle between professional and avocational interests during the 1910s over the AIA's popular magazine, *Art and Archaeology* (David Robinson to Edgar Lee Hewett, 17 August 1917. Box 26, ELH). Ultimately it ceased publication.

The expansion of archaeology in the American field (Willey and Sabloff 1993) and increasingly complex politics within the AAA led to the creation of the Society for American Archaeology in 1934. In many ways this new organization followed the now-traditional model, with membership drawn largely from the academy and an emphasis on intellectual topics. The fact that most of its members continued to participate in the AAA implies that the foundation of the new organization reflected a political divide rather than an intellectual split or a quest for a different organizational model. Increasing confidence on the part of archaeologists and a recognition of the benefits of independent representation also inspired the new organization.

The New World focus of the SAA's journal, *American Antiquity*, provided new opportunities for publication. Initially it featured both professional and avocational contributions. The first issue of *American Antiquity* included an article by an amateur, P. F. Titterington (who also underwrote the cost of this issue) on "Certain Bluff Mounds of Western Jersey County, Illinois." In 1935, W. C. McKern, the first Editor of *American Antiquity*, wrote:

> it is difficult to see how the work of the specialist can progress satisfactorily, if indeed it can survive, without the support of a constantly growing element of amateur students.
>
> AMERICAN ANTIQUITY, acting as the instrument of the Society for American Archaeology, hopes it may serve to some extent in providing the means of a mutually beneficial contact between professionals and amateur students of American archaeology [McKern 1935: 82; see also Sabloff 1985].

Despite McKern's hopes, concern for avocational participation did not flourish within the SAA. The AIA maintained its local chapters and in 1948 launched *Archaeology* as a popular magazine to fill the void left by the demise of *Art and Archaeology* and to mirror the professional *American Journal of Archaeology*. The SAA took no similar steps.

The rising tide of professionalism was also reflected in the complex fight over ethics and standards that was waged from the 1950s through the 1970s, ultimately leading to the creation of the Society of Professional Archaeologists (SOPA) in 1976 (Davis 1982). In this case it was the evolution of archaeology outside the academy that prompted the debate. To a certain extent the growth of the cultural resource management (CRM) field represented a return to an older model of the profession, one in which alternative career paths flourished outside the university system, thus challenging the predominantly academic focus of the organization itself (see Altschul and Patterson, this volume).

Gender bias remained a considerable force, particularly since American archaeology was even more of a male preserve than anthropology as a whole. Outreach to Native American communities was equally of low priority. In these areas the SAA resembled other professional societies of its founding era, but the demands of practitioners, trends within the profession, and the topical focus of the organization would ultimately demand evolution for the society to succeed in the long run.

The Past 25 Years

Since the 50th Anniversary meeting of the Society for American Archaeology in Denver, Colorado (1985) and the subsequent publication (1986) of *American Archaeology: Past and Future*, edited by David Meltzer, Don Fowler, and Jeremy Sabloff, the field of American archaeology and its leading society have undergone a number of important changes. We now turn to a discussion of several of the most significant trends in SAA's activities in the past quarter century and relate them to broader trends in the discipline.

A turning point in the recent history of the SAA was the 1988 adoption by the SAA Executive Committee of the "Management Study of Short-range and Long-range Needs for Organization and Operation," commonly known as the "Evans Report" (after its author John Evans). The extraordinary leadership of then SAA presidents Don Fowler and Dina Dincauze and the members of the Executive Committee, along with the vision of Jerry Miller (the Executive Director of the SAA at the time), led the Society to the commissioning of the report, the undertaking of a survey of Society members, a host of discussions at the annual meetings and special seminars, the eventual adoption of the report, and the formation of a Long-range Planning Task Force (chaired by Fred Wendorf) to devise a strategy for the implementation of the report's principal action items.

In effect, the adoption of the Evans Report and the by-laws revisions it entailed changed the SAA from an organization whose professional commitment was primarily directed at the academic community to a more completely professional one with a variety of new goals and commitments (also see the important essays in Kehoe and Emmerichs 1999, among others).

This process has been evolutionary and often unnoticed. It is of interest to note that in the 50th anniversary volume, only the chapters by Don Fowler (on conservation) and Ruthann Knudson (on CRM) tackle at any length the key non-"intellectual" issues faced by the discipline. The motivations for and causes of the heightened post–1985 attention to issues of professionalism can be seen as pragmatic, political, and academic/intellectual. From a practical perspective, the SAA needed to significantly increase its membership in order to survive (as the Evans Report forcefully argued), while increasing its ability to serve its broad and varied constituencies. In order to do so, it had to better serve the interests of archaeologists throughout the Americas.

Broadening the franchise of the organization required several structural changes. The growth in importance and influence of non-academic archaeologists was particularly dramatic during this era. Whether employed by one of a number of federal agencies, from the National Park Service to the Forest Service, to the Bureau of Land Management to the Bureau of Reclamation to the Army Corps of Engineers, or state historic preservation offices or private firms or university groups specializing in environmental impacts, or historic preservation or private utilities with large land holdings, these practicing archaeologists have grown rapidly in numbers in the past several decades and their memberships in the SAA have grown apace (Altschul and Patterson, this volume).

The organization has also had to make itself more accessible to the wide range of nonprofessional or amateur archaeologists. Besides an interest in their membership dues, another pragmatic reason for increased attention to amateur enthusiasts was the importance of their voice in favorably influencing the political powers that be in Washington, D.C. (both in Congress and the federal agencies) to support archaeological work and protect archaeological resources (the SAA also significantly increased its own lobbying efforts in Washington, D.C. at this time).

Moreover, since a significant quantity of archaeological fieldwork is undertaken by local amateur groups, the better the communication between the SAA and amateurs, the better the possibility of further strengthening this research. Among the positive responses in this area was the creation of the Council of Affiliated Societies in 1991 (Davis and Kornfeld 2007). The establishment of this group was due in no small part to the energy and vision of Earl Lubensky. Over the years, this group has acted as an important liaison between the SAA and a number of key state, provincial, and city archaeological societies, among others, in both the United States and Canada.

The SAA also recognized that if it was to be the Society for *American* Archaeology and not just United States archaeology, it had to do much more to involve colleagues from Canada and Latin America. Thus, in recent years, a variety of initiatives have involved colleagues throughout the Americas, from holding annual SAA meetings in leading Canadian cities such as Montreal, Toronto, and Vancouver; to creating the new journal *Latin American Antiquity* in 1990; to establishing a Committee on the Americas in order to bring issues and concerns of Latin American archaeologists to the attention of the SAA; and to formal discussions with the National Institute of Anthropology and History (INAH) of Mexico about mutual concerns.

One of the major developments for the SAA in the past 25 years has been its efforts (albeit belated) to better communicate and work with Native American groups (see, for example, Watkins 2000 for an excellent overview of the general issues involved in such attempts [Silliman and Ferguson, this volume]). The SAA's efforts to build bridges to these communities can be seen in the creation of the Native American Scholarship Fund (through the leadership of David Hurst Thomas) and the establishment of the Committee on Native American Relations. The committee charge clearly states its goals:

> The Committee on Native American Relations works to increase understanding by archaeologists of the issues of concern to Native Americans, to promote understanding by Native Americans of the value and relevance of archaeology, and to foster better relationships between both groups.

Another key area has been the repatriation of Native American burial remains and material culture (see Bray 2001 and Killion 2008, among others). The SAA played a role in helping in the drafting of a workable repatriation bill in the U.S. Congress and then working for its passage and signing into law as the Native American Graves Protection and Repatriation Act of 1990. It also has established a Committee on Repatriation.

While archaeology as a discipline has grown increasingly aware of the role of gender in the peoples of the past that it studies (see, for example, Conkey and Spector 1984; Gero and Conkey 1991), the SAA also has recognized that it must be involved in greater efforts toward gender equity in the profession (Altschul and Patterson, this volume). The creation of the SAA Committee on the Status of Women in Archaeology (COSWA) more than 30 years ago (and reestablished in 1991) is just one example of developments within the Society in this regard (also see Zeder 1997).

The SAA also has increased its involvement in education, both in terms of professional preparation and in terms of the broader public. The student constituency—both graduate and undergraduate, especially the former—has received increasing attention. The last quarter century has seen, for example, the establishment of an SAA Student Affairs Committee, an annual Student Research Award, a competitive, issue-oriented "ethics bowl" held at the annual meeting, and an annual Student Paper award. These are just a few of the steps that the SAA has taken in attempts to reach out to archaeology students. The involvement of the SAA in public education efforts had a number of motivations, spanning the pragmatic, political, and intellectual realms. Through the strong efforts of Ed Friedman and many others, the SAA formed the Public Education Committee in 1989. Since its founding, this very active committee has organized and coordinated a host of activities that have enabled aspects of archaeological research to become part of primary and secondary school curricula and to make school children, in particular, and the interested public, in general, more aware than ever before of archaeological fieldwork and its results.

All of these changes can be traced to the growth of new perspectives on the nature of archaeology—its practice and the discipline's relations to the entities supporting it and the peoples affected by its work. Members of the SAA have had a growing, and still ongoing, realization of how—in myriad kinds of ways—their own work was increasingly embedded in modern society. This awareness did not suddenly appear in the 1980s, as it had a long history in American archaeology, with a recent lineage that includes luminaries such as Fred Johnson and J. O. Brew, as well as Carl Chapman, Bob McGimsey, and Hester Davis. But it clearly has blossomed in the years following the SAA's 50th anniversary.

Although some form of processual thinking still dominates American archaeology, the influence of postmodern thinking is evident in a wide range of archaeological practices in the Americas (see, for example, the discussion in Sabloff 2005). This situation is clearly recognized in the term "processual plus" (Hegmon 2003), denoting the integration of some postmodern thought into the processual paradigm.

In particular, the overwhelming majority of American archaeologists now recognize that their work is no "ivory tower" pursuit but is embedded in political and economic matrices (see, for example, McGuire 1992, 2008; Patterson 2002, 2003; Schmidt and Patterson 1995). On the one hand, from government policies, to funding sources, to employers' objectives, archaeologists work within tight political and economic parameters. On the other hand, the places they undertake fieldwork, the data they uncover, and the interpretations they produce can all have significant political and economic consequences for a wide variety of communities today. While the archaeologists are studying the past, they are not working there—and they understand more clearly than ever that their work impacts the present (see Sabloff 2008).

Clearly, the professional make-up of the field has changed in recent decades and continues to do so, while the number of archaeologists with graduate degrees (M.A.s or Ph.D.s) has been growing. However, the number of available academic positions has not come close to matching that pace, and the percentage of archaeologists going into the world of practicing archaeology has been increasing. Moreover, the funding of much archaeological research now comes either from governmental sources or private CRM companies. In order to survive and thrive, the SAA has had to recognize the importance of non-academic-based archaeologists and their work and to make SAA activities and meetings useful to both academic and practicing archaeologists (Altschul and Patterson, this volume).

In the face of the continuing destruction of the archaeological record throughout the world, which seems to march on inexorably through new constructions, warfare, neglect, and looting, archaeologists have become much more sensitive to this loss and more militant than ever before about the need to preserve and protect the record of humanity's history, both in the ground and in museums and repositories. The SAA has responded to the strong emotional feelings of its members in regard to slowing the rate of destruction, on the one hand, and the challenge of doing something about it, on the other hand, in a number of ways, including public education, workshops at annual meetings, lobbying at both federal and state levels in the United States, and support of key legal proceedings.

The past quarter-century of changes in the SAA discussed above are most clearly codified in two key documents. The first is the Society's Code of Ethics, which was adopted in 1996 (see http://saa.org/AbouttheSociety/PrinciplesofArchaeologicalEthics/tabid/203/Default.aspx) (see Lynott and Wylie 2000; also see Vitelli and Colwell-Chanthaphonh 2006). The Code emphasizes eight principles:

1. providing adequate stewardship of the archaeological record and collections;
2. pursuing public accountability, especially in regard to groups affected by archaeological research;
3. fighting against the commercialization of archaeological materials;
4. promoting public education and outreach;

5. sharing intellectual property (archaeological data) rather than treating it as a personal possession;
6. publically reporting and publishing archaeological materials;
7. preserving records and enhancing access to them; and
8. providing proper training and resources in investigating archaeological resources.

The second document is the SAA's Mission and Goals statement, which was revised as recently as 2007. The statement reads as follows (http://saa.org/AbouttheSociety/tabid/54/Default.aspx):

Mission Statement

The mission of the Society for American Archaeology is to expand understanding and appreciation of humanity's past as achieved through systematic investigation of the archaeological record. The society leads the archaeological community by promoting research, stewardship of archaeological resources, public and professional education, and the dissemination of knowledge. To serve the public interest, SAA seeks the widest possible engagement with all segments of society, including governments, educators, and indigenous peoples, in advancing knowledge and enhancing awareness of the past.

Goals

1. SAA advances archaeological research and disseminates archaeological knowledge to the professional community and to the public at large.
2. SAA improves the practice of archaeology and promotes archaeological ethics.
3. SAA is dedicated to the conservation of the archaeological record.
4. SAA serves as a bond among archaeologists worldwide in all segments of the archaeological community.
5. SAA effectively serves the needs of the diverse constituencies that comprise its membership.
6. SAA is an effective advocate for archaeology in the legislative and public policy arenas.
7. SAA provides an effective and flexible structure for the Society's operations and initiatives.

As this discussion indicates, American archaeologists have become increasingly interested in making their fieldwork, analyses, and interpretations relevant and responsible in today's world. In the past 25 years, as the SAA's leadership has become aware of these developments and has helped position the Society as a force for change, the SAA's mission and activities have enlarged. In so doing, the SAA has become more of a professional society than a learned one, and it also has been supporting and helping to implement professional attempts to make archaeology relevant to a host of problems confronting the modern world, from conservation, to agricultural sustainability, to ethnic strife and warfare, among many others.

Thinking Backwards and Forwards

It is both heartening and disconcerting to discover that the issues being addressed by the SAA have been with it not only since the founding of the organization but since the dawn of interest in American archaeology. The continuities are substantial, and some of the topics discussed by the members of the original American Ethnological Society in Albert Gallatin's parlor might well be echoed in conference symposia at the SAA's 75th anniversary meeting in St. Louis. Transcripts of testimony regarding the Antiquities Act of 1906 could be inserted into the congressional record pertaining to modern archaeological legislation with little editing. Some of the issues that bedeviled these early organizations, such as scholarly communication and maintenance of membership, also continue to be of concern.

The organizational structure that has proven so successful in the case of the SAA is not the only shape that archaeology in the United States has adopted. Some alternative models remain in existence, and the evolution of SOPA into the Register of Professional Archaeologists (ROPA) in 1998 illustrates an approach focused more tightly on the issue of professional accreditation. Some regional societies, such as the various state archaeological councils, also emphasize professional issues, monitoring local antiquities preservation, standards of accountability, and generally supporting archaeological "causes" without necessarily emphasizing scholarship. A contrasting case is provided by the annual Pecos Conference (Woodbury 1985, 1993), which attracts several hundred participants annually to talk about archaeology in the Greater Southwest but has almost no organizational apparatus at all and plays a minimal role in maintaining the profession. A similar function is provided by the Mid-Atlantic Conference, an annual meeting that provides a venue for scholarly presentations. Some regional organizations, such as the Arkansas Archeological Society, are quite dynamic, providing a range of professional services. Their success in part reflects issues of scale, since national organizations inevitably fail to address significant local issues in detail. Participation in such organizations can also reflect a rejection of the inherent "status structure" of the profession, which accords priority to national organizations.

Indeed, some avocational archaeological societies are thriving, creative centers for research that are almost entirely independent of national, professional organizations. The Archaeological Society of Virginia, for instance, has numerous chapters, conducts field schools, gives grants to students, and holds scholarly meetings. Publications are a specialty of others, such as the Pacific Coast Archaeological Society in southern California, which oversees the *Pacific Coast Archaeological Society Quarterly*, or the Colorado Archaeological Society, which publishes *Southwestern Lore*. It is likely that such endeavors could not be sustained by "academic" archaeology, for instance, or a national organization such as the SAA, and thus represent an essential element of the infrastructure of the discipline.

In the twenty-first century we recognize many of the inherent difficulties of professional organizations of which our ancestors had only limited awareness. The critical importance of engaging the Native American community is a product of the belated acknowledgment of responsibility shaped by cultural, political, and intellectual perspectives emergent in the late twentieth century that would have been alien to our nineteenth-century forbears (although it is of interest to note that the first President of the SAA, Arthur C. Parker, was a Seneca from New York; see Hertzberg 1979) (in this volume, see chapters by Silliman and Ferguson, Sebastian, and Wilcox). Issues pertaining to gender representation are equally a product of the times, although accounts of nineteenth-century path breakers such as Alice Fletcher and Virginia McClurg hint at counternarratives that we are only beginning to explore (for instance, Reyman 1992; Franklin and Paynter, this volume).

Within this complex historical context the SAA continues to grow. At a certain level the national organization combines the varied strengths of regional societies and conferences and successfully operates in a way that appears to be quite satisfying on the whole to its membership today. Historical lessons suggest that such circumstances may be ephemeral, but the bustle in the hallways of annual meetings indicate considerable vitality.

As the SAA moves towards its 100th anniversary in 2035, some of the issues raised here will undoubtedly play out. Can the Society become increasingly tilted toward its professional responsibilities without losing all its intellectual roots? Will its growing size constrain scholarly exchange, especially at its annual meetings? Will outreach to the public in general and its engagement with Native American groups in particular, as well as growing involvement with wide-ranging public policy issues, become an inherent and fully accepted part of professional responsibilities? While we cannot answer such queries, especially in regard to the state of the SAA a quarter century from now, we are encouraged that the Society has been willing to confront a number of long-standing issues and that its growth in the past 25 years has been steady and positive.

References Cited

Primary Sources

BL   Braun Library, Southwest Museum/Autry Museum of the West
ELH   Edgar Lee Hewett Papers, Fray Angelico Chavez Library, Museum of New Mexico
OHS Ohio Historical Society
SSL   Stone Science Library, Boston University

Secondary Sources

Barnhart, Terry A.
   1998 In Search of the Mound Builders: The State Archaeological Association of Ohio, 1875–1885. *Ohio History* 107:105–170.
   2005 *Ephraim George Squier and the Development of Americanist Anthropology*. University of Nebraska Press, Lincoln.

Bieder, Robert E.
   1986 *Science Encounters the Indian, 1820–1880*. University of Oklahoma Press, Norman.

Bieder, Robert E., and Thomas G. Tax
   1974 From Ethnologists to Anthropologists: A Brief History of the American Ethnological Society. In *American Anthropology: The Early Years*, edited by John V. Murra, pp. 11–12. *Proceedings of the American Anthropological Society, 1974*.

Bray, Tamara L. (editor)
   2001 *The Future of the Past: Archaeologists, Native Americans, and Repatriation*. Garland Publishing, New York.

Browman, David L.
  2002   Frederic Ward Putnam: Contributions to the Development of Anthropological Institutions and Encouragement of Women Practitioners. In *New Perspectives on the Origins of Americanist Archaeology*, edited by David L. Browman and Stephen Williams, pp. 209–241. University of Alabama Press, Tuscaloosa.
Carter, Edward Carlos
  1993   *"One Grand Pursuit": A Brief History of the American Philosophical Society's first 250 Years, 1743–1993*. American Philosophical Society, Philadelphia.
Conkey, Margaret W., and Janet D. Spector
  1984   Archaeology and the Study of Gender. In *Advances in Archaeological Method and Theory*, Vol. 7, edited by Michael B. Schiffer, pp. 1–38. Academic Press, New York.
Darnell, Regna, and Frederick W. Gleach
  2002   Editor's Introduction. In *Celebrating a Century of the American Anthropological Association: Presidential Portraits*, edited by Regna Darnell and Frederick W. Gleach, pp. ix–xxii. American Anthropological Association, Arlington, Virginia.
Davis, Hester A.
  1982   Professionalism in Archaeology. *American Antiquity* 47:158–163.
Davis, Hester A., and Marcel Kornfeld
  2007   The Council of Affiliated Societies: Past, Present, and Future. *The SAA Archaeological Record* 7(3):35–36.
Dyson, Stephen L.
  1998   *Ancient Marbles to American Shores: Classical Archaeology in the United States*. University of Pennsylvania Press, Philadelphia.
Evans, Joan
  1956   *A History of the Society of Antiquaries*. Oxford University Press, Oxford.
Gero, Joan, and Margaret Conkey (editors)
  1991   *Engendering Archaeology: Women and Prehistory*. Blackwell, Oxford.
Goldstein, Daniel
  1994   "Yours for Science": The Smithsonian Institution's Correspondents and the Shape of Scientific Community in Nineteenth Century America. *Isis* 85(4):573–599.
Haber, Samuel
  1991   *The Quest for Authority and Honor in the American Professions, 1750–1900*. The University of Chicago Press, Chicago.
Harmon, David, Francis P. McManamon, and Dwight P. Pitcaithley
  2006   *The Antiquities Act: A Century of American Archaeology, Historic Preservation, and Nature Conservation*. University of Arizona Press, Tucson.
Hegmon, Michelle
  2003   Setting Theoretical Egos Aside: Issues and Theory in North American Archaeology. *American Antiquity* 68:213–243.
Hertzberg, Hazel W.
  1979   Nationality, Anthropology, and Pan-Indianism in the Life of Arthur C. Parker (Seneca). *Proceedings of the American Philosophical Society* 123:47–72.

Hinsley, Curtis M., Jr.
   1985   From Shell-Heaps to Stelae: Early Anthropology at the Peabody Museum. In *Objects and Others: Essays on Museums and Material Culture*, edited by George W. Stocking, Jr., pp. 49–74. University of Wisconsin Press, Madison.
   1986   Edgar Lee Hewett and the School of American Archaeology in Santa Fe, 1906–1912. In *American Archaeology Past And Future*, edited by David J. Meltzer, Don L. Fowler, and Jeremy A. Sabloff, pp. 217–236. Smithsonian Institution Press, Washington, D.C.
   1994   *The Smithsonian and the American Indian: Making a Moral Anthropology in Victorian America*. Smithsonian Institution Press, Washington, D.C.

Hunter, Michael
   1971   The Royal Society and the Origins of British Archaeology. *Antiquity* 65:113–121.

Judd, Neil M.
   1967   *The Bureau of American Ethnology: A Partial History*. University of Oklahoma Press, Norman.

Kehoe, Alice B., and Mary Beth Emmerichs (editors)
   1999   *Assembling the Past: Studies in the Professionalization of Archaeology*. University of New Mexico Press, Albuquerque.

Killion, Thomas W. (editor)
   2008   *Opening Archaeology: Repatriation's Impact on Contemporary Research and Practice*. SAR Press, Santa Fe.

Lamb, Daniel S.
   1906   The Story of the Anthropological Society of Washington. *American Anthropologist* 8:564–579.

Lange, Charles H., and Carroll L. Riley
   1996   *Bandelier: the Life and Times of Adolf Bandelier*. University of Utah Press, Salt Lake City.

Levine, Philippa
   1986   *The Amateur and the Professional: Antiquarians, Historians, and Archaeologists in Victorian England, 1838–1886*. Cambridge University Press, Cambridge.

Lynott, Mark J., and Alison Wylie (editors)
   2000   *Ethics in American Archaeology*, second edition. Society for American Archaeology, Washington, D.C.

McGuire, Randall H.
   1992   *A Marxist Archaeology*. Academic Press, San Diego.
   2008   *Archaeology as Political Action*. University of California Press, Berkeley.

McKern, W. C.
   1935   Editorial. *American Antiquity* 1:81–83.

McKusick, Marshall
   1970   *The Davenport Conspiracy*. Report #1, Office the State Archaeologist, Iowa City, Iowa.

Meltzer, David J.
   1998   Introduction: Ephraim Squier, Edwin Davis, and the Making of an American Classic. In *Ancient Monuments of the Mississippi Valley*, by Ephraim G. Squier and Edwin Davis, pp. 1–97. Smithsonian Institution Press, Washington, D.C.

Meltzer, David J., and Robert C. Dunnell (editors)
  1992 *The Archaeology of William Henry Holmes*. Smithsonian Institution Press, Washington, D.C.
Meltzer, David J., Don D. Fowler, and Jeremy A. Sabloff (editors)
  1986 *American Archaeology Past and Future: A Celebration of the Society for American Archaeology 1935–1985*. Smithsonian Institution Press, Washington, D.C.
Milanich, Jerald T.
  2001 A Peek at the Past. *Archaeology* 54(5):38–39.
Patterson, Thomas C.
  2002 *Toward a Social History of Archaeology in the United States*. Wadsworth/Thomson Learning, Belmont, California.
  2003 *Marx's Ghost: Conversations with Archaeologists*. Berg, Oxford.
Reyman, Jonathan (editor)
  1992 *Rediscovering Our Past: Essays on the History of American Archaeology*. Avebury, Aldershot, England.
Sabloff, Jeremy A.
  1985 American Antiquity's First Fifty Years: An Introductory Comment. *American Antiquity* 50:228–236.
  2005 Processual Archaeology. In *Archaeology: The Key Concepts*, edited by Colin Renfrew and Paul Bahn, pp. 212–219. Routledge, London.
  2008 *Archaeology Matters: Action Archaeology in the Modern World*. Left Coast Press, Walnut Creek, California.
Schmidt, Peter R., and Thomas C. Patterson (editors)
  1995 *Making Alternative Histories: The Practice of Archaeology and History in Non-Western Settings*. School of American Research Press, Santa Fe.
Sheftel, Phoebe S.
  1979 The AIA 1879–1979: a Centennial Review. *American Journal of Archaeology* 83(1):3–17.
Smith, Duane A.
  1988 *Mesa Verde National Park: Shadows of the Centuries*. University Press of Kansas, Lawrence.
Snead, James E.
  1999 Science, Commerce, and Control: Patronage and the Development of Anthropological Archaeology in the Americas. *American Anthropologist* 101:256–271.
  2001 *Ruins and Rivals: The Making of Southwest Archaeology*. University of Arizona Press, Tucson.
  2002 The "Western Idea": Local Societies and American Archaeology. In *Excavating our Past: Perspectives on the History of the Archaeological Institute of America*, edited by Susan Heuck Allen, pp. 123–140. Archaeological Institute of America, Boston.
Vitelli, Karen D., and Chip Colwell-Chanthaphonh (editors)
  2006 *Archaeological Ethics*, second edition. AltaMira Press, Lanham, Maryland.
Watkins, Joe
  2000 *Indigenous Archaeology: American Indian Values and Scientific Practice*. AltaMira Press, Walnut Creek, California.

Willey, Gordon R., and Jeremy A. Sabloff
   1993 *A History of American Archaeology*, third edition. W.H. Freeman & Co., San Francisco.

Woodbury, Richard
   1985 Regional Archaeology Conferences. *American Antiquity* 50:434–444.
   1993 *60 Years of Southwestern Archaeology: A History of the Pecos Conference.* University of New Mexico Press, Albuquerque.

Zeder, Melinda
   1997 *The American Archaeologist: A Profile*. Altamira Press, Walnut Creek, California.

4

Consultation and Collaboration with Descendant Communities

STEPHEN W. SILLIMAN *and* T. J. FERGUSON

Archaeologists who belong to the Society for American Archaeology, as well as other major professional organizations, have an ethical mandate to consult with the descendants of the people who lived in the archaeological sites we investigate. This mandate is articulated in the principle of accountability in the Society's "Principles of Archaeological Ethics" (http://saa.org/AbouttheSociety/PrinciplesofArchaeologicalEthics/tabid/203/Default.aspx). The principle commits us "to make every reasonable effort, in good faith, to consult actively with affected group(s), with the goal of establishing a working relationship that can be beneficial to the discipline and to all parties involved" (Watkins et al. 1995:33). Several elements are open for interpretation in this principle, including who counts as a descendant, what constitutes reasonable effort, how consultation is defined, who determines which groups are affected, and how benefit is evaluated. Nonetheless, the principle stands as a guide for best practice, despite the complex array of political, economic, social, and cultural milieus that surround archaeologists working in all areas of the world. In addition, many who work in the United States also find themselves with a legal mandate to conduct government-to-government consultation with Indigenous descendant groups to comply with the National Historic Preservation Act of 1966 (NHPA), the Native American Graves Protection and Repatriation Act of 1990 (NAGPRA), and other federal legislation (see Sebastian, this volume; Wilcox, this volume).

The synergy of these ethical and legal mandates sets the stage for a variety of productive consultative and collaborative relationships between archaeologists and descendant communities of all varieties (and encourages individuals from these communities to become archaeologists in their own right). While archaeologists consult with communities because of legal and professional requirements, they collaborate because they want to. The voluntary nature of collaborative work deepens consultation beyond what Watkins (2000) calls "legislated ethics." For Native Americans, the sovereignty explicitly recognized in government-to-government consultation may only be implied in collaboration (Gonzalez et al. 2006:392), but the latter remains important. However, members of these communities can often tell when consultation is bureaucratic and formulaic rather than a practice that archaeologists enjoy, encourage, value, and benefit from doing. Either way, collaboration and consultation require more than "public outreach." While outreach benefits various groups, particularly school children, disenfranchised groups, local residents, and the general public, it tends to create a one-sided delivery from archaeologists to others. This forecloses important "feedback" from those recipients, particularly since the delivered product—knowledge, artifact, and experience—exists already in a relatively final form before delivery to the public. In contrast, collaboration begins earlier and entails more intellectual, practical, and personal interaction between archaeologists and the communities with which they work.

In this chapter, we answer a number of questions about collaboration between archaeologists and descendant communities, including how those communities are defined, what collaboration entails, how collaboration can be conducted in various ways, and how this work leads to multivocal narratives and multicultural practices. We focus largely on North America and Native Americans, but the implications extend far beyond that continent. Looking back on 75 years of the Society for American Archaeology's history, we argue that effective consultation and productive collaboration with descendant groups has improved and will continue to improve archaeology by expanding the repertoire of questions we ask, developing new methods to investigate those questions, opening the interpretation of results to include Indigenous and other perspectives on theory and history, and making the discipline accountable outside of itself. We admit that this position is both reflective and directive.

What are Descendant and Traditionally Associated Communities?

Conceptualizing descendant communities is complicated. They are more than simply the biological progeny of the people who lived in the sites we study (Borgstede 2002; Meskell and Van Damme 2008; Singleton and Orser 2003). Beyond genetics, these communities are defined by their historical, cultural, and symbolic associations to places that they consider ancestral, and these values and beliefs must be taken into account in addition to the biological heritage of individual people. Descendant communities can be local, residing in proximity to ancestral sites, or they may be distant or diasporic, having migrated hundreds or thousands of kilometers away from the ancient or recent homes of their ancestors. The identification of descendant communities is contingent on the interpretation of social and historical contexts, as well as the self-identification of social groups, and these can be hotly contested issues (Chirikure and Pwiti 2008). Descendant communities in the Americas, for instance, encompass many groups, including Indian tribes, progeny of enslaved African-Americans, offspring of Hispanic colonizers, sons and daughters of pilgrims and pioneers, more recent immigrants of the last century, and the complex intermixtures of some or all of these. Deciding which social groups form communities that are related to the past groups that we study has political and intellectual consequences that warrant careful consideration. In particular, anthropological concepts of descent must be balanced with Indigenous and folk concepts of ancestry in order to establish fair and equitable dialogue with people who are interested in and may be affected by what we do.

Traditionally associated communities, a concept fostered by the National Park Service (1998), differ from descendant groups in that they do not necessarily claim biological descent from the people who lived in the archaeological sites we investigate. Instead, these communities have traditional ties to archaeological sites that occur in the area in which they live, perhaps for many generations, and they often have deep emotional attachments to these places. We should seek out and consult with traditionally associated communities much as we do with descendant groups, although some of the parameters will vary, particularly when questions of "firstness" come into play. Still, we need to consult these communities about research that impacts archaeological sites so their cultural values and beliefs can be taken into account as we design and implement research.

What is Collaboration?

Collaboration—working jointly on a project—has a long history in archaeology. In fact, we argue that archaeology has always been about collaboration, but politics and disciplinary tradition structure who participates in that collaboration, and only recently has community collaboration become more common. Traditionally, one type of collaboration in archaeology has grown out of the enormous amount of information generated from archaeological fieldwork—that is, data spanning a number of disciplines including soil science, geology, zoology, botany, architecture, material culture studies, chemistry, ecology, and more. The ability to use multiple sources of information to their fullest potential is frequently well beyond the expertise of a single archaeologist, so collaboration often takes the form of specialist-to-specialist interactions (see Zeder et al., this volume) and has produced the interdisciplinary nature of archaeology today.

Another type of collaboration stems from the impossibility of doing fieldwork alone. Digging complex stratigraphy, screening hundreds of kilograms of sediments, recovering artifacts, mapping discoveries, completing paperwork, and backfilling requires coordination among many team members. This labor is regularly provided by undergraduate, graduate, and sometimes secondary students who are taught and supervised by professional archaeologists in formal field schools; by skilled and semi-skilled field technicians employed by cultural resource management firms; by volunteers of all ages who seek archaeological experience; and by local populations hired as seasonal workers by national and international archaeological teams. Until recently, these "reservoirs of cheap labor" (Chirikure and Pwiti 2008:467; Shepherd 2003) or workers at the trowel's edge (Berggren and Hodder 2003) have not been considered as legitimate stakeholders of the pasts being investigated.

Collaboration with descendant communities has become an increasingly popular addition in the last 40 years spurred largely by the inclusion of Native American tribes, First Nations, and other descendant communities in the historic preservation program of the United States and other countries, and by an ethical commitment on the part of archaeologists to implement an inclusive theoretical program relevant to Indigenous peoples and local stakeholders. Collaboration with descendant communities, particularly Indigenous ones, has become a global project wherein archaeologists seek to work with local people who have a direct interest in and involvement with the archaeology, history, and lands that we study (Meskell and Van Damme 2008; Smith and Jackson 2008).

As Colwell-Chanthaphonh and Ferguson (2008) point out, collaboration occurs along a continuum of practice from resistance, to communicating research plans, to full-fledged involvement of descendant groups in the design, implementation, and interpretation of results. At one end of the continuum is a mode of resistance in which the goals of archaeology develop in opposition to descendant groups and traditionally associated communities. As a result, information about heritage resources is secreted by all parties, and stakeholders have no voice in interpreting the past. Although resistance seems like the antithesis of collaboration, this mode of interaction happens when two or more groups are pitted against one another. This opposition forms a basis for building communities nevertheless, be they communities of Indigenous people opposing archaeologists or communities of archaeologists opposing Indigenous peoples or a blurring with archaeologists allied with and assisting Indigenous groups, all of which were evident in the recent controversies surrounding the Ancient One, or Kennewick Man (Burke et al. 2008; Chatters 2001). The communities created or empowered by opposition sometimes produce a rapprochement between archaeologists and Indigenous peoples that allows them to cooperate on future projects on an equal basis.

In the participatory mode, archaeologists confer with descendant groups and invite them to be involved in research activities, but they develop the goals of research independently. By virtue of participation, descendant groups gain a voice in the interpretation of research results. This voice is strengthened when a project achieves full collaboration, with research goals and methods developed and implemented jointly by archaeologists and descendant group members. Collaborative research provides a means by which to best meet the needs of all parties interested in archaeological research. To achieve mutual benefit does not necessarily mean that all parties benefit equally or completely, but it does mean that participants have open dialogue, make respectful compromises, and seek a useful process and final product. Beyond collaboration, some tribes elect to exercise Indigenous control over archaeology on their lands as part of self-determination. This Indigenous control often entails hiring archaeologists to assist tribes in meeting their goals, resulting in collaborative research. Some of the archaeologists

Indigenous groups hire are community members, but others are not (e.g., Bendremer and Thomas 2008; Two Bears 2008).

The various modes of interaction along the collaborative continuum are not mutually exclusive in that some projects start out in one mode and then progress to another mode as research unfolds. Other projects have some components that are participatory and others that are collaborative. Individual archaeologists often work sequentially in various modes as new projects develop with new opportunities for engagement with descendant communities. True collaborative research is predicated on all parties developing a fundamental trust with one another, and this trust requires a long-term research commitment on the part of archaeologists working with descendant groups.

When do Archaeologists Collaborate?

In North America—much like in Australia, South America, Central America, and Africa—archaeology developed in a colonial context where the preeminent goal was to maximize scientific knowledge by extracting artifacts from archaeological sites and removing them for study and curation in museums, often far from their original place of origin. Little thought was given to how the disturbance of ancestral places and the displacement of material culture impacted descendant groups, particularly since most archaeological research in North America until the mid-twentieth century focused on studying Native American pasts whose descendants had a muted political voice. Although descendant groups and traditionally associated peoples often provided labor for archaeological excavations, these groups were rarely involved in setting or implementing the scientific research agenda. In most instances, their labor has long been forgotten. Decisions about which sites to study and how those sites were investigated remained the purview of archaeologists who were primarily concerned with advancing scientific goals.

Over time in the United States, the unregulated removal of archaeological materials on federal and tribal land came to be viewed as a threat to the integrity of the archaeological record, and thus an impediment to scientific study. In response, Congress passed a series of laws to protect archaeological sites, beginning with the Antiquities Act of 1906 and continuing through the National Historic Preservation Act of 1966 (NHPA), as amended in 1992 (King 2008; Sebastian 2004). The federal historic preservation program defined by these laws initially conceived of places of past human occupation as scientific resources that could be managed much like natural resources to conserve scientific values and maximize research potential. Only after the amendment of the NHPA in 1992 did federally recognized tribes gain the ability to participate fully in the national historic preservation program by developing tribal historic preservation offices (THPO). THPOs strengthen the control of tribes over cultural resources management and archaeological research on their land (Ferguson 2000).

The field of cultural resource management (CRM) developed in the United States after 1966, and an increasing number of archaeologists began to work in the governmental and private sectors to provide the professional services needed to implement the federal historic preservation program (Snead and Sabloff, this volume). In the 1970s several tribes established tribal archaeology programs to capture the economic benefits of CRM and facilitate development of infrastructure on their lands by having archaeologists assist with historic preservation compliance activities. The archaeologists who worked for tribal programs applied research to meet tribal goals and objectives, including developing tribally owned contract archaeology businesses and historic preservation offices; assisting with repatriation of human remains, funerary objects, and sacred artifacts; helping to develop tribal museums; and conducting research for litigation of land and water rights (Anyon et al. 2000; Downer 1997; Forsman 1997; Jones and McBride 2006; Stapp and Burney 2002). CRM work sponsored by tribes entails participatory and collaborative modes of research, and the cultural experience of archaeologists working directly for or with Indigenous peoples had a profound influence that served to balance scientific and Indigenous beliefs and values about how and why archaeology should be conducted. This experience shaped their professional ethics profoundly (Adams 1984). Some of these archaeologists began to espouse a paradigm of covenantal archaeology in which tribes and archaeologists worked under explicit agreements about the goals and methods governing archaeology on tribal lands (Bendremer and Thomas 2008; Powell et al. 1993; Zimmerman 2000).

Participation of tribes in the historic preservation program is legally mandated, with consultation required at specific points in the compliance process (Ferguson 2009). Archaeologists are required to confer with federally recognized tribes about the management and investigation of archaeological sites impacted by federal undertakings. In the course of discussing managerial decisions, many tribes, including those that do not employ their own archaeologists, decide to become directly involved in research, moving the process from participation in the historic preservation program into collaboration in archaeological research (Kerber 2006). Tribal members help develop research designs, determine appropriate methods, participate in fieldwork, and share authorship in report preparation (Dowdall and Parrish 2002; Ferguson et al. 2004; Swidler et al. 2000).

Outside of CRM, some archaeologists occasionally applied their work and collaborated with descendant groups to meet goals defined by Indigenous communities. The most notable of these were the archaeologists employed as expert witnesses during the Indian Claims Commission established in 1946 to quiet title to lands taken from tribes without payment during the nineteenth and twentieth centuries (Ellis 1974; Ross 1973). The research goals and methods of these archaeologists were informed by their collaborative work, and in some instances archaeologists were granted permission to excavate archaeological sites on tribal land that were theretofore off-limits to scientific study (Ellis and Brody 1964).

The passage of NAGPRA in 1990, with its provisions mandating consultation with tribes and traditional religious leaders during the process of repatriating human remains and sacred objects, led to a tremendous increase in the number of archaeologists directly interacting with descendant groups. One of the unintended consequences of NAGPRA has been an increase in collaborative research as the social and political ties forged in consultation carry forward into new research projects of interest to both archaeologists and descendant groups (Killion 2008). Collaboration arising out of NAGPRA has infused archaeology with new methods, theory, and epistemological viewpoints. A similar process to the CRM context occurs in museum settings, where consultation pursuant to NAGPRA requires that archaeologists and other museum employees engage in sustained dialogue with federally recognized tribes concerning culturally affiliated human remains, funerary objects, objects of cultural patrimony, and sacred objects in museum collections. This dialogue leads to new collaborative engagements in which tribes participate in the documentation of collections, design of new exhibits, and other museum activities (Kreps 2003; Lippert 2008).

Collaborative approaches forged in the area of Americanist CRM and NAGPRA have been embraced by university-based archaeologists, who have conceptualized and articulated the goals of collaborative research as a critical means of making archaeology socially relevant and democratic (Colwell-

Chanthaphonh and Ferguson 2008; Dongoske et al. 2000; Hodder 2002; Silliman, ed. 2008; Zimmerman 2008a). The historical trajectory of the development of collaborative archaeology in Canada mirrors much of what transpired in the United States (Lilley 2000; Nicholas and Andrews 1997; Peck et al. 2003). Especially notable in Canada was the early adoption of archaeological training in formal educational programs as a form of Indigenous empowerment (Nicholas 1997). Bound by ethical rather than legal requirements to consult with descendant groups, archaeologists based in the academy follow the same general process as described for CRM. The goals and outcomes of archaeological research are negotiated with descendant groups to create projects that are both culturally relevant and conducted in a manner to enhance Indigenous and local community goals and objectives (Dillehay 2008; Heckenberger 2004, 2008; McDavid 2002). Academic archaeologists have also embraced collaborative approaches in training students at field schools in the social and intellectual skills they need to practice archaeology in the twenty-first century (Bendremer and Thomas 2008; Bruseth et al. 2000; Herle 1994; Mills 2000; Mills et al. 2008; Preucel et al. 2005; Pyburn 2003; Rossen 2008; Silliman and Sebastian Dring 2008; see also Altschul and Patterson, this volume). These skills include innovative research design, low-impact archaeological methods, incorporation of Indigenous oral narratives into archaeological interpretation, and integration of multiple sources of information in archaeological research (Lightfoot 2008).

Why Collaborate?

Collaborative archaeology employs a variety of research and participatory techniques because a multiplicity of peoples have a stake in how heritage sites and objects are defined, managed, studied, and interpreted (Colwell-Chanthaphonh and Ferguson 2008:7; Watkins 2003). Common to the various practices of collaborative archaeology is a research model that balances ethics, methods, and archaeological theory with the concerns of descendant groups and traditionally associated communities. Because the legal arena of consultation is complicated and historically focused on Native American concerns, we discuss collaboration more broadly within and outside of consultation. Since we define collaboration as a function of wants, we must ask the following question: What makes archaeologists *want* to collaborate, given the highly variable and exclusionary ways they have handled various community, public, and scholarly constituents over the last century?

We consider theoretical interests and political commitments separately even though they frequently intertwine in the practices of individual archaeologists. Ethics play an unquestionably critical role in guiding current and future ideas and practices about collaboration and deserve attention in their own right (e.g., Colwell-Chanthaphonh and Ferguson 2004; Zimmerman 2006; Zimmerman et al. 2003), but we concern ourselves here with what makes ethics of community work and cooperation desirable and workable. An impetus for increased collaboration between professional and academic archaeologists and a variety of descendant communities comes from developments in theory and politics inside and outside of archaeology. Elements shared across these perspectives include political awareness, social justice, reflexivity, and multivocality.

Post-processual theory has contributed to community archaeology, as demonstrated by Ian Hodder's work at Çatalhöyük in Turkey. Hodder developed important elements of practice as he navigated a variety of communities, including local residents, politicians, New Age Goddess followers, and artists (Hodder 2002, 2003). This multicommunity, multistakeholder responsiveness has not garnered a significant following in North America, where archaeologists focus their attention primarily on descendant communities. Hodder's collaborative model employing the metaphor of "at the trowel's edge" (Berggren and Hodder 2003) has had more appeal, however, acknowledging the need to incorporate community members and other collaborators at all levels of the archaeological process. A recent book, *Collaborating at the Trowel's Edge* (Silliman, ed. 2008), has used this model to frame the ways that North American archaeologists work with Native communities, develop research designs, excavate in the field, narrate histories, and teach students. This particular goal is actually more postcolonial than postprocessual per se, and such terminologies and approaches are increasing as this decade draws to a close (see Preucel and Cipolla 2008). Moreover, following more pragmatist philosophical and critical race studies, Carol McDavid (1997, 2002) developed a community-based approach in Brazoria, Texas, that uses web technology and critical dialogue to incorporate descendant groups in her research on an eighteenth-century plantation. Although the collaborative elements developed later in McDavid's (2007) research, the goal has been to recognize and encourage the project as a "historically situated conversation" involving the local community, both descendant and non-descendant, African-American and White, historically enslaved and enslaving (see also Franklin and Paynter, this volume).

Alongside the general theoretical parameters established by the postprocessual agenda are the contributions of feminist and Marxist archaeologists to thinking about and doing collaborative archaeology. Spector's (1993) pivotal early work reveals how a feminist agenda encourages collaborative research with Native American communities, including knowledge sharing, self-reflexivity, and multivocality. Recently, Conkey's (2005) assessment of feminist and Indigenous archaeologies reveals additional commonalities. Marxist archaeologists also developed approaches to communities, frequently framed by class rather than ethnicity, which encourage sharing power and asserting a political goal in archaeological practice. The Colorado Coal Field War Project, centered on the early twentieth-century workers' strike and subsequent massacre in southern Colorado, used this approach (Ludlow Collective 2001; McGuire 2008; Saitta 2005), demonstrating the value of thinking about archaeology as a craft coproduced with and for communities (Shanks and McGuire 1996). In this project, archaeologists considered the mining community as a descendant group based on a shared class position as unionized laborers rather than on biological or cultural heritage (McGuire 2008:10; Franklin and Paynter, this volume).

Politics have also helped to shape collaborative archaeologies. The politics of "public archaeology" have led some archaeologists to account for how archaeology can and should serve a variety of publics (Little and Zimmerman, this volume). Some versions of this political approach promote the relevance of archaeology to public interests, in part to ensure that the various publics continue to support the enterprise of archaeology. In these formulations, archaeology is already seen to be a part of certain communities, usually framed as generalized, if not national, communities (e.g., McManamon 2000, 2003). In a more radical way, archaeologists like McGuire (2008) anchor their community archaeology in Marxist theory to argue for praxis, the use of archaeology to intervene in the world. Similarly, others from critical archaeological traditions use community archaeology projects to develop a more democratic archaeology and a more democratic society (McDavid 2002:312). This comprises part of an effort to situate archaeological practice within a wide spectrum of community interests and civic engagement (Little and Shackel 2007).

The activist politics of particular communities, mainly Indigenous and minority, have ushered in new forms of cooperative archaeological projects. Some communities have requested, if not demanded, more accountability from archaeologists and more openness in the archaeological process that permits their participation as researchers, consultants, stakeholders, and historical or political authorities. This is exemplified in the African Burial Ground controversy that erupted in New York City in the early 1990s. Minimal consultation and mismanagment of the African Burial Ground project metamorphosed through community insistence into collaboration (Franklin and Paynter, this volume; LaRoche and Blakey 1997; Perry 1997). Other collaborations between archaeologists and African-American communities have developed in a more positive context (Cuddy and Leone 2008; Shackel and Gadsby 2008). Matthews (2008), for instance, has revisited the nature of collaboration and community work with African-American communities in New Orleans, Louisiana, by emphasizing critical anthropological understandings of the politics of difference rather than relying on "rigid identity markers" to define communities and collaborations. Similarly, Mullins (2007) has approached the "color line" in Indianapolis to unpack assumptions and to encourage community participation and development in multicultural urban contexts.

The most noticeable impact of activist politics in American archaeology appears in the form of Indigenous archaeology, a term widely used now to refer to archaeologies with, for, and by Native people (Nicholas 1997, 2008; Silliman 2008; Smith and Wobst 2005; *contra* McGhee 2008). Community politics at national and at local levels spurred many archaeologists in the 1980s and 1990s to form productive working relationships with Indigenous communities. The struggles behind the passage of NAGPRA reveal these early antagonisms as communities fought to have their voices heard and their repatriation claims recognized (Sebastian, this volume; Wilcox, this volume). The development of Indigenous archaeology after 2000 has been grounded more in an ethic of cooperation and a recognition of the value and legitimacy of Indigenous claims and knowledge, due in large part to Watkins' (2000) seminal contribution. The increasing interest in archaeology by Native American and First Nations communities has transformed archaeological practice. Several volumes dedicated entirely to the practical, theoretical, and methodological dimensions of Indigenous archaeology have appeared in the last decade (Dongoske et al. 2000; Ferguson and Colwell-

Chanthaphonh 2006; Kerber 2006; Silliman 2008; Smith and Wobst, eds. 2005), along with other edited volumes (Colwell-Chanthaphonh and Ferguson 2008; Shackel and Chambers 2004) and journal issues (Atalay 2006) that have made notable contributions to Native American community archaeology.

Archaeology as Multivocal and Multicultural Practices

Far from compromising the standards of archaeological practice as a few detractors seem to argue (McGhee 2008), collaborations with a variety of communities, including descendant and traditionally associated groups, have expanded the questions asked, the methods used to answer them, and the interpretation of subsequent results (Zimmerman 2008a). Based on the contexts of history, theory, and practice discussed earlier, we suggest that working closely with descendant communities adds a valuable dimension to our multidisciplinary partnering. It can provide historical information, local environmental and geographical information, sharing of power and resources, participatory historical narration, political and symbolic capital, reflexive insight into the archaeological process, and progress toward social justice and restitution for disenfranchised groups. Therefore, why the collaborative approach has taken so long to develop in Americanist archaeology is puzzling given the long history of archaeology's connection to anthropology in the United States. How can archaeologists proceed without recognizing that they are entering communities and landscapes with different cultural, religious, historical, and practical orientations? The very fact of needing permission to access land demonstrates that the acquisition of archaeological data grounded therein comes with political and social consequences. Archaeologists should not assume that their research does not "do work" in the political and cultural world, and that they are powerless to silence or summon important histories and objects. Doing archaeology as anthropology necessitates paying careful attention to the *living* people who descend from the past and not just to the past.

If we are to emphasize the "public" in public archaeology (Little 2002), we need to share—and this does not mean *give up entirely*, since archaeologists have valuable skills and knowledges—the interpretive authority and physical products of archaeology. This means that coauthorship with community members and peer review by descendant communities may be critical elements for collaborative projects. Sometimes we find that community members want to cowrite scholarly publications (e.g., Bendremer and Thomas 2008; Silliman and Sebastian Dring 2008). At other times, a community person involved in directing the research may wish to be listed as an author much in the same way that the directors of scientific laboratories will be listed on publications written by postdoctoral researchers working on their research team. With authorship comes responsibility for the contents of a publication, so Indigenous people and other descendant communities approach this opportunity as part of their serious commitment to a project.

An interesting development in collaborative archaeologies is the creation of knowledge in the context of application, as what many might term "applied anthropology." Archaeological problem definition, methods, and findings all improve when the communities involved with archaeologists use the research. We find that archaeology can give back to descendant communities in profound ways, including sharing knowledge produced during the archaeological process. Such knowledge can be used as a resource for cultural preservation, resource management, site protection, alternative histories, repatriation efforts, economic incentives, political capital, education, and more. When crafted in collaborative contexts, knowledge resonates strongly with community needs (Shanks and McGuire 1996).

An important component of equity and reciprocation involves sharing the financial benefits of archaeology. Paying a fair wage for the work of Indigenous consultants, when appropriate, and seeking funds to pay for tribal research, participation, and travel of community members to professional meetings so they can participate in the dissemination of knowledge and interact with the wider archaeological community require dedicated effort on the part of collaborating archaeologists. Peers who review grant proposals need to be aware that these are essential to the collaborative process, and are thus a legitimate part of project budgets, even if expensive. Conducting archaeological research in collaborative contexts also permits the *practice*, not just the results, of archaeology to serve a greater good. The process of working with communities is as important as the products of that work (Silliman 2008:9–11). Many communities use archaeological field and laboratory training to build capacity for its members who may then seek education and careers in archaeology or any number of other fields. Community volunteers or interns on projects with strong educational components, such as field schools, offer low-cost training options for economically disenfranchised communities (Silliman and Sebastian Dring 2008). Encouraging community members to be conversant in archaeology's jargon gives them the opportunity to join or to contest those languages. The discipline can only benefit, even if that means undergo harsh critique, when more of "the public" knows about what we do.

When archaeology takes place in a community context, we come to realize that we need to mitigate the effects of archaeological work on people past and present. Although archaeologists conceive of their practice as scientific, nonharmful, and ethical, communities may evaluate our work using different values. Beyond the obvious concerns with disturbing human remains, Indigenous communities often have to take steps to ameliorate the cultural, political, and spiritual impacts of fieldwork, such as digging holes in the earth (Dowdall and Parrish 2002; Million 2005; Silliman and Sebastian Dring 2008). Respecting power, even when scientifically trained archaeologists may not recognize its cultural dimensions, is important. Reflecting about collaboration with archaeologists, Leigh Kuwanwisiwma (2008), the director of the Hopi Cultural Preservation Office, notes that this endeavor requires equality, respect, and reciprocity. Trust, the underpinning of all collaborative relationships, can only be established when archaeologists work with Indigenous people over many years. Members of descendant communities need to see how archaeologists react to the myriad challenges that inevitably arise in collaborative work so that they know the archaeologist will honor the commitments entailed in ethical and equitable research.

Conclusion

We conclude this chapter with optimism and caution. We are optimistic that archaeology will continue to improve with more collaboration and community involvement, becoming better in empirical and scientific applications, as well as cultural and human practices. To accomplish this, we need more theoretical treatment of what collaborations are and what they can produce, and more methodological guidance for how to do community archaeology in the many diverse contexts, some of which involve rather internally heterogeneous communities, that archaeologists face (Marshall 2002; Watkins and Ferguson 2005). We also need more explicit attention to what has been termed "ethnographic archaeologies" or the systematic and critical approach to the ways that archaeological knowledges, results, and practices take form in the world of politics, emotions, values, heritage, and science (Castañeda and Matthews 2008; Mortenson and Hollowell 2009). In addition, we should not lose sight of the possibility, too, that archaeology does not just work in communities, but also creates them (Zimmerman 2008b). Archaeology should become a practice that does more than take away objects, bodies, history, rights, and power from communities, a characterization of the field that still resonates strongly with Indigenous and minority groups, as Tuscarora singer/songwriter Pura Fé passionately captured in her song "You Still Take." Archaeology should *give back* to communities in responsible and helpful ways. Giving back to communities means many things, and we leave it to readers to continue exploring those possibilities and expanding its horizons.

We must approach this future cautiously as well. By working to integrate the varying perspectives of groups from diverse professional and cultural backgrounds, collaborative archaeology creates opportunities that sometimes lead to unique tensions outside the realm of most academic research or expertise (Adler and Bruning 2008). We need to recognize that collaboration will not always lead to unitary approaches or complete consensus (Brown and Robinson 2006; Kuwanwisiwma 2008; McGuire 2003), and that archaeologists may find themselves at the limits of what interpretations that they, in good faith, can support. Therefore, we need to approach these matters through explicit protocols, open discussions, flexibility, and, most importantly, respect. While our chapter focuses on Indigenous groups, the basic approach we espouse is also effective in working with other communities whose beliefs run counter to standard archaeological interpretation. As Zimmerman (2008c:77) remarks in an essay about interaction with non-Indian "fringe" groups, archaeology has powerful tools that should be used with respect and humility to produce work that communities can use to create their own pasts and meanings for it. The difficult but workable challenge is to do this in a manner that simultaneously respects the scientific basis of our discipline.

As David Hurst Thomas (2008:xii) observes, collaborative archaeology can be transformative, accompanied by significant changes in ethics, methodologies, and actual interpretive results. Thomas counsels, however, that we should not assume that the shift of our profession toward a more inclusive and reciprocal archaeology is either universal or permanent. All archaeologists concerned with the broad range of social and intellectual values inherent in collaborative archaeology need to share these principles with their colleagues and students in order to carry the paradigm forward in the future development of our discipline.

References Cited

Adams, E. Charles
    1984 Archaeology and the Native American: A Case at Hopi. In *Ethics and Values in Archaeology*, edited by Ernestine L. Green, pp. 236–242. Free Press, New York.

Adler, Michael, and Susan Bruning
    2008 Navigating the Fluidity of Social Identity: Collaborative Research into Cultural Affiliation in the American Southwest. In *Collaboration in Archaeological Practice: Engaging Descendant Communities*, edited by Chip Colwell-Chanthaphonh and T. J. Ferguson, pp. 35–54. AltaMira Press, Lanham, Maryland.

Anyon, Roger, T. J. Ferguson, and John R. Welch
    2000 Heritage Management by American Indian Tribes in the Southwestern United States. In *Cultural Resource Management in Contemporary Society: Perspectives on Managing and Presenting the Past*, edited by Francis P. McManamon and Alf Hatton, pp. 120–141. Routledge, London.

Atalay, Sonya (guest editor)
    2006 Decolonizing Archaeology. Special issue, *American Indian Quarterly* 30 (3&4).

Bendremer, Jeffrey C., and Elaine L. Thomas
    2008 The Tribe and the Trowel: An Indigenous Archaeology and the Mohegan Archaeological Field School. In *Collaborating at the Trowel's Edge: Teaching and Learning in Indigenous Archaeology*, edited by Stephen W. Silliman, pp. 50–66. Amerind Studies in Archaeology 2. University of Arizona Press, Tucson.

Berggren, Åsa, and Ian Hodder
    2003 Social Practice, Method, and Some Problems of Field Archaeology. *American Antiquity* 68:421–434.

Borgstede, Greg
    2002 Defining the Descendant Community in a Non-Western Context: The Maya of Highland Guatemala. *Teaching Anthropology: Society for Anthropology in Community Colleges Notes* 9(1):27–29, 38.

Brown, III, John, and Paul A. Robinson
    2006 "The 368 Years' War": The Conditions of Discourse in Narragansett Country. In *Cross-Cultural Collaboration: Native Peoples and Archaeology in the Northeastern United States*, edited by Jordan E. Kerber, pp. 59–75. University of Nebraska Press, Lincoln.

Bruseth, James E., James E. Corbin, Cecile E. Carter, and Bonnie McKee
    2000 Involving the Caddo Tribe during Archaeological Field Schools in Texas: A Cross-Cultural Sharing. In *Working Together: Native Americans and Archaeologists*, edited by Kurt E. Dongoske, Mark Aldenderfer, and Karen Doehner, pp. 129–138. Society for American Archaeology, Washington, D.C.

Burke, Heather, Claire Smith, Dorothy Lippert, Joe Watkins, and Larry Zimmerman (editors)
 2008 *Kennewick Man, Perspectives on the Ancient One*. Left Coast Press, Walnut Creek, California.
Castañeda, Quetzil E., and Christopher Matthews (editors)
 2008 *Ethnographic Archaeologies: Reflections on Stakeholders and Archaeological Practices*. AltaMira Press, Lanham, Maryland.
Chatters, James C.
 2001 *Ancient Encounters: Kennewick Man and the First Americans*. Simon & Schuster, New York.
Chirikure, Shadreck, and Gilbert Pwiti
 2008 Community Involvement in Archaeology and Cultural Heritage Management: An Assessment from Case Studies in Southern Africa and Elsewhere. *Current Anthropology* 49(3):467–485.
Colwell-Chanthaphonh, Chip, and T. J. Ferguson
 2004 Virtue Ethics and the Practice of History: Native Americans and Archaeologists along the San Pedro Valley of Arizona. *Journal of Social Archaeology* 4(1):5–27.
 2008 Introduction: The Collaborative Continuum. In *Collaboration in Archaeological Practice: Engaging Descendant Communities*, edited by Chip Colwell-Chanthaphonh and T. J. Ferguson, pp. 1–32. AltaMira Press, Lanham, Maryland.
Conkey, Margaret
 2005 Dwelling at the Margins, Action at the Intersection? Feminist and Indigenous. *Archaeologies: Journal of the World Archaeological Congress* 1(1):9–59.
Cuddy, Thomas W., and Mark P. Leone
 2008 New Africa: Understanding the Americanization of African Descent Groups through Archaeology. In *Collaboration in Archaeologial Practice: Engaging Descendant Communities*, edited by Chip Colwell-Chanthaphonh and T. J. Ferguson, pp. 203–223. AltaMira Press, Lanham, Maryland.
Dillehay, Tom
 2008 *Monuments, Empires, and Resistance: The Araucanian Polity and Ritual Narratives*. Cambridge University Press, New York.
Dongoske, Kurt E., Mark Aldenderfer, and Karen Doehner (editors)
 2000 *Working Together: Native Americans and Archaeologists*. Society for American Archaeology, Washington, D.C.
Dowdall, Katherine M., and Otis O. Parrish
 2002 A Meaningful Disturbance of the Earth. *Journal of Social Archaeology* 3(1):99–133.
Downer, Alan S.
 1997 Archaeologists—Native American Relations. In *Native Americans and Archaeologists: Stepping Stones to Common Ground*, edited by Nina Swidler, Kurt E. Dongoske, Roger Anyon, and Alan S. Downer, pp. 23–34. AltaMira Press, Walnut Creek, California.
Ellis, Florence Hawley
 1974 Anthropology of the Laguna Land Claims. In *American Indian Ethnohistory, Indians of the Southwest: Pueblo Indians III*, edited by David Agee Horr, pp. 9–120. Garland, New York.

Ellis, Florence Hawley, and J. J. Brody
  1964   Ceramic Stratigraphy and Tribal History at Taos Pueblo. *American Antiquity* 29:316–327.
Ferguson, T. J.
  2000   NHPA: Changing the Role of Native Americans in the Archaeological Study of the Past. In *Working Together: Native Americans and Archaeologists*, edited by Kurt E. Dongoske, Mark Aldenderfer, and Karen Doehner, pp. 25–36. Society for American Archaeology, Washington, D.C.
  2010   Improving the Quality of Archaeology in the United States through Consultation and Collaboration with Native Americans and Descendant Communities. In *Archaeology and Cultural Resource Management: Visions for the Future,* edited by Lynne Sebastian and William D. Lipe. SAR Press, Santa Fe, in press.
Ferguson, T. J., and Chip Colwell-Chanthaphonh
  2006   *History is in the Land: Multivocal Tribal Traditions in Arizona's San Pedro Valley*. University of Arizona Press, Tucson.
Ferguson, T. J., Chip Colwell-Chanthaphonh, and Roger Anyon
  2004   One Valley, Many Histories: Tohono O'odham, Hopi, Zuni and Western Apache History in the San Pedro Valley. *Archaeology Southwest* 18(1):1–15.
Forsman, Leonard A.
  1997   Straddling the Current: A View from the Bridge Over Clear Salt Water. In *Native Americans and Archaeologists: Stepping Stones to Common Ground*, edited by Nina Swidler, Kurt E. Dongoske, Roger Anyon, and Alan S. Downer, pp. 105–111. AltaMira Press, Walnut Creek, California.
Gonzalez, Sara L., Darren Modzelewski, Lee M. Panich, and Tsim D. Schneider
  2006   Archaeology for the Seventh Generation. *American Indian Quarterly* 30 (3/4):388–415.
Heckenberger, Michael
  2004   Archaeology as Indigenous Advocacy in Amazonia. *Practicing Anthropology* 26(3):35–39.
  2008   Entering the Agora: Archaeology, Conservation, and Indigenous Peoples in the Amazon. In *Collaboration in Archaeological Practice: Engaging Descendant Communities*, edited by Chip Colwell-Chanthaphonh and T. J. Ferguson, pp. 243–272. AltaMira Press, Lanham, Maryland.
Herle, Anita
  1994 Museums and Shamans: A Cross-Cultural Collaboration. *Anthropology Today* 10(1):2–5.
Hodder, Ian
  2002   Ethics and Archaeology: The Attempt at Çatalhöyük. *Near Eastern Archaeology* 65(3):174–181.
  2003   Archaeological Reflexivity and the "Local" Voice. *Anthropological Quarterly* 76(1):55–69.
Jones, Brian D., and Kevin A. McBride
  2006   Indigenous Archaeology in Southern New England: Case Studies from the Mashantucket Pequot Reservation. In *Cross-Cultural Collaboration: Native Peoples*

and Archaeology in the Northeastern United States, edited by Jordan E. Kerber, pp. 265–280. University of Nebraska Press, Lincoln.

Kerber, Jordan E. (editor)
2006   *Cross-Cultural Collaboration; Native Peoples and Archaeology in the Northeastern United States.* University of Nebraska Press, Lincoln.

Killion, Thomas (editor)
2008   *Opening Archaeology: Repatriation's Impact on Contemporary Research and Practice.* SAR Press, Santa Fe.

King, Thomas F.
2008   *Cultural Resource Laws and Practice.* 3rd ed. Rowman and Littlefield Publishers, Lanham, Maryland.

Kreps, Christina F.
2003   *Liberating Culture: Cross-Cultural Perspectives on Museums, Curation, and Heritage Preservation.* Taylor & Francis, London.

Kuwanwisiwma, Leigh J.
2008   Collaboration Means Equality, Respect, and Reciprocity, A Conversation about Archaeology and the Hopi Tribe. In *Collaboration in Archaeological Practice: Engaging Descendant Communities*, edited by Chip Colwell-Chanthaphonh and T. J. Ferguson, pp. 151–169. AltaMira Press, Lanham, Maryland.

LaRoche, Cheryl, and Michael L. Blakey
1997   Seizing Intellectual Power: The Dialogue at the New York African Burial Ground. *Historical Archaeology* 31(3):84–106.

Lightfoot, Kent G.
2008   Collaborative Research Programs; Implications for the Practice of North American Archaeology. In *Collaboration at the Trowel's Edge: Teaching and Learning in Indigenous Archaeology*, edited by Stephen W. Silliman, pp. 211–227. Amerind Studies in Archaeology 2. University of Arizona Press, Tucson.

Lilley, Ian (editor)
2000   *Native Title and the Transformation of Archaeology in the Postcolonial World.* Oceania Monographs 50. University of Sydney, Sydney.

Lippert, Dorothy
2008   Not the End, Not the Middle, But the Beginning; Repatriation as a Transformative Mechanism for Archaeologists and Indigenous Peoples. In *Collaboration in Archaeological Practice: Engaging Descendant Communities*, edited by Chip Colwell-Chanthaphonh and T. J. Ferguson, pp. 119–130. AltaMira Press, Lanham, Maryland.

Little, Barbara J.
2002   *Public Benefits of Archaeology.* University Press of Florida, Gainesville.

Little, Barbara J., and Paul Shackel (editors)
2007   *Archaeology as a Tool of Civic Engagement.* Rowman and Littlefield Publishers, Lanham, Maryland.

Ludlow Collective
2001   Archaeology of the Colorado Coal Field War, 1913–1914. In *Archaeologies of the Recent Past*, edited by Victor Buchli and Gavin Lucas, pp. 94–107. Routledge, London.

Marshall, Yvonne
  2002 What is Community Archaeology? *World Archaeology* 34:211–219.

Matthews, Christopher
  2008 The Location of Archaeology. In *Ethnographic Archaeologies: Reflections on Stakeholders and Archaeological Practices*, edited by Quetzil E. Castañeda and Christopher Matthews, pp. 157–182. AltaMira Press, Lanham, Maryland.

McDavid, Carol
  1997 Descendants, Decisions, and Power: The Public Interpretation of the Archaeology of the Levi Jordan Plantation. *Historical Archaeology* 31(3):114–132.
  2002 Archaeologies that Hurt; Descendants that Matter: A Pragmatic Approach to Collaboration in the Public Interpretation of African-American Archaeology. *World Archaeology* 34:303–314.
  2007 Beyond Strategy and Good Intentions: Archaeology, Race, and White Privilege. In *Archaeology as a Tool of Civic Engagement*, edited by Barbara J. Little and Paul Shackel, pp. 67–88. Rowman and Littlefield Publishers, Lanham, Maryland.

McGhee, Robert
  2008 Aboriginalism and the Problem of Indigenous Archaeology. *American Antiquity* 73:579–597.

McGuire, Randall H.
  2003 Why Can't We Be Friends? In *Indigenous People and Archaeology: Honouring the Past, Discussing the Present, Building for the Future*, edited by Trevor Peck, Evelyn Siegfried, and Gerald A. Oetalaar, pp. 92–101. Archaeological Association of the University of Calgary, Calgary.
  2008 *Archaeology as Political Action*. University of California Press, Berkeley.

McManamon, Francis P.
  2000 Archaeological Messages and Messengers. *Public Archaeology* 1(1):5–20.
  2003 Archaeology, Nationalism, and Ancient America. In *The Politics of Archaeology and Identity in a Global Context*, edited by Susan Kane, pp. 115–137. Archaeological Institute of America, Boston.

Meskell, Lynn, and Lynette Sibongile Masuku Van Damme
  2008 Heritage Ethics and Descendant Communities. In *Collaboration in Archaeological Practice: Engaging Descendant Communities*, edited by Chip Colwell-Chanthaphonh and T. J. Ferguson, pp. 131–150. AltaMira Press, Lanham, Maryland.

Million, Tara
  2005 Developing an Aboriginal Archaeology: Receiving Gifts from White Buffalo Calf Woman. In *Indigenous Archaeologies: Decolonizing Theory and Practice*, edited by Claire Smith and H. Martin Wobst, pp. 5–14. Routledge, London and New York.

Mills, Barbara J.
  2000 The Archaeological Field School in the 1990s: Collaboration in Research and Training. In *Working Together: Native Americans and Archaeologists*, edited by Kurt E. Dongoske, Mark Aldenderfer and Karen Doehner, pp. 121–128. Society for American Archaeology, Washington, D.C.

Mills, Barbara J., Mark Altaha, John R. Welch, and T. J. Ferguson
  2008 Field Schools without Trowels: Teaching Archaeological Ethics and Heritage

Preservation in a Collaborative Context. In *Collaborating at the Trowel's Edge: Teaching and Learning in Indigenous Archaeology*, edited by Stephen W. Silliman, pp. 25–49. Amerind Studies in Archaeology 2. University of Arizona Press, Tucson.

Mortenson, Lena, and Julie Hollowell
   2009 *Ethnographies and Archaeologies: Heritage and the Archaeological Past.* University Press of Florida, Gainesville.

Mullins, Paul R.
   2007 Politics, Inequality, and Engaged Archaeology: Community Archaeology along the Color Line. In *Archaeology as a Tool of Civic Engagement*, edited by Barbara J. Little and Paul Shackel, pp. 89–108. Rowman and Littlefield Publishers, Lanham, Maryland.

National Park Service
   1998 NPS-28: Cultural Resource Management Guideline. National Park Service, Washington, D.C.

Nicholas, George P.
   1997 Education and Enpowerment: Archaeology with, for, and by the Shuswap Nation. In *At a Crossroads, Archaeology and First Peoples in Canada*, edited by George P. Nicholas and Thomas D. Andrews, pp. 85–104. Archaeology Press, Simon Fraser University, Burnaby, Canada.
   2008 Native Peoples and Archaeology. In *Encyclopedia of Archaeology*, Volume 3, edited by Deborah M. Pearsall, pp. 1660–1669. Elsevier, Inc., New York.

Nicholas, George P., and Thomas D. Andrews
   1997 *At a Crossroads, Archaeology and First Peoples in Canada.* Archaeology Press, Simon Fraser University, Burnaby, Canada.

Peck, Trevor, Evelyn Siegfried, and Gerald A. Oetelaar (editors)
   2003 *Indigenous Peoples and Archaeology: Honouring the Past, Discussing the Present, Building for the Future.* The Archaeological Association of the University of Calgary, Calgary, Canada.

Perry, Warren
   1997 Archaeology as Community Service: The African Burial Ground Project in New York City. *North American Dialogue* 2(1).

Powell, Shirley, Chrisina E. Garza, and Aubrey Hendricks
   1993 Ethics and Ownership of the Past: The Reburial and Repatriation Controversy. In *Archaeological Method and Theory* 5, edited by Michael Schiffer, pp. 1–42. University of Arizona Press.

Preucel, Robert W., and Craig N. Cipolla
   2008 Indigenous and Postcolonial Archaeologies. In *Archaeology and the Postcolonial Critique*, edited by Matthew Liebmann and Uzma Z. Rizvi, pp. 129–140. AltaMira, Lanham, Maryland.

Preucel, Robert W., Lucy F. Williams, and William Wierzbowksi
   2005 The Social Lives of North American Objects. In *Objects of Everlasting Esteem: Native American Voices on Identity, Art, and Culture*, edited by Lucy F. Williams, William Wierzbowski, and Robert Preucel, pp. 1–26. University of Pennsylvania Museum of Archaeology and Anthropology, Philadelphia.

Pyburn, K. Anne
   2003   What Are We Really Teaching in Archaeological Field Schools? In *Ethical Issues in Archaeology*, edited by Larry J. Zimmerman, Karen D. Vitelli and Julie Hollowell-Zimmer, pp. 213–224. AltaMira Press, Walnut Creek, California.

Ross, Norman A.
   1973   *Index to the Expert Testimony before the Indian Claims Commission.* Clearwater Publishing Company, New York.

Rossen, Jack
   2008   Field School Archaeology, Activism, and Politics in the Cayuga Homeland of Central New York. In *Collaborating at the Trowel's Edge: Teaching and Learning in Indigenous Archaeology*, edited by Stephen W. Silliman, pp. 103–120. Amerind Studies in Archaeology 2. University of Arizona Press, Tucson.

Saitta, Dean J.
   2005   Labor and Class in the American West. In *North American Archaeology*, edited by Timothy R. Pauketat and Diana DiPaolo Loren, pp. 359–385. Blackwell, Malden.

Sebastian, Lynne
   2004   Archaeology and the Law. In *Legal Perspectives on Cultural Resources,* edited by Jennifer R. Richmond and Marion P Forsyth, pp. 3–16. AltaMira, Walnut Creek, California.

Shackel, Paul A., and Erve Chambers (editors)
   2004   *Places in Mind: Public Archaeology as Applied Anthropology.* Routledge, New York.

Shackel, Paul A., and David A. Gadsby
   2008   "I Wish for Paradise": Memory and Class in Hampden, Baltimore. In *Collaboration in Archaeological Practice: Engaging Descendant Communities*, edited by Chip Colwell-Chanthaphonh and T. J. Ferguson, pp. 225–242. AltaMira Press, Lanham, Maryland.

Shanks, Michael, and Randall H. McGuire
   1996   The Craft of Archaeology. *American Antiquity* 61:75–88.

Shepherd, Nick
   2003   "When the Hand that Holds the Trowel is Black…": Disciplinary Practices of Self-Representation and the Issue of "Native" Labour in Archaeology. *Journal of Social Archaeology* 3(3):334–352.

Silliman, Stephen W.
   2008   Collaborative Indigenous Archaeology: Troweling at the Edges, Eyeing the Center. In *Collaborating at the Trowel's Edge: Teaching and Learning in Indigenous Archaeology*, edited by Stephen W. Silliman, pp. 1–21. Amerind Studies in Archaeology 2. University of Arizona Press, Tucson.

Silliman, Stephen W. (editor)
   2008   *Collaborating at the Trowel's Edge: Teaching and Learning in Indigenous Archaeology.* Amerind Studies in Archaeology 2. University of Arizona Press, Tucson.

Silliman, Stephen W., and Katherine H. Sebastian Dring
   2008   Working on Pasts for Futures: Eastern Pequot Field School Archaeology in Connecticut. In *Collaborating at the Trowel's Edge: Teaching and Learning in Indige-*

nous Archaeology, edited by Stephen W. Silliman, pp. 67–87. Amerind Studies in Archaeology 2. University of Arizona Press, Tucson.

Singleton, Theresa A., and Charles H. Orser

    2003 Descendant Communities: Linking People in the Present to the Past. In *Ethical Issues in Archaeology*, edited by Larry J. Zimmerman, Karen D. Vitelli, and Julie Hollowell-Zimmer, pp. 143–152. AltaMira Press, Walnut Creek, California.

Smith, Claire, and Gary Jackson

    2008 The Ethics of Collaboration; Whose Culture? Whose Intellectual Property? Who Benefits? In *Collaboration in Archaeological Practice: Engaging Descendant Communities*, edited by Chip Colwell-Chanthaphonh and T. J. Ferguson, pp. 171–199. AltaMira Press, Lanham, Maryland.

Smith, Claire, and H. Martin Wobst

    2005 Decolonizing Archaeological Theory and Practice. In *Indigenous Archaeologies: Decolonizing Theory and Practice*, edited by Claire Smith and H. Martin Wobst, pp. 5–16. Routledge, London.

Smith, Claire, and H. Martin Wobst (editors)

    2005 *Indigenous Archaeologies: Decolonizing Theory and Practice*. Routledge, London and New York.

Spector, Janet D.

    1993 *What This Awl Means: Feminist Archaeology at a Wahpeton Dakota Village*. Minnesota Historical Society Press, Minneapolis.

Stapp, Darby C., and Michael S. Burney

    2002 *Tribal Cultural Resource Management, The Full Circle of Stewardship*. AltaMira Press, Walnut Creek, California.

Swidler, Nina, David C. Eck, T. J. Ferguson, Leigh J. Kuwanwisiwma, Roger Anyon, Loren Panteah, Klara Kelley, and Harris Francis

    2000 Multiple Views of the Past: Integrating Archaeology and Ethnography in the Jeddito Valley. *CRM* 9:49–53.

Thomas, David Hurst

    2008 Foreword. In *Collaboration in Archaeological Practice: Engaging Descendant Communities*, edited by Chip Colwell-Chanthaphonh and T. J. Ferguson, pp.vii-xii. AltaMira Press, Lanham, Maryland.

Two Bears, Davina R.

    2008 'Íhoosh'aah, Learning by Doing: The Navajo Nation Archeology Department Student Training Program. In *Collaborating at the Trowel's Edge: Teaching and Learning in Indigenous Archaeology*, edited by Stephen W. Silliman, pp. 188–207. Amerind Studies in Archaeology 2. University of Arizona Press, Tucson.

Watkins, Joe

    2000 *Indigenous Archaeology: American Indian Values and Scientific Practice*. AltaMira Press, Walnut Creek, California.

    2003 Archaeological Ethics and American Indians. In *Ethical Issues in Archaeology*, edited by Larry J. Zimmerman, Karen D. Vitelli, and Julie Holowell-Zimmerman, pp. 129–142. AltaMira Press, Walnut Creek, California.

Watkins, Joe, and T. J. Ferguson
  2005 Working with and Working for Indigenous Communities. In *Handbook of Archaeological Methods, Volume 2*, edited by Herbert D. G. Maschner and Christopher Chippindale, pp. 1372–1406. AltaMira Press, Walnut Creek, California.
Watkins, Joe, Lynne Goldstein, Karen Vitelli, and Leigh Jenkins
  1995 Accountability: Responsibilities of Archaeologists to Other Interest Groups. In *Ethics in American Archaeology: Challenges for the 1990s*, edited by Mark J. Lynott and Alison Wylie, pp. 33–37. Society for American Archaeology, Washington, D.C.
Zimmerman, Larry J.
  2000 A New and Different Archaeology? With a Postscript on the Impact of the Kennewick Dispute. In *Repatriation Reader, Who Owns American Indian Remains?*, edited by Devon A. Mihesuah, pp. 294–306. University of Nebraska Press, Lincoln.
  2006 Sharing Control of the Past. In *Archaeological Ethics*, 2nd ed., edited by Karen D. Vitelli and Chip Colwell-Chanthaphonh, pp. 170–175. AltaMira, Walnut Creek, California.
  2008a Multivocality, Descendant Communities, and Some Epistemological Shifts Forced by Repatriation. In *Opening Archaeology: Repatriation's Impact on Contemporary Research and Practice*, edited by Thomas Killion, pp. 91–108. SAR Press, Santa Fe.
  2008b Real People or Reconstructed People? Ethnocritical Archaeology, Ethnography, and Community Building. In *Ethnographic Archaeologies: Reflections on Stakeholders and Archaeological Practices*, edited by Quetzil E. Castañeda and Christopher Matthews, pp. 183–204. AltaMira Press, Lanham, Maryland.
  2008c Unusual or "Extreme" Beliefs about the Past: Community Identity, and Dealing with the Fringe. In *Collaboration in Archaeological Practice: Engaging Descendant Communities*, edited by Chip Colwell-Chanthaphonh and T. J. Ferguson, pp. 55–86. AltaMira Press, Lanham, Maryland.
Zimmerman, Larry J., Karen D. Vitelli, and Julie Hollowell-Zimmer (editors)
  2003 *Ethical Issues in Archaeology*. AltaMira, Walnut Creek, California.

5

Crossing Boundaries and Academic Fair Trade

JOSÉ LUIS LANATA *and* ROBERT D. DRENNAN

The political configuration of the modern world molds human activities in practically every sphere of endeavor, certainly including the practice of archaeology. The dynamics of modern national boundaries impede archaeological research and communication in numerous ways, and create multiple inequities in the opportunities available to archaeologists situated in different places. In the spirit of attempting to overcome or at least ameliorate these impediments and inequities, the editors of this volume proposed a chapter on "erasing boundaries." We have adjusted this title a bit for two reasons. First, the boundaries are so intimately involved in the practice of archaeology—and not always in entirely negative ways—that they require particular attention. And second, as archaeologists, we obviously cannot really erase all the boundaries anyway. We can, however, reduce the damage boundaries do to the archaeological endeavor by making them easier to cross.

Boundaries and Archaeology

Boundaries—in all their forms—and the difficulty of crossing them, impede the practice of archaeology most fundamentally by restricting communication. It is a commonplace that the free and open communication of information and ideas fosters progress in science, and boundaries represent impediments to this flow of information and ideas. Both "science" and "progress" are, of course, concepts regarded with deep suspicion by some archaeologists—the discipline does include the most remarkable diversity of activities, aims, and outlooks. But it is difficult to argue that there is *any* kind of academic or scholarly activity (no matter how scientific, unscientific, or anti-scientific) that thrives on limitations to the free and open flow of information and ideas. And lest this be branded an ethnocentric "Western" notion, note that it is espoused by the Premier of the State Council of the People's Republic of China: "Science has no boundaries. ... Just as collisions generate sparks, exchange and communication enrich imagination and creativity" (Wen 2008). The intellectual interaction that creates communities of scholars is the lifeblood of any academic discipline. This intellectual interaction takes place through various channels. There is the actual face-to-face interaction that occurs in conferences, collaborative research, and other sorts of scholarly visits. As essential as such face-to-face interaction is to the creation and maintenance of a scholarly community, much larger quantities of information and ideas flow to much larger audiences through publication. Across practically the entire range of channels, national boundaries represent pinch points in the flow of information and ideas. Publications are often not very well distributed within the boundaries of the country where they are published, but they always have a much harder time crossing those boundaries. Many contexts for meeting and interacting with colleagues are national, and not international—even when foreign archaeologists attend. We emphasize national boundaries here, but other kinds create problems for archaeology as well. Some national boundaries are also linguistic boundaries, and thus create especially high hurdles to communication. The archaeological regions of specialization into which we divide the world may or may not correspond to national boundaries, but they also create their own communities of scholars, whose boundaries are difficult to cross.

National boundaries work in some obvious ways, as well as in some subtle and subconscious but extremely powerful ways, to create national archaeological communities. Archaeologists in one nation are subject to a national set of political, social, economic, cultural, educational, and administrative conditions in which archaeology is carried out. Such conditions vary quite strongly between countries, and give national archaeological communities special concerns often not shared with their neighbors across the border. The effect of strong national archaeological communities with well-developed national channels of communication can be to reduce rather than increase communication across national boundaries.

The archaeologists of practically all nations regularly reinforce the boundaries between national archaeological communities in the curricula designed to train the archaeologists of the future. The information many students of archaeology find in the classroom often emphasizes, sometimes overwhelmingly, the archaeological past of their own nation at the expense of even immediate neighbors, trimming off the parts of the past that lie on the wrong side of modern national boundaries. The phenomena archaeologists study very frequently—if not always—transcend modern national boundaries since past social, cultural, economic, and/or political entities and their interactions often had spatial distributions that differ sharply from the patterns of today's political organization. It is easy to detect, for example, ways in which the patterns of communication and interaction among archaeologists studying the ancient Maya are bent by the modern boundaries that divide Mexico, Guatemala, Belize, Honduras, and El Salvador.

Wide-ranging comparative research is made especially challenging by the difficulties in access to information created by boundaries. These arise in part directly from the economic and political foibles of modern national boundaries, but finally an even more severe obstacle to meaningful comparative research is the difficulty of entering and comprehending a series of different national or regional specialist conversations about the practice of archaeology that have differing impacts on visions of what happened in the past in different places.

The diversity of theoretical perspectives and orientations contained within the discipline of archaeology creates yet another layer of complications (Pauketat and Meskell this volume). With so much variety, it may not even be possible to imagine a single community of archaeological scholars exchanging ideas and information. At the very least there would be a number of fissures in such a community, produced by the selectivity we all must employ in deciding just what, in that flux of information and ideas, to pay attention to. Because of the wide variety of circumstances in which archaeology is practiced in different countries, and because of purely random factors as well, it is inevitable that some theoretical orientations will develop strongly in some national archaeological communities while others are more robustly developed elsewhere. This can lead to a national or ethnic identification of entire theoretical perspectives (often in the context of arguing against them) that makes such theoretical fissures in networks of communication align even more strongly and damagingly with national boundaries.

Clearly, however, the diversity of theoretical perspectives could instead lead to patterns of strong interaction between archaeologists across the globe that cross over national and academic boundaries.

Boundaries, Archaeology, and National Identities

The national character of archaeological communities is strongly reinforced where archaeology plays an important role in constructing national identity. There is a large literature on this subject, concentrating primarily on its political and ethical dimensions. As archaeologists, we are urged to live up to our responsibilities in aiding and supporting the use of archaeology in establishing cultural identity when the national or other entities involved are regarded as laudable, but to resist being co-opted into support of entities whose aims are politically or ethically dubious (or worse—sometimes much worse). Apart from the immense complexity of the ethical issues that may be raised, a great deal of the funding that supports archaeology in much of the world is motivated by concerns of heritage, identity, and cultural pride. And this puts archaeologists in the same position as Willie Sutton, who (probably apocryphally) answered the question of why he robbed banks by saying "Because that's where the money is." For archaeology, the money is very often from the coffers of nation-states, and the result is that the archaeological enterprise is often, first and foremost, beholden to national heritage, national identity, and national cultural pride.

The form that archaeological orthodoxy in the service of national identity takes is, of course, shaped differently under varying political circumstances and histories. The contexts are almost unimaginably varied, ranging from support of massed national political, economic, or military power (as in the construction of an Aryan-centric national prehistory in Hitler's Germany) to resistance against it (as connected to Native American land reclamation efforts). In Mexico, national identity has been built on indigenous cultural achievements in opposition to Spanish colonial heritage in a postcolonial environment that began long before the term "postcolonial" became fashionable. A general amalgam of indigenous cultural heritage has been contrasted to Spanish colonial heritage and emphasized, often at the expense of the impressive indigenous cultural diversity of the territory that is now Mexico. In Peru and Bolivia, positive attention to indigenous heritage in constructing national identity has gone in waves, and has come under attack at times as a cynical manipulation of indigenous heritage to help sustain a system of European oppression of indigenous peoples beyond the end of the colonial era. Situating Lima and La Paz as political successors to Cuzco or Wari and Tiwanaku, respectively, gives archaeology special prominence, but it is hardly an unalloyed benefit to efforts to understand the precolonial (but often indigenously imperialist) past of the central Andes. National identity in the United States has traditionally been focused far more heavily on European colonial heritage. The current politics of archaeology have more to do with appreciating and promoting the rights of indigenous and other groups disadvantaged under the dominant political, economic, and cultural regime (Franklin and Paynter, this volume; Sebastian, this volume; Wilcox, this volume; Silliman and Ferguson, this volume). Conservative governments in both Argentina and Chile have projected their modern national boundary farther into the past than the existence of either nation. Both have used archaeological and other anthropological research on Mapuche origins (conveniently organized nationally) to counter land claims on the grounds that the Mapuche are an ethnic group of Chile and thus not entitled to land in Argentina or vice versa. In China, a major current in archaeological research (almost entirely state-sponsored) is tracing back to its roots the trajectory of what can be identified as culturally Chinese, an effort with direct implications for relationships between the dominant Han Chinese and China's officially designated cultural minorities.

In all its variety, though, as has often been noted, the use of archaeology in the construction of narratives of national identity is a highly exclusionary activity (e.g., Kojan and Angelo 2005:394)—one not likely to encourage entirely open flows of information and ideas across national boundaries (or for that matter, within them either) as some readings of the past become politically incorrect. The importance of archaeology in this arena, then, can add to the difficulty of crossing boundaries. Indeed, it can create one of the most difficult challenges archaeologists must face in attempting to cross boundaries.

Boundaries, Archaeology, and Inequalities

For obvious reasons, the archaeological communities of large, rich, and powerful nations are in an advantageous position. Such nations have many more institutions that help support archaeology, especially universities, and substantial numbers of these institutions have considerable resources with which to support what they do. Their governments have more resources available to support fields like archaeology, and their powerful economies provide other sources of support as well. The archaeological communities that exist within the boundaries of such nations can be quite large, making it easier to sustain not only the scholarly and professional organizations that facilitate interaction but also the commercial and noncommercial entities whose publications provide the major channel for the flow of information and ideas. The quantity of information and ideas flowing through these channels in a large archaeological community is much greater than in a small one, and access to it is easier. Archaeologists fortunate enough to be members of such national communities are truly swimming in the deep end of the pool. They have opportunities not available to archaeologists whose national archaeological communities are much smaller and less well endowed. Such inequalities of access to ideas, information, and resources can feed upon themselves in what it was once fashionable to call a "deviation-amplifying system" that not only perpetuates but intensifies the inequalities.

This would be true of the internal dynamics of archaeological communities (or "invisible colleges," the term Díaz-Andreu [2007] has adopted for them) if they existed on entirely different planets with no possibility of communication between them. And, although we do not often pause to notice, the vast majority of practicing archaeologists in practically all countries are not much engaged in interaction with colleagues across national boundaries. They are specialists in the archaeology and heritage management of some part of their own country; the colleagues with whom they interact face-to-face are their own compatriots; the meetings they attend are in their own nations (or even their own regions); and the literature they read is published and circulates primarily in their own countries. The limitations this situation imposes on the invisible colleges of the large, rich, and powerful nations are easier to overlook than the much more severe impediments it presents to archaeology in small nations with more restricted resources.

It is a relatively small proportion of archaeologists who are well connected to genuinely international flows of information and ideas. These are mostly archaeologists who in one way or another are participating members in two or more national invisible colleges. If they come from large, rich, and powerful nations, they may carry out field research in other countries. Their ability to do this likely springs from access to public or private resources targeted toward scholarly research (as contrasted with heritage concerns), which are useable internationally. If they come from nations with more limited archaeological opportunities, they are more likely to be studying or participating in conferences outside their own countries. While we take it for granted that all such activities that can foster the international flow of information and ideas deserve encouragement, we must also recognize the asymmetrical relationships symbolized and reinforced by these different roles occupied predominantly by the boundary-crossers from "central" and "peripheral" countries.

Broad Trends in the Americas (and Elsewhere)

The concerns of the Society for American Archaeology are primarily focused in the Americas, and thoughts of boundary crossing in the Americas quickly turn to bilateral relationships between North America and Latin America. Three general trends in Latin American archaeology during the period since the mid-1990s are of particular relevance here. First, although it varies from country to country, there is a broad increase in the presence of North American and European archaeological research teams in Latin America. Second, the same period has seen substantial increases in the number of Latin American university graduates engaged in master's, doctoral, and postdoctoral studies in North America and Europe. Third, resources for training in archaeology have increased in Latin American universities. This has occurred not only at the undergraduate level, with the founding of new programs in archaeology, but also at the postgraduate level, with a substantial increase in the range of opportunities for master's and doctoral studies in archaeology. This somewhat more recent trend is clearly related to, and made possible by, the return of Latin American students who have completed postgraduate degrees abroad. All of these trends vary substantially from country to country as a consequence of their different economic circumstances and their varied historical trajectories and academic traditions. Archaeologists from different Latin American nations have been trained very differently (some, for example, under the special educational rules of military governments), and they work under very different circumstances (including dangerous ones such as near zones of *guerrilla* or drug traffic). Nonetheless, the three interrelated trends are seen broadly across Latin America, and have spawned a new set of invisible colleges with varying academic impacts.

The increase in foreign participation in archaeological research has changed the face of archaeology at the regional and local level to varying degrees and in different ways in different countries. The level of participation of Latin American archaeological professionals in research alongside their colleagues from other countries has also soared in many nations, partly owing to legal requirements for national counterparts to foreign researchers, but also as the natural outcome of the increased numbers of Latin American archaeologists carrying out postgraduate study abroad. Success at integrating international research teams in real collaboration has varied substantially. Genuine international collaboration requires moving well beyond simply simultaneous presence in the field of archaeologists from different countries, and many perfectly successful efforts at international cooperation in carrying out archaeological fieldwork have fallen far short of the intellectual engagement that is the hallmark of real collaboration (Silliman and Ferguson, this volume). Such intellectual engagement on an equal footing is the essence of the "academic fair trade" of our title (an expression we borrow from Claudia Briones who used it in a lecture at the Centre of Latin American Studies at the University of Cambridge in January, 2008). Legal regulations, bilateral international cooperation agreements, and other top-down institutional arrangements, however well-intentioned, do not guarantee that genuine collaboration will take place. Informal, personal considerations are of much greater importance to the success of a truly collaborative effort, and the development of international research teams from the bottom up (growing out of collegial and personal relationships among the people involved) is more likely to be fully successful. Latin American archaeologists who have realized postgraduate study abroad are particularly favorably positioned to facilitate such efforts, as are foreign archaeologists who have invested time not just in carrying out fieldwork but also in really joining the national archaeological invisible college where they do their research. We wrote this paragraph specifically with our experiences in Latin America in mind, but every single word applies equally well to relationships between national and foreign archaeologists in a number of other parts of the world. East and Southeast Asia come especially quickly to mind.

Linguistic boundaries continue to be especially difficult to cross and throw especially challenging impediments in the path toward academic fair trade. As a consequence of forces much broader than just in archaeology, English has obviously become, for the moment, a global *lingua franca* in many different arenas, from the internet to air traffic control to diplomacy to banking to chemistry. Just how permanent this situation is, only time will tell. Given the realities of the world at the beginning of the twenty-first century, however, no one should pretend surprise that archaeologists who are native speakers of English publish less in other languages apart from their own than do native speakers of Spanish, Portuguese, French, German, Italian, Dutch, Norwegian, Danish, etc. It is easy to predict that archaeologists native to large and highly developed linguistic invisible colleges will publish primarily (or even almost exclusively) in that language, while archaeologists whose native linguistic invisible colleges are smaller and lack publication outlets of such wide dissemination will show a greater inclination to publish in languages foreign to them. For some, at least, practicality trumps ideals, and "the need to communicate is probably more important than the need to perpetuate a victim mentality," as Chirikure (2008:182) has put it. This does not, however, make the practical or symbolic impact of the pattern any less unfortunate (Bernbeck 2008; Holtorf 2008).

Even if English is, in one sense or another, the "language of science," much important archaeological information is available only in other languages, and many very interesting archaeological conversations take place in other languages. Archaeologists limited to the information available in just one language or able to participate only in the conversations that take place in a single language are just that: limited, in terms of access to the flow of information and ideas. This issue has often reared its head in the bilateral relationship between an invisible college composed largely of North Americans who carry out research in Latin America (or several of them actually, since there is not as much communication as one might wish between North American archaeologists whose work lies in different parts of Latin America) and an invisible college of Latin American archaeologists (or again, perhaps several regionally distinct ones). All North American archaeologists who carry out research in Latin America need the information and ideas available in the archaeological literature published in the regions where they work. This is not just a question of courtesy to colleagues in the nations where foreigners do research (although there *is* that); it is a practical necessity. Some North American archaeologists recognize this; many appear not to (despite having been preached at about it for many years). The archaeologists of many parts of Latin America are also harmed if they lack access to the substantial archaeological literature on their regions published in English in

North America. (Something similar might be said about Europe, but the quantity of material published on Latin American archaeology in Europe is far smaller, so let's keep things simpler for the moment by focusing on North and Latin America.) The development of two invisible colleges in different languages concerning the archaeology of various parts of Latin America interferes with the flow of information and ideas and impedes the development of academic fair trade.

Again, we have written specifically in terms of the relationship between North American and Latin American archaeologists, but much the same could be said about many other parts of the world. Hansen (2008) has made a similar point about the archaeology of Egypt. And again, East Asia comes quickly to mind as an example of dual invisible colleges operating in different languages. As foreign participation in the archaeology of China, for example, has increased over the past decade or two, a newly vigorous and extremely stimulating conversation about China's past has developed in English. This conversation is, in many respects, starkly different from the one that has long existed in Chinese. The two are by no means oblivious of each other, but information and ideas do not flow very readily from one to the other. There is almost no flow at all of ideas or information from either of these two conversations about China to any of the various invisible colleges built around the archaeology of, say, the central Andes. (We will return later to the special opportunities and challenges of global comparative research.)

Language boundaries are especially vexing in the broader panorama of theoretical discussions (in contrast to regionally based ones). Here as well the second broad trend in Latin American archaeology referred to above has had an impact. The return to their countries of origin of Latin American students who have completed postgraduate degrees (or briefer periods of specialized training) abroad has expanded the participation of Latin American archaeologists in theoretical debates of varied character—be they processual, postprocessual, or processual-plus (*sensu* Hegmon 2003). The series of meetings on *Teoría Arqueológica en América del Sur* that have taken place in different countries since 1998 provides tangible evidence of this. Latin American archaeologists are much more involved in these more global archaeological invisible colleges of varied theoretical stripes than those of any other part of the world outside Europe, North America, and Australia. A different, and perhaps preferable, way to express this observation is that what many of us think of as global theoretical debate in archaeology is another invisible college, largely anglophone but with a freshly vigorous and expanding (although by no means entirely new) sector in Spanish in Latin America. A strong current in the Latin American theoretical literature expresses frustration at a sense of marginalization in that largely anglophone debate, and at the same time seeks theoretical approaches that maintain a distinctly Latin American identity. An idea often expressed in Chinese archaeology grows from similar roots: the notion that Western models may have utility in understanding China's past, but that finally models with a distinctively Chinese character are required.

Ideas do flow from debates in English into the Latin American theoretical discussion in Spanish, not because articles are much translated into Spanish (they are not), but because participants in the Latin American discussion bring them there, primarily from English. (Even French social philosophers arrive in the Latin American debates more strongly from the anglophone archaeological literature than directly from France or the archaeological literature in French, which has not paid them nearly as much attention as archaeologists writing in English and Spanish have.) Stimulation from the Latin American debates has not flowed as effectively into the conversation in English, even though some of its participants have showed admirable willingness to publish in English. The bulk of the attention North American archaeologists give to the archaeological literature in Spanish goes to publications rich in data about their regions of specialty rather than to theoretical writing. This shows clearly in the pattern of sales of archaeology publications from Latin America distributed by the University of Pittsburgh: abstractly theoretical works from Latin America do not sell nearly as well as site reports.

As if there were not already enough vexatious complexity to this issue, theoretical debate, unlike regional studies, is (or at least should be) linguistically multilateral. The information flow issue in, say, Peruvian archaeology has a strongly bilateral character dominated by relationships between the Peruvian invisible college and a very largely North American one. Thinking about it tends to concentrate quickly on the Spanish-English/Peru-North America axis, relegating other nationalities and Portuguese, French, German, and Japanese to the sidelines. This is a dangerous oversimplification, but its practitioners can usually get away with it because the number of players relegated to the sidelines is relatively small. Even this excuse disappears when we consider what should be much broader theoretical debates, not tied to the archaeology of any one region, within Latin America or beyond. However effectively, symmetrically, or bidirectionally the English-Spanish language boundary is crossed in theoretical debate among Latin American and English-speaking archaeologists, this will not automatically enable its ideas to flow readily to archaeologists (of whatever nationality or native language) specializing in China, Russia, Egypt, or France.

The trend of vigorous university development in Latin America is attributable to varied factors, including economic growth, increased need for more highly educated professionals in many fields, and the return of democratic governments to some countries where they had been absent. In many countries anthropology and archaeology programs have proliferated and/or expanded. The larger dynamic of university-level education in which they exist varies greatly from country to country, not without its impact on the conditions in which archaeologists work. Recent UNESCO (2008) data indicate that only 31 percent of young people across Latin America advance to university-level studies, but the figure varies from 64 percent in Argentina to 47 percent in Chile to 26 percent in Mexico and 25 percent in Brazil. This proportion is increasing almost everywhere at a substantial rate of growth, although perhaps in patterns that will only accentuate the differences between countries in access to higher education: growth is 15 percent in Argentina, 12 percent in Uruguay, 11 percent in Brazil, 9 percent in Chile, and 8 percent in Mexico. The differences in the proportion of entering students who graduate with degrees are dramatic, for example, 74 percent in Chile vs. 21 percent in Argentina.

SAA annual meetings show the impact of all these various trends. At the 2006 (Puerto Rico) and 2007 (Austin) meetings some 35 percent of symposia, poster sessions, and forums were on specifically Latin American subjects and about 38 percent involved Latin America in some way—not very different from the figures for North American subjects. Although in absolute terms the number of Latin Americans participating in the annual meeting is not large, the increase in recent years has been conspicuous. Attendance by non-Latin Americans at archaeological meetings in Latin America has also increased. Beyond the Americas, East Asian archaeology and archaeologists have been considerably more visible at recent SAA meetings than they were earlier. The Society for East Asian Archaeology is an organization of primarily Western origin, but its 2008 meeting in Beijing shattered previous attendance records. And broadly international organizations like the World

Archaeological Congress continue to grow, although sometimes more focused on the politics of archaeology than on understanding the human past. Does this mean that crossing boundaries is becoming much easier and more common? The answer to this question is complicated. From a nationalist perspective it is easy to brand many of these trends as nothing more than another manifestation of North American academic imperialism, but this view is simplistic. Underlying economic issues are important. The application of neo-liberal economic policies across Latin America during the 1990s, together with increasing numbers of university graduates, made possible the participation of much larger numbers of Latin American archaeologists in the SAA meetings. Their numbers dropped off after the economic crisis of 2001–2002, which was felt in much of Latin America. This could repeat itself in more exaggerated fashion with the much more globally felt impact of the financial crash of 2008, which is playing itself out as we write.

Crossing Boundaries and Academic Fair Trade in the Twenty-first Century

We cannot conclude this essay with a grand overarching solution to the difficulties of crossing boundaries in archaeology, but our hope is to do more than simply rail against them. In practical terms, our situation is that of a boy with his finger in the dike, but in reverse. We aim, not to stop the leaks that allow information and ideas to flow across boundaries, but to increase them. Our concluding thoughts, then, should be taken as suggestions for poking holes in the dikes. We cannot dismantle the dikes entirely; it is not clear that truly erasing boundaries would make the world a better place, even if we could. Fortunately, the dikes do not need to be entirely removed. Quite a satisfying flood can be produced simply by poking holes wherever and whenever the opportunity presents itself. At least five particular opportunities for poking holes occur to us.

1. Curriculum Design

The curricula that introduce students to archaeology are often narrowly focused and reinforce the artificial limits of national, regional, and linguistic boundaries. It will often be natural for studies of the past to emphasize regions closer to home over those much farther away, and deep knowledge of one or more regions of specialty is essential for archaeological research. Some students, however, are intensively schooled in the archaeology of their own nations with very little attention given even to those parts of cultures that extend across national boundaries into neighboring countries. Archaeological curricula that are more global in scope are often carved up into archaeological regions that are presented in such a way as to suggest that the study of one has little real relevance to the study of another. Linguistic boundaries are more complicated to deal with for students, who may or may not yet have much facility with a language other than their own. Students who are taught in English, though, are especially at risk of developing the attitude that English gives them access to everything important in archaeology (as well as its corollary, that publishing in English is to communicate to all the world's archaeologists). Every time an archaeologist steps into a classroom is an opportunity to poke a hole in a dike, for the next generation at least.

2. Crossing Boundaries Physically

Archaeologists who actually take passport in hand and cross national boundaries physically obviously play pivotal roles. This is true whether they go to participate in meetings, for scholarly visits of moderate length, to study, to teach, or to carry out research. Scholarly visits of a few months to a year have been very helpful during the past decade or two at beginning to poke holes in the dikes between China and North America or Europe. As noted above, radically expanded opportunities in recent years for Latin American archaeologists to pursue postgraduate study abroad have also poked many holes in the dikes—not only the dikes between the students' own countries and North America or Europe but between countries within Latin America as well. It is fervently to be hoped that opportunities for postgraduate training within Latin America will expand, as they seem vigorously to be doing now in at least some countries, in part owing to the efforts of archaeologists there who have postgraduate degrees that they could not have obtained at home at the time they studied. The aim, however, should not be postgraduate programs so that no archaeologists have to go abroad to study. This would simply plug up some of the most promising holes already poked in the dike, to the particular detriment of national invisible colleges dependent on only a few universities (or even on only a single one) for domestic archaeological training.

International research projects often miss excellent opportunities when their leaders cross boundaries only in the physical sense. Those who travel for such purposes may have regrettably little contact with their colleagues in the universities, museums, and other institutions of the countries where they carry out research. Sometimes requirements for collaboration are treated simply as bureaucratic obstacles to be gotten over as expeditiously as possible by getting some national archaeologist's name on the project. Better opportunities for postgraduate training for the students of many countries are fundamental to the establishment of equitable and genuine collaboration in such research, but so is real effort on the part of both foreign and national archaeologists. At their best, international research projects can open doors to real participation in different national invisible colleges by participants on all sides, but this does not automatically happen just because international projects exist.

Physically crossing boundaries, of course, is particularly expensive, and thus especially sensitive to economic trends. With recent economic development in the European Union and the direction of resources toward academia, along with vigorous economic growth in several parts of Latin America, the flow of archaeologists between Europe and Latin America has enlarged substantially. A small but significant number of Latin American undergraduate and graduate students have begun to study in other Latin American countries. This increasingly multilateral dynamic helps to diffuse the bilaterally asymmetrical character of the previously dominant scholarly exchanges between North and Latin America. Some of the international flow of students as well as senior scholars, of course, becomes permanent, and such expatriate scholars are especially well positioned to poke holes in the dikes between their native and adopted national invisible colleges. This has been particularly visible in the case of Chinese archaeologists in the West during the past decade. The international flow of scholars is difficult to quantify, but perhaps the experience of the University of Pittsburgh can be illustrative. During the past 15 years, 40 students specializing in Latin American archaeology have received Ph.D.s from the University of Pittsburgh. Of these 40, 19 are of U.S. or Canadian nationality; 20 are from Latin America. Most now work in universities, museums, or institutes in their native countries, but four of the Latin Americans are in permanent positions in North American universities, while two of the North Americans have made permanent moves in the opposite direction. Although archaeologists cannot tame the cycles of national and global economies that cause the levels of resources available to archaeology to vary, they do have great impact on how strongly the available resources are directed toward poking holes in dikes by physically crossing boundaries.

3. Inter-Institutional Collaboration

Inter-institutional collaborations can provide both frameworks and resources that facilitate the crossing of boundaries. The emergence of the European Union has led to the development of cooperative graduate programs involving universities in different countries. Students are permitted or required to take courses at different universities, and fellowship opportunities for students from the developing world have increased. Such collaboration between universities is rare in the Americas. There are no international educational entities to facilitate it, and within nations, the urges toward competition between universities can be stronger than those toward collaboration. We could think, for example, of the number of professionals and students interested in the dynamics of Inka expansion and how their horizons could be expanded and the quality of their work enhanced if even four or five universities could cooperate in a joint research and training effort. A slightly different approach is represented by academic networks created by formal agreements between institutions in Argentina, Brazil, Chile, Colombia, Uruguay, and some other Latin American nations. These provide resources for workshops that enhance interaction between already-existing research teams working on similar issues in complementary ways. They also facilitate the sharing of expensive equipment and laboratory facilities, as in a proposed joint international laboratory for archaeological genetics that could process samples from different Latin America countries (Zeder et al., this volume). These networks are still in their infancy and have yet to fully demonstrate their ability to produce results, but they certainly have the potential to poke holes in dikes. Perhaps even more important, they foster complex multilateral relationships that promise to contribute greatly to academic fair trade.

4. Publications, Languages, and Distribution

Publications have been and continue to be the major avenue of information flow both within and across boundaries. We have complained for decades about their expense, but they are much more cost effective than physically crossing boundaries. Publications do not automatically cross language boundaries, though, since they cannot all be in all languages. Article-length publications can appear with multilingual abstracts at little additional cost (as they do in the SAA's journals). Summaries or translations of articles from elsewhere are published by some journals or as volumes of collected papers. Commercial publishers produce translated editions of a small number of archaeological books, although the selection is erratic. For example, Spanish translations of "handbooks" or other synthetic publications on Latin American archaeology are not available, and North American textbooks seem substantially less represented in the Spanish-language editions available in Latin America than European ones. Publications of primary interest to regional specialists can be published in the language of the region, even if produced by foreign researchers (as with many publications from the Centre d'Études Mexicaines et Centraméricaines or the Institut Français d'Études Andines). Publications of importance both regionally and internationally can be produced in fully bilingual editions (as with the volumes copublished by the University of Pittsburgh and various institutions in Latin America). None of these represents a comprehensive solution to crossing language boundaries, but each pokes one more little hole in a dike somewhere. The costs of these options vary substantially, but the limiting factor often is the priority given by an archaeological author to crossing the language boundary. English-speaking archaeologists whose research areas are in Latin America have an especially poor record of publishing in Spanish, although there are numerous venues in which they might seek publication of their work.

Distribution of publications is also often highly constrained by national boundaries, and the difficulty of acquiring international publications is a time-honored excuse used by archaeologists of all nations for not knowing or using what they contain. Commercial publication of books and journals in archaeology is concentrated in North America and Europe; they are available for purchase, but prices are sometimes exorbitant. Institutionally published books and journals are often more economical, but they may be difficult or impossible to order (they are sometimes impossible to obtain at the institution where they were published, even though several boxes full must be stashed under a staircase somewhere). Archaeologists can at least try to direct the work they produce toward venues where it is both readily available and reasonably priced. And it is not beyond the capacity of institutions or departments run by archaeologists to make their publications available for purchase. Cooperation between institutions can enlarge these holes in the dikes.

5. New Information Technology

The information technology exists to alleviate many of the difficulties associated with traditional publications, as well as to help us cross boundaries in other ways. In some ways, the technology has far outstripped our abilities to figure out how to put it to effective use, let alone institute the necessary changes in social and economic organization. The costs of paper, ink, and mailing can easily be eliminated from the publication process by electronic dissemination, but the biggest costs have always been editorial—the whole set of tasks involved in turning a pile of submitted manuscripts of varying quality into a smaller number of peer-reviewed, professionally produced, readily accessible books or journal articles. If there are no books or journals on paper to sell, then alternative sources of income must be sought. Large commercial publishers have complex systems for charging for access to books and journals on-line; the smaller-scale publication programs of institutions and academic societies are at a substantial disadvantage here, and have a lot of catching up to do. Some institutions are able to cover editorial costs without sales and make their publications openly available free. In some cases these are institutions whose paper publications have been notoriously difficult to obtain, and one has to wonder about the permanent availability of publications they provide on-line. Open-access on-line journals are still few in archaeology and must face the same issues of institutional permanence as well as compete with the established reputations for quality built up over time by traditional journals.

On-line access has also changed the structure of information inequalities in some unexpected ways. Latin American scholars, for example, have traditionally had much more limited access than those of Europe or North America to the global scholarly literature in their fields. International books and journals can be painfully slow to arrive; moments of institutional, political, or economic crisis interrupt the flow and create permanent gaps in libraries' collections, gaps often filled by professors' own libraries. At least some well-financed major universities in Latin America have moved aggressively to take advantage of advances in information technology and cooperation with libraries elsewhere to substantially narrow the gap between their faculties' access to information and that of university faculties in North America and Europe. At the same time, the gap between scholars at major universities and less well-financed ones in terms of information access has widened (within every country, and this is true within Europe and North America as well). This information access gap between major and minor institutions globally threatens to become wider than the information access gap between academically "central" and "peripheral" countries, if in fact this is not already the case. This is one way in which the impact of national boundaries may be diminishing, but it hardly seems cause for celebration. (We can now *all* have even more dramatic inequalities of information access right within our own countries.) The rising tide of technology is lifting all boats, but some much more than others. Thus some boundaries become easier to cross; others, more difficult.

The digital world also affects the substance of publishing in little-noticed ways. As archaeological publishing has shifted more strongly toward journals and collected volumes of papers, concentrated more tightly in the hands of a smaller number of commercial publishers, our scholarly product has become more strongly and rigidly packaged into articles of a few thousand words. This happens at the expense of books—books that provide either lengthy and reflective treatments of particular subjects or reports of primary research in the field. A diminishing quantity of such books puts us at risk of de-emphasizing the large and integrative ideas of our discipline at the same time as we lose its fundamental data base. The shift away from book-length publications is commonly attributed to the length of time and amount of money required to produce a book, but, thanks to current information technology, it has never been quicker, easier, or more economical to produce a book, or simpler to make it available for sale worldwide. New information technology perhaps offers better ways to present and preserve our basic data than in traditional site reports, but we are still in the process of figuring out just how. On-line archaeological databases include an amazing spectrum of information, from continental-scale sets of projectile points, to the complete inventories of artifacts from a single site, to reference collections of phytoliths or pollen, to the collections catalogs of museums. These are vital research and teaching resources, usually freely available, aimed at everyone from elementary school children to advanced researchers. Not surprisingly, their forms of organization and the nature of the information included vary substantially, interfering with their collective utility for any one purpose. It is tempting to gather some key players around a table and try to organize all this chaos (e.g., Kintigh 2006), but we should not expect effective solutions to emerge from committees; they will have to evolve. Whatever form they take, it will certainly have an impact on crossing boundaries and academic fair trade.

In conclusion, information technology leads us to a final broad thought about crossing boundaries and academic fair trade—this one more fully optimistic. Email and other very common internet tools have completely transformed the dynamics of working in collaborative research teams. They certainly do not erase the boundaries of nations, languages, regional specializations, or other invisible colleges. They do, however, make it far easier than ever before for individuals personally equipped with the necessary linguistic and knowledge skills to cross all these kinds of boundaries. The possibilities for forming collaborative research teams that cross all such boundaries have increased exponentially, and those research teams can engage in deeper and more intensive collaboration than ever before. We are particularly optimistic about the vigorous development of collaborative programs of comparative archaeological research that transcend regional specializations because this context provides powerful incentives to poke holes in dikes between all kinds of invisible colleges: regionally specialized, national, linguistic, methodological, theoretical, and all the rest. The strongly multilateral character that relationships in such research teams can take contributes greatly to academic fair trade because it is a potent antidote to the asymmetries of many traditional axes of bilateral relationships in archaeology—particularly those between national and foreign invisible colleges focused on the archaeology of a single region.

Acknowledgments. We would like to thank Wendy Ashmore, Dorothy Lippert and Barbara Mills for their invitation to participate in this volume and the comments they and two anonymous reviewers made to an early version of this contribution.

References Cited

Bernbeck, Reinhard
    2008 Archaeology and English as an Imperial *Lingua Franca. Archaeologies: Journal of the World Archaeological Congress* 4:168–170.

Chirikure, Shadreck
    2008 Language and Archaeology in Southern Africa: The Search for Post-colonial Reality. *Archaeologies: Journal of the World Archaeological Congress* 4:182–185.

Díaz-Andreu, Margarita
    2007 Internationalism in the Invisible College. *Journal of Social Archaeology* 7:29–48.

Hansen, Nicole B.
    2008 Arabic and Its Role in Egyptology and Egyptian Archaeology. *Archaeologies: Journal of the World Archaeological Congress* 4:171–174.
Hegmon, Michelle
    2003 Setting Theoretical Egos Aside: Issues and Theory in North American Archaeology. *American Antiquity* 68:213–243.
Holtorf, Cornelius
    2008 The Cunning Means of Domination. *Archaeologies: Journal of the World Archaeological Congress* 4:190–200.
Kintigh, Keith W.
    2006 The Promise and Challenge of Archaeological Data Integration. *American Antiquity* 71:567–578.
Kojan, David, and Dante Angelo
    2005 Dominant Narratives, Social Violence, and the Practice of Bolivian Archaeology. *Journal of Social Archaeology* 5:383–408.
UNESCO
    2008 *Global Education Digest 2009: Comparing Education Statistics across the World.* UNESCO Institute for Statistics, Quebec.
Wen Jiabao
    2008 Science and China's Modernization. *Science* 322:649.

6

Inequality and Archaeology

MARIA FRANKLIN *and* ROBERT PAYNTER

If archaeology is to play a role that is more significant in terms of both the social sciences and American society as a whole, it is essential that archaeologists understand and take account of the social significance of their discipline [Trigger 1986:209].

The volume celebrating the 50th anniversary of the founding of the SAA (Meltzer et al. 1986) tracked issues that still puzzle us today and matters that we have moved beyond. Some of the changes from the previous volume to this, the 75th anniversary volume, are due to the accumulation of new information and internal debates within the discipline. Just as importantly, some are due to factors emanating from American society and beyond that have affected the practice and ideas of American archaeologists, altering with whom we work, how we conduct that work, and what we have come to know.

Articles directly addressing our theme of inequality in the 50th anniversary volume included Wright's (1986) comparative study of state origins in the core civilizations of Mesopotamia, the Indus Valley, Mesoamerica, and the Central Andes. Wright argued that in order to comprehend the rise of social stratification, more rigorous multiscalar research that included finer-grained regional histories would be needed. One significant trend that he noted and supported involved an increase in "integrated archaeological and ethnohistoric studies" that would allow archaeologists to better address ethnicity, ideology, and sociopolitical processes (Wright 1986:359). Yet Wright cautioned against ethnocentrism in interpreting the historical and oral records, and controlling the "historical knowledge of great importance to living people" (Wright 1986:359). Leone (1986) surveyed the growing discontent with the "new archaeology" and the rising interests in symbolic, structural, and critical archaeologies. He advocated a research strategy that starts with understanding archaeology's embeddedness within the political economy of archaeology-producing cultures that then seeks to unmask those cultures' ideologies (professional and popular) about the nature of social inequality. Finally, Trigger (1986) previewed his soon-to-appear history of archaeology, and emphasized the entanglement of archaeological ideas and practice in the U.S.'s colonization of Native America.

Twenty-five years later we can see that Wright, Leone, and Trigger grasped the general trends for the future of the archaeology of inequality, if not the details. For instance, the field has moved in the direction of writing fine-grained regional histories, but from the inside-out or bottom-up rather than as a means to test general theory (Beaudry et al. 1991; Mrozowski 2006:5; Saitta 2007a:20–21). Our data sets are increasingly diversified, with ethnohistoric, archival, and oral history sources more integrated with our archaeological research, and this has raised important implications with regard to multivocality and knowledge production. There have been more reflexive studies of the practice of archaeology, though few address how our ideas reverberate with the "culture wars" of the past two-and-a-half decades. Questions concerning identity, ideology, and power are more evident in the literature. The practice that has received the most attention concerns relations with Native communities of North America, mostly because of the efforts by members of Native communities, whose concerns were given the weight of law with the passage of the Native American Graves Protection and Repatriation Act of 1990 (NAGPRA) (see chapter by Wilcox, this volume).

The proliferation of site-specific and detailed regional studies makes regional comparison too daunting a task for this review. Instead, we draw on our specialization in the archaeology of the post-Columbian world to assess how our unequal world has changed and how this has affected how we theorize and practice archaeology. The relations of capitalist production, the dynamics of the nation-state, discrimination, and exploitation based on the shifting boundaries of race, gender, and sexual preference, and the ongoing attempts to decolonize the U.S. and the world at large are all significant forces that give our historical epoch its distinctive characteristics. We are particularly interested in those projects that have confronted social inequality through critical self-reflection, and by decentering archaeological authority, valorizing alternative (non-archaeological) knowledge claims and epistemologies, and by overtly addressing issues that resonate with contemporary struggles for social justice. As other authors included in this volume are considering inequality and its implications in community collaboration, the public benefits of archaeology, and the impact of NAGPRA and cultural resource management, we focus on the investigations of class, race, and gender and their related politics (past and present) in shaping contemporary archaeology. In reviewing the literature on class analysis, and feminist and African diasporic archaeologies, there are, of course, overlapping concerns between these subgenres as well as with this chapter and others included in this volume.

What Do We Mean by Inequality?

Matters of social equality and inequality have a deep resonance in social theory (Beaudry et al. 1991; Mrozowski 2006:5; Saitta 2007a:20–21) as well as the political ideologies of Western nation-states (Williams 1983:117–119). Studying these, rather than complexity or large-scale societies, immediately gives research a connection to deep metaphors as well as explicit theories that affect life in and outside the academy. To be clear, for us inequality means unequal access to strategic resources and resultant differentials in structured abilities to exercise power. Strategic resources are material, social, and ideological, and are defined only in the context of specific social circumstances. Inequalities may be noted in any social interaction; those of interest to us are the ones that have an enduring character, evident in successive interactions, structured by social institutions and ideological constructions that emerge from and transcend any single social encounter (Tilly 1998).

Historicizing Archaeologies of Inequality

It is undeniable that archaeology is related to, and situated within, broader historical processes, and that archaeologists are, to varying degrees, compliant with and resistant to nationalism, capitalism, neocolonialism, and other hegemonic forces at work in the world. A number of scholars have charted the genealogies of archaeology with these tensions in mind, implicating archaeology's role in power relations writ large, and advocating for alternatives (e.g., McGuire 2008; McGuire et al. 2005; Patterson 1995, 2003;

Schmidt and Patterson 1995; Trigger 1989). These biting critiques of archaeology's sociopolitics, and the critical analyses of its history are instances of disciplinary reflexivity (Meskell 2002), and coincide with attempts to clarify our agendas and to locate our politics in moving beyond business as usual. Thus, in writing about eliminating inequality through archaeology, we hope to illustrate the relationships between history, context, and practice as others have done before us.

Along with our case studies, therefore, we summarize some of the major political currents that have influenced archaeology, either by constraining or enabling its emancipatory potential. For example, neoliberalism's reach has had the effect of curtailing the entry of individuals with working-class backgrounds into the profession, while simultaneously (and relatedly) inhibiting class analysis in archaeology. On the other hand, the civil rights, black power, and women's movements helped to legitimize scholarship by and of racial minorities and women and created the institutional spaces (in the academy, museums, etc.) needed to foster this research. Taking ownership of these legacies is relevant to reconfiguring the politics of archaeology since many of us seek to ally ourselves with various local, national, and global struggles for equality that are anchored to and inspired by these and other activist heritages; their repercussions are still evident. Nevertheless, while organized labor movements pitted against neoliberalism and class exploitation, and anti-racist and feminist activisms have all influenced the social, economic, and political terrain of the U.S., over much of its history archaeology has managed to diffuse its own potential for contributing to these and other causes. Even well-intentioned research focused on historically subjugated social groups can lose much of its political currency if lacking in engagement with concerns and struggles relevant in today's world. Such studies may well help to diversify representations of the past but do little to challenge hierarchical relations in the present. Archaeology, as with other hegemonic institutions, has the ability to absorb and mainstream research considered radical and threatening to the status quo while deflecting much of its transformative potential in the process (this is arguably the case with the majority of gender archaeology). Importantly, we cannot leave all of the "political work" to archaeologists collaborating with the public. It's all political work, but we can choose our politics. In writing about difference and power in the past we are potentially writing emancipatory narratives for the present (Saitta 2007a:1–7).

Finally, not only is archaeology different 25 years after the SAA's last assessment of the field, but so too are the ways in which archaeological knowledge is produced, who is producing it, and the direct and indirect involvement of the state and corporations in our field. It is to the play between these forces that we now turn.

Class

Historical Context. A major factor contributing to today's alignment of class relations in the U.S. is a political economy known as neoliberalism. It involves the commodification and rationalization of various realms of life by curtailing the economic regulatory functions of the state and thereby encouraging private entrepreneurial activities. David Harvey presents neoliberalism as based on the philosophy that

> human well-being can best be advanced by liberating individual entrepreneurial freedoms and skills within an institutional framework characterized by strong private property rights, free markets, and free trade. The role of the state is to create and preserve an institutional framework appropriate to such practices [Harvey 2005:2].

The recent worldwide sweep of neoliberalism was grounded in a longer history of capitalist class process. The post-Depression World War II political economies of Western Europe and the U.S. were based on compromises between core nation capital and labor that limited elites' abilities to accumulate wealth in the name of promoting growth for the national economy. When this two-decade system of core accumulation began to stagnate in the 1970s, it threatened elites and provided the impetus for unraveling the compromise. Though some nations of Western Europe continued to regulate the market and redistribute wealth, the U.S., and increasingly other polities around the globe, sought to curtail the regulatory functions of the state and thereby "liberate" the forces of the market, releasing individual and corporate entrepreneurial energies, and permitting accumulation and concentration for the elites at the expense of the middle and working classes on a grand scale.

Though the crises and the neoliberal responses originated in the 1970s, it was with the Reagan Administration of the 1980s and more so with the Bush I, Clinton, and Bush II administrations that these policies came to seem like common sense in the United States. The tactics that increasingly dismantled the "welfare state" included defunding the state to weaken its regulatory and social service functions, systematically dismantling labor unions, exporting high-wage jobs to low-wage paying countries, carrying out the work of core-nation, low-wage paying jobs with immigrants, creating gains in labor productivity by substituting computers for bureaucratic labor, and increasingly financializing the accumulation process (Foster and Magdoff 2008, 2009; Harvey 2005).

Archaeology felt these impacts in a number of ways (Patterson 1995:129–144). Most generally, neoliberalism negatively affected the incomes of the working and middle classes (e.g., Massey 2007; Wolff 2007), which has had a complex, but nonetheless real, effect on who has been willing and able to practice the quintessentially middle-class profession of contemporary American archaeology (McGuire 1992; McGuire and Walker 1999; Patterson 1995:98–100, 1999; Saitta 2007a:1–2). The institutional base of academic archaeology has generally been eroded as universities were particularly targeted for reorganization and defunding (Harvey 2005:44). The management of archaeological resources, mandated in federal and state legislation in the 1960s and 1970s, was increasingly conducted in the private sector (Zeder 1997:172, 207–209) (see also Altschul and Patterson, and Snead and Sabloff in this volume), which itself encountered financial difficulties with the defunding of public sector projects. Unions, as a means to push back against neoliberal initiatives, have only been a player in public sector universities and colleges, have had insignificant effects in private sector cultural resource management, and are illegal for private sector faculty (McGuire 2008:98–140).

These institutional changes have also had diffuse but traceable effects on the ideological constructions of archaeology. For instance, a case can be made that archaeology's retreat from theories of structure and toward theories of agency is in part a response to the rise of neoliberal ideologies of hyperindividualism and "choice" (Eagleton 1996; Harvey 1989; McGuire and Wurst 2002; Patterson 1995). Additionally, since most Americans today think of themselves as middle class, or as members of communities comprised of aggregates of individuals, it is not surprising that archaeology, as a discipline of the middle class, similarly underutilizes class analysis to understand the past (American Social History Project 1992:508; Davis 1986; Fones-Wolf 1994; McGuire 2008:104–107; Saitta 2007a:109). Perusing electronic databases of archaeological literature only reinforces the sense that class analysis does not figure prominently in our field.

There are of course exceptions. Archaeologists studying the pre-Columbian world of Mesoamerica and Latin America use notions of class to understand some of the driving forces of this region's history (e.g., Blackmore 2008; Brumfiel 1991, 2006; Patterson 1985, 1986a, 1986b, 1991). A few archaeologists have brought class to the study of the North American past (e.g., Cobb 2000; McGuire 1989; McGuire and Saitta 1996; Muller 1997; Saitta 1994, 1997, 2001, 2005; Saitta and Keene 1990). Moreover, a small but growing number of archaeologists are investigating recent wars that have pitted capitalist against socialist political economies, as in the Spanish Civil War (Gassiot-Ballbe and Steadman 2008), the Dirty Little War in Argentina (Doretti and Snow 2003), the Cold War (Schofield and Cocroft 2007), and the politics of looting in the present Iraq war (Bahrani 2003; Emberling and Hanson 2008; Steele 2008).

The majority of archaeological studies of class examine the post-Columbian world, an increasingly rich literature that has generated its own reviews (Mrozowski 2006; Orser 1996; Paynter 2000a, 2000b; Wurst, 1999, 2002, 2006; Wurst and Fitts 1999). Particularly notable examples include studies of class relations and industrialization (Beaudry et al. 1991; Mrozowski 2006; Mrozowski and Beaudry 1990; Mrozowski et al. 1996), and class struggles within the contexts of plantation slavery and tenancy (Delle 1998, 1999; Orser, ed. 1990; Orser 1991, 1999). Researchers with Archaeology in Annapolis, Maryland, have produced scholarship within the realm of public archaeology on class and inequality since the 1980s, including studies on the relationship between race and class (Leone 1988, 1999, 2005; Leone and Hurry 1998; Matthews 2001; Mullins 1999a, 1999b, 1999c; Palus et al. 2006; Potter 1994, 1999; Shackel 1993; Shackel et al. 1998).

Labor Pitted against Capital. Saitta (2007a:8–17, 2007b) argues that archaeology must be both explanatory and emancipatory if it is to fulfill its own social responsibilities and those of intersubjective science. These two goals are most obviously met in studies of how people and communities have struggled for social justice in the face of exploitation. The labor strike is such a case where resistance meets the structures of domination in extraordinarily complex historical moments. Just such empirical and interventionist work is being conducted by the Ludlow Collective (McGuire 2008:188–221; Saitta 2007a) concerning the Colorado Coalfield Strike of 1913–1914 and its ongoing implications for labor relations to this day.

The Ludlow Collective has conducted a multiscalar archaeological study of the strike and the associated eight-month-long armed conflict, uncovering evidence of the tactics and strategies used by both sides in this bloody confrontation. They have discovered that the strikers strategically used space, locating their tent colonies to control access to the coalfields. They also organized well-ordered community settlement patterns to overcome stereotypes of disorderly immigrants and cleverly rotated the community settlement orientation to thwart surveillance by their opponents. The strikers fostered social solidarity within the camps by discouraging residential segregation by ethnicity and encouraging participation in a common mass culture. The miners displayed their skills in constructing semi-subterranean housing that provided warmth and storage spaces for them and their families. Their food remains told of provisioning by the union along with evidence of covert support from the surrounding community. Their "eclectic variety of vessel forms, including individual settings and serving vessels" (Saitta 2007a:79) spoke less of Victorian middle-class gentility and more of a persistent European peasant dining practice. And contrary to assertions that figure prominently in stories about the confrontation, the archaeology found no convincing evidence for striker rifle pits, "explosive bullets," or mass graves.

In addition to discovering tangible aspects of this important labor action, the Ludlow Collective has collaborated with the United Mine Workers to assist in registering the site as a National Historic Landmark and developing interpretive exhibits at the site. More than a mundane exercise in public outreach, they have conducted these pro-labor interventions in neoliberalism's atmosphere of hostility to organized labor, a hostility that has been manifested by the "decapitation" of some of the statues at the Ludlow memorial.

The archaeology of the Ludlow strike is one of the very few instances where the work of archaeology has both contributed to the history of organized labor and engaged directly with today's labor movement. It is more common for such engagements to occur in projects connected with the current struggles concerning racial justice and gender equality.

Race and African American Archaeology

Historical Context. To date, the majority of archaeologists interested in race research African American sites and/or work with African Americans in public archaeology programs. Yet, even though U.S. black activism during the

1960s helped generate interest in African American archaeology, it was not until the 1990s that antiracist scholarship gained any ground in the discipline (Orser 1998a:662). Although a number of archaeologists have since made a concerted effort to investigate race and racism in the past (e.g., Babson 1990; Byrne 2003; Davidson 2004; chapters in Delle et al. 2000; Epperson 1990, 1997, 1999, 2001; Funari 1999; Hall 2000; Leone et al. 2005; Mullins 1999a, 2008; Orser, ed. 2001; Orser 2004; Paynter 2001; Paynter et al. 1996; Perry and Paynter 1999; see chapters in Scott 1994; Silliman 2006; Voss 2008; Wilkie 2004) and to challenge racial inequities in the present (e.g., Barile 2004; chapters in Little and Shackel 2007; McDavid 1997, 2002, 2007; Mullins 2007; chapters in Shackel and Chambers 2004; Young 2004), critical race studies still remain rather peripheral to archaeology despite the centrality of race as a structuring principle with troubled histories in both the U.S. and abroad. We provide here a brief historical synthesis of 1960s black political mobilization in an attempt to further clarify its role in creating the impetus and institutional space for archaeological research on nonwhite ethnic groups (especially African Americans).

The civil rights movement brought sweeping reformations to U.S. society. Archaeologists have commented on its influence in "shaping" CRM laws (Shackel 2004:4) and shifting research emphases to historically subjugated groups (Patterson 1995), especially African Americans in the late 1960s (Ferguson 1992:xxxv–xxxvi; Franklin 1997a:39; Singleton 1999:1–2). Theresa Singleton (1995) noted that it was direct African-American involvement in archaeological projects that ensured its growth as a serious field of inquiry. Nor can we elide the significant contributions of race vindicationist scholars such as W.E.B. Du Bois and St. Clair Drake to African diaspora scholarship and politics (Leone et al. 2005; Mullins 2008). We concur with all of these authors, but would expand the argument to include the Black Power movement as an influential force in African diaspora studies (see also Ferguson 1992:xxxviii), especially given its role in the establishment of black studies departments nationwide.

The civil rights movement is usually spotlighted in the American narrative of democracy and equality, yet the Black Power movement has typically been scuttled from the storyline. This is no doubt due to the mainstream collective memory of black cultural nationalists as hyper-militant, antiwhite, and far too politically radical. Yet the Black Power movement also included black student activists who sought to valorize black consciousness, culture, history, and aesthetics. That is, the movement was diverse in terms of its advocates, gender politics, rhetoric, objectives, and forms of antiracist activism, and any attempt to reduce it to the headlines of the period in question is problematic at best.

The two political formations converged in what some have referred to as the Black Studies movement of the 1960s and 1970s (Drake 1978:100–101; Walters 1993:365). Civil rights led to the desegregation of colleges and universities, and the mainly urban, black students who entered the academy were heavily influenced by black cultural nationalists. Black students at white-dominated institutions already serving as sites of conflict increasingly agitated for black studies programs. The Black Students Union, the Third World Liberation Front, and the Black Panther Party staged sit-ins and protests at San Francisco State University, which led to the nation's first department of black studies in 1969 (Rojas 2007:46) as well as the creation of the School of Ethnic Studies. The florescence of ethnic and women's studies soon followed.

In 2000, there were more than 225 black/Africana studies programs in the U.S. (Nelson 2000:84–85) as black political mobilization helped to legitimize scholarship on and by African and African-descended peoples (Aldridge and Young 2000). It was within this context that archaeologists were inspired by "ethnic pride movements" (Orser 1998a:65) to undertake the study of subjugated histories, as the way was paved by disenfranchised groups who fought for recognition and justice. Yet while black politics influenced the development of ethnic and cultural studies in historical archaeology, its explicitly antiracist agenda did not play a significant or immediate role in the way that archaeologists theorized the past or problematized archaeology's role in the present.

Laboring Against Racism. Charles Fairbanks' investigation of slavery at Kingsley Plantation, Florida, in the late 1960s is credited as pioneering African diaspora archaeology, yet the historical archaeologists who began to focus on non-white ethnic groups sidelined the analysis of "race" (for an early exception, see Otto 1984). In the 1970s and 1980s, archaeologists interested in identity issues instead turned to class and status analyses, identifying cultural continuity or acculturation, and studies of ethnicity (Little 1994; Orser 2004; Singleton and Bograd 1995). While the reasons for the lack of attention to race may vary in detail, they all relate to archaeology's colonialist and nationalist roots (Paynter 2000a:20–21), and a reluctance to confront the racial politics of archaeology. For example, race is perceived as too controversial or sensitive a topic while ethnicity serves as a less politically charged alternative to researching social identity and relations (Orser 2001:7; Singleton 1999). The subsequent de-emphasis on race was in part due to processualism and its commitment to scientific neutrality that made headway in historical archaeology in the 1970s (e.g., South 1977). Nevertheless, power remained heavily implicated in this ethnicity over race equation. Terrence Epperson (2004) observed that archaeologists are resistant to interrogating their own racial privilege if it means relinquishing the reins of authority to descendent groups. This resonates with Edmund Gordon's (1997:153) critique of a white-dominated anthropology: "The seeming inability of most mainstream anthropologists to fully confront the colonial nature of the discipline is explicable when one recognizes that such a coming to terms would offer them few advantages." Before racism can be challenged at all, therefore, archaeologists need to be more self-reflexive and explicit in defining their political agendas (Bell 2008; Franklin 1997a; Potter 1991; Wilkie 2004), and be willing to concede that a counter-hegemonic archaeology requires coalition-building with communities of color. It also requires a social constructionist approach to race that accounts for the realities of structural racism (e.g., Epperson 2004; Mullins 1999a, 2008).

It was not until the 1990s that critical investigations of race grounded in antiracist politics began to gain ground in historical archaeology. The most significant intervention was exemplified by the work of Michael Blakey, Warren Perry, Cheryl LaRoche, Mark Mack, Lesley Rankin-Hill, Jean Howson, and others at Howard University and John Milner Associates who worked on the African Burial Ground (ABG) in New York (Blakey 1997; Blakey and Rankin-Hill 2004; Epperson 1999; La Roche and Blakey 1997; Leone et al. 2005; Mack and Blakey 2004; Medford 2004; Perry et al. 2006). The racial politics that erupted over the excavation and interpretation of the site are well known. What has received less attention is the analysis and theorization of race that the team undertook that differed significantly from the traditional bioarchaeological approach. To start, the team's research design was inclusively informed by members of the black descendent community and framed within both engaged anthropology and the "African American tradition of scholar activism" (LaRoche and Blakey 1997:86–87; Mack and Blakey 2004:11). Thus, the question concerning the geographical origins of the individuals interred at the site was decidedly not addressed using the typical biological approach of "racing" individuals that is essentialist, ahistorical, and noncontextual (Blakey 2001). Instead, researchers considered "the historical interactions of biology and culture such that data on each inform the other and, most importantly, such that human biology is interpreted within historically specific, sociocultural contexts" (Mack and Blakey 2004:10–11; see also Blakey 2001). This meant that interpretations of the mitochondrial DNA, skeletal and dental evidence, and cultural signatures (including dental modification and burial practices) were contextualized locally within colonial-era slavery in New York and more broadly within the linkages between Africa and its diaspora. Both the researchers and the descendent community were concerned with the social construction of cultural identities rather than static racial categories, in reconstructing individual life histories rather than obscuring these experiences by using a "populational" methodology (Mack and Blakey 2004:16). Moreover, in recovering this history and testifying to the brutality of slavery in a state where this narrative has been largely erased, the ABG project team, in collaborating with the descendent community, succeeded in producing not only a more politically relevant archaeology, but also "indisputably better science" (Epperson 2004:103).

The African Burial Ground project is significant for exemplifying the fact that in order to challenge racial inequality we must both de-essentialize race while recognizing how race nevertheless structures societies in very tangible and destructive ways (see also Crenshaw et al. 1995; Guinier and Torres 2002; Sanjek 1996). In this case Blakey and his team chose to forego racing human remains, and in doing so denied the biological essentialism of racial categories. Importantly, however, they did not challenge the black community's political mobilization around race, and instead validated the concerns over racism expressed by their "ethical clients."

Mark Leone's (2005) *The Archaeology of Liberty in an American Capital* speaks to both theorizing about difference and inequality and coupling theory with practice in the form of community collaboration. Leone assessed capitalism's reach in Annapolis from about 1700 to 1920 through an analysis of the dominant ideology of possessive individualism. While he proposed that ideology worked effectively in masking "the material truth of unequal wages and high rents" (Leone 2005:162) among non-elite whites, he was also concerned with "seeing others who were outside of the blindness of ideology and had alternatives to capitalism within democracy" (Leone

2005:33). That is, Leone's (2005:247) goals were not only to produce a critique of capitalism but to discover "a view of how to build a world different from it." This is the juncture at which Leone's work is more specifically relevant to our discussion of eliminating inequalities.

After reflecting upon the role of archaeology in public life and his own struggles with instituting change through archaeology, Leone and his team of Annapolis researchers were able to partner with the local African American community (see also Mullins 1999a:8–9), which provided the questions and concerns—including "We want to know what is left from Africa"—that guided the analysis and interpretation of black Annapolitan sites (Leone 2005:xiii, 60–61, 189–191). And with this renewed focus on African Americans, archaeologists subsequently discovered resistance to capitalism through the recovery of what they referred to as spiritual caches and bundles. Representative of African cosmological belief systems and rituals, these findings provided the evidence for an alternative, coherent identity and "lifeworld," or culture (Leone 2005:187, 192–266; Leone et al. 2001). As with the ABG project team's interpretations, Leone theorized that these spiritual practices were evidence of African diasporic ethnogenesis within the context of slavery and racism. Enslaved blacks, in particular, saw through capitalism's exploitation, and recognized the contradiction embedded within the ideology of individualism that promoted liberty and freedom in a democratic society while denying it to those racialized as black (Leone 2005:260). Thus, in critiquing dominant society, blacks produced a religious worldview that existed within but also outside of capitalism.

There were a number of tensions that archaeologists needed to resolve in order to work toward democraticizing archaeology (Leone 2005:193). One involved whether archaeology could prove useful to the black descendent community, and if so, would using it run the risk of maintaining hegemony "by absorbing people of African descent into the results of archaeology and into the middle-class sciences, some of whose results they had been able to avoid so far" (Leone 2005:193)? Thus, the responsibility of teaching young African Americans about archaeology went to Maisha Washington, a black woman who was a former curator of the Banneker-Douglass Museum. This opened up a space for black Annapolitans to envision/write an alternative history to the dominant narrative, including that of the archaeologists. Strategies such as this will remain open to debate as to their efficacy in diffusing archaeology's hegemonic role in society.

In this post-civil rights era, race remains a fundamental challenge in the U.S. Race currently plays a central role in political representation, quality of education, healthcare, including AIDS education and treatment, environmental justice, affordable housing, racial profiling, police brutality, incarceration rates, and the list goes on. The devastation left behind in the wake of Katrina clearly illuminated the sedimentation of racial inequality. It is a wonder then that as recently as 2004, Charles Orser (2004:7) could emphatically state, "A general reluctance to engage the historical and theoretical natures of race has permeated American historical archaeology, a field whose practitioners investigate places and times most definitely impacted by strategies of racialization." One of the major problems, therefore, has been a neglect to take stock of the crises in black America today. Relative to this is a failure to interrogate white privilege. As Epperson (1997:10) once wrote, "if we are to subvert, renounce, and eventually abolish whiteness we need to challenge the 'naturalness' of this pernicious social construction and strive to understand its origins and history." We have discussed case studies on race and inequality within African diaspora archaeology where it figures most prominently, but critical studies of whiteness are equally imperative and archaeologists are beginning to play a significant role in this area (Bell 2005; Brandon 2004; Epperson 1990, 1997, 2001; Orser 2004; Paynter 2001; Scott 2001).

Feminist Archaeology

Historical Context. The second wave women's movement of the 1960s and 1970s in protest of women's subjugation in both private and public life "fuelled feminist intellectual enquiry and the encounter with these political realities within the academy confirmed the identity of feminist scholarship as the intellectual wing of the women's movement" (Crowley 1999:132). Coinciding with the civil rights and then Black Power movements, feminist activism drew inspiration from these as well as its own heritage of identity politics in mobilizing (Adams 1989) and in demanding the creation of women's studies programs (with the first founded in 1970 at what is now San Diego State University). American feminist anthropology grew out of and contributed to this political and intellectual confluence, as feminists offered courses on the anthropology of women and published groundbreaking texts on the subject (e.g., Reiter 1975; Rosaldo and Lamphere 1974; see also Lewin 2006; Quinn 1977; Visweswaran 1997; Wylie 1991).

Yet in the 1970s, processual archaeology dominated the scene in the U.S., and it took over a decade after the feminist intervention in anthropology before Margaret Conkey and Janet Spector's (1984) significant and critical assessment of androcentrism in our discipline appeared in print (Conkey 2003:868). Their critique and their framework for an archaeology of gender drew mainly from feminist anthropology. Yet given the timing of their publication, Conkey and Spector were well aware of the problems associated with the second wave's universalizing notions of both womanhood and sexual asymmetry and were able to call attention to them (1984:16–21). By then, women of color were increasingly challenging the second wave, charging its mainly white, middle-class female constituents with racism, homophobia, and classism, and in the process, giving rise to third wave feminism and its focus on difference. Black feminists have been instrumental in calling for intersectional analyses, for attending to the complexity of subject formation along the lines of race, class, sexuality, gender, etc., and the ways in which oppression operates simultaneously along these lines. Although black women's involvement in the second wave women's movement has been obscured (Baxandall 2001; Nadasen 2002), and their political and theoretical contributions within the academy minimized (McClaurin 2001), black feminist theory, and third wave feminism in general, have still managed to assert some influence in feminist archaeology (Battle 2004; Brandon 2004; Conkey 2005; Franklin 2001; Voss 2006, 2008). Thus, feminist archaeology currently represents both the second and third waves (but see Engelstad 2007:224–226), with the former typically focused on women and the latter on issues of gender, intersectionality, and difference (Gilchrist 1999:6–7; Meskell 1999:53–106, 2002:282–283).

One might reasonably assume that the burgeoning interest in engendering archaeology since the 1980s was due to the larger influx of women into archaeology who were practicing feminists. Alison Wylie (1997) discovered, however, a more complicated scenario when she surveyed participants of the 1989 Chacmool Conference on The Archaeology of Gender. She observed that while senior scholars at the vanguard of engendering the discipline positioned themselves as feminists, most of the conference attendees (who were predominantly female) did not, or were ambivalent about identifying as feminists, although they were nonetheless interested in gender and archaeology (Wylie 1997:93–95; see also Conkey and Gero 1997). Thus, while a critical mass of women in the profession did result in a heightened awareness of gender issues in archaeology, as Wylie (1997:95) noted, this sense of a gendered standpoint was "not an explicitly feminist standpoint." The consequence of this decoupling of an interest in gender from a feminist politics reverberates even more strongly today than it did 20 years ago (Engelstad 2007). Archaeologists, most of them women, have produced a tidal wave of gender analyses (the majority focused on women) that exists mainly outside the realm of feminist archaeology (Conkey 2003; Conkey and Gero 1997:424–425). While the inclusion of women in the past is certainly central to most feminists, Conkey (2003:876) legitimately argues that not only is gender typically undertheorized in this research, but it "is still often just another variable that has been added to an unreflexive, somewhat positivist approach" (see also Meskell 1999:84–85). This has to matter to anyone committed to transforming archaeology and transformative uses of archaeology in the present.

Feminist Politics, Theory, and Practice. One answer to the question regarding what it means to practice archaeology as a feminist (in recognition that there are multiple positions in feminist archaeology) is aptly provided by Alison Wylie (2007:211) who states that there are "four widely shared commitments" in "doing archaeology as a feminist" (see also Conkey 2003; Conkey and Gero 1997). The first commitment involves problem orientations around issues relevant to women, or more broadly, to those victimized by gender oppression (see also Meskell 1999:82–87, and Tomásková 2007:274). In what must be coupled with the first commitment, Wylie writes that "feminists should ground their research in the situated experience of women and those marginalized by conventional sex/gender structures" (Wylie 2007:211; see also Wylie 1992). Wylie is careful to note that while women's experiences should be foregrounded, it should not follow that any experience is granted epistemic primacy (Wylie 2007:212). The third commitment relates to the ethics and politics of archaeological practice and entails accountability, collaboration, and egalitarianism in working toward a more democratic archaeology (Wylie 2007:212). In this sense, feminist archaeology is allied with the concerns of Indigenous archaeology (Atalay 2006; Conkey 2005; Dongoske et al. 2000; Lippert 2008; Watkins 2000, 2005; Zimmerman 2008) and other critical archaeologies such as the case studies discussed previously. Finally, Wylie argues for critical reflexivity, for feminists to comprehend the ways in which their situated locations, experiences, positionalities, and interests "are constitutive of the research process and of the understanding it produces" (Wylie 2007:212; see also Conkey and Gero 1997:429–430; Joyce and Tringham 2007; Tomásková 2007).

Laurie Wilkie's (2003) *The Archaeology of Mothering: An African-American Midwife's Tale* is certainly in league with Wylie's understanding of feminist archaeology, and exemplifies the kind of scholarship that is required in working toward social justice. Wilkie's study is about mothering and the constellation of meanings, practices, representations, identities, and symbolisms that revolve around the social construction of "mother." Wilkie focused on the life of Lucrecia Perryman, a black woman who was both mother and midwife during the nineteenth and early twentieth century in Alabama. Black feminist theorizing played a key role in shaping Wilkie's questions and interpretations, and also in contextualizing her politics, which involved de-essentializing black womanhood, denaturalizing dominant constructions of "woman" and "mother," and clarifying the entanglements of race, class, and gender and their roles in structuring multiple forms of identity and oppression.

Wilkie's self-reflection was expressed not only in how she situated herself with respect to her analysis, but also in her vigilance in interposing the relevance of her questions and interpretations to present-day issues central to black women's everyday lives. One of her concerns was challenging pervasive stereotypes that degrade black women (Collins 1991:67–90; hooks 1981:51–71, 83–86) since "controlling images" (Wilkie 2003:74) serve to naturalize hierarchies and justify discrimination. One such example is the myth of the matriarch that blames black women for maintaining female-headed households which then lead to the fragmentation of the nuclear family (Wilkie 2003:47–48; see also hooks 1981:71–83, 178–181). Another is what Patricia Hill Collins (2004:130–131) refers to as the "Bad Black Mother," or "BBM." Attributed to poor and working-class mothers, BBMs are stereotypically abusive, sexually promiscuous, neglectful of their children, and at fault for perpetuating the cycle of poverty that will be inherited by their kids (see also Mullings 1995). With its origins dating back to slavery, this stigmatized representation of black women as inferior mothers has led to public policies aimed at curtailing welfare, and in asserting control over their fertility and reproduction (Collins 2004:133; Mullings 1995:132; Wilkie 2003:211). Thus, Wilkie's research on black mothering and womanhood is imbued with a strong sense of urgency and is aligned with current black feminist politics.

Altogether, the evidence presented by Wilkie challenged the notions of a fractured black community and irresponsible mothering among poor and working-class blacks in the past that called into question the validity of contemporary stereotypes drawn and reproduced from them. Her study is representative of a growing body of feminist archaeology aimed at undermining assumptions about gender, race, sexuality, and class, and that is explicitly concerned with disrupting essentialisms (and their attendant inequalities) in the present by challenging their presumed continuities into the past (e.g., Beaudry 2006; Joyce 2008; Meskell 1999, 2002; Pyburn 2004; Voss 2008). Feminists have also made important inroads in other areas of practice that figure largely in our attempts to address hegemony and inequality.

Feminist archaeologists have set in their sights a range of challenges for transforming the ways we conceptualize and practice archaeology (e.g., Moser 2007; Tomàskovà 2007) that have broader implications for the profession and its social and political relevance. For instance, the politics of writing, of generating authoritative texts that mystify archaeology's many ambiguities while bringing closure to our (re)constructions of the past is a key subject of interest to feminists who recognize the power play this entails (e.g., Joyce 2002; Spector 1993; Wilkie 2003; see also Gero 2007). Rosemary Joyce and Ruth Tringham (2007) creatively tackled this issue as it relates to multivocality by presenting the past in multilinear narratives (versus the traditional unilinear narrative) via digital media. Non-archaeologists travel their own routes to meanings and interpretations by navigating hypertext; this action simultaneously de-centers the archaeologists' knowledge claims while validating diverse ways of knowing the past. Relatedly, feminists have sought to democratize the classroom by encouraging active engagement and collaboration among students/instructors in contrast to using traditional pedagogies based on passive learning where the instructors are the assumed authorities (Arnold 2005; Conkey and Tringham 1996; Hendon 2005). These practices certainly have their counterparts in postcolonial, critical, or more broadly, "post-processual" archaeologies, and it is likely that shared commitments will lead to more synergy between the various camps in the near future (see also Conkey 2005).

Although eliminating inequality for feminist archaeologists is emphatically not only about gender-related issues, they still dominate the agenda, and for good reason. Feminists who pioneered the archaeology of gender conceived of it as a means of addressing androcentrism and gender oppression. Yet, as previously discussed, too many gender analysts have disassociated themselves and their research from feminist scholarship and politics (Hays-Gilpin 2000; Wylie 1997, 2007:211). This is a significant problem given that gender discrimination has been well documented in what is now a gender-balanced profession in the U.S. (see discussion below). And make no mistake about it: we cannot compartmentalize gender inequity issues in the present and theorizing about gender in the past as if they are separate projects. Peripheralized as feminist archaeology is, however, no one could claim at this juncture that there simply aren't enough theoretically and methodologically rigorous feminist research models and practices to inspire and emulate.

Remarks

The case studies above are but some of the projects where archaeologists have understood the necessity to engage the contemporary world, developing empirical knowledge that contributes to economic justice as well as racial and gender equality (Little and Shackel 2007). The social movements of the 1960s and 1970s and neoliberalism were important forces that reshaped the United States' cultural landscape and political economy and have had lasting impacts on archaeology. By considering the implications of these various forces for the emergence and trajectories of archaeologies of inequality, we hoped to further illustrate how embedded the discipline is within broader historical processes.

In addition, though we have emphasized one dimension or another in these studies, we acknowledge the need to understand the intersection of race, class, and gender as structuring principles that have shaped the American past. Intersectional analysis still escapes too much of our theory and method, thereby limiting the complexity in the telling of specific histories. Attention to such will be a hallmark of the next 25 years of work.

Moreover, race, class, and gender are by no means the only modes of identity or political fields affecting archaeological theory and practice. Others include the continuing attempts to undo the political relations of European colonization (Schmidt and Patterson 1995; Smith and Wobst 2005; Watkins 2000, 2005) and responses to the real and imminent effects of global warming (e.g., Dawdy 2006); all deserve attention. For now we turn our attention to the question of how the changing alignments of race, class, and gender have influenced who is practicing archaeology in the twenty-first century.

Diversity Issues in Archaeology

Over the last 30 years, the professional face of archaeology and its institutional base have shown signs of both continuity and change. While the academy and museums are still important venues for the practice of archaeology, the vast majority of U.S. archaeology is now conducted under the auspices of CRM (Patterson 1999:164–167). Neoliberalism and civil rights legislation (which opened more doors for women and minorities in higher education) are all implicated, though to varying degrees, in how the profession has transformed.

With regard to gender, Patterson (1995:81,108) tracked the gender parity shift in the field from women comprising 9.7 percent in 1936 to a relatively stable 11–15 percent from 1946–1969, and becoming increasingly a large percentage of the field in the 1970s to reach 28.3 percent in 1976. Melinda Zeder's (1997:9–11) survey analysis of SAA members strikingly demonstrated that by 1994, women were 49 percent of the student respondents and 36 percent of the professional respondents. Significantly, Zeder noted that professional women were approaching 50 percent of the younger cohorts, those between the ages of 20 and 39. Clearly the social movements and cultural changes that brought more women into middle-class professions have also impacted archaeology. Still, there are gender disparities in terms of employment opportunities and placement (Wylie 1997:82–83), workplace segregation (Gero 1985; Wylie 1997), citation practices (Hutson 2002), the marginalization of gender and feminist theory (Conkey 2007; Conkey and Gero 1997), promotions, funding, and in the training of students (Nelson et al. 1994).

Neoliberalism, and especially its cuts to state budgets, has affected who has access to earning a B.A. in anthropology, the gateway degree for most professional archaeology positions. Many state budgets dropped precipitously in the recession of the late 1980s to early 1990s, with a concomitant drop in state support for public higher education. Despite the prosperity of the mid-to-late 1990s, most higher education budgets were slow to "catch up," if they did. The recession of the early twenty-first century saw another round of state budget cuts with more cutbacks in funding for higher education. Many of these public institutions sought to make up for the state support by shifting the cost of education to the students through tuition and fee increases that far outpaced the growth of inflation or of most family incomes

(Zumeta 2003). At the University of Massachusetts, Amherst, there is an increasing tendency for middle-class families, who previously could afford to send their children to private schools, to instead send them to public universities. Faculty and students worry that the higher "objective" scores of students from relatively more wealthy school systems crowd out the applications of students from financially deprived ones. The working class seems to be increasingly attending state and community colleges, which have few or no full-time archaeologists and little if any laboratory or field programs.

In addition, our anecdotal experience is that the cost of attending college and the accompanying burden of debt has led students away from "esoteric" fields like archaeology into the apparently more lucrative futures offered by professional schools. This has certainly been a concern for students of color, as many are the first in their families to earn college degrees. Moreover, a number of them choose fields in which they believe they can make a difference in their communities, and historically, archaeology has not presented itself as having contemporary relevance (Franklin 1997b). These pressures are only increasing the trend Zeder (1997:14) noted for "archaeologists to come from increasingly higher socioeconomic backgrounds."

The number of archaeologists of color is still depressingly low. As Zeder observed, "For a discipline dedicated to the study of human diversity over the ages, American archaeology is starkly homogenous in its own ethnic make-up" (Zeder 1997:13). Of the 1,644 respondents in the mid 1990s, "2 were African American, 4 were of Asian heritage, 15 were Hispanic (with 5 coming from Latin American countries), and 10 people classified themselves as Native Americans" (Zeder 1997:13). By our estimate, there are currently about a dozen or so African American Ph.D. archaeologists, and about the same from Native American communities (see Altschul and Patterson, this volume).

We suggest that another reason for the low participation of people of color in the profession, deserving deeper exploration, is that American archaeology is what Enoch Page identifies as a White Public Space (Page 2006; Page and Thomas 1994; Page 1999). Within this space, institutional practices support Eurocentric cultural perspectives that concretize orders of racial and economic inequality (James and Gordon 2007). Many agree that such economic and social closure limits the practice, imagination, and sensitivity necessary to understand the cultural breadth that is the subject matter of archaeology. For example, as NAGPRA has brought to the fore, we often treat human remains as inanimate rather than animate beings (Peters 2006). Another limitation is a readiness to privilege the imperatives of labor and management efficiency in understanding factories, plantations, etc., and not considering the possibilities for and residues of foot dragging and sabotage (Nassaney and Abel 1993). Yet another constraint concerns the valuing of notions of time as a linear phenomenon in contrast to stressing cyclicity and recurrence in our interpretations (Joe Watkins, personal communication 2008).

Conclusions

Eliminating inequalities through archaeology is undoubtedly an ambitious goal. It is undeniably easier to demonstrate the emancipatory potential of archaeology at the "frontlines," where archaeologists are engaged in interacting with the public, than it is to argue the same for other vehicles for archaeological scholarship, including the majority of our publications and conference papers. However, it is our position that archaeologists committed to social justice who emphatically locate their research in politically relevant ways to contemporary struggles to end discrimination are actually "doing" something productive. Even writing for other archaeologists has political implications: the discipline is still fairly conservative and can hardly be described as antiracist, -classist, -sexist, or anti-heteronormative. It remains a challenge for us to democratize archaeology, let alone tackle the deep-seated inequalities pervasive in all of the areas of the world in which we work. Yet, transforming the discipline is a start (e.g., Atalay 2006; Conkey and Gero 1997; Conkey and Spector 1984; Dongoske et al. 2000; McGuire 2008; Million 2005; Watkins 2000), and the theoretical labor that goes into de-essentializing categories of difference, denaturalizing structural hierarchies, and exposing and critiquing hegemony can and has worked hand-in-hand with applied archaeology in the public realm. It is important to remember that the New York African Burial Ground project, with its political, theoretical, methodological, and historical innovations, was from start to end a cultural resource management project guided by service to the community. There is no divide between theory and practice, and if the objective is to work toward eliminating inequalities, the theories that we choose to work recursively with our practice must attend to the entanglement of power and difference.

We are writing at a point in time when U.S. headlines recently, and prematurely, exclaimed Obama's victory as proof that we have entered a "post-racial" era. Moreover, the celebration of Obama's win overshadowed the passage of Proposition 8 banning same-sex marriage in California. We are also in the midst of a global capitalist crisis that underscores the transnational connections and unequal power relations between political economies here and abroad. The political and social landscape continues to shift, but it remains that inequality is a moving force in the politics of nation-states. This means that whether archaeologists take this issue on directly as research projects or not, the discipline cannot escape being implicated in the contemporary struggles over inequality. In order for archaeology to have more traction with the contemporary world, we must labor to understand the historical trajectories and social forms of inequality that have shaped it, and we must move forward with the theoretical tools and practices that help to deconstruct inequality.

Acknowledgments. We would like to thank our editors, Wendy Ashmore, Barbara Mills, and Dorothy Lippert, for inviting us to coauthor this chapter and for their encouragement, patience, and their vision for transforming archaeology. We also wish to acknowledge the support and collegiality of Tom Patterson, Ventura Perez, Enoch Page, and Whitney Battle-Baptiste, each of whom inspired what we presented here. We received generous assistance in locating sources on political movements, and the formation of ethnic and black studies, from Kimbra Smith, Rodolfo Rosales, Matthew Countryman, Cathryn Watson, Tehama Lopez, Carlos Vazquez, Camilo Arturo Leslie, and Kiley Guyton Acosta, and we are grateful for their support. Finally, we are indebted to two anonymous reviewers who provided us with insightful comments and constructive feedback, all of which helped to strengthen this manuscript.

References Cited

Adams, M. L.
   1989 There's No Place Like Home: On the Place of Identity in Feminist Politics. *Feminist Review* 31:22–33.

Aldridge, Delores P., and Carlene Young
   2000 Historical Development and Introduction to the Academy. In *Out of the Revolution: The Development of Africana Studies*, edited by Delores P. Aldridge and Carlene Young, pp. 3–12. Lexington Books, Lanham, Maryland.

American Social History Project
   1992 *Who Built America?: Working People and the Nation's Economy, Politics, Culture, and Society, Vol. 2: From the Gilded Age to the Present.* Pantheon Books, New York.

Arnold, Bettina
   2005 Teaching with Intent: The Archaeology of Gender. *Archaeologies* 1(2):83–93.

Atalay, Sonya
  2006 Indigenous Archaeology as Decolonizing Practice. *American Indian Quarterly* 30(3):280–310.
Babson, David W.
  1990 The Archaeology of Racism and Ethnicity on Southern Plantations. *Historical Archaeology* 24:20–28.
Bahrani, Zainab
  2003 Looting and Conquest. The Nation Online, Electronic document, http://www.thenation.com/doc/20030526/bahrani. Accessed April 2, 2009.
Barile, Kerri S.
  2004 Race, the National Register, and Cultural Resource Management: Creating an Historic Context for Postbellum Sites. *Historical Archaeology* 38:90–100.
Battle, W. L.
  2004 "A Yard to Sweep": Race, Gender and the Enslaved Landscape. Unpublished Ph.D. dissertation, Department of Anthropology, University of Texas at Austin.
Baxandall, Rosalyn
  2001 Re-Visioning the Women's Liberation Movement's Narrative: Early Second Wave African American Feminists. *Feminist Studies* 27(1):225–245.
Beaudry, Mary C.
  2006 *Findings: The Material Culture of Needlework and Sewing.* Yale University Press, New Haven, Connecticut.
Beaudry, Mary C., Lauren J. Cook, and Stephen A. Mrozowski
  1991 Artifacts and Active Voices: Material Culture as Social Discourse. In *The Archaeology of Inequality*, edited by Randall H. McGuire and Robert Paynter, pp. 150–191. Blackwell, Oxford.
Bell, Alison
  2005 White Ethnogenesis and Gradual Capitalism: Perspectives from Colonial Archaeological Sites in the Chesapeake. *American Anthropologist* 107:446–460.
  2008 On the Politics and Possibilities for Operationalizing Vindicationist Historical Archaeologies. *Historical Archaeology* 42:138–146.
Blackmore, Chelsea
  2008 Challenging "Commoner": An Archaeological Examination of Social Identity and Class Formation at the Northeast Group, Chan, Belize. Unpublished Ph.D. dissertation, University of California, Riverside.
Blakey, Michael L.
  1997 Commentary: Past Is Present. *Historical Archaeology* 31:140–145.
  2001 Bioarchaeology of the African Diaspora in the Americas: Its Origins and Scope. *Annual Review of Anthropology* 30:387–422.
Blakey, Michael L., and Lesley M. Rankin-Hill (editors)
  2004 *New York African Burial Ground Skeletal Biology Final Report, Volumes 1–2.* Howard University, Washington, D.C. Submitted to United States General Services Administration Northeastern and Caribbean Region, Contract No. GS-02P-93-CUD-0071. Electronic copies available from http://www.africanburialground.gov/ABG_FinalReports.htm, accessed June 19, 2009.

Brandon, Jamie C.
   2004   Reconstructing Domesticity and Segregating Households: The Intersections of Gender and Race in the Postbellum South. In *Household Chores and Household Choices: Theorizing the Domestic Sphere in Historical Archaeology*, edited by Kerri S. Barile and Jamie C. Brandon, pp. 197–209. University of Alabama Press, Tuscaloosa.

Brumfiel, Elizabeth M.
   1991   Weaving and Cooking: Women's Production in Aztec Mexico. In *Engendering Archaeology: Women and Prehistory*, edited by Joan M. Gero and Margaret W. Conkey, pp. 224–251. Blackwell, Oxford.
   2006   Cloth, Gender, Continuity, and Change: Fabricating Unity in Anthropology. *American Anthropologist* 108:862–877.

Byrne, Denis R.
   2003   Nervous Landscapes: Race and Space in Australia. *Journal of Social Archaeology* 3:169–193.

Callinicos, Alex
   1995   *Theories and Narratives: Reflections on the Philosophy of History*. Duke University Press, Durham, North Carolina.

Cobb, Charles R.
   2000   *From Quarry to Cornfield: The Political Economy of Mississippian Hoe Production*. University of Alabama Press, Tuscaloosa, Alabama.

Collins, Patricia H.
   1991   *Black Feminist Thought: Knowledge, Consciousness, and the Politics of Empowerment*. Routledge, New York.
   2004   *Black Sexual Politics: African Americans, Gender, and the New Racism*. Routledge, New York.

Conkey, Margaret W.
   2003   Has Feminism Changed Archaeology? *Signs* 28(3):867–880.
   2005   Dwelling at the Margins, Action at the Intersection? Feminist and Indigenous Archaeologies, 2005. *Archaeologies* 1(1):9–59.
   2007   Questioning Theory: Is There a Gender of Theory in Archaeology? *Journal of Archaeological Method and Theory* 14:285–310.

Conkey, Margaret W., and Joan M. Gero
   1997   Programme to Practice: Gender and Feminism in Archaeology. *Annual Review of Anthropology* 26:411–437.

Conkey, Margaret W., and J. Spector
   1984   Archaeology and the Study of Gender. In *Advances in Archaeological Method and Theory*, edited by Michael B. Schiffer, pp. 1–38. vol. 7. Academic Press, New York.

Conkey, Margaret W., and Ruth E. Tringham
   1996   Cultivating Thinking/Challenging Authority: Some Experiments in Feminist Pedagogy in Archaeology. In *Gender and Archaeology*, edited by Rita P. Wright, pp. 224–250. University of Pennsylvania Press, Philadelphia.

Crenshaw, Kimberle, Neil Gotanda, Gary Peller, and Kendall Thomas (editors)
   1995   *Critical Race Theory: The Key Writings that Formed the Movement*. The New Press, New York.

Crowley, H.
   1999 Women's Studies: Between a Rock and a Hard Place or Just Another Cell in the Beehive? *Feminist Review* 61:131–150.

Davidson, James M.
   2004 "Living Symbols of Their Lifelong Struggles": In Search of the Home and Household in the Heart of Freedman's Town, Dallas, Texas. In *Household Chores and Household Choices: Theorizing the Domestic Sphere in Historical Archaeology*, edited by Kerri S. Barile and Jamie C. Brandon, pp. 75–106. University of Alabama Press, Tuscaloosa.

Davis, Mike
   1986 *Prisoners of the American Dream: Politics and Economy in the History of the US Working Class*. Verso, New York.

Dawdy, Shannon Lee
   2006 The Taphonomy of Disaster and the (Re)formation of New Orleans. *American Anthropologist* 108:719–730.

Delle, James A.
   1998 *An Archaeology of Social Space: Analyzing Coffee Plantations in Jamaica's Blue Mountains*. Plenum Press, New York.
   1999 The Landscapes of Class Negotiation on Coffee Plantations in the Blue Mountains of Jamaica, 1790–1850. *Historical Archaeology* 33:136–158.

Delle, James A., Stephen A. Mrozowski, and Robert Paynter (editors)
   2000 *Lines that Divide: Historical Archaeologies of Race, Class, and Gender*. University of Tennessee Press, Knoxville.

Dongoske, Kurt E., Mark Aldenderfer, and Karen Doehner (editors)
   2000 *Working Together: Native Americans and Archaeologists*. Society for American Archaeology, Washington, D.C.

Doretti, Mercedes, and Clyde Snow
   2003 Forensic Anthropology and Human Rights: The Argentine Experience. In *Hard Evidence: Case Studies in Forensic Anthropology*, edited by Dawnie W. Steadman, pp. 290–310. Prentice-Hall, Upper Saddle River, New Jersey.

Drake, S. C.
   1978 Reflections on Anthropology and the Black Experience. *Anthropology and Education Quarterly* 9(2):85–109.

Eagleton, Terry
   1996 *The Illusions of Postmodernism*. Blackwell, Cambridge, Massachusetts.

Emberling, Geoff, and Katharyn Hanson (editors)
   2008 *Catastrophe! The Looting and Destruction of Iraq's Past*. Oriental Institute Museum of the University of Chicago.

Engelstad, Ericka
   2007 Much More than Gender. *Journal of Archaeological Method and Theory* 14:217–234.

Epperson, Terrence W.
   1990 Race and the Disciplines of the Plantation. *Historical Archaeology* 24:29–36.
   1997 Whiteness in Early Virginia. *Race Traitor* 7:9–20.

1999 The Contested Commons: Archaeologies of Race, Repression, and Resistance in New York City. In *Historical Archaeologies of Capitalism*, edited by Mark P. Leone and Parker B. Potter, Jr., pp. 81–110. Plenum Press, New York.
2001 "A Separate House for the Christian Slaves, One for the Negro Slaves": The Archaeology of Race and Identity in Late Seventeenth-Century Virginia. In *Race and the Archaeology of Identity*, edited by Charles E. Orser, Jr., pp. 54–70. University of Utah Press, Salt Lake City.
2004 Critical Race Theory and the Archaeology of the African Diaspora. *Historical Archaeology* 38:101–108.

Ferguson, Leland
1992 *Uncommon Ground: Archaeology and Early African America, 1650–1800*. Smithsonian Institution Press, Washington, D.C.

Fones-Wolf, Elizabeth A.
1994 *Selling Free Enterprise: The Business Assault on Labor and Liberalism, 1945–1960*. University of Illinois Press, Urbana, Illinois.

Foster, John Bellamy, and Fred Magdoff
2008 Financial Implosion and Stagnation: Back to the Real Economy. *Monthly Review* 60(7):1–29.
2009 *The Great Financial Crisis: Causes and Consequences*. Monthly Review Press, New York.

Franklin, Maria
1997a "Power to the People": Sociopolitics and the Archaeology of Black Americans. *Historical Archaeology* 31:36–50.
1997b Why Are There So Few Black American Archaeologists? *Antiquity* 71:799–801.
2001 A Black Feminist-Inspired Archaeology? *Journal of Social Archaeology* 3:108–125.

Fried, Morton H.
1967 *The Evolution of Political Society*. Random House, New York.

Funari, Pedro Paolo A.
1999 Maroon, Race and Gender: Palmares Material Culture and Social Relations in a Runaway Settlement. In *Historical Archaeology: Back from the Edge*, edited by Pedro Paolo A. Funari, Martin Hall and Sian Jones, pp. 308–327. Routledge, London.

Gassiot-Ballbé, Emengol, and Dawnie W. Steadman
2008 The Political, Social and Scientific Contexts of Archaeological Investigations of Mass Graves in Spain. *Archaeologies* 4(3):429–444.

Gero, Joan M.
1985 Socio-politics and the Woman-at-Home Ideology. *American Antiquity* 50:342–350.
2007 Honoring Ambiguity/Problematizing Certitude. *Journal of Archaeological Method and Theory* 14:311–327.

Gilchrist, Roberta
1999 *Gender and Archaeology: Contesting the Past*. Routledge, London.

Gordon, Edmund T.
  1997 Anthropology and Liberation. In *De-colonizing Anthropology: Moving Further Toward An Anthropology for Liberation,* edited by Faye V. Harrison, pp. 150–169. 2nd ed. American Anthropological Association, Washington, D.C.
Guinier, Lani, and Gerald Torres
  2002 *The Miner's Canary: Enlisting Race, Resisting Power, Transforming Democracy.* Harvard University Press, Cambridge.
Hall, Martin
  2000 *Archaeology and the Modern World: Colonial Transcripts in South Africa and the Chesapeake.* Routledge, London.
Harvey, David
  1989 *The Condition of Postmodernity.* Basil Blackwell, Oxford.
  2005 *A Brief History of Neoliberalism.* Oxford University Press, Oxford.
Hays-Gilpin, Kelley
  2000 Feminist Scholarship in Archaeology. *Annals of the American Academy of Political and Social Science* 571:89–106.
Hendon, Julia A.
  2005 Fact or Speculation? How a Feminist Perspective Can Help Students Understand What Archaeologists Know and Why They Think They Know It. *Archaeologies* 1(2):21–32.
hooks, b.
  1981 *Ain't I A Woman: Black Women and Feminism.* South End Press, Boston.
Hutson, Scott
  2002 Gendered Citation Practices in American Antiquity and Other Archaeological Journals. *American Antiquity* 67:331–342.
James, Joy, and Edmund T. Gordon
  2007 Afterword: Activist Scholars or Radical Subjects? In *Engaging Contradictions: The Case for Activist Research,* edited by Charles R. Hale, pp. 367–373. University of California Press, Berkeley.
Joyce, Rosemary A.
  2002 *The Languages of Archaeology.* Blackwell, Oxford.
  2008 *Ancient Bodies, Ancient Lives: Sex, Gender, and Archaeology.* Thames and Hudson, New York.
Joyce, Rosemary A., and Ruth E. Tringham
  2007 Feminist Adventures in Hypertext. *Journal of Archaeological Method and Theory* 14:328–358.
LaRoche, Cheryl J., and Michael L. Blakey
  1997 Seizing Intellectual Power: The Dialogue at the New York African Burial Ground. *Historical Archaeology* 31:84–106.
Leone, Mark P.
  1986 Symbolic, Structural and Critical Archaeology. In *American Archaeology Past and Future: A Celebration of the Society for American Archaeology, 1935–1985,* edited by David J. Meltzer, Don D. Fowler, and Jeremy A. Sabloff, pp. 415–438. Smithsonian Institution Press, Washington, D.C.
  1988 The Georgian Order as the Order of Merchant Capitalism in Annapolis,

Maryland. In *The Recovery of Meaning: Historical Archaeology in the Eastern United States*, edited by Mark P. Leone and Parker B. Potter, Jr., pp. 235–261. Smithsonian Institution Press, Washington, D.C.

1999 Ceramics from Annapolis, Maryland: A Measure of Time Routines and Work Discipline. In *Historical Archaeologies of Capitalism*, edited by Mark P. Leone and Parker B. Potter, Jr., pp. 195–216. Kluwer Academic/Plenum Publishers, New York.

2005 *The Archaeology of Liberty in an American Capital: Excavations in Annapolis*. University of California Press, Berkeley.

Leone, Mark P., Gladys-Marie Fry, and Timothy Ruppel

2001 Spirit Management among Americans of African Descent. In *Race and the Archaeology of Identity*, edited by Charles E. Orser, Jr., pp. 143–157. University of Utah Press, Salt Lake City, Utah.

Leone, Mark P., and Silas D. Hurry

1998 Seeing: The Power of Town Planning in the Chesapeake. *Historical Archaeology* 32:34–62.

Leone, Mark P., Cheryl J. LaRoche, and Jennifer J. Babiarz

2005 The Archaeology of Black Americans in Recent Times. *Annual Review of Anthropology* 34:575–598.

Lewin, Ellen

2006 Introduction. In *Feminist Anthropology: A Reader*, edited by Ellen Lewin, pp. 1–38. Blackwell, Malden, Massachusetts.

Lippert, Dorothy

2008 The Rise of Indigenous Archaeology: How Repatriation Has Transformed Archaeological Ethics and Practice. In *Opening Archaeology: Repatriation's Impact on Contemporary Research and Practice*, edited by Thomas W. Killion, pp. 151–160. School for Advanced Research Press, Santa Fe, New Mexico.

Little, Barbara J.

1994 People with History: An Update on Historical Archaeology in the United States. *Journal of Archaeological Method and Theory* 1:5–40.

Little, Barbara J., and Paul A. Shackel (editors)

2007 *Archaeology as a Tool of Civic Engagement*. Altamira Press, Lanham, Maryland.

McClaurin, Irma

2001 Introduction: Forging a Theory, Politics, Praxis, and Poetics of Black Feminist Anthropology. In *Black Feminist Anthropology*, edited by Irma McClaurin, pp. 1–23. Rutgers University Press, New Brunswick, New Jersey.

McDavid, Carol

1997 Descendants, Decisions, and Power: The Public Interpretation of the Archaeology of the Levi Jordan Plantation. *Historical Archaeology* 31:114–131.

2002 Archaeologies That Hurt; Descendants That Matter: A Pragmatic Approach to Collaboration in the Public Interpretation of African-American Archaeology. *World Archaeology* 34:303–314.

2007 Beyond Strategy and Good Intentions: Archaeology, Race, and White Privilege. In *Archaeology as a Tool of Civic Engagement*, edited by Barbara J. Little and Paul A. Shackel, pp. 67–88. Altamira Press, Lanham, Maryland.

McGuire, Randall H.
  1989 The Greater Southwest as a Periphery of Mesoamerica. In *Centre and Periphery*, edited by T. C. Champion, pp. 40–66. Allen and Unwin, London.
  1992 *A Marxist Archaeology*. Academic Press, San Diego, California.
  2008 *Archaeology as Political Action*. University of California Press, Berkeley.
McGuire, Randall H., Maria O'Donovan, and LouAnn Wurst
  2005 Probing Praxis in Archaeology: The Last Eighty Years. *Rethinking Marxism* 17(3):355–372.
McGuire, Randall H., and Dean Saitta
  1996 Although They Have Petty Captains, They Obey Them Badly: The Dialectics of Prehispanic Western Pueblo Social Organization. *American Antiquity* 61:197–216.
McGuire, Randall H., and Mark Walker
  1999 Class Confrontations in Archaeology. *Historical Archaeology* 33:159–183.
McGuire, Randall H., and LouAnn Wurst
  2002 Struggling with the Past. *International Journal of Historical Archaeology* 6(2):85–94.
Mack, Mark E., and Michael L. Blakey
  2004 The New York African Burial Ground Project: Past Biases, Current Dilemmas, and Future Research Opportunities. *Historical Archaeology* 38:10–17.
Massey, Douglas S.
  2007 *Categorically Unequal: The American Stratification System*. Russell Sage Foundation, New York.
Matthews, Christopher N.
  2001 Political Economy and Race: Comparative Archaeologies of Annapolis and New Orleans in the Eighteenth Century. In *Race and the Archaeology of Identity*, edited by Charles E. Orser, Jr., pp. 71–87. University of Utah Press, Salt Lake City, Utah.
Medford, Edna G. (editor)
  2004 *New York African Burial Ground History Final Report*. Howard University, Washington, D.C. Submitted to United States General Services Administration Northeastern and Caribbean Region, Contract No. GS-02P-93-CUD-0071. Electronic copies available from http://www.africanburialground.gov/ABG_FinalReports.htm, accessed June 19, 2009.
Meltzer, David J., Don D. Fowler, and Jeremy A. Sabloff (editors)
  1986 *American Archaeology Past and Future: A Celebration of the Society for American Archaeology, 1935–1985*. Smithsonian Institution Press, Washington, D.C.
Meskell, Lynn
  1999 *Archaeologies of Social Life*. Blackwell, Oxford.
  2002 The Intersections of Identity and Politics in Archaeology. *Annual Review of Anthropology* 31:279–301.
Million, Tara
  2005 Developing an Aboriginal Archaeology: Receiving Gifts from White Buffalo Calf Woman. In *Indigenous Archaeologies: Decolonizing Theory and Practice*, edited by Claire Smith and H. Martin Wobst, pp. 43–55. Routledge, London.

Moser, Stephanie
   2007   On Disciplinary Culture: Archaeology as Fieldwork and Its Gendered Associations. *Journal of Archaeological Method and Theory* 14:235–263.

Mrozowski, Stephen A.
   2006   *The Archaeology of Class in Urban America*. Cambridge University Press, New York.

Mrozowski, Stephen A., and Mary C. Beaudry
   1990   Archeology and the Landscape of Corporate Ideology. In *Earth Patterns*, edited by William Kelso and Rachel Most, pp. 189–208. University Press of Virginia, Charlottesville.

Mrozowski, Stephen A., Grace H. Ziesing, and Mary C. Beaudry
   1996   *Living on the Boott: Historical Archaeology at the Boott Mills Boardinghouses, Lowell, Massachusetts*. University of Massachusetts Press, Amherst.

Muller, Jon
   1997   *Mississippian Political Economy*. Plenum, New York.

Mullings, Leith
   1995   Households Headed by Women: The Politics of Race, Class, and Gender. In *Conceiving the New World Order: The Global Politics of Reproduction*, edited by Faye D. Ginsburg and Rayna Rapp, pp. 122–139. University of California Press, Berkeley.

Mullins, Paul R.
   1999a   *Race and Affluence: An Archaeology of African America and Consumer Culture*. Kluwer Academic/ Plenum Publishers, New York.
   1999b Race and the Genteel Consumer: Class and African-American Consumption. *Historical Archaeology* 33:22–38.
   1999c   "A Bold and Gorgeous Front": The Contradictions of African America and Consumer Culture. In *Historical Archaeologies of Capitalism*, edited by Mark P. Leone and Parker B. Potter, Jr., pp. 169–193. Kluwer Academic/Plenum Publishers, New York.
   2007   Politics, Inequality, and Engaged Archaeology: Community Archaeology Along the Color Line. In *Archaeology as a Tool in Civic Engagement*, edited by Barbara J. Little and Paul A. Shackel, pp. 89–108. Altamira Press, Lanham, Maryland.
   2008   Excavating America's Metaphor: Race, Diaspora, and Vindicationist Archaeologies. *Historical Archaeology* 42:104–122.

Nadasen, Premilla
   2002   Expanding the Boundaries of the Women's Movement: Black Feminism and the Struggle for Welfare Rights. *Feminist Studies* 28(2):271–301

Nassaney, Michael S., and Marjorie R. Abel
   1993   The Political and Social Contexts of Cutlery Production in the Connecticut Valley. *Dialectical Anthropology* 18:247–289.

Nelson, Sarah M., Margaret C. Nelson, and Alison Wylie (editors)
   1994   *Equity Issues for Women in Archeology*. Archeological Papers of the American Anthropological Association no. 5. American Anthropological Association, Arlington, Virginia.

Nelson, William E.
- 2000 Black Studies, Student Activism, and the Academy. In *Out of the Revolution: The Development of Africana Studies*, edited by Delores P. Aldridge and Carlene Young, pp. 79–91. Lexington Books, Lanham, Maryland.

Orser, Charles E., Jr.
- 1991 The Continued Pattern of Dominance: Landlord and Tenant on the Postbellum Cotton Plantation. In *The Archaeology of Inequality*, edited by Randall H. McGuire and Robert Paynter, pp. 40–54. Blackwell, Oxford.
- 1996 *A Historical Archaeology of the Modern World*. Plenum Press, New York.
- 1998a The Challenge of Race to American Historical Archaeology. *American Anthropologist* 100:661–668.
- 1998b The Archaeology of the African Diaspora. *Annual Reviews in Anthropology* 27:63–82.
- 1999 Archaeology and the Challenges of Capitalist Farm Tenancy in America. In *Historical Archaeologies of Capitalism*, edited by Mark P. Leone and Parker B. Potter, Jr., pp. 143–167. Kluwer Academic/Plenum Publishers, New York.
- 2001 Race and the Archaeology of Identity in the Modern World. In *Race and the Archaeology of Identity*, edited by Charles E. Orser, Jr., pp. 1–13. University of Utah Press, Salt Lake City, Utah.
- 2004 *Race and Practice in Archaeological Interpretation*. University of Pennsylvania Press, Philadelphia.

Orser, Charles E., Jr. (editor)
- 1990 Historical Archaeology on Southern Plantations and Farms. *Historical Archaeology* 24(4).
- 2001 *Race and the Archaeology of Identity*. University of Utah Press, Salt Lake City, Utah.

Otto, John S.
- 1984 *Cannon's Point Plantation 1794–1860: Living Conditions and Status Patterns in the Old South*. Academic Press, Orlando, Florida

Page, Enoch H.
- 2006 Toward a Unified Paradigm of Race. *American Anthropologist* 108:530–533.

Page, H. E.
- 1999 No Black Public Sphere in White Public Space: Racialized Information and Hi-Tech Diffusion in the Global African Diaspora. *Transforming Anthropology* 8(1&2):111–128.

Page, H. E., and R. B. Thomas
- 1994 White Public Space and the Construction of White Privilege in U.S. Health Care: Fresh Concepts and a New Model of Analysis. *Medical Anthropology Quarterly* 8:109–116.

Palus, M. M., Mark P. Leone, and M. D. Cochran
- 2006 Critical Archaeology: Politics Past and Present. In *Historical Archaeology*, edited by Martin Hall and Stephen W. Silliman, pp. 84–104. Blackwell, Malden, Massachusetts.

Patterson, Thomas C.
- 1985 Pachacamac: An Andean Oracle Under Inca Rule. In *Recent Studies in Andean*

Prehistory, edited by D. Peter Kvietok and Donald H. Sandweiss, pp. 159–176. Cornell University Press, Ithaca, New York.

1986a Ideology, Class Formation and Resistance in the Inca State. *Critique of Anthropology* 6:75–85.

1986b Class and State Formation: the Case of pre-Incaic Peru. *Dialectical Anthropology* 10:275–282.

1991 *The Inca Empire: The Formation and Disintegration of a Pre-Capitalist State.* Berg, New York.

1995 *Toward a Social History of Archaeology in the United States.* Harcourt Brace, New York.

1999 The Political Economy of Archaeology. *Annual Review of Anthropology* 28:155–174.

2003 *Marx's Ghost: Conversations with Archaeologists.* Berg, New York.

Paynter, Robert

2000a Historical and Anthropological Archaeology: Forging Alliances. *Journal of Archaeological Research* 8:1–37.

2000b Historical Archaeology and the Post-Columbian World of North America. *Journal of Archaeological Research* 8:169–217.

2001 The Cult of Whiteness in Western New England. In *Race and the Archaeology of Identity*, edited by Charles E. Orser, Jr., pp. 125–142. University of Utah Press, Salt Lake City, Utah.

Paynter, Robert, Susan Hautaniemi, and Nancy Ladd Muller

1996 The Landscapes of the W.E.B. Du Bois Boyhood Homesite: An Agenda for an Archaeology of the Color Line. In *Race*, edited by Steven Gregory and Roger Sanjek, pp. 285–318. Rutgers University Press, New Brunswick, New Jersey.

Perry, Warren R., Jean Howson, and Barbara A. Bianco (editors)

2006 *New York African Burial Ground Archaeology Final Report, Volumes 1–4.* Howard University, Washington, D.C. Submitted to United States General Services Administration Northeastern and Caribbean Region, Contract No. GS-02P-93-CUD-0071. Electronic copies available from http://www.africanburialground.gov/ABG_FinalReports.htm, accessed June 19, 2009.

Perry, Warren, and Robert Paynter

1999 Artifacts, Ethnicity, and the Archaeology of African Americans. In *"I, Too, Am America": Archaeological Studies of African-American Life*, edited by Theresa A. Singleton, pp. 299–310. University Press of Virginia, Charlottesville, Virginia.

Peters, Ramona L.

2006 Consulting with the Bone Keepers: NAGPRA Consultations and Archaeological Monitoring in the Wampanoag Territory. In *Cross-Cultural Collaboration: Native Peoples and Archaeology in the Northeastern United States*, edited by Jordan E. Kerber, pp. 32–43. University of Nebraska Press, Lincoln, Nebraska.

Potter, Parker B., Jr.

1991 What is the Use of Plantation Archaeology? *Historical Archaeology* 25:94–107.

1994 *Public Archaeology in Annapolis: A Critical Approach to History in Maryland's Ancient City.* Smithsonian Institution Press, Washington, D.C.

1999 Historical Archaeology and Identity in Modern America. In *Historical Archae-*

ologies of Capitalism, edited by Mark P. Leone and Parker B. Potter, Jr., pp. 51–79. Kluwer Academic/Plenum Publishers, New York.

Pyburn, K. Anne
  2004 Introduction: Rethinking Complex Society. In *Ungendering Civilization*, edited by K. Anne Pyburn, pp. 1–46. Routledge, New York.

Quinn, Naomi
  1977 Anthropological Studies on Women's Status. *Annual Review of Anthropology* 6:181–225.

Reiter, Rayna R. (editor)
  1975 *Toward an Anthropology of Women.* Monthly Review Press, New York.

Rojas, Fabio
  2007 *From Black Power to Black Studies: How a Radical Social Movement Became an Academic Discipline.* Johns Hopkins University Press, Baltimore.

Rosaldo, Michelle Zimbalist, and Louise Lamphere (editors)
  1974 *Woman, Culture, and Society.* Stanford University Press, Stanford.

Saitta, Dean J.
  1994 Agency, Class, and Archaeological Interpretation. *Journal of Anthropological Archaeology* 13:201–227.
  1997 Power, Labor, and the Dynamics of Change in Chacoan Political Economy. *American Antiquity* 62:7–26.
  2001 Communal Class Processes and pre-Columbian Social Dynamics. In *Re/Presenting Class: Essays in Postmodern Marxism*, edited by J. K. Gibson-Graham, S. Resnick and R. Wolff, pp. 247–263. Duke University Press, Durham, North Carolina.
  2005 Marxism, Tribal Society, and the Dual Nature of Archaeology. *Rethinking Marxism* 17(3):385–397.
  2007a *The Archaeology of Collective Action.* University Press of Florida, Gainesville.
  2007b Ethics, Objectivity and Emancipatory Archaeology. In *Archaeology and Capitalism: From Ethics to Politics*, edited by Yamis Hamilakis and Philip Duke, pp. 267–280. Left Coast Press, Walnut Creek, California.

Saitta, Dean J. and Arthur S. Keene
  1990 Power and Surplus Flow in Prehistoric Communal Societies. In *The Evolution of Political Systems: Sociopolitics in Small-Scale Sedentary Societies*, edited by Steadman Upham, pp. 203-224. Cambridge University Press, Cambridge.

Sanjek, Roger
  1996 The Enduring Inequalities of Race. In *Race*, edited by Steven Gregory and Roger Sanjek, pp. 1–17. Rutgers University Press, New Brunswick, New Jersey.

Schmidt, Peter R., and Thomas C. Patterson (editors)
  1995 *Making Alternative Histories: The Practice of Archaeology and History in Non-Western Settings.* School of American Research Press, Santa Fe, New Mexico.

Schofield, John, and Wayne Cocroft (editors)
  2007 *A Fearsome Heritage: Diverse Legacies of the Cold War.* Left Coast Press, Walnut Creek, California.

Scott, Elizabeth M.
  2001 "An Indolent Slothfull Set of Vagabonds: Ethnicity and Race in a Colonial

Fur-Trading Community." In *Race and the Archaeology of Identity*, edited by Charles E. Orser, Jr., pp. 14–33. University of Utah Press, Salt Lake City, Utah.

Scott, Elizabeth M. (editor)
  1994 *Those of Little Note: Gender, Race, and Class in Historical Archaeology*. University of Arizona Press, Tucson.

Shackel, Paul A.
  1993 *Personal Discipline and Material Culture: An Archaeology of Annapolis, Maryland, 1695–1870*. University of Tennessee Press, Knoxville.
  2004 Introduction: Working with Communities. In *Places in Mind: Public Archaeology as Applied Anthropology*, edited by Paul A. Shackel and Erve J. Chambers, pp. 1–16. Routledge, New York.

Shackel, Paul, and Erve J. Chambers (editors)
  2004 *Places in Mind: Public Archaeology as Applied Anthropology*. Routledge, New York.

Shackel, Paul A., Paul R. Mullins, and Mark S. Warner (editors)
  1998 *Annapolis Pasts: An Historical Archaeology of Annapolis, Maryland*. University of Tennessee Press, Knoxville.

Silliman, Stephen W.
  2006 Struggling with Labor, Working with Identities. In *Historical Archaeology*, edited by Martin Hall and Stephen W. Silliman, pp. 147–166. Blackwell, Malden, Massachusetts.

Singleton, Theresa A.
  1995 The Archaeology of Slavery in North America. *Annual Review of Anthropology* 24:119–140.
  1999 An Introduction to African-American Archaeology. In *"I, Too, Am America": Archaeological Studies of African-American Life*, edited by Theresa A. Singleton, pp. 1–17. University Press of Virginia, Charlottesville.

Singleton, Theresa A., and Mark D. Bograd
  1995 *The Archaeology of the African Diaspora in the Americas*. Guides to the Archaeological Literature of the Immigrant Experience in America, Number 2. The Society for Historical Archaeology, Ann Arbor, Michigan.

Smith, Claire, and H. Martin Wobst (editors)
  2005 *Indigenous Archaeologies: Decolonising Theory and Practice*. Routledge, London.

South, Stanley S.
  1977 *Method and Theory in Historical Archaeology*. Academic Press, New York.

Spector, Janet D.
  1993 *What This Awl Means: Feminist Archaeology at a Wahpeton Dakota Village*. Minnesota Historical Society Press, St. Paul.

Steele, Caroline
  2008 Archaeology and the Forensic Investigation of Recent Mass Graves: Ethical Issues for a New Practice of Archaeology. *Archaeologies* 4(3):414–428.

Tilly, Charles
  1998 *Durable Inequality*. University of California Press, Berkeley.

Tomásková, Sylvia
  2007 Mapping a Future: Archaeology, Feminism, and Scientific Practice. *Journal of*

Archaeological Method and Theory 14:264–284.

Trigger, Bruce G.

    1986 Prehistoric Archaeology and American Society. In *American Archaeology Past and Future: A Celebration of the Society for American Archaeology, 1935–1985*, edited by David J. Meltzer, Don D. Fowler and Jeremy A. Sabloff, pp. 187–215. Smithsonian Institution Press, Washington, D.C.

    1989 *A History of Archaeological Thought*. Cambridge University Press, Cambridge.

Visweswaran, Kamala

    1997 Histories of Feminist Ethnography. *Annual Review of Anthropology* 26:591–621.

Voss, Barbara L.

    2006 Engendered Archaeology: Men, Women, and Others. In *Historical Archaeology*, edited by Martin Hall and Stephen W. Silliman, pp. 107–127. Blackwell, Malden, Massachusetts.

    2008 *The Archaeology of Ethnogenesis: Race and Sexuality in Colonial San Francisco*. University of California Press, Berkeley.

Walters, Ronald W.

    1993 *Pan-Africanism in the African Diaspora*. Wayne State University Press, Detroit.

Watkins, Joe

    2000 *Indigenous Archaeology: American Indian Values and Scientific Practice*. Alta Mira Press, Walnut Creek, California.

    2005 Through Wary Eyes: Indigenous Perspectives on Archaeology. *Annual Review of Anthropology* 34:429–449.

Wilkie, Laurie A.

    2003 *The Archaeology of Mothering: An African-American Midwife's Tale*. Routledge, New York.

    2004 Considering the Future of African American Archaeology. *Historical Archaeology* 38:109–123.

Williams, Raymond

    1983 *Keywords: A Vocabulary of Culture and Society. Revised Edition*. Oxford University Press, New York.

Wolf, Eric R.

    1990 Distinguished Lecture: Facing Power-Old Insights, New Questions. *American Anthropologist* 92:586–596.

Wolff, Edward N.

    2007 *Recent Trends in Household Wealth in the United States: Rising Debt and the Middle-Class Squeeze*. Levy Economics Institute Working Paper no. 502. Bard College, Annandale-on-Hudson, New York.

Wright, Henry T.

    1986 The Evolution of Civilizations. In *American Archeology Past and Future: A Celebration of the Society for American Archaeology, 1935–1985*, edited by David J. Meltzer, Don D. Fowler and Jeremy A. Sabloff, pp. 323–365. Smithsonian Institution Press, Washington, D.C.

Wurst, LouAnn

    1999 Internalizing Class in Historical Archaeology. *Historical Archaeology* 33:7–21.

2002 "For the Means of Your Subsistence ... Look Under God to Your Own Industry and Frugality": Life and Labor in Gerrit Smith's Peterboro. *International Journal of Historical Archaeology* 6(3):159–172.

2006 A Class All Its Own: Explorations of Class Formation and Conflict. In *Historical Archaeology*, edited by Martin Hall and Stephen W. Silliman, pp. 190–206. Blackwell Publishing, Malden, Massachusetts.

Wurst, LouAnn, and R. K. Fitts (editors)
1999 Confronting Class. *Historical Archaeology* 33(1).

Wylie, Alison
1991 Gender Theory and the Archaeological Record: Why is There No Archaeology of Gender? In *Engendering Archaeology: Women and Prehistory*, edited by Joan M. Gero and Margaret W. Conkey, pp. 31–54. Basil Blackwell, Oxford.

1992 The Interplay of Evidential Constraints and Political Interests: Recent Archaeological Research on Gender. *American Antiquity* 57:15–35.

1997 The Engendering of Archaeology: Refiguring Feminist Science Studies. *Osiris* 12:80–99.

2007 Doing Archaeology as a Feminist: Introduction. *Journal of Archaeological Method and Theory* 14:209–216.

Young, Amy L.
2004 The Beginning and Future of African American Archaeology in Mississippi. *Historical Archaeology* 38:66–78.

Zeder, Melinda
1997 *The American Archaeologist: A Profile*. Altamira Press, Walnut Creek, California.

Zimmerman, Larry J.
2008 Multivocality, Descendent Communities, and Some Epistemological Shifts Forced by Repatriation. In *Opening Archaeology: Repatriation's Impact on Contemporary Research and Practice*, edited by Thomas W. Killion, pp. 91–107. School for Advanced Research Press, Santa Fe.

Zumeta, William
2003 Higher Education Finances: In Recession Again. *The NEA 2003 Almanac of Higher Education*:53–66.

7

In The Public Interest: Creating A More Activist, Civically Engaged Archaeology

BARBARA J. LITTLE *and* LARRY J. ZIMMERMAN

> *[W]e have responsibilities towards the communities, individuals, and institutions directly implicated by archaeological work into the recent past in helping them come to terms with the obscured and often painful circumstances of contemporary life. Under these circumstances, archaeology should be socially relevant. It must earn its keep [Victor Buchli 2007].*
>
> *Out beyond ideas of wrongdoing and rightdoing, there is a field. I will meet you there.*
> —Jalal ad-Din Mohammad Balkhi (Rumi) [Barks 2004:36]

Archaeologists apparently feel the need for archaeology to "earn its keep," an idea that has a substantial history. We have dubbed our work public and have described it as applied, engaged, and more recently, activist, political, or vindicationist (e.g., Blakey 2001; Mullins 2008; Stottman 2010). The labels illustrate archaeologists' hopes to rationalize and legitimize our work to contemporary people. As an archaeologist, if one subscribes to the notion that the past is a public heritage and recognizes that the public pays most of the bills for what archaeologists do, then surely, and almost by definition, what archaeologists do must be done in the public interest. Archaeology, then, might be thought of as public service, with the needs of publics and their concerns paramount. Principle 2 of the Society for American Archaeology's (1996) Principles of Archaeological Ethics (PAE) codifies accountability to those publics.

One problem, however, is that public interest is profoundly difficult to define, as both the publics and their interests are legion. Even the very idea that an archaeologically known past is a public heritage, and for which archaeologists are stewards, might be open to question (see Kehoe 1998:212–214 for a discussion). We choose two epigraphs to highlight both our responsibility and our desire to act with appropriate humility (Zimmerman 2005). It is difficult to know if the actions we take toward relevance and public interests are right actions, and yet pretending that we might carry on our work without regard to such interests seems indefensible.

Legalistic definitions of public interest seem to be of limited utility. What publics? What interest? Defined by whom? With regard to publics, in an attempt to be inclusive, Principle 4, Public Education and Outreach, of the PAE lists several: "Many publics exist for archaeology including students and teachers; Native Americans and other ethnic, religious, and cultural groups who find in the archaeological record important aspects of their cultural heritage; lawmakers and government officials; reporters, journalists, and others involved in the media; and the general public." Add to these tourists and tourism councils, museums, parks, planners, and a range of scholars including historians, ecologists, economists, and geographers (Costanza et al. 2007; Little 2002; McManamon 1991).

Definitions of interest are as diverse as those of publics and can be characterized in a variety of ways. The scope of interest ranges from local to international, from professionally ethical to illegal. It is worth remembering that various publics' interests in archaeology do not necessarily coincide with those of archaeologists. Interests connect with values that may change with community composition, including different communities of scholars and policymakers. Some interest is explicitly that of political activists, as exemplified in the work by Ludlow Collective with the United Mine Workers (e.g., Saitta 2007; see also Hamilakis and Duke 2007, McGuire 2008). It ranges from long-term interest in sustaining cultural identity to short-term gains such as immediate economic interest in employment or turning archaeology toward a profit motive (see, for example, MacLean and Yago 2008 for such financial "innovations"). The categories are not neatly bounded; for example, economic interest in tourism intersects with political claims, social boundaries, and spiritual concerns. "Public interest," then, is a definitional moving target shifting over time and across places and communities.

Characterizing archaeologists' efforts to serve the public is a challenge because there is great variety in agendas and intended publics. Efforts include, for example, community-driven projects with antiracism goals and academically driven projects with goals to inform far-reaching policy to enhance human resiliency in the face of global climate change. Projects might focus on an immediate specific problem such as alleviating neighborhood litter or creating a viable seed bank to protect crop variation; they may be long-term and transdisciplinary, focused on reclaiming and creating meaningful heritage in nations devastated by war and occupation; they may aim to plan defensible interventions in land use to prevent soil degradation and regain agricultural viability; they may seek to educate children about the value of cultural diversity. Such variety emphasizes the scope of archaeology and the potential usefulness of a discipline that values appropriately flexible time depth, spatial scale, material conditions, and social/political context.

In this context of defining our topic, it is fair to ask how to define archaeology. Are dictionary definitions of archaeology as the systematic study of the past by analysis of recovered material evidence useful? Can only archaeologists define archaeology? Do only some types of archaeology answer to the public, while some are walled off via scientific or bureaucratic privilege and jargon? Is archaeology about heritage in general or that associated with specific groups? Should archaeology deal with only the tangible? Is it defined in terms of amateur versus professional? Might it be bounded by a time period or spatial unit, by theoretical perspective, research domain, or analytic specialization? Is an "Indigenous" archaeology something to be defined differently than scientific or Western or colonizing archaeology? There are many definitions even along the spectrum of a particular orientation like feminist archaeology, some of which focus on liberal reform and some toward reconceptualizing the structures of archaeology and scholarly practice (e.g., Little 1994). How much does—or should—archaeology carry on its shoulders?

The questions are myriad, complex, often confusing, and sometimes contradictory; providing facile answers to them is next to impossible and not a goal of this chapter. Answers and ways to arrive at them are as unique as the publics, the archaeologists serving them, and the situation at hand, defying any formulaic approach. Offering some parameters for expanding the ways in which archaeologists and publics might work toward mutually defined interests, however, is a more reasonable task and is one of the primary goals of the chapter. In some ways, these parameters define the cutting, or maybe even the bleeding, edge of a socially responsible and responsive archaeology.

Accountability and engagement with publics involves "politics," including "identity politics" (McGuire 2008; Meskell 2002). Although archaeologists may differ on how to structure their work, given that our discipline is inextricably interwoven with the political, there can be very little disagreement anymore about those inescapable connections (Pauketat and Meskell, this volume). As Sander van der Leeuw and Charles Redman (2002:602) state it, the constructive question with which we can accept our political responsibilities can be framed as, "What can we do?" The search for relevance by archaeologists does not necessarily result in archaeology that is explicitly formulated as political action (cf. Hamilakis and Duke 2007). We don't attempt to clarify the varieties of archaeological political intention or consequence in this chapter. However, we maintain that if the information archaeology generates has any value at all, it cannot be value neutral. If it cannot be value neutral, it legitimately can be contested by communities and their members. If it has value, it can offer potential for community building and may provide useful perspectives on contemporary concerns. If archaeology has value, it is political, and politics is sometimes about internally conflicting interrelationships among a society's members and ways of seeking solutions (cf. Franklin and Paynter, this volume).

Earning Our Keep: A Brief History of American Archaeology as Politics

Doing politics, including identity politics, is not new for American archaeology. Our origins as a profession are directly linked to doing identity politics stemming from activity carried out at the public's behest to investigate an advanced (read "white") race that preceded the Indians, ultimately to be displaced by them. The Moundbuilder Myth (Silverberg 1968) was one thread in justifying displacement of Indians from the land as part of an incipient notion of Manifest Destiny. Intensive archaeological and ethnographic research provided an answer to the Moundbuilder question: ancestors of contemporary Indians had built the mounds and were the first inhabitants of the continent. American archaeology's first encompassing project demonstrated the utility of archaeology. Stemming from public needs and very political in its implications, the project went a long way toward putting an end to a powerful colonialist myth, though hardly an end to either colonialist American archaeology or colonialist treatment of Indigenous people.

The Moundbuilder myth was an element of larger political constructs about race, unilinear evolution, and Social Darwinism. In essence, archaeology's help in debunking the myth was a political act, aimed toward the solution of what Franz Boas and others thought of as a contemporary social problem. It was, however, also part of a purposeful process of documenting what many believed was a disappearing race, another myth that continued to colonize Native American pasts. By the time of the 1906 Antiquities Act, and its definitions of archaeological remains as resources that needed protection, archaeologists had made the political choice to define the past as a public heritage. Over the next few decades archaeologists worked to refine their methods and also promoted the past as public heritage, prompting archaeological projects within programs such as the Works Progress Administration and Civilian Conservation Corps during the Great Depression (Fagette 1996), then Post-World War II salvage projects such as those of the River Basin Surveys (Thiessen 1999).

By the late 1940s, there was growing frustration about archaeology's theoretical direction and calls for a reexamination of its goals and methods (Taylor 1983), which reached a crescendo in the late 1960s with a demand for a New Archaeology. The intent of the New Archaeology to be relevant to broader social questions was noble; many New Archaeologists were trying to understand the processes of culture change with an eye toward solution of social problems. But, paraphrasing Alice Kehoe (1998), it got lost in its notions of the past as knowable through positivist approaches and a belief that archaeology's product could be objective and true.

Processual archaeology's development paralleled the development of cultural resource management (CRM) and the cultural heritage industry. CRM continued the theme of salvage archaeology site preservation from the early twentieth century and expanded its core definition of the archaeological past as a public heritage, and Charles McGimsey coined the term "public archaeology" (King 1983:143; McGimsey 1972:4). Although archaeologists paid more attention to the Archeological and Historic Preservation Act than the National Historic Preservation Act (NHPA), the regulatory focus on information as the key to archaeological significance under the latter served to define archaeologists as the primary stewards of the archaeological record. CRM became the dominant force in archaeology, providing primary employment for archaeologists and funds for research (e.g., Altschul 2005; Knudson 1986; Little 2009a; see Altschul and Patterson and Snead and Sabloff, this volume).

Although academic and CRM archaeologists were enmeshed in their own politics, each thought they were apolitical, objective, and working for the public good. One problem for most groups external to the hegemonic center was that most archaeologists were practicing a politics of exclusion. As far as American Indians were concerned, archaeologists did not recognize Indigenous ways of knowing the past as valid and claimed all pasts as public, even those particular Indian nations thought of as their own. From the 1960s onward, a growing American Indian political consciousness brought challenges, and Indians directly confronted archaeology over the issue of repatriation. The Native American Graves Protection and Repatriation Act (NAGPRA) of 1990 resulted. The impact of repatriation on archaeology has been profound (Killion 2008; Watkins 2000; Sebastian, this volume; Wilcox, this volume). Of course, archaeology is also implicated in the exclusion of women as well as non-white men, the poor, and otherwise disenfranchised (e.g., Franklin and Paynter, this volume). An increasing number of works counter such exclusion. As a beginning, in the late 1960s Charles Fairbanks began work on Florida's Kingsley Plantation slave cabins in order to enter the larger anthropological and political debate about whether Africans could have retained any of their own culture after the horrors of the transatlantic slave trade. Theresa Singleton (1999) has named the early period of African American archaeology as "moral mission archaeology" because it sought to give voice to the voiceless, albeit also inadvertently restricting the types of questions asked of diasporic sites.

By the 1980s, and reflecting postmodern trends academically, the limitations of processual archaeology were becoming clear, with a recognition that a wide range of approaches could provide useful perspectives on multi-threaded, multivocal pasts. Post-processual archaeology (for want of a better term) came with the recognition that people might find meaning in the past and that learning how people create such meanings could expand archaeological knowledge.

For generations, archaeologists have called for our work to be relevant but the interpretation of that call has changed. Jeremy Sabloff (2008:17) is one of those joining the current call for "action archaeology" by which he means "involvement or engagement with the problems facing the modern world through archaeology," where "archaeologists work *for* living communities not just *in* or near them" [emphases in original]. As he points out, the term "action archaeology" has a substantial history. He raised what he calls the "prophetic" term a decade earlier in his Archaeology Distinguished Lecture (Sabloff 1998), attributing it to Kleindienst and Watson's (1956) call to make archaeology relevant. Some other calls for archaeological relevance in the decades between that one and his own came in the early 1970s near the start of the "New Archaeology," which initially claimed to seek general laws of human behavior. If properly generated and interpreted, those laws could benefit the human condition and could provide understanding, if not solutions, to its problems. John Fritz and Fred Plog called for relevance in their 1970 article "The Nature of Archaeological Explanation." Soon thereafter, Richard Ford (1973) discussed archaeology's pre-1900 role in overthrowing theological epistemologies in favor of Darwinian explanations as a primary example in his "Archeology Serving Humanity" article, which was his own call for relevance. Fritz and Plog (1970:412) cautioned: "We suggest that unless archaeologists find ways to make their research increasingly relevant to the modern world, the modern world will find itself increasingly capable of getting along without archaeologists." Their warning reverberates throughout archaeological practice today.

Parameters of an Archaeology in the Public Interest

American archaeologists rarely have been reluctant to set ambitious goals for our highly ambiguous practice. The questions we ask have defined what's worth asking (and what's worth funding) and have implicitly dismissed many other questions valued by many publics outside of professional archaeological practice. Listening to those questions and working with those publics to design methodologies and interpret findings can foster the diversity and flexibility of archaeology. Part of such growth is seen in the ways in which archaeologists currently seek to make a positive difference in the world. Within the genealogy of the discipline, projects focused on ecological sustainability are based in some of the ongoing analytic strengths developed in the New Archaeology. Value added in the public interest comes from more focused and intentional efforts to contribute to pressing ecological issues (e.g., Costanza et al. 2007; Hegmon et al. 2008; Redman and Kinzig 2003; van der Leeuw and Redman 2002). Although ideas about neutral science long blinded archaeologists to the cultural impact of their own discipline, realization of archaeology's political embeddedness has opened up the field to setting our sights on lofty aims of creating justice, building peace, and promoting human rights as well as mitigating human suffering anticipated with massive ecological change.

We propose that this trend reflects a quest for wisdom. It is not unrelated to archaeologists' work with Native peoples and the values curated by many Indigenous cultures. Gary Holthaus (2008:29) characterizes the all too familiar rift between sustainability and the modern worldview:

> For the longest-surviving cultures, the sciences, the humanities, and the arts were shot through with the sacred. Nature and the sacred, wisdom and the sacred, were inseparably linked. In our time the sacred has come uncoupled from wisdom; wisdom uncoupled from knowledge; knowledge unhooked from information; information unhooked from facts; facts disconnected from data; data disassociated from firsthand observation and experience. Our culture seems to have forsaken wisdom in favor of all the latter—at a time when wisdom is our greatest need and would be its greatest asset.

Barbara Little (2002:16) summarizes a discussion of archaeology's public benefits: "The study of archaeology has the potential to teach about the contingency of all human endeavor. As we expand our view of the past to include the struggles, successes, and failures of all peoples from all times and situations, our wisdom—and compassion—ought also to expand." Can archaeology contribute to wisdom? To a humane and sustainable culture? We are optimistic that it can do so. The power of the discipline becomes more clear the more we see how it has contributed to colonialist and oppressive culture; we believe that our practice can continue to be rehabilitated. Archaeology, particularly in cooperation with sister practices of historic preservation, public history, tourism, education, and museology, can raise consciousness and awareness about gender, race and white privilege, class, religious faction, and other boundaries. Differently framing the past can encourage different ways of seeing, thinking about, and acting in the present.

Because archaeology straddles many boundaries, it has the potential of reconfiguring the often paralyzing divisions between scientific, humanistic, artistic, and spiritual worldviews. For example, Chip Colwell-Chanthaphonh and T. J. Ferguson (2004) promote an ethical framework to reconcile scientific and humanistic aspects of Native American pasts. Taking a humanist perspective on the power of archaeology, Little (2007) uses the West African concept of *sankofa* as a tool to enhance the relevance of archaeology by learning from the past. *Sankofa* is an Akan (Ghana) word that refers to the concept of reclaiming the past and understanding how the present came to be so that we can move forward. It came into the lexicon of archaeology through the African Burial Ground project in lower Manhattan (e.g., Blakey 2004). *Sankofa* is a way for keeping the past and present connected in a public scholarship that seeks to shine light into the dark corners of cultural imperialism and ideologies that undermine human rights.

Colleagues in other fields see the value of an archaeological perspective in addressing present-day issues but may be unwilling to wait for archaeologists to be certain enough about our data and its meanings to offer workable solutions. Non-archaeologists have used archaeology, though not always cautiously. Jared Diamond (2005) seeks to change the way people and governments make decisions as he uses archaeology to argue for an urgent response to the earth's ecological crisis in his book *Collapse*. Archaeologists have answered Diamond's books, working toward a more realistic concept of sudden change (McAnany and Yoffee 2009). No one is more aware of the ambiguities of archaeology than archaeologists. Some non-archaeologists are far more clear about their agenda than archaeologists working on similar topics. Agricultural researchers Marcel Mazoyer and Laurence Roudart (2006), for example, offer the ambitious synthesis, *A History of World Agriculture from the Neolithic Age to the Current Crisis*, with the explicit aim to overcome agricultural inequalities and peasant poverty. Contributors to *Agrarian Landscapes in Transition* (Redman and Foster 2008) are equally ambitious in their research but are broader and less committal about specific issues. In that volume, Redman (2008:9) asks, "Bold decisions must be made during the next few years. Will they be reactive or anticipatory? Will they focus on rescuing biophysical systems to the exclusion of socioeconomic systems? Will they attempt to reconcile protection and restoration with development and livelihood?" Also working on agricultural issues, Paul Minnis (Minnis et al. 2006:17) highlights connections between archaeology and ensuring the food supply, including increasing our available crops. Such work might influence concepts and actions guiding human relationships with the land and influence how agricultural and other practices might be sustainable over the long term (see also Zeder et al. this volume).

Non-archaeologists have also drawn on archaeology in attempts to change the overarching cultural narrative of the modern world. In her widely influential book, *The Chalice and the Blade*, Riane Eisler (1995:xv) uses archaeology as one of the disciplines to lay out her argument that the past "provides verification that a better future *is* possible – and is in fact firmly rooted in the haunting drama of what actually happened in our past." Archaeologists can be as ambitious in our approach to narrative and metaphor. As an example, overcoming white privilege requires deep cultural changes to which archaeology can contribute. Former SAA President Robert Kelly (1998) has stated directly, "It seems too simplistic, but archaeology's purpose today is to play a role in ending racism. Everything follows from this fact" (see also, e.g., Blakey 2001; Epperson 1991; McDavid and Babson 1997; Mullins 2008; Franklin and Paynter, this volume). As archaeology seeks to claim an active role in the modern world, it must take seriously the demands of practicing antiracism and antidiscrimination. Such a stance requires more than trying to eliminate biases from our work; it requires active engagement against the structures of oppression interwoven throughout our society.

Archaeology has a role to play in community building and civic renewal (e.g., Colwell-Chanthapohn and Ferguson 2008; Little and Shackel 2007) and, via both local and larger efforts, in the connections between heritage and human rights (e.g., Silverman and Ruggles 2007) and global justice movements (e.g., AGJ 2005; Funari 2009; Little 2009b, 2010; Musteata 2009; Pikirayi 2009). Even in violently polarized communities, archaeology may help build bridges, as exemplified in ongoing work between Israeli and Palestinian archaeologists (e.g., Bohannan 2008; PUSH 2007; Scham and Yahya 2003). As the Global Justice Movement seeks to pull together across causes and across the globe, archaeology can demonstrate inclusion by including everyone in the past as well as the present. Archaeology also adds the strength of interdisciplinary teams. The Integrated History and Future of People on Earth (IHOPE) project approaches the goal of sustainability through researching and modeling human-environment interactions (Costanza et al. 2007). With social and environmental justice goals in mind, we then make an argument for the future and not for the past as we provide evidence for the human continuum, for survival against the odds, and for hope (Little 2009b, 2010).

Archaeology can examine the deep history of contemporary issues and draw upon our discoveries and approaches to come up with new narratives to help improve present and future environmental and social conditions and to respond intelligently to climate change. Innocent Pikirayi (2009) raises the challenge to archaeologists to serve the United Nations Millennium Development Goals: eradication of extreme poverty and hunger; achieving universal primary education, promoting gender equity and empower women, reducing child mortality; improving maternal health; combating HIV/AIDS, malaria and other diseases; ensuring environmental sustainability; and, developing a global partnership for development. It is not enough to research such issues in order to point out the ways that we are shaped by history. Finding solutions to such problems also requires engagement with communities from local to international so that archaeologists can work with others to craft informed goals and actions. During the past two decades, the World Archaeological Congress (WAC) has sought to address many of these matters, and even though its origins were controversial (Ucko 1987), WAC has been internationally influential in focusing the attention of many archaeologists on such issues (Zimmerman 2006).

An Archaeology of Ten Minutes Ago

Archaeological projects can have grand social justice goals, but usually they are relatively simple and mundane. In spite of this, they can have potentially important ramifications for people's daily lives. Archaeology has a powerful set of tools that can answer questions about pasts, certainly, but those same tools can provide powerful information about the present, or more precisely, the past of ten minutes ago. The most widely cited example is the Garbage Project (e.g., Rathje and Murphy 2001) with its clear political agenda to make people aware of garbage and landfill problems and to change behaviors in order to solve those problems. In some cases, ethnoarchaeological projects changed orientation from searching for analogues to interpret the past to explicit attention to the present (e.g., Gonzalez-Ruibal 2006). Other research tying together past and present through material culture has also been influential (e.g., Schiffer 1999). Richard Gould (2005) and others used archaeology in recovery efforts after the 9/11 World Trade Center tragedy. Archaeological methods can assist in the aftermath of mass fatality or natural disasters such as the post-Hurricane Katrina and Rita recovery efforts

(Dawdy 2006). Archaeologists have now been involved in recovery of remains of victims of ethnic cleansing and political executions for over 20 years as well as involving themselves in a variety of other forensic cases (e.g., Conner 2007).

Archaeology is about things past, to be sure, but it doesn't necessarily need to be about things 100 or 1,000 years ago. Rather, archaeology can work at a boundary between past and present, which requires a fundamental understanding that humans constantly create archaeological sites. Time is not the important variable, but the uses and distribution of cultural materials are. An "archaeology of ten minutes ago," to borrow the title of David Gadsby's and Jodi Barnes' session at the 2008 meeting of the Society for Historical Archaeology, thus becomes a way of thinking about the material world we live in, and "casts the human world as a place where people interact with and accumulate material culture, from trash piles, to items on a knick-knack shelf, to paintings on a wall. Archaeology is all around us, constantly created in that brief moment between the past and the future, and is forever changing as it recedes into the past" (Patel 2007:51). In other words, archaeology that is about "now," not just "back then," can be a highly relevant archaeology. A few additional examples illustrate that a public interest archaeological project can have origins with the public or from archaeologists themselves.

Inspired by the Garbage Project, Jay Stottman (2007) developed the University of Louisville Litter Project, which aims to use the methods of archaeology to analyze the problem of litter and work with the community to advocate solutions. Frustrated by neighborhood meetings in which people complained but were unwilling to take responsibility or action, Stottman decided to design an archaeological project to discover the source of the litter, widely assumed by the neighborhood to be bar and restaurant patrons. He involved undergraduate students in collecting and analyzing data and then using what they learned to propose solutions. In spite of the anger aroused by discarded alcohol bottles in the neighborhood, students found that this category comprised only 4 percent of the litter. Observations showed that the location and maintenance of trash receptacles along with the wind contributed to the litter problem. Students proposed solutions including more trash cans, more strategic placement of the municipal trash cans, and more frequent pick up. Armed with good information, and inspired by the study and new ways of approaching their common concern, residents, business owners, and the city government worked together to implement solutions and solve the neighborhood litter problem. Stottman, Sarah Miller, and Gwynn Henderson (2007) designed a lesson plan for students based on the project. The exercise addresses several objectives, including the demonstration of archaeology's applicability to social change.

The Graffiti Archaeology Project is being conducted by non-archaeologists. Started in San Francisco by Cassidy Curtis, 65 photographers have photographed graffiti at the same locations in San Francisco, New York, Los Angeles, London, and other cities from the late 1990s to the present. The product is a polished website (http://www.otherthings.com/grafarc/) that allows viewers to see the changes in graffiti over time (also see posting in Flickr). Curtis makes no claim to being an archaeologist, noting in a FAQ about the site that he doesn't have a degree in archaeology. When he named the site, he was "really just being cute." He makes no claim that the project is like traditional archaeology and even expresses uneasiness when archaeologists mention it. Is this really archaeology? Close enough, it would seem, to draw the interest of *Archaeology* magazine. Writer Samir Patel (2007) interviews several archaeologists about the project, whose comments range from curiosity about what kinds of research questions the project might address to a worry that academic theorizing might detract from the project. Curtis recognizes that the project illustrates, but doesn't explain, the culture of the "writers," the graffiti artists who create the work. Of additional interest is that the location of graffiti sites is not divulged, considered privileged by the photographers in order to prevent the authorities from coming in to paint over, or "buff" them, likened by Patel to archaeologists protecting site locations to prevent looting.

Certainly there are commonalities between graffiti project data and methods and the way archaeology works, but the project is not traditional archaeology and lacks focus. Yet, were archaeologists to actively participate in analysis of the information, a great deal might come of it that would help in understanding expressive culture and why people seem compelled to "tag" public property and space. Given the antiquity of graffiti, the project might be useful in planning public spaces and providing outlets for protest and declarations of identity. There may also be useful analogies that might help in understanding the impulses and techniques of more ancient creators of rock art, which is often layered, much like contemporary graffiti.

Graffiti also has a presence in a project on the archaeology of homelessness, in which homeless people use it to transmit information or to mark ethnicity. Started by Larry Zimmerman (2004) in St. Paul, Minnesota, in 2003, and continued in Indianapolis, Indiana (Albertson 2009; Zimmerman and Welch 2006, 2008), the ongoing project is an examination of the material culture of homelessness and its distribution and disposition in campsites used by homeless people living away from shelters. The project began as a spinoff of excavations at the James J. Hill mansion in St. Paul prior to restoration of massive garden walls at the site. Surface survey of the overgrown, brushy gardens revealed a wide range of debris outside the ordinary for "usual" surface trash, including an abundance of castoff clothing, sleeping bags, drug paraphernalia, alcohol bottles, and remains of fires and cooking. Daily encounters with homeless people on the site indicated that most of the material was from their occupancy. Excavations revealed little material from the time of the Hills' ownership, but long-term occupancy by homeless people, from the time after the property was turned over to the Archdiocese of St. Paul and the gardens abandoned in the 1920s. Investigations of the site indicated two semi-permanent campsites, one in a partially collapsed "mushroom cave" built into one of the garden walls and another in the depression formed as the roots of a fallen tree pulled free.

When Zimmerman moved to Indianapolis, he began investigations of homelessness just east of city center, working with a formerly homeless archaeology student, Jessica Welch, to locate campsites of homeless people. In a roughly ten-by-ten block area, the survey documented 5 route sites, 40 short-term sites, and 16 camp sites, the vast majority of them adjacent or very near the railway that provided relatively easy pedestrian access to downtown. The route sites were very temporary "stopping places" for eating, elimination, and hanging out. Short-term sites were used for eating or sleeping for a night or two either in the open or in temporary shelters, but with no indication of permanency. Campsites utilized existing structures for longer-term occupancy or were open sites with some level of construction, and showed consistent evidence of use for sleeping, food preparation, and consumption. Researchers disturbed nothing, but photographically documented the sites.

Early on, investigators recognized that there were unusual patterns in some sites. In particular, the campsites and short-term sites showed ingenuity in construction or utilization of unusual activities, including expression in the form of well-made graffiti similar to that documented on the Graffiti Archaeology project and less common objects such as a "hat tree" with artistic arrangement of baseball-style caps on a small tree. More commonly, some objects indicated the harsh realities of living homeless, especially in areas away from shelters, and these took the project beyond curiosity into the realm of social problems.

Small, unused bottles of shampoo and hair conditioner of the type found in hotels rooms were relatively common. Why they were there at all was puzzling until investigators discovered that local churches provided them, asking parishioners to collect such items when they stayed in hotels so that the church could distribute them. The problem is that in their camps, the homeless rarely had access to enough water to use them. Similarly, unopened or haphazardly opened food cans were common, also from donations; no can openers accompanied the cans, not even of the small, inexpensive, disposable military type. Other behaviors also indicated that homeless people often cached important items at or near sites so that they didn't have to carry them around as they went downtown to panhandle.

Application of archaeological methods indicated that social service agencies could do better in providing aid and recognizing the needs of homeless people, especially away from shelters where almost no systematic investigations have been made by any discipline. Even simple changes might make the life of homeless people more bearable. As it happens, the project also raised the ire of local officials by suggesting that donation boxes placed downtown would do little either to help the homeless or to be successful in keeping down the number of homeless people who panhandle downtown and apparently scare off convention-goers. The funds generated are small and given to shelters. Except in the worst weather, homeless people tend to avoid shelters for a range of reasons, often because shelter and handouts come with religious proselytizing. On publication of a story about the boxes (Ward 2008) that included discussion of the homeless archaeology project, a local homeless activist reported that the shelters and others in the "homeless industry" were upset about the archaeological observations because they feel that shelters offer the best hope for homeless people.

What is apparent from the project is that the lives of the homeless have numerous similarities to the lives of foraging peoples studied using ethnoarchaeological methods. Although they do not have consistent, kin-based social support networks, they usually are very knowledgeable about their landscape (Valado 2006), learning consistent and intermittent sources for food and creating spaces where there is some level of security and comfort. They also are capable in using resources that many others might not consider. Archaeological investigation may increase the appreciation and respect for skills of both the homeless and people from the past. The investigators recognize that the project is far from complete. In particular, ethnographic research would be especially useful to answer questions already raised. Partnerships with other disciplines might be especially useful, especially with social work, sociology, geography, and political science, with a goal toward development of practical public policy regarding homelessness.

Creating a More Activist, Civically Engaged Archaeology

Over the past 25 years, American archaeology has been emerging from its complicity in a colonial structure of social "injustice." Archaeology is no longer a public heritage benefitting archaeologists first. Rather, archaeology is shifting toward benefitting various publics first, providing powerful tools and the expertise in using them. For example, archaeologists and educators have been cooperating in the public interest for decades. The initial motivation for archaeologists was the belief that an educated public would be less likely to loot and vandalize sites or participate in the antiquities trade. The collaboration has turned toward serving the needs of teachers and students, as well as adult learners in informal educational settings (e.g., Burke and Smith 2007; Moe 2002; Smardz and Smith 2000; Allen and Joyce, this volume).

Through collaboration, archaeologists seek ways for publics to use archaeology to provide meaning for their own lives. Sometimes publics take archaeology into their own hands, as is happening with Indigenous people and with other communities as well (Silliman and Ferguson, this volume). Intellectually the shift is profound, still focused on accountability to archaeology's many publics, but putting control of the process into the publics' hands. How can archaeologists serve while maintaining ethical responsibility for our participation? Practitioners from other fields offer their experience. Randy Stoecker (1999) struggles with the question of how academics can be relevant in participatory research that aims towards turning control over to the community. He discusses his own roles within participatory research

(PR) as a practice dedicated to social change through democratizing the knowledge process. Similarly, many public historians have long dedicated themselves to a shared authority (Frisch 1990).

What does archaeology get out of public service? Elizabeth Brumfiel (2005:136) observes that "archaeologists should not be satisfied with perfunctory efforts to address diverse, politically engaged publics. Politics may sometimes debase archaeological research, but collaboration with politically engaged groups sometimes contributes new, richer, better interpretations of the archaeological record." More broadly, there may be more meaningful engagement with the past and among the publics who value it. We may expect more opportunities to make a difference if there is increased public support for more widely valued archaeology. Fully participating in the ways in which people create and use their past(s) and current material circumstances may well be where archaeology can or will make the greatest contributions regarding social justice, which is of course a lofty goal. To achieve such a goal takes letting go of sole control of why and how archaeology gets done.

Archaeologists are working out what it means to serve communities by struggling through the complexities of the work (e.g., McGhee and McDavid 2009; Sandlin and Bey 2006). Jennifer Sandlin and George Bey (2006:271) analyze archaeologists as adult learners as they struggle through experience and practice to transform archaeological practice and move from "archaeology as technical competency towards archaeology as informed practical action." They remark (2006:271) upon the "ongoing problem that community archaeology is, as Marshall (2002) notes, primarily perceived as existing within the realm of cultural resource management as opposed to academic archaeology." An increasing number of projects, however, make it clear that such work can and does take place in any setting. Fred McGhee and Carol McDavid (2009) discuss participatory research in the CRM and academic/nonprofit sectors, respectively. While acknowledging the postcolonial critique and Nicholas and Hollowell's (2007) call for completely rethinking the archaeological process, McGhee proposes an approach from an applied rather than academic perspective, partly because communities tend not to be interested in academic theory. He observes that African American and Native American communities are fully aware of the colonialism and scientific racism embedded within CRM but opt to work within the system rather than seeking to eliminate it. Arguing for the suitability of public archaeology to community organizing and participatory research, McGhee points out that CRM archaeologists are accustomed to subordinating their own research interests to others' interests and understand that their work has consequences. McGhee focuses on the process of CRM, while McDavid advocates for experimenting with ways to apply critical race theory in archaeological contexts, particularly in nonprofit community-based projects.

Writing about the treatment of Hopi and Zuni cultural landscapes within a CRM context, T. J. Ferguson and Roger Anyon (2001) appeal to governmental officials to understand that tribal perspectives are qualitatively different from those of academic scholarship. The tribes, for example, resist defining boundaries for significant places, in part because the boundaries shift according to temporal context of the stories they embody. Partly because archaeological features are significant parts of cultural landscapes, tribes are able to use the legal frameworks of the NHPA and NAGPRA to make the bureaucratic process work, albeit imperfectly, toward preserving their culturally meaningful places.

Of course, many of the current laws and regulations were not written with tribal perspectives in mind, although some changes have made the process more inclusive. Richard Stoffle (2005) comments on the federal government partially returning stewardship to tribal governments through legislation and regulation. Amendments to the NHPA in 1992 gave authority for tribes to establish Tribal Historic Preservation Offices (THPO) to take over all or some of the responsibilities of State Historic Preservation Offices (SHPO). As Darby Stapp and Michael Burney (2002) point out, the process and outcomes are likely to be different for tribes because tribes have different agendas and different ways of understanding stewardship. Stoffle observes that a deep epistemological shift is necessary to define valid data and interpretation in CRM from a tribal perspective. He writes (2005:139), "American Indian people are just beginning to systematically argue for the value of their epistemologies, much as they argued 20 years ago for cultural and biological connections with artifacts and bodies. They are trying to undo the cant of conquest as well as the physical act of encroachment."

Whether working in CRM, government, museum, or academic settings, archaeologists take several approaches to work in the public interest. Many involve direct collaboration with communities of different sorts. Academic and governmental entities can set up boundary organizations as a management tool to facilitate collaboration and coproduction of knowledge and social order. These function on the edges between science and government in policy advisory work and ought to include all interested stakeholders. Not surprisingly, the success of such tools depends on human contingencies such as leadership (Guston 2001; Schnieder 2008). David Guston (2001: 402) explains that "The boundary organization draws its stability not from isolating itself from external political authority but precisely by being accountable and responsive to opposing, external authorities." In some ways historic preservation offices for tribes, states, and federal agencies (THPO, SHPO, and FPO) could function this way in relationship to federal regulations, in collaboration with CRM firms and the communities in which archaeological compliance work takes place.

Continuing a long tradition of interdisciplinary work, archaeologists collaborate with a wide variety of practitioners and theorists, from scientists to community elders. Zeder and colleagues (this volume) discuss work for problems we face today from climate change and other ecological transformations, all with far-reaching social ramifications. Such work raises implications for the ways in which local community concerns and global concerns need to intersect. Archaeology can be of service in bridging these concerns if it can lend a perspective that considers local and global scales simultaneously.

As participants in Arizona State University's Long-Term Vulnerability and Transformation Project, Michelle Hegmon and colleagues (2008:313) ask, "Why are some changes [major transformations and institutional collapses] much more dramatic and fraught with suffering than others?" The severity of transformations is measured through demographic scale of impacts, population displacement, cultural change, and physical suffering, including injury, illness, and death. They investigate the concepts of rigidity traps and path dependence, each of which involve human agency and decision making. Comparing rigidity in three ancient southwestern populations—Mimbres, Mesa Verde, and Hohokam—Hegmon and her colleagues (2008:321) summarize that, "rigidity—lack of flexibility, suppression of innovation, and resistance to change—may delay change or transformation for some time but not forever. Furthermore, in such rigidity trap situations, the transformation, when it inevitably comes, is severe and associated with human suffering." They ask if we are in a rigidity trap today, marked by absence of social options, limits of buffering strategies, attachment to traditions, attachment to technology, attachment to place, and path dependence. The latter "describes how the development of certain technologies, institutions, or land-use patterns (esp. in combination) often establishes a trajectory that becomes increasingly difficult to change, even if change is recognized as desirable. One contemporary example is our electrical grid system. Anticipatory governance is today considered one way of minimizing the development of path dependence, and knowledge of cases, such as those described here, may contribute to such governance" (Hegmon et al. 2008:322). Questions of governance raise issues about the scale at which democratic decision making and policy formation are carried out. Some public interests would be better served if global, federal, tribal, state, and local decision making were coordinated or at least drew on mutually acceptable knowledge (and wisdom). We don't want to overstate the potential importance of archaeology but do want to emphasize that collaborative, multiscale approaches can indeed have great impact.

Another tool is translational research (TRIP 2008). Translational research takes knowledge generated from interdisciplinary scientific inquiry or humanistic scholarship and transforms it into practices and solutions with a stated goal of making a difference in people's lives. Researchers generate knowledge and utilize evidence to develop meaningful practices that address problems or issues in everyday life and collaborate or form partnerships to successfully translate the researcher's evidence or evidence generated by others into meaningful practices. Archaeology can build community and social capital and can be used to organize publics around contemporary issues. Identifying problems to be solved requires true collaboration with the people who have the problem, which in turn requires developing partnerships. To do this archaeologists have to share power, let the partners help build research agendas and set goals, and work with them and other scholars to interpret evidence and craft solutions, then try to figure out whether or not the solutions helped.

How do archaeologists learn how to do translational research? Fortunately, social organizers have provided useful information (e.g., Stoecker 1999). They understand that political issues are contested across lines of power and address unbalanced or unequal social relationships. Organizers make judgments about which political issues can be most effectively contested and will have the greatest impact on altering power relationships, that is, which issues can be "won" given the resources and support of a community. The key is to aim high with long-term goals and build an organization through achievable solutions using strategies and tactics that feed into the larger plan. The goal of organizing is that with enough planning an organization will grow, gain power, and be able to go after increasingly larger and more meaningful issues. Translational scholars must listen to their collaborators to determine which issues to focus on, build mutual respect and trust, and develop the human capital already present in a community. Studying activist literature produced by social organizers is useful and gives clues as to how to achieve a translational archaeology (see for example, Alinsky 1946, 1971, an organizer of the Back of the Yards neighborhood in Chicago during the 1930s and an infamous figure as the father of community and grassroots organizing).

Another way archaeologists can work in the public interest, particularly in informal educational settings like museums, parks, and tourist destinations, is to build opportunities for transformative learning for both publics and archaeologists (see Sandlin and Bey 2006). Transformative learning, which develops autonomous thinking, is relevant for understanding how we really can learn from the past, rather than having the past simply reinforce the status quo (e.g., Mezirow 1991). Transformative learning does not necessarily come about as a result of traditional teaching per se, but is fostered by opportunities within a safe learning environment with a community of learners. The transformation refers to changes in a person's frame of reference, beliefs, attitudes, and emotional reactions through critical reflection about experiences. A major life crisis or transition can trigger a disorienting dilemma, bring about the transformation of one's perspectives, and change one's life. Such learning is important, for example, to the success of the Truth and Reconciliation Commissions. It is also important to the relearning of history in such a way that it does not disparage Native Americans, women, or other groups based on stereotypical biased histories. Social history, particularly that done in connection with the civil rights and women's liberation movements, was crucial to raising consciousness both within specific groups and in the broader community (see Franklin and Paynter, this volume). By bringing authentic experiences into private and public awareness, these movements challenged assumptions and encouraged changes in perception (Little 2007).

Archaeology in the public interest takes many forms, from targeting specific local or global issues, to creating overarching cultural narratives, to privileging human rights and global justice. We are confident that as archaeologists increasingly embrace public service in our work, we will develop more innovative and effective methods for effective public scholarship. We anticipate that such work will strengthen the discipline through synergy with those who are working on shared social problems with different methods, different perspectives and worldviews, and different visions.

Acknowledgments. We wish to thank the editors for their invitation to participate and especially for their encouragement (and patience). We also thank two anonymous reviewers as well as Paul Shackel and Teresa Moyer for their helpful comments. Barbara Little learned about boundary organizations from Peggy Nelson and thanks her for supplying some essential references. This chapter's contents and opinions do not necessarily reflect the views or policies of the U.S. National Park Service. Larry Zimmerman wishes to honor the memories of Jan Hammil and Maria Pearson who helped him to remain optimistic about the future of archaeology, and thanks Jessica Welch and Courtney Singleton for their insistence that archaeology can and should be activist.

References Cited

AGJ (Archaeologists for Global Justice)
   2005 Website: Archaeologists for Global Justice. Electronic document, http://www.shef.ac.uk/archaeology/global-justice.html, accessed June 7, 2009.

Albertson, Nicole
   2009 Archaeology of the Homeless. *Archaeology* 62(6):42–43.

Alinsky, Saul D.
   1946 *Reveille for Radicals.* University of Chicago Press, Chicago.
   1971 *Rules for Radicals: A Pragmatic Primer for Realistic Radicals.* Vintage Books, New York.

Altschul, Jeffrey H.
   2005 Significance in American Cultural Resource Management: Lost in the Past. In *Heritage of Value, Archaeology of Renown: Reshaping Archaeological Assessment and Significance,* edited by Clay Mathers, Timothy Darvill, and Barbara J. Little, pp. 192–210. University Press of Florida, Gainesville.

Barks, Coleman, with Reynold Nicholson, A. J. Arberry, and John Moyne
   2004 *The Essential Rumi: New Expanded Edition.* HarperOne, New York.

Blakey, Michael
   2001 Bioarchaeology of the African Diaspora in the Americas: Its Origins and Scope. *Annual Review of Anthropology* 30:387–422.
   2004 Introduction. In *The New York African Burial Ground Skeletal Biology Final Report,* Vol. 1, edited by M. Blakey and L. Rankin-Hill, pp. 2–37. For the United States General Services Administration, Northeast and Caribbean Region.

Bohannon, John
   2008 Team Unveils Mideast Peace Plan. *Science* 320(5874):302.

Brumfiel, Elizabeth M.
  2005 Archaeology and Its Publics: Taking Dissent Seriously. *American Anthropologist* 107:133–136.
Buchli, Victor
  2007 Opinion. *Conservation Bulletin* 56:14.
Burke, Heather, and Claire Smith (editors)
  2007 *Archaeology to Delight and Instruct: Active Learning in the University Classroom.* Left Coast Press, Walnut Creek, California.
Colwell-Chanthaphonh, Chip, and T. J. Ferguson
  2004 Virtue Ethics and the Practice of History: Native Americans and Archaeologists along the San Pedro Valley of Arizona. *Journal of Social Archaeology* 4:5–27.
Colwell-Chanthaphonh, Chip, and T. J. Ferguson (editors)
  2008 *Collaboration in Archaeological Practice: Engaging Descendant Communities.* AltaMira Press, Lanham, Maryland.
Conner, Melissa
  2007 *Forensic Methods: Excavation for the Archaeologist and Investigator.* AltaMira Press, Lanham, Maryland.
Costanza, Robert, Lisa J. Graumlich, and Will Steffen (editors)
  2007 *Sustainability or Collapse? An Integrated History and Future of People on Earth.* Report of the 96th Dahlem Workshop. MIT Press, Cambridge, Massachusetts, in cooperation with Dahlem University Press, Berlin.
Dawdy, Shannon Lee
  2006 The Taphonomy of Disaster and the (Re)Formation of New Orleans. *American Anthropologist* 108:719–730.
Diamond, Jared
  2005 *Collapse: How Societies Choose to Fail or Succ*eed. Penguin, New York.
Eisler, Riane
  1995 [1987] *The Chalice and the Blade: Our History, Our Future.* Harper Collins, New York.
Epperson, Terrence W.
  1991 Race and the Disciplines of the Plantation. *Historical Archaeology* 24:29–36.
Fagette, Paul
  1996 *Digging for Dollars: American Archaeology and the New Deal.* University of New Mexico Press, Albuquerque.
Ferguson, T. J., and Roger Anyon
  2001 Hopi and Zuni Cultural Landscapes: Implications of History and Scale for Cultural Resource Management. In *Native Peoples of the Southwest; Negotiating Land, Water, and Ethnicities*, edited by Laurie Weinstein, pp. 99–122. Bergin and Garvey, Westport, Connecticut.
Ford, Richard I.
  1973 Archeology Serving Humanity. In *Research and Theory in Current Archeology*, edited by Charles L. Redman, pp. 83–94. John Wiley, New York.
Frisch, Michael
  1990 *A Shared Authority: Essays on the Craft and Meaning of Oral and Public History.* SUNY Press, Albany.

Fritz, John M., and Fred Plog
   1970   The Nature of Archaeological Explanation. *American Antiquity* 35:405–412.
Funari, Pedro Paulo A.
   2009   Comments on What Can Archaeology do for Justice, Peace, Community, and the Earth? *Historical Archaeology* 43(4):120–121.
Gonzalez-Ruibal, Alfredo
   2006   The Past is Tomorrow. Towards an Archaeology of the Vanishing Present. *Norwegian Archaeological Review* 39:110–125.
Gould, Richard A.
   2005   Archaeology Prepares for a Possible Mass Fatality Disaster. *The SAA Archaeological Record* 5(4):10–12.
Guston, David H.
   2001   Boundary Organizations in Environmental Policy and Science: An Introduction. Special Issue: Boundary Organizations in Environmental Policy and Science (Autumn 2001). *Science, Technology, & Human Values* 26(4):399–408.
Hamilakis, Yannis, and Philip Duke (editors)
   2007   *Archaeology and Capitalism, From Ethics to Politics*. Left Coast Press, Walnut Creek, California.
Hegmon, Michelle, Matthew A. Peeples, Ann P. Kinzig, Stephanie Kulow, Cathryn M. Meegan, and Margaret C. Nelson
   2008   Social Transformation and Its Human Costs in the Prehispanic U. S. Southwest. *American Anthropologist* 110:313–324.
Holthaus, Gary
   2008   *Learning Native Wisdom; What Traditional Cultures Teach Us about Subsistence, Sustainability, and Spirituality*. University Press of Kentucky, Lexington.
Kehoe, Alice Beck
   1998   *The Land of Prehistory: A Critical History of American Archaeology*. Routledge, New York.
Kelly, Robert
   1998   Native Americans and Archaeologists: A Vital Partnership. *SAA Bulletin* 16(4):24–26.
Killion, Thomas (editor)
   2008   *Opening Archaeology: Repatriation's Impact on Method and Theory*. SAR Press, Santa Fe.
King, Thomas F.
   1983   Professional Responsibility in Public Archaeology. *Annual Review of Anthropology* 12:143–164.
Kleindienst, Maxine R., and Patty Jo Watson
   1956   Action Archaeology: The Archaeological Inventory of a Living Community. *Anthropology Tomorrow* 5:75–78.
Knudson, Ruthann
   1986   Contemporary Cultural Resource Management. In *American Archaeology Past and Future: A Celebration of the Society for American Archaeology 1935–1985*, edited by David J. Meltzer, Don D. Fowler, and Jeremy A. Sabloff, pp. 395–413. Smithsonian Institution Press, Washington, D. C.

Little, Barbara J.
   1994 Consider the Hermaphroditic Mind: Comment on "The Interplay of Evidential Constraints and Political Interests: Recent Archaeological Research on Gender." *American Antiquity* 59:539–544.
   2002 Archaeology as a Shared Vision. In *Public Benefits of Archaeology*, edited by Barbara J. Little, pp. 3–19. University Press of Florida, Gainesville.
   2007 *Historical Archaeology: Why the Past Matters*. Left Coast Press, Walnut Creek, California.
   2009a Public Archaeology in the United States. In *Heritage Studies: Methods & Approaches,* edited by Marie Louise S. Sørensen and John Carman. Routledge, London, in press.
   2009b What Can Archaeology Do for Justice, Peace, Community, and the Earth? *Historical Archaeology* 43(4):115–119.
   2010 Public Benefits of Public Archaeology. In *Oxford Handbook of Public Archaeology,* edited by John Carman, Carol McDavid, and Robin Skeates. Oxford, in press.

Little, Barbara J., and Paul A. Shackel (editors)
   2007 *Archaeology as a Tool of Civic Engagement*. AltaMira Press, Lanham, Maryland.

Maclean, Caitlin, and Glenn Yago
   2008 Financial Innovations for Developing Archaeological Discovery and Conservation. Financial Innovations Lab Report, Volume 7. Milken Institute, Santa Monica, California.

Marshall, Yvonne (editor)
   2002 Community Archaeology. Thematic Issue. *World Archaeology* 34(2).

Mazoyer, Marcel, and Laurence Roudart
   2006 *A History of World Agriculture from the Neolithic Age to the Current Crisis*. Translated by James H. Membrez. Monthly Review Press, New York.

McAnany, Patricia A., and Norman Yoffee (editors)
   2009 *Questioning Collapse: Human Resilience, Ecological Vulnerability and the Aftermath of Empire*. Cambridge University Press, Cambridge.

McDavid, Carol, and David Babson (editors)
   1997 In the Realm of Politics: Prospects for Public Participation in African American Archaeology. Thematic Issue. *Historical Archaeology* 31(3).

McGhee, Fred L., and Carol McDavid
   2009 Strategies of Practice: Implementing Postcolonial Critique, CRM, Public Archaeology and Advocacy, in *World Archaeological Congress (WAC) Handbook on Postcolonialism and Archaeology*, edited by Uzma Rizvi and Jane Lydon. Left Coast Press, Walnut Creek, California, in press.

McGimsey, Charles Robert
   1972 *Public Archeology*. Seminar Press, New York.

McGuire, Randall H.
   2008 *Archaeology as Political Action*. University of California Press, Berkeley.

McManamon, Francis P.
   1991 The Many Publics for Archaeology. *American Antiquity* 56:121–130.

Meskell, Lynn
 2002 The Intersections of Identity and Politics in Archaeology. *Annual Review of Anthropology* 31:279–301.
Mezirow, Jack
 1991 *Transformative Dimensions of Adult Learning*. Jossey-Bass, San Francisco.
Minnis, Paul E., Barbara J. Little, Robert Kelly, Scott E. Ingram, Dean Snow, Lynne Sebastian, and Katherine A. Spielmann
 2006 Answering the Skeptic's Question. *The SAA Archaeological Record* 6(5):17–20.
Moe, Jeannie M.
 2002 Project Archaeology: Putting the Intrigue of the Past in Public Education. In *Public Benefits of Archaeology*, edited by Barbara J. Little, pp. 176–186. University Press of Florida, Gainesville.
Mullins, Paul R.
 2008 Excavating America's Metaphor: Race, Diaspora, and Vindicationist Archaeologies. *Historical Archaeology* 42:104–122.
Musteata, Sergiu
 2009 Let's Do Our Job Better And Then There Will Be No Reasons To Talk About Relevancy Of Archaeology. *Historical Archaeology* 43(4):122–124.
Nicholas, George, and Julie Hollowell
 2007 Ethical Challenges to a Postcolonial Archaeology: The Legacy of Scientific Colonialism. In *Archaeology and Capitalism, From Ethics to Politics*, edited by Yannis Hamilakis and Philip Duke, pp 59–82. Left Coast Press, Walnut Creek, California.
Patel, Samir S.
 2007 Writing on the Wall: The Graffiti Archaeology Project Challenges the Discipline of Archaeology. *Archaeology* 60(4):50–53.
Pikirayi, Innocent
 2009 What can Archaeology do for Society in Southern Africa? *Historical Archaeology* 43(4):125–127.
PUSH (Promoting dialogue and cultural Understanding of our Shared Heritage)
 2007 Our Shared Heritage. An Anthology of the [Mideast] Region's Shared Natural and Cultural Heritage. Electronic document, http://www.pushproject.org/publications/assets/Our%20Shared%20Heritage%20Nov%2007.pdf , accessed June 6, 2009.
Rathje, William, and Cullen Murphy
 2001 *Rubbish: The Archaeology of Garbage*. University of Arizona Press, Tucson.
Redman, Charles L., and David R. Foster (editors)
 2008 *Agrarian Landscapes in Transition: Comparison of Long-Term Ecological and Cultural Change*. Oxford University Press, New York.
Redman, Charles L., and Ann P. Kinzig
 2003 Resilience of Past Landscapes: Resilience Theory, Society, and the Longue Durée. *Conservation Ecology* 7(1):14. Electronic document, http://www.consecol.org/vol7/iss1/art14 , accessed June 7, 2009.
Sabloff, Jeremy A.
 1998 Distinguished Lecture in Archeology: Communication and the Future of American Archaeology. *American Anthropologist* 100:869–875.

2008 *Archaeology Matters: Action Archaeology in the Modern World*. Left Coast Press, Walnut Creek, California.

Saitta, Dean J.
2007 *The Archaeology of Collective Action*. University Press of Florida, Gainesville.

Sandlin, Jennifer A., and George J. Bey, II
2006 Trowels, Trenches and Transformation: A Case Study of Archaeologists Learning a More Critical Practice of Archaeology. *Journal of Social Archaeology* 6:255–276.

Scham, Sandra Arnold, and Adel Yahya
2003 Heritage and Reconciliation. *Journal of Social Archaeology* 3:399–416.

Schiffer, Michael B.
1999 *The Material Life of Human Beings: Artifacts, Behavior, and Communication*. Routledge, London.

Schneider, Anne L.
2008 Why do Some Boundary Organizations Result in New Ideas and Practices and Others only Meet Resistance? Examples from Juvenile Justice. *The American Review of Public Administration* 39(1):60–79.

Silverberg, Robert
1968 *Mound Builders of Ancient America: The Archaeology of a Myth*. New York Graphic Society, Greenwich, Connecticut.

Silverman, Helaine, and D. Fairchild Ruggles (editors)
2007 *Cultural Heritage and Human Rights*. Springer, New York.

Singleton, Theresa A.
1999 An Introduction to African-American Archaeology. In *"I, Too, Am America": Archaeological Studies of African-American Life*, edited by Theresa A. Singleton, pp. 1–17. University of Virginia Press, Charlottesville.

Smardz, Karolyn, and Shelley J. Smith (editors)
2000 *The Archaeology Education Handbook: Sharing the Past with Kids*. AltaMira Press, Walnut Creek, California.

Society for American Archaeology
1996 *Principles of Archaeological Ethics*. Electronic document, http://www.saa.org/aboutSAA/committees/ethics/principles.html, accessed October 20, 2008.

Stapp, Darby C., and Michael S. Burney
2002 *Tribal Cultural Resource Management: The Full Circle to Stewardship*. AltaMira Press, Walnut Creek, California.

Stoecker, Randy
1999 Are Academics Irrelevant? Roles for Scholars in Participatory Research. *American Behavioral Scientist* 42(5):840–854.

Stoffle, Richard W.
2005 Review essay of *Places that Count: Traditional Cultural Properties in Cultural Resource Managemen*, by Thomas F. King, and *Tribal Cultural Resource Management: The Full Circle to Stewardship*, by Darby C. Stapp and Michael S. Burney. *American Anthropologist* 107:138–140.

Stottman, M. Jay
2007 The Culture of Littering: Using Archaeology to Help Solve Contemporary

Problems. Paper presented at the Society for Historical Archaeology annual meetings, Williamsburg, VA.

Stottman, M. Jay (editor)
 2010 *Archaeologists as Activists: Can Archaeology Change the World?* University of Alabama Press, Tuscaloosa.

Stottman, M. Jay, Sarah E. Miller, and A. Gwynn Henderson
 2007 Culture of Litterbugs. In *Archaeology to Delight and Instruct: Active Learning in the University Classroom*, edited by Heather Burke and Claire Smith, pp. 180–200. Left Coast Press, Walnut Creek, California.

Taylor, Walter W.
 1983 *A Study of Archaeology*. Reprinted, Southern Illinois University Press, Carbondale. Originally published 1948, Memoir 69, American Anthropological Association, Menasha, Wisconsin.

Thiessen, Thomas D.
 1999 Emergency Archeology in the Missouri River Basin: The Role of the Missouri Basin Project and the Midwest Archeological Center in the Interagency Archeological Salvage Program, 1946–1975. Midwest Archaeological Center, Lincoln. Electronic Document, http://www.nps.gov/history/mwac/publications/pdf/spec2.pdf, accessed January 14, 2009.

TRIP (Translating Research into Practice)
 2008 Translating Research into Practice Database. Electronic document, https://db.liberalarts.iupui.edu/trip/CASlogin.asp, accessed November 12, 2008.

Ucko, Peter J.
 1987 *Academic Freedom and Apartheid*. Duckworth, London.

Valado, Martha Trenna
 2006 *Factors Influencing Homeless People's Perception and Use of Urban Space*. Doctoral dissertation, Department of Anthropology, The University of Arizona. Retrieved October 3, 2007, from ProQuest Digital Dissertations database, Publication No. AAT 3218224.

van der Leeuw, Sander, and Charles L. Redman
 2002 Placing Archaeology at the Center of Socio-Natural Studies. *American Antiquity* 67:597–605.

Ward, Camille
 2008 City Pans Panhandling. *Nuvo*, July 23, 2008. Electronic document, http://www.nuvo.net/articles/city_pans_panhandling/ accessed November 12, 2008.

Watkins, Joe
 2000 *Indigenous Archaeology; American Indian Values and Scientific Practice*. AltaMira Press, Walnut Creek, California.

Zimmerman, Larry J.
 2004 Archaeological Evaluation of the Hillside Garden Areas at the James J. Hill House (21RA21), St. Paul, Minnesota. *The Minnesota Archaeologist* 63:118–136.
 2005 First, Be Humble: Working with Indigenous Peoples and Other Descendant Communities. In *Indigenous Archaeologies: Decolonizing Theory and Practice*, edited by Claire Smith and H. Martin Wobst, pp. 301–314. Routledge, London.

2006 Liberating Archaeology, Liberation Archaeologies and WAC. *Archaeologies* 2(1):85–95.

Zimmerman, Larry J., and Jessica Welch

2006 Toward an Archaeology of Homelessness. *Anthropology News* 47(2):54.

2008 Social Problems and Creating an Archaeology of 'Now', Not Just 'Back Then': An Archaeology of Homelessness. Paper presented at the World Archaeological Congress 6, Dublin, Ireland.

8

Archaeology and Historic Preservation Law: Twenty-Five Years of Interesting Times

LYNNE SEBASTIAN

Article II of the bylaws of the Society for American Archaeology lays out the ten objectives of the Society and concludes by saying:

> In pursuit of its objectives, the Society shall promote and support all legislative, regulatory, and voluntary programs that forbid and discourage all activities that result in the loss of scientific knowledge and of access to sites and artifacts.

Not only does SAA recognize in its most fundamental document the critical importance to archaeology of legal and regulatory protections, throughout its 75-year history the Society has been actively involved in the passage of legislation protecting the archaeological record from looting and destruction and promoting the scientific study of the physical remains of our, and the world's, heritage. SAA's government affairs program has long been considered one of its most important member services.

The impact of laws and regulations on archaeology in the United States began more than 100 years ago with the passage of the Antiquities Act of 1906, and expanded with the passage of the Historic Sites Act in 1935—the year after the SAA was founded. Subsequent congressional actions mandated data collection for archaeological sites that would be impacted by certain types of government actions, required identification of archaeological sites that might be affected by all kinds of government actions and consideration of measures to mitigate those effects, and strengthened penalties for looting of sites on public and tribal lands. Among other things, this growing body of legislation created an entirely new set of career paths for archaeologists and generated exponential increases in funding for archaeology (Altschul and Patterson, this volume) and in the amount of archaeology being done. The cultural resource management (CRM) field was born (Snead and Sabloff, this volume).

Although occasional "salvage" projects designed to rescue archaeological materials from large-scale land disturbance had been carried out since the New Deal programs of the 1930s, the legal foundations for CRM were established in the 1960s and early 1970s by the passage of the Reservoir Salvage Act in 1960, the Historic and Archeological Data Preservation Act in 1974, the National Environmental Policy Act (NEPA) in 1969, and especially the National Historic Preservation Act (NHPA) in 1966. Section 106 of the NHPA requires that federal agencies take into account the effects of their actions on all kinds of historic properties, including archaeological sites. The basic Section 106 procedure, as developed over the past 40 years, is a consultation-based process that includes identification of "old stuff," a determination as to whether the identified old stuff is eligible for listing on the National Register of Historic Places, an evaluation of the nature of the effects of the federal action on any eligible (or national register listed) properties, and a negotiated decision about how those effects might be avoided, minimized, or mitigated.

NEPA, on the other hand, is not a historic preservation law per se, but rather requires that agencies evaluate the impacts of their actions on all aspects of the human environment, including historic and cultural resources. NEPA is the umbrella law under which all federal agency planning takes place. For a brief summary of all the U.S. laws pertaining to historic preservation see Sebastian (2002); for more detailed discussion see King (1998); and for the history of these laws and SAA's role see Davis (2010).

The practice of federally mandated archaeology was well established at the time of SAA's 50th anniversary, but the legal context within which both CRM and academic archaeology are practiced has changed significantly during the intervening 25 years, with the passage of amendments to the NHPA in 1992, promulgation of revised regulations implementing Section 106 of NHPA in 1986 and 1999, and the passage of the Native American Graves Protection and Repatriation Act (NAGPRA) in 1990. Since I have spent the quarter century between the 50th and 75th anniversaries of the SAA working with and teaching about the NHPA and Section 106 and its regulation, both in a State Historic Preservation Office and as a private consultant, I will be describing the changes in historic preservation law and regulations in this chapter while Michael Wilcox addresses the issues raised by the passage of NAGPRA in Chapter 9.

Since compliance with Section 106 of the NHPA is the basis for the livelihood of the majority of archaeologists in the U.S. as well as the source of funding for the vast majority of archaeology being done in this country today, it is worth looking back on the history of this very interesting 25-year period. If there is anything that we know, as archaeologists, it is that this history is even now shaping our future.

The 1986 Section 106 Regulation

The 50th anniversary of the SAA occurred just as the Advisory Council on Historic Preservation (ACHP), which was created by the NHPA and is charged with promulgating regulations implementing Section 106, was preparing to do just that. The first legally binding Section 106 regulation (36 CFR Part 800), had been published only six years earlier in January of 1979. Prior to that time the ACHP's "procedures" for carrying out Section 106 had been advisory rather than regulatory, but in response to a presidential memorandum and supported by a subsequent amendment to NHPA giving ACHP rule-making authority, the Council issued binding regulations for the first time in 1979.

Two years later, almost to the day, the Reagan administration took over the reins of the executive branch and began pursuing its anti-regulatory (and some would say anti-environmental) approach to government. Noting that nothing in the plain language of Section 106 required identification of historic properties or mitigation of effects or consultation or any of the other detailed procedures found in the ACHP's regulation, the administration attempted to replace the regulatory procedures with a process by which federal agencies would simply send the ACHP a letter describing their undertaking and receive back a letter "commenting" on the undertaking. For good measure the administration also proposed a federal budget that would zero out the Historic Preservation Fund appropriation supporting the activities of State Historic Preservation Offices (SHPOs), one of the major consulting partners in the Section 106 process.

As Tom King (2000:21) has pointed out, if the administration had been less heavy-handed, they might have succeeded in effectively neutralizing Section 106. But by proposing to dismantle the *entire* regulatory process and refusing to appropriate *any* funding from the HPF trust fund set aside by Congress to support historic preservation activities, they created a strong, grassroots-driven "push back." Congressional representatives and senators who supported historic preservation spent the next eight years diligently putting HPF funding back into the federal budget every year, and the ACHP staff managed to rewrite the Section 106 regulation (creating the 1986 version) in a way that kept most of the core elements of the regulatory process in place.

Having learned from this experience how vulnerable the Section 106 process was because it extended beyond the statutory language of the NHPA, the preservation community ensured that, in 1992 when the law was being amended in several other ways, language was inserted into Section 110 (at §110[a][2][E]) that would provide statutory support for the Section 106 process. This language, which enumerates the tasks that a federal agency must include in its Section 106 procedures, proved to be very useful more than a decade later when another very anti-regulatory attack was mounted against Section 106. Although many in the CRM community feared in 2006 that the language of Section 106 would be changed in a way that would fatally weaken the process, SAA and a few other organizations in the preservation community stood firm on the protection afforded by the 1992 amendment to Section 110, and eventually the crisis was resolved through carefully crafted amendments to other sections of the law, leaving Section 106 intact.

While the 1986 regulation did, as noted above, maintain the core Section 106 process—identify historic places, determine whether they are eligible to the National Register of Historic Places, determine whether they will be adversely effected, and propose measures to avoid or reduce those effects—it also introduced important streamlining measures. The first of these involved what are called "consensus determinations of eligibility." As originally written, Section 106 only required consideration of effects on properties *listed* on the national register. This greatly limited the effectiveness of the law, especially for archaeological sites. In 1972, however, President Nixon signed Executive Order 11593, which instructed agencies to consider the effects of their undertakings on properties *eligible* for listing on the national register as well. Ultimately the law was amended (in 1976) to include this language, but the ACHP's original nonbinding procedures were based on this executive order.

The 1979 regulation established a process for determinations of eligibility that went like this: The federal agency, in consultation with the SHPO, evaluates the significance of each historic property by applying the criteria of eligibility to the national register established by the National Park Service. If the agency and the SHPO agree that the property isn't eligible to the Register, then the undertaking can proceed. If either or both parties believe the property meets the criteria or if there is a question as to whether it meets the criteria or not, the agency is *required* to secure a determination of eligibility from the Secretary of the Interior (in actuality from the Keeper of the National Register), confirming whether or not the property actually meets the criteria. Needless to say, this created a *serious* bottleneck in the process.

The 1986 regulation formalized a de facto and much more expeditious process—the one still in use today—whereby properties are considered eligible or not eligible for the purposes of Section 106 if the agency and the SHPO agree on their eligibility status. Only if no consensus can be reached between agency and SHPO does the agency need to request a determination from the Keeper of the National Register. This consensus process is vital to the smooth functioning of Section 106. Given the thousands of historic properties identified every year and the very small size of the National Register staff, the whole system would bog down in about a week without it. On the other hand, the consensus process has also given rise to concerns about the validity and consistency of determinations of eligibility within the Section 106 process, especially for archaeological sites (Sebastian 2010).

A second streamlining measure in the 1986 regulation had to do with findings of effect. Section 800.9(c) offered a new provision whereby "effects of an undertaking that would otherwise be found to be adverse may be considered as being not adverse." The regulation then outlined three cases where this provision would apply, the critical one for our purposes here being,

> when the historic property is of value only for its potential contribution to archeological, historical, or architectural research and when such value can be substantially preserved through the conduct of appropriate research, and such research is conducted in accordance

with applicable professional standards and guidelines [36 CFR Part 800.9(c)(1), version 1986].

Under the 1979 regulation, a finding of adverse effect was a Big Deal. The agency had to prepare what was called a "preliminary case report," host a public meeting and on-site inspection if requested to do so by the ACHP, prepare a memorandum of agreement (MOA) detailing proposed mitigation measures and publish it in the Federal Register. Rather than simply accepting the MOA at the staff level, the ACHP Executive Director could ask that the full ACHP or a panel of ACHP members review and respond to the MOA. Not surprisingly, all of this created *another* bottleneck.

The provision for turning "adverse effect" into "no adverse effect" through data recovery was one way that the 1986 regulation attempted to deal with this bottleneck. Although both adverse effect and no adverse effect findings were still reviewed by the ACHP, the review process for "no adverse effect" findings was much simpler, it didn't require an MOA or publication in the Federal Register or a public meeting, and the review happened at the ACHP staff level. The 1986 regulation also allowed the agency and SHPO to conclude an agreement without the ACHP participating and brought the full Council (as opposed to staff) into the process only in relatively rare cases.

For archaeologists, this provision of the 1986 regulation meant that few federal projects that involved only archaeological sites were found to have an adverse effect. With an approved data recovery program, a development project could end up destroying large numbers of archaeological sites and still be found to have "no adverse effect." As the application of this provision played out during the years that this version of the regulation was in effect (1986–1999), some people—mostly archaeologists and Native Americans—argued that this made it too easy for agencies to simply "dig, document, and destroy" archaeological sites rather than make a serious effort to avoid affecting these properties.

Personally I never found that claim to be persuasive. Archaeological excavation is so expensive that it does a fine job of militating against any tendency that an agency might have to see excavation rather than avoidance as the easy way out. The cost of data recovery is a far stronger deterrent than the relatively minor annoyance of having to jump through a few more bureaucratic hoops. I do think there was a down side to this narrow focus on data recovery as *the* mitigation for adverse effects on archaeological sites, however. Agencies and consultants became so focused on research designs, excavation techniques, and analytical methods that we lost track of the broader scope of possible mitigation measures, some of which have greater public benefits than standard, government-issue data recovery (Little 2002). In any case, this provision for turning an "adverse effect" into a "no adverse effect" through data recovery was eliminated when the regulation was revised again in 1999.

Another important difference between the 1986 regulation and its 1979 predecessor was in the provisions for involvement of federally recognized Indian tribes. The 1979 regulation included the words "Indian tribes" only once. In the very last section, under the heading "Public Participation," the regulation said

> The Council, Federal agencies, and the State Historic Preservation Officers should seek assistance from the public including other Federal agencies, units of local and State government, public and private organizations, individuals and federally recognized Indian tribes in evaluating National Register and eligible properties, determining effects, and developing alternatives to avoid or mitigate an adverse effect [36 CFR 800.15, 1979 version].

The 1986 regulation, on the other hand, had an entire section (36 CFR 800.1[c][2][iii]) on participation by Indian tribes and made a clear distinction between the role of tribes and that of the public as well as between tribes and other interested parties. This section of the 1986 regulation required that agencies be sensitive to tribal preservation concerns, treat tribal governments as consulting parties for undertakings on tribal land, work with established tribal preservation procedures, and involve tribes as interested parties for undertakings off tribal lands. The regulation also raised the possibility that tribes could participate in lieu of the SHPO in Section 106 activities on tribal lands. Overall, the regulation required participation by Indian tribes or described the nature of that participation in seven different sections.

The 1992 NHPA Amendments

While the ink was still wet on the Federal Register publication of the 1986 version of 36 CFR Part 800, events were already in motion that would lead to amendment of the NHPA in 1992 and require yet another rewrite of the regulation as a result. The 1992 amendments added several additional provisions to the law, many of which would have significant impacts on Section 106, even though that section was not amended. I have already described one of these: language was added to Section 110 describing what must be included in agency Section 106 procedures. As noted above, this amendment provided statutory support for the process established in earlier versions of the ACHP's regulation. Other amendments obligate federal agencies to withhold assistance from applicants who engage in anticipatory demolition—that is, destruction of a historic property for the purpose of avoiding Section 106 compliance—and provide a process through which agencies may withhold certain information about historic properties from public disclosure.

By far the most far-reaching impacts on the Section 106 compliance process—and thus on American archaeology—came from the 1992 amendments having to do with participation by Indian tribes and Native Hawaiian organizations. The amendments at §101(d)(1-5) directed the Secretary of the Interior to assist tribes in developing their own historic preservation programs, to develop a process whereby tribes may assume some or all of the functions of the SHPO for federal projects and programs on tribal land, to include tribes in the apportionment of Historic Preservation Fund grants and contracts, and to arrange for Section 106 compliance on tribal lands to be carried out under tribal regulations rather than under 36 CFR Part 800 where appropriate.

All of these provisions have changed and fostered the involvement of individual Native Americans and of Indian tribes in cultural resource management and archaeology (see Ferguson [1999] for a discussion of immediate impacts and long-term trends). But none of them have had anything like the impact on Section 106 or cultural resource management or American archaeology created by a seemingly simple statement in the final section of these amendments: "Properties of traditional religious and cultural importance to an Indian tribe or Native Hawaiian organization may be determined to be eligible for inclusion on the National Register" (NHPA 101[d][6]).

In order to understand where this provision came from and why, we have to start in 1978 when Congress passed the American Indian Religious Freedom Act or AIRFA, which reads in part:

> It shall be the policy of the United States to protect and preserve for American Indians their inherent right of freedom to believe, express,

and exercise the traditional religions of the American Indian, Eskimo, Aleut, and Native Hawaiians, including but not limited to access to sites, use and possession of sacred objects, and the freedom to worship through ceremonials and traditional rites [AIRFA §1].

Although this statute helped to resolve the problems of native people who had been denied access to sacred sites on public lands or harassed or intruded upon during the conduct of ceremonies or personal rituals, it did not address the problem of destruction of sacred sites through federal actions.

Congress directed federal agencies to

evaluate their policies and procedures in consultation with native traditional religious leaders in order to determine appropriate changes necessary to protect and preserve Native American religious cultural rights and practices [AIRFA §2].

But where traditional practices and places came into conflict with multiple use mandates on federal lands, AIRFA did not have the statutory or regulatory muscle to tip the balance. In the case of *Lyng v. Northwest Indian Cemetery Protective Association*, for example, U.S.D.A. Forest Service was building roads for logging on public lands in California in an area where several tribes carried out ceremonies and personal rituals. In 1988 the Supreme Court ruled that logging was in the public interest and that, unless the Forest Service's intent was to infringe upon native religious practices or coerce individuals to act against their beliefs, the agency could carry out projects that would impact or even destroy sacred sites.

By this time, many tribes and native individuals had become familiar with Section 106 as a result of the tribal consultation provisions in the 1986 version of the ACHP's regulation. Here was a law called the National Historic *Preservation* Act; why couldn't it be used to *preserve* sacred sites? The answer to that question was often that NHPA couldn't be used because the National Register regulation 36 CFR 60 and the guidance document based on it, *Bulletin 15 How to Apply the National Register Criteria for Evaluation*, include what is called the "religious exception":

Ordinarily . . . properties owned by religious institutions or used for religious purposes . . . shall not be considered eligible for the National Register. However, such properties will qualify if they . . . [are] a religious property deriving primary significance from architectural or artistic distinction or historical importance [National Park Service 1997:26].

Since sacred sites are, by definition, used for religious purposes, many people in the preservation community considered this to be a show stopper when it came to using Section 106, which is based on National Register eligibility, to protect sacred sites.

The response from those hoping to use the Section 106 process in this way was twofold: creation of a new National Register Bulletin on evaluating and documenting traditional cultural properties (Parker and King 1990) and lobbying for an amendment to the NHPA stating that places of religious *and* cultural significance to Indian tribes and Native Hawaiians *could* be found eligible to the National Register. The emphasis on combined cultural and religious significance was intended to avoid the "establishment clause" constitutional issue that had created the religious exception in the first place.

One of the interesting things about this two-pronged approach to solving the problem is that National Register Bulletin 38, which defines a traditional cultural property as

> a district, site, building, structure, or object that is eligible for inclusion in the National Register of Historic Places because of its association with cultural practices or beliefs of a living community that (a) are rooted in that community's history, and (b) are important in maintaining the continuing cultural identity of the community [Parker and King 1990:1].

is more inclusive than the later NHPA amendment. Bulletin 38 says that all kinds of traditional communities may have historically important places that meet the definition of a traditional cultural property. The 1992 amendment, however, is restricted to places of religious and cultural significance to Indian tribes and Native Hawaiian organizations.

In 1992 we had an entirely new property type (with its own National Register bulletin, no less) that had to be considered in the Section 106 process. And we had a number of important new provisions in NHPA, including one authorizing tribes to take over the role of the SHPO on tribal lands. It was clear that another major revision of the Section 106 regulation would be needed. When the process began, I don't think any of us imagined that it would take more than seven years, but it did.

The 1999 Section 106 Regulation

Most people also didn't think that promulgation of the revised regulation would result in a major lawsuit, but that happened as well (*National Mining Association v. Slater* in the U.S. District Court for the District of Columbia and *National Mining Association v. John M. Fowler, et al.*, in the U.S. Court of Appeals). As a result of these suits (and through a series of legal machinations that only we Section 106 wonks and a small army of attorneys really understand or care about), the 1999 regulation has undergone several relatively minor amendments. The most current version was published in the Federal Register in 2004. The basic provisions of 36 CFR Part 800, however, are still those of the version published in 1999, so I will use that date to refer to the current regulation.

There are a number of important differences between the provisions of the 1999 regulation and those of the 1986 version. As mentioned previously, the provision for turning an "adverse effect" finding for an undertaking into a "no adverse effect" finding by carrying out an approved data recovery program was removed. The main impact of this change for archaeologists has been that all undertakings involving mitigation of adverse effects through data recovery now require notification to the ACHP that the undertaking will have an adverse effect and development of an MOA.

Another major change concerns participation by the ACHP in review of standard Section 106 cases. The 1979 regulation not only provided for Council staff review of all undertakings that affected historic properties, but provided a process for review by a subcommittee or even the full ACHP at the discretion of the Council's Executive Director. The 1986 version provided for staff review of all "adverse effects" and "no adverse effects" but called for full ACHP review only in unusual circumstances. The 1999 regulation largely withdraws even the Council staff from case-by-case Section 106 review. Undertakings that have "no adverse effect" are no longer subject to ACHP review unless there is a dispute. As for "adverse effect" undertakings, when the ACHP is notified by an agency about an undertaking that will have an adverse effect, staff use a set of criteria established in Appendix A of the regulation to decide whether to participate in consultations about resolving those effects or not. In general, it has become relatively rare for the ACHP staff to participate in these consultations, and the full ACHP becomes involved only in high-profile cases or in situations where consultations have reached an impasse.

It is no surprise, given the major thrust of the 1992 NHPA amendments, that the most significant changes in the 1999 regulation have had to do with Native American participation. As a proxy measure for the magnitude of the change, we might note that the 1979 regulation used the words "Indian tribes" only once, and viewed tribes as a subset of "the public." The 1986 regulation recognized the unique legal status of tribes as separate from the public or even other types of interested parties and used the words "Indian tribe" or "tribe" 23 times. But the 1999 regulation contains the words "Indian tribe" more than 100 times (and somewhat ironically, "the public" appears only 63 times).

Section 106 and Sacred Sites

No one asked my opinion at the time, but if they had, I would not have recommended Section 106 as a mechanism for addressing the shortcomings of AIRFA. From a Native American perspective, Section 106 has serious shortcomings of its own. For one thing, the process requires a lot of disclosure of potentially sensitive information. Among the most inappropriate questions that one can ask about many Native American sacred sites are "Where is it?" and "Why is it important?" And the first two questions asked in the Section 106 process are "Where is it?" and "Why is it important?" Another problem is that, despite its name, the National Historic Preservation Act does not actually involve any requirement to preserve anything. So in the Section 106 process, after native practitioners have made the difficult choice to disclose sensitive information about the location and significance of a sacred site, all they get is a promise that the effects of the undertaking on that site will be "considered." Well, they don't want the adverse effects on their sacred site to be "considered"; they want their sacred site to be *preserved!* Hello??

Inclusion of sacred sites in the Section 106 process can also be problematic from an agency perspective. Federal agencies exist to carry out a particular mission, whether it is multiple-use land management or national security or provision of safe, effective transportation systems or whatever. Section 106 is, according to the 1999 regulation, a process for accommodating the needs of federal undertakings with historic preservation concerns through consultation. But because of the special needs of sacred sites—for privacy, quiet, preservation in perpetuity, etc.—accommodation between them and federal mission-related development projects is frequently impossible.

Another "round peg and square hole" aspect of this situation is that Section 106 is a process designed for "historic properties," that is, districts, sites, buildings, structures, or objects that are listed on or eligible for listing on the National Register of Historic Places. And sacred "sites" very often occur at the scale of enormous landscapes hundreds of square miles in extent, again making accommodation with the needs of federal undertakings extremely problematic. Indeed, many native belief systems include the notion that the whole earth and everything on it is sacred, making any modern development problematic and rendering questions about discrete sacred "sites" or individual traditional cultural properties nonsensical to some extent.

Nevertheless, the most recent version of 36 CFR Part 800 requires us, in no uncertain terms, to find solutions to these problems. Additionally, as anthropologists, CRM archaeologists want to make the best possible use of the opportunities that Section 106 offers to afford some protection to vulnerable religious and cultural sites. And when it works, when an important sacred site actually *is* preserved as a result of this less-than-perfect regulatory fit, we have a tremendously rewarding outcome for all parties.

So What about CRM and NAGPRA?

One of The SAA Press's reviewers for this book commented, very reasonably, that "NAGPRA is central to much of this volume, but no one talks specifically about its impact on CRM and how that might differ from its impact on non-CRM archaeology." I'm not sure what he or she thought the answer would be, but I suspect that this reviewer, like most of our academic colleagues, will be surprised by my response.

Nobody talked about it because NAGPRA has relatively little impact on CRM archaeology, especially in the eastern U.S., where the amount of federal and tribal land is miniscule. Remember that unlike NHPA and NEPA, NAGPRA applies only on federal and tribal land. Even in the West, where the proportion of such lands is much greater, most CRM projects intersect with NAGPRA only if Native American burials (and quite rarely, items of cultural patrimony) are encountered during testing or data recovery, triggering compliance with Section 3. Even then, however, because of tribal sovereignty and the government-to-government nature of legally mandated consultation, the federal agency carries out the consultations and compliance, so that the average CRM practitioner has almost no involvement with NAGPRA.

Which brings me to the Great Exception: CRM archaeologists who are employed by federal agencies, particularly land-managing agencies. Many federal archaeologists spend considerable amounts of their time in consultations with Native Americans and have been consulting with tribes since the passage of AIRFA in 1978 and especially since the passage of the Archeological Resources Protection Act (ARPA) in 1979. The 1986 version of the Section 106 regulation increased the amount of consultation that took place, as did NAGPRA in 1990, the amendments to NHPA in 1992, the executive orders on Indian sacred sites in 1996 and on consultation with tribes in 2000, and especially the 1999 revision of the Section 106 regulation. Tribal consultation is a major component of current-day CRM archaeology, but this is largely because of the requirements of the Section 106 regulation; NAGPRA plays only a limited role. And because both federal agencies and tribes tend to take the government-to-government nature of their relationship very seriously, most CRM archaeologists—for most CRM projects—have limited involvement in the consultation process beyond implementing the agreements that are reached as a result of it.

Section 106, Archaeology, and Challenges for the Future

One of the things that writing this essay has made clear to me is the danger of prognostication. As I have looked back on where we were in the CRM world at the time of SAA's 50th anniversary, I would not have anticipated (and in fact did not anticipate!) many of the directions in which the field has gone. Prognostication is the order of the day, however, so I will make a brave attempt. The Section 106 process has historically been *pulled* in new directions by internal trends arising from the regulation—review bottlenecks or lessened involvement by the ACHP, for example—and *pushed* in new directions by external political and economic trends, and I would expect both of these forces to shape the next 25 years.

By far the most striking internal trend arising from the 1999 regulation has been the greatly increased involvement of Native Americans in the Section 106 process. This involvement has given rise to a number of challenges that native people, archaeologists, and federal agencies will need to work together to solve. One of these I have already touched upon: the landscape-sized scale of sacred "sites" in the worldview of many tribes. How are agencies to go about finding an accommodation between the needs of development projects and historic preservation concerns about a 1,000-square-mile historic property for which no mitigation of adverse effects is possible?

The other challenge that arises from this landscape scale of concerns has to do with the identification of historic properties. Because the National Register is designed around sites, districts, structures, buildings, and objects, we are used to thinking small when it comes to historic properties. The tendency in Section 106, when faced with an enormous, landscape-scale concern, is to draw an arbitrary boundary around an area encompassing the proposed development project and then interview elders and others about traditional cultural properties *within* that bounded space (Silliman and Ferguson, this volume).

What often happens next is that all of the concerns about the sacredness of the entire enormous landscape and about the threats that this landscape faces from a myriad of factors become focused on that one, small bounded space and the proposed development project right in the center of it. Our ethnographic process under Section 106 is creating sacred "sites" that are hugely significant because they embody all of the sacredness of a landscape hundreds or thousands of times bigger than the arbitrarily bounded space. And these newly minted sacred sites quickly become reified, especially in the views of the media and anti-development groups, who decry the monumental insensitivity of a proposed development project "right in the middle" of Tribe X's most sacred place. Well, of *course* it is in the middle; the bounded space was drawn specifically to surround the development project! We have to find a way to deal with identification and assessment of effects at the scale of the property of concern—the landscape itself.

Another challenge for archaeologists is the issue of balance between the valid claims and concerns of native people and our professional obligation to the archaeological record and to the broader American public. We've seen a huge pendulum swing from the 1979 regulation, which gave Indian tribes a single, "also-ran" mention as a subset of the public, to the current situation where, for example, the ACHP's recently adopted policy on the treatment of human remains is based entirely on Native American views. Despite strenuous efforts, SAA and the Society for Historical Archaeology were unable to secure inclusion of even a single principle in that ACHP policy reflecting the value of scientific analysis of human remains or substantially acknowledging that a large proportion of the human remains recovered during Section 106 projects are Euroamericans, African Americans, or others of non-Native American descent.

This issue of balance also arises in intellectual property claims by tribes wishing to control dissemination of archaeological data recovered with federal money and/or from federal lands. In addition to issues about control of data, requests for reburial or repatriation of entire archaeological assemblages, sometimes without analysis, are becoming increasingly common. Some archaeologists (e.g., Zimmerman 2006) have encouraged their colleagues to give up their heavy emphasis on scientific methods and interpretations and rely more on Indigenous knowledge. Others (e.g., McGhee 2008) argue that faith-based knowledge systems and empirically based knowledge systems cannot be amalgamated without diminishing both. We need to work together to find a center point in this pendulum's arc, and clearly this is a challenge that will shape CRM's and SAA's next 25 years.

The external political and economic "push" that will shape the direction of Section 106 and CRM archaeology in the near future is coming into focus even as we are completing the chapters of this book in the late fall of 2008. In less than two months a new administration will come to Washington emphasizing economic recovery and energy independence. One of the likely mechanisms for economic recovery will be massive investment in infrastructure—rebuilding and repairing our transportation systems, our schools, our hospitals. Impacts on archaeology and other kinds of historic properties from new construction and from rehabilitation of historic bridges, buildings, and structures will be substantial.

Energy independence will involve major investments in conventional oil and gas exploration and development, the search for better and cleaner approaches to coal power and nuclear power, and incentives for investment in alternative energy sources. One of the things that many individuals and organizations who are pushing for alternative energy have not really considered is the huge environmental and historic preservation related impacts of those energy developments and their associated new power lines and other ancillary facilities. Solar farms, for example, will have substantial, unavoidable impacts on archaeological sites.

The need to move these economic and energy-related projects forward rapidly will put great pressure on federal planning and environmental compliance programs. We have a system that has become very bureaucratic and inflexible, and we are going to be asked to "change," to be more flexible and creative and contribute to the solution of our country's most pressing problems.

Conclusions

There is a reason why legislative and regulatory initiatives are specifically mentioned in the bylaws of the Society for American Archaeology and why the Government Affairs Program is considered one of the core member service programs of the SAA. Archaeological remains are fragile, nonrenewable, and vulnerable to disturbance from development, looting, and vandalism. The archaeological record contains a vast library of information about the past and about the human experience in the Americas over a thousand generations. Legal protections are essential if archaeologists, whether we work in academia or CRM or other fields within the profession, are to continue learning from this rich and irreplaceable record and sharing its remarkable stories with the American public over the next 25 years.

References Cited

Davis, Hester A.
   2010   Archaeologists Looked to the Future in the Past. In *Archaeology and Cultural Resource Management: Visions for the Future*, edited by Lynne Sebastian and William D. Lipe. SAR Press, Santa Fe, in press.

Ferguson, T. J.
   1999   NHPA: Changing the Role of Native Americans in the Archaeological Study of the Past. *SAA Bulletin* 17(1):33–37.

King, Thomas F.
   1998   *Cultural Resource Laws & Practice: An Introductory Guide.* AltaMira Press, Walnut Creek, California.
   2000   *Federal Planning and Historic Places: The Section 106 Process*. AltaMira Press, Walnut Creek, California.

Little, Barbara J. (editor)
   2002   *Public Benefits of Archaeology.* University Press of Florida, Gainesville.

McGhee, Robert
   2008   Aboriginalism and the Problems of Indigenous Archaeology. *American Antiquity* 73:579–597.

National Park Service
   1997   How to Apply the National Register Criteria for Evaluation. *National Register Bulletin 15*. National Park Service, Washington, D.C.

Parker, Patricia L., and Thomas F. King
   1990 Guidelines for Evaluating and Documenting Traditional Cultural Properties. *National Register Bulletin 38*. National Park Service, Washington, D.C.

Sebastian, Lynne
   2002 Preserving America's Past: Supplemental Materials on Cultural Resource Management and Federal Historic Preservation Laws. SAA's M.A.T.R.I.X. Project. Electronic document, http://www.indiana.edu/~arch/saa/matrix/01/SAAcurriculum.pdf
   2010 Deciding What Matters: Archaeology, Eligibility, and Significance. In *Archaeology and Cultural Resource Management: Visions for the Future*, edited by Lynne Sebastian and William D. Lipe. SAR Press, Santa Fe, in press.

Zimmerman, Larry J.
   2006 Sharing Control of the Past. In *Archaeological Ethics,* edited by Karen D. Vitelli and Chip Colwell-Chanthaphonh, pp. 170–175. 2nd ed. AltaMira Press, Walnut Creek, California.

9

NAGPRA and Indigenous Peoples: The Social Context and Controversies, and the Transformation of American Archaeology

MICHAEL WILCOX

Even today when supposedly great strides have been made to recognize the rights of Indians to recover the skeletal remains of their ancestors and to repossess items of sacred value or cultural patrimony, the wishes of Native Americans are often ignored by the scientific community. In cases where Native Americans have attempted to regain items that were inappropriately alienated from the tribe, they have often been met with resistance from museums.... The bill before us is not about the validity of museums or the value of scientific inquiry, rather, it is about human rights.... for museums that have dealt in good faith with Native Americans, this legislation will have little effect. For museums and institutions which have consistently ignored the requests of Native Americans, the legislation will give Native Americans greater ability to negotiate.

[Statement of Senator Inouye, 136 Congressional Record S17174, Daily Edition, October 26th 1990].

It is impossible to overestimate the impact of NAGPRA upon the profession of archaeology. For many of us who entered the field after 1990, there is a clear distinction between the kind of archaeology practiced before NAGPRA (Public Law 601-101) and the kind of archaeology practiced today. In many ways NAGPRA reflects dramatic changes in American attitudes about the 4.5 million Native Americans in the United States. Passed by a unanimous vote in House and Senate and signed into law by a Republican President (G.H.W. Bush), NAGPRA was presented to the American public by Senators Inouye and McCain as human rights legislation (Trope and Echo-Hawk 1992:22). The law recognizes tribal consent as a precondition of archaeological research on tribal lands and requires consultation with tribes on all federal lands. Further, NAGPRA required that all museums and universities receiving federal funds, except for the Smithsonian Institution which has its own repatriation law, make inventories of their collections and send summaries of all Native American sacred and ceremonial objects, objects of cultural patrimony and unassociated funerary items to tribes most likely to be affiliated with those items.

Human remains were to be similarly inventoried and lists of those remains were to be sent to "culturally affiliated" tribes. Private collections were exempted and tribes recognized by the states (but not the federal government), were not covered by the law. The determination of cultural affiliation, sacredness, and what cultural patrimony is were left largely undefined. The ambiguity in the law has raised a number of important questions for both archaeologists and Native Americans: Can the materials collected and analyzed by archaeologists provide links between modern Native Americans and their more remote ancestors? Do changes in material culture signal cultural transformations and adaptations or do they signal the migration or incorporation of new communities? Can modern ethnic classifications be projected backward into the past? Are archaeologists to assume that Native Americans originated in the New World (as some tribes maintain) and have inhabited the same landscapes since time immemorial? Should an overwhelmingly Anglo-American community of scholars be called upon to define the parameters of Native American culture? Given the lack of communication between archaeologists and Native Americans for much of the twentieth century, how could archaeologists determine cultural continuity with groups many had never really met or interacted with? There was simply no formal training to prepare archaeologists to do this type of work or to answer these types of questions. Adding to the difficulties faced by archaeologists were the often angry polemical tracts written by Native American scholars such as Vine Deloria (1969, 1970, 1992). Deloria's positions often saddled contemporary archaeologists with the sins of our intellectual ancestors and ignored the important roles archaeologists have played as conservators, advocates, and scholars of Native American cultures. Still, determining the relationships between contemporary peoples and the past, the social, historical, and political contexts of archaeological practice, and the role of memory and myth in the construction of human identities were not among the "Big Questions" of Americanist archaeology in 1990.

Although it is certainly true that archaeologists were active in negotiating the language of the law, repatriation as a concept was not initiated by a ground swell of support from within the discipline (Zimmerman 1989:60–67; Zimmerman et al. 2003). Crafted in consultation with Native Americans, NAGPRA was not motivated by any internal theoretical movement within the field. Nor was there much support for revisions to the SAA's 1986 Statement Concerning the Treatment of Human Remains:

> Whatever their ultimate disposition, all human remains should receive appropriate scientific study, should be responsibly and carefully conserved and should be accessible only for legitimate scientific or educational purposes. The SAA opposes universal or indiscriminate reburial of human remains, either from ongoing excavations or from extant collections. …The scientific importance of human remains should be determined by their potential to aid in present and future research [Society for American Archaeology Executive Committee 1986:7–8].

The idea that archaeologists should enumerate and make explicit the historical connections between Native Americans and the archaeological resources of North America with the goal of repatriating materials to living Native American groups was interpreted by the leadership of the SAA and some of its members as a threat to the future of the discipline—or as a return to a kind of archaeology discredited and abandoned by proponents of processual or "scientific" archaeology. These concerns were raised privately and publicly in a number of articles reflecting a wide range of beliefs on NAGPRA and what it would mean for the future of archaeology (Buikstra 1981; Clark 1996; Goldstein and Kintigh 1990, Meighan 1984, 1992; Willey 1981:26).[1]

It is not surprising, then, that nearly 20 years since its passage that the SAA, represented in the pages of *American Antiquity*, in our annual meetings, and in the public pronouncements of elected leaders, presents a discipline moving in two distinct directions. On one hand, many archaeologists now communicate and interact closely with Indian tribes in virtually every phase of research—often finding themselves working in much the same manner as ethnographers did in the late nineteenth and early twentieth centuries (Silliman and Ferguson, this volume). Oral history projects, collaborative research, nondestructive analysis, low-impact mapping projects, and conservation are all at the heart of a lot of contemporary archaeological fieldwork. Museums, once some of the most vocal critics of NAGPRA (museum workers had nightmares of artifacts flying off the shelves and back into the ground), now regularly consult with and develop educational and collaborative programs with Native Americans. Having worked on the Repatriation Committee at Harvard's Peabody Museum (1993–1999), I was witness to a wholesale transformation in attitude and relationship between the museum and Native Americans. This dialogue was as good for the health of the museum community as it was for Native Americans. Unfortunately, for many museums, it was the first time this kind of communication had taken place.

Notions of what constitutes fieldwork and even the location of the field itself have been radically transformed since 1990 (Pauketat and Meskell, this volume). Archaeological projects often begin with discussions with tribal councils and governors, community representatives, elders, and educators. Talking with people, and learning about the history of a community, as well as the actions or misdeeds of one's professional ancestors, are all a part of contemporary fieldwork. Government archaeologists, museum workers, and contract archaeologists have been at the forefront of this shift in archaeological practice. Other archaeologists, some of whom enjoyed unrestricted access to very large collections of human remains in museums and other large institutions, have continued to fight repatriation. Members of this more conservative group have at times assumed a reactionary position vis-à-vis NAGPRA, have engaged in legal battles with Native Americans and have dominated both public and academic discourse—often positioning themselves as defenders of scientific research, as stewards of "the archaeological record," and as scholars most responsible for articulating universal narratives of humankind (Goldstein and Kintigh 1990; McGhee 2008; Meighan 1984,1992). This split is most noticeable in the governance of the SAA, in the recognition (and non-recognition) of what constitutes legitimate research in our journal *American Antiquity*, and in the recent phenomenon of litigation and press releases by the SAA in support of "archaeological litigation."

Despite these more confrontational actions, the legal processes initiated by consultation have also helped generate the development of a whole generation of Indigenous archaeologists who work as Tribal Historical Preservation Officers ("Tipoes"), as professionals within tribal or CRM companies, and as students who have entered the ranks of academic archaeology. One could argue that NAGPRA was part of a larger social movement calling for the inclusion of Native Americans in the representation of their cultures (see Sebastian, this volume). Ultimately these changes represent a significant shift in what has become a more open and less insular archaeology—a discipline that is more responsive to a larger population of stakeholders and whose intellectual vitality is capable of both self criticism and theoretical and methodological innovation.

Acknowledging the Political in Archaeological Research

While much of the antiquities legislation of the early twentieth century facilitated the development of the professional field of archaeology, the passage of NAGPRA represented a dramatic shift in the recognition of Native Americans as equal partners in the management of archaeological resources. It may come as some surprise to learn that the same laws that helped launch the industry of cultural resource management (CRM) and expanded the membership of the SAA, would eventually lead to the passage of NAGPRA (see Sebastian, this volume). But once the subjects of cultural and religious significance were raised in the 1986 amendments to Section 106 and Native Americans were acknowledged as "stakeholders" (a term rarely heard in archaeological circles before), a legal path was cleared for the passage of NAGPRA. The right to study, interpret, represent, and curate the remains of human cultures continues to be the primary mission of archaeology. And although much of the language used in defense of archaeologists as stakeholders emphasizes "scientific interests" in relation to Native American "spiritual claims," these rhetorical positions tend to marginalize historical and ethnographic analysis as legitimate forms of archaeological research (ironically the same lines of evidence used to make connections between contemporary peoples and the past). They also create an oppositional relationship between *science* and *religion* and *scientific evidence* vs. *Native American religious values.* The equation or conflation of archaeology with science (exclusively) obscures a whole range of beliefs among archaeologists about the nature of contemporary archaeological research, mischaracterizes Native American beliefs about science (and religion), and ignores the prominent role archaeologists have played in the representation of Native American culture and history. Fortunately, contemporary archaeology is much more accommodating and open to collaboration and communication with Native Peoples and descendent communities now than it has been in the past. At the time that NAGPRA was passed, many archaeologists justifiably considered themselves to be great advocates of Native American culture and history (many still are). But little of the training archaeologists received then (and in some institutions still do) had anything to say about the informative potential of communication with contemporary Indians.

Isolated from descendent communities, archaeologists saw themselves as stewards of more authentic, ancestral versions of Indian culture. For some archaeologists cultural authenticity is rooted in technological or religious performance (can you still make or do you still use object x?).

Many of these assumptions are cultural constructs and many of the thornier or messier issues raised by NAGPRA are best understood as emanating from American stereotypes about Native Americans (or Indigenous Peoples) in general. The lack of interaction is explained in part by the nature of archaeological data and partially by the invocation of archaeology as a purely scientific practice.

Do the Data Talk Back?

Throughout the twentieth century, archaeologists had enjoyed unrestricted access to archaeological materials and resources for a few simple reasons: (1) artifacts and sites did not "talk back" to archaeologists in the same manner that ethnographic subjects had (at least not yet); (2) Native Americans lacked the political power and educational credentials to negotiate on equal terms with government agencies, universities, museums, and archaeologists; and (3) archaeological data was a "material" that could be conceived of, conserved, alienated, and protected as property. The same could not be said for ethnographic projects. Negotiated interactions play a much larger role in ethnographic research. Contemporary human subjects protocols require an explicit consideration of the effects of research upon a community. The crises of representation that had challenged social and cultural anthropologists to question the power imbalances between scholar and anthropological subject had been safely avoided by proponents of the New Archaeology (Clifford 1988; Geertz 1983; Hodder 1986; Marcus and Fischer 1986).

The position (and self-representation) of archaeologists as "scientists" provided a powerful and enduring barrier to criticisms leveled by Native Americans, but that same insularity had failed to generate widespread public support or sympathy for the exclusive rights of archaeologists over human remains.[2] Juxtaposed with the legacy of the scientific racism of the nineteenth century (see Senator Inouye's testimony), this rhetorical strategy was no match for the powerful symbolism of human rights struggles invoked by Indian activists and lawyers. Borrowing from the organizational scripts of the civil rights movements of the 1960s, Native Americans began to assert a larger political presence in the disposition and treatment of human remains and cultural properties in the late 1960s. Using the GI Bill, many veterans of World War II broke down barriers to higher education. Urban migrations and federal termination policies of the 1950s brought more students into contact with the dynamic culture of 1960s activism. The passage of AIRFA (The American Indian Religious Freedom Act 1978) was accomplished by the same kinds of pan-ethnic social awareness generated during this time. For Native American leaders such as Suzanne Harjo, Walter R. Echo-Hawk Jr., and James Riding In (each of whom continues to be involved in NAGPRA implementation), NAGPRA is an extension of the activist movements generated in the zeitgeist of the 1960s (Riding In et al. 2004).

The exuberance of the 1960s was reflected in the self-confidence and iconoclasm of the New Archaeology—critical self-reflection was not among its stronger attributes. The search for universal narratives of human social and cultural evolution led archaeologists deeper into quantitative analyses of technology, material, and environment, but often did so at the expense of local histories. By the 1980s a whole generation of archaeologists had been trained to regard contemporary Native Americans as largely irrelevant in the interpretation of the past. This attitude has persisted through several decades of archaeological theorizing—spanning from Binford's (1967) rejection of historical analysis to Upham's (1987) rejection of ethnographic information in the study of Pueblo prehistory. The search for connections between contemporary Indians and the past (the much maligned Direct Historical Approach) was abandoned as passé by the late 1970s. With only few exceptions (Deloria 1992; Echo-Hawk 2000; Sprague 1974; Watkins 2003), discussions with contemporary Indians about the practice of archaeology have had a comparatively limited visibility within the pages of *American Antiquity*.

This dissonance could not have come at a more inopportune time for North American archaeologists interested in protecting the status quo—euphemistically referred to as the "local, case by case approach" (Kintigh 1990:6). The position of the SAA prior to NAGPRA was that national legislation was not needed and that disputes over the possession, display, and interpretations of Native American artifacts and materials should be resolved by interested parties at the local level. This approach was in fact at the heart of Native American complaints. The tribes had little political or legal clout in areas where their relatively small numbers placed them at a distinct disadvantage at the state level. Nor did it address the situation where museums held large collections outside of the state in which the tribes were located. For many tribes, the local, case-by-case approach was part of the problem. By the time that repatriation legislation was introduced, archaeologists in North America were at the margins of a rapidly evolving international debate about the legacy of colonialism and the representation of Indigenous peoples in archaeological research. By 1992, the 500-year anniversary of Columbus had helped raise the political profile of Native Americans; the United Nations Declaration of 1993 as the Year of the Indigenous Person provided further momentum. Given the ease with which the spread of ideas and political power have been facilitated by technologies of connection, it seems unlikely that Indigenous Peoples will return to the largely invisible status of the early twentieth century. The increasingly sophisticated lobbying and political power exerted by tribes through water rights and gaming provide little promise that NAGPRA will be repealed or modified to reflect the interests of conservative archaeologists. If the previous (2000–2008) political climate of deregulation and lax government oversight failed to weaken NAGPRA, it seems highly unlikely that the next 25 years will provide a return to a pre-NAGPRA archaeology.

Strategies, Posturing and Protectionism, and the Future of Archaeology

Outside of the United States, the 1980s witnessed several proactive moves by archaeologists to speak to the interests and concerns of Indigenous Peoples and the political role of archaeological research within contemporary society. The development of the World Archaeological Congress in 1986 and the passage of the Vermillion Accords in South Dakota in 1989 helped set the stage for the kind of reasoned negotiation and cooperation that characterizes much of the archaeology of the post-NAGPRA age (Zimmerman 2006). The involvement of Native Americans within the SAA has expanded as the result of NAGPRA. Before 1990 there were exactly zero Native Americans employed as archaeology professors within the entire system of 2,804 American Universities. A more recent survey of the membership of the Coalition of Indigenous Archaeologists reveals 13 current Ph.Ds in archaeology, approximately 30 graduate students in various stages of training, and four Native Americans employed in tenure-track university positions. This represents a modest but significant change in American archaeology. The current membership of the SAA's Indigenous Populations Interest Group is 1,300—one of the Society's largest. The development of collaborative methods (Colwell and Ferguson 2008; Ferguson 1999; Ferguson and Colwell-Chanthaphonh 2006; Lightfoot 2005; Silliman 2008; Silliman and Ferguson, this volume) and Indigenous archaeology (Watkins 2000; Wilcox 2009) are both largely regarded as positive manifestations of repatriation dialogue and the social movements responsible for NAGPRA, but there is still significant institutional resistance to some of these changes.

To date, many of the references to these changes and much of the scholarly work regarding collaboration are found in the pages of the Society's newsletter, *The SAA Archaeological Record*. The location of reports and articles dealing with the rapidly evolving relationship between archaeologists and contemporary Indigenous Peoples is, to some, a troubling phenomenon. The section "Working Together," initiated as a forum in which examples of cooperation between Native Peoples and archaeologists could be showcased, has become the default location for many reports and articles dealing with contemporary Indigenous peoples. The belief that this type of work is either "archaeopolitics" or is somehow not regarded with the same weight as other forms of archaeological inquiry has been be interpreted by some as "a retreat to data"—an attempt by some archaeologists to "circle the wagons" and insulate archaeological scholarship in reaction to changes in a political landscape (Shepherd 2003). To date, the only article within *American Antiquity* examining Indigenous archaeology or the changes engendered by the entrance of Native Americans into the field has been highly negative (McGhee 2008).

Some of this conservatism has been reflected in the internal governance of the SAA. In the 18 years since the passage of NAGPRA, only a single Native

American has been appointed to serve on the SAA's Repatriation Committee. This appointment was made in 2008.[3] The SAA has asserted its interests through the filing of a series of *amicus briefs* (literally "friend of the court") supporting the claims of the plaintiffs in the Kennewick case (*Bonnichsen et al v. United States of America*), issuing press releases supporting such controversial issues as the Jelderk's Decision on Kennewick, and criticizing the Department of Interior's proposed rule for the Disposition of Culturally Unidentifiable Human Remains. The proposed rule was met with general approval by many tribes—and individual Native Americans. Some of the public statements by the SAA have asserted views few Native Peoples can reasonably be expected to support. A press release issued on behalf of the SAA in 2002 stated that "Judge Jelderks' decision in the Kennewick case will go a long way toward restoring the balance between the interests of science and those of Native Americans that Congress mandated when it passed NAGPRA in 1990" (SAA 2002). In addressing the controversy surrounding the return of "culturally unidentifiable" human remains, the SAA similarly released a statement asserting a more conservative interpretation of cultural affiliation: "The proposed regulations have a potential for abuse by groups that have very little connection to any sort of legitimate Indian identity . . . concerned parties should not be forced to work with groups that have a weak claim to Indian identity" (SAA 2007).

These positions locate a largely Euro-American population of archaeologists as arbiters of "authentic" and "inauthentic" claims to Indian identity—a position few archaeologists and Native Americans are comfortable with. Much of the dispute over cultural affiliation lies not in the demonstrable connections between tribes and the materials, but in the fact that many tribes were either terminated by the U.S. government in the twentieth century (but still enjoy state recognition), or as in California, are recognized by the state, but had negotiated treaties locked in a vault (and consequently never ratified) in Washington D.C. in the 1850s (Prucha 1997). These specific cases are likely to generate conflicts between archaeologists and Native Americans about the roles that archaeological and historical narratives play in the recognition of "official histories" and claims to tribal sovereignty.

The leadership of the SAA should recognize that not all of its members support either these kinds of legal decisions or their endorsement by the SAA. The academy is founded upon the belief that debate and discussion are signs of a healthy and vibrant intellectual community. Proclamations supporting only one part of the discipline's views are probably not an accurate reflection of the diversity of views within the SAA on NAGPRA (or Jelderks), nor are they particularly helpful for those of us who work with Native Americans. It is likely that the next 25 years will only witness an increase in the presence of Native Americans within the SAA. I am hopeful that the discipline will welcome these changes and explore these issues in the spirit of academic debate.

Conclusion

In examining the past 25 years of archaeological legislation one thing is clear: in 1985, no one could have envisioned the magnitude of the changes brought about by first, the revisions to Section 106, and second, the dramatic shift in the representation of Native Americans in all phases of archaeological research. Archaeology has become more responsive to a larger constituency of stakeholders. The contributions of archaeologists to the so-called Big Questions (e.g., the origin of modern humans, the development of social complexity, the role of technology and environment in human social change) are still among the most valuable contributions archaeologists can make to humankind. This is beyond dispute. But the whole notion of stakeholders calls to mind the role of archaeology within contemporary society. The questions raised by cultural anthropologists in the 1980s regarding representation, Indigenous peoples, and the importance of explicit ethical commitments are all important facets of contemporary archaeology. What is the relationship between contemporary peoples and the past? How are these relationships constructed? What role does memory or place play in the construction of human identity? How are sacredness, cultural, religious, and ethnic distinctions manifested in a material world? Will DNA clarify cultural concepts or will its application embolden new forms of racial consciousness? These are all questions raised by NAGPRA. As a discipline, we have absolutely nothing to gain by avoiding these ideas or by relegating them to the margins of "archaeopolitics." Archaeologists may consider ourselves "stewards" or "caretakers" of archaeological resources, but we should not lose sight of the fact that through analysis and interpretation, we help *create* the archaeological record. Our ability to reflect the diversity of human experiences regarding memory, the shifting nature of material meaning, heritage, the construction of cultural differences, gender, and ethnicity depend upon a greater recognition of a diverse constituency. Let's hope that the next time, we don't have to wait for a law to realize that as archaeologists, we must reflect those changes and are uniquely positioned to address these other Big Questions.

References Cited

Binford, Lewis R.
    1967   Reply to K.C. Chang's "Major Aspects of the Interrelationship of Archaeology and Ethnology." *Current Anthropology* 8:234.

Buikstra, Jane
    1981   A Specialist in Ancient Cemetery Studies Looks at the Reburial Issue. *Early Man* 3(3):26–27.

Clark, Geoffrey A.
    1996   NAGPRA and the Demon Haunted World. *Society for American Archaeology Bulletin* 14(5):3.

Clifford, James
    1988   *The Predicament of Culture: Twentieth-century Ethnography, Literature, and Art.* Harvard University Press, Cambridge.

Colwell-Chanthaphonh, Chip, and T. J. Ferguson (editors)
    2008   *Collaboration in Archaeological Practice: Engaging Descendant Communities.* AltaMira Press, Lanham, Maryland.

Deloria, Jr., Vine
    1969   *Custer Died for Your Sins: An Indian Manifesto.* Macmillan, New York.
    1970   *We Talk, You Listen: New Tribes, New Turf.* Macmillan, New York.
    1992   Indians, Archaeologists and the Future. *American Antiquity* 57:595–598.

Dye, David H.
    1989   The National Museum of the American Indian: Reburial and Repatriation. *Bulletin of the Society for American Archaeology* 7(6):5.

Echo-Hawk, Roger
    2000   Ancient History in the New World: Integrating Oral Traditions and the Archaeological Record in Deep Time. *American Antiquity* 65:267–290.

Ferguson, T. J.
    1999   NHPA: Changing the Role of Native Americans in the Archaeological Study of the Past. *SAA Bulletin* 17(1):33–37.

Ferguson, T. J., and Chip Colwell-Chanthaphonh
    2006   *History is in the Land: Multivocal Tribal Traditions in Arizona's San Pedro Valley.* University of Arizona Press. Tucson.

Geertz, Clifford
    1983   *Local Knowledge: Further Essays in Interpretive Anthropology.* Basic Books, New York.

Goldstein, Lynne, and Keith Kintigh
    1990   Ethics and the Reburial Controversy. *American Antiquity* 55:585–591.

Hodder, Ian
   1986 *Reading the Past: Current Approaches to Interpretation in Archaeology.* Cambridge University Press, Cambridge and New York.

Kintigh, Keith
   1990 A Perspective on Reburial and Repatriation. *Bulletin of the Society for American Archaeology* 8(2):6–7.

Lightfoot, Kent G.
   2005 *Indians, Missionaries, and Merchants: The Legacy of Colonial Encounters on the California Frontiers.* University of California Press, Berkeley.

Lovis, William A.
   1990 How Far Will it Go? A Look at S. 1980 and Other Repatriation Legislation. *Bulletin of the Society for American Archaeology* 8(2):8-10.

Marcus, George E., and Michael M. J. Fischer
   1986 *Anthropology as Cultural Critique: An Experimental Moment in the Human Sciences.* University of Chicago Press, Chicago.

McGhee, Robert
   2008 Aboriginalism and the Problems of Indigenous Archaeology. *American Antiquity* 73:579–597.

Meighan, C. W.
   1984 Archaeology: Science or Sacrilege? *Ethics and Values in Archaeology,* edited by Ernestene L. Green, pp. 208–223. The Free Press, London.
   1992 Some Scholars' Views on Reburial. *American Antiquity.*57:704–710.

Plog, Stephen, and Don Rice
   1990 Redefining the Nature of American Archaeology. *Bulletin of the Society for American Archaeology* 8(2):1.

Prucha, Francis Paul
   1997 *American Indian Treaties: The History of a Political Anomaly.* University of California Press. Berkeley.

Reid, J. J.
   1992 Editor's Corner: Recent Findings on North American Prehistory. *American Antiquity* 57:195–196.

Riding In, James, Walter Echo-Hawk, Suzan Shown Harjo, and Cal Seciwa
   2004 Protecting Native American Human Remains, Burial Grounds and Sacred Places (panel discussion). *Wicazo Sa Review* 19(2):169–183.

Shepherd, Nick
   2003 State of the Discipline: Science, Culture and Identity in South African Archaeology, 1870–2003. *Journal of Southern African Studies* 29:823–844.

Silliman Stephen (editor)
   2008 *Collaborating at the Trowel's Edge: Teaching and Learning in Indigenous Archaeology.* Amerind Studies in Archaeology 2. University of Arizona Press, Tucson.

Society for American Archaeology Executive Committee
   1986 SAA Statement Concerning the Treatment of Human Remains. *Bulletin of the Society for American Archaeology* 4(3):7–8.

Society for American Archaeology
   2002 SAA Responds to the Kennewick Man Court Decision. Society for American

Archaeology. http://www.saa.org/repatriation/KennewickPressRelease.html.

2007 Society for American Archaeology Statement on Department of Interior Proposed Rule For the Disposition of Culturally Unidentifiable Human Remains and Funerary Objects. http://www.saa.org/repatriation/index.html.

Sprague, R.
  1974 American Indians and American Archaeology. *American Antiquity* 39:1–2.

Trope, Jack, and Walter Echo-Hawk
  1992 The Native American Graves Protection and Repatriation Act: Background and Legislative History. *Arizona State Law Journal* 24(1:)35–77.

Upham, Steadman
  1987 The Tyranny of Ethnographic Analogy. In Coasts, Plains, and Deserts: Essays in Honor of Reynold J. Ruppé, edited by Sylvia W. Gaines, pp. 265–279. *Anthropological Research Papers*, No. 38, Arizona State University, Tempe.

Watkins, Joe
  2000 *Indigenous Archaeology: American Indian Values and Scientific Practice*. AltaMira Press, Walnut Creek, California.
  2003 Beyond the Margin: American Indians, First Nations, and Archaeology in North America. *American Antiquity* 68:273–285.

Wilcox, Michael V.
  2009 *The Pueblo Revolt and the Mythology of Conquest: Indigenous Archaeology and the Narratives of Contact*. University of California Press, Berkeley.

Willey, P.
  1981 Another View by One of the Crow Creek Researchers. *Early Man* 3(3):26.

Zimmerman, Larry J.
  1989 Made Radical by My Own: An Archaeologist Learns to Understand Reburial. In *Conflict in the Archaeology of Living Traditions,* edited by Robert Layton, pp. 60–67. Unwin Hyman, London.
  2006 Sharing Control of the Past. In *Archaeological Ethics,* second edition, edited by Karen D. Vitelli and Chip Colwell-Chanthaphonh, pp. 170–175. AltaMira Press, Walnut Creek, California.

Zimmerman, Larry J., Karen D. Vitelli, and Julia J. Hollowell-Zimmer (editors)
  2003 *Ethical Issues in Archaeology*. AltaMira Press, Walnut Creek, California.

Notes

1. Kintigh, as a representative of the SAA in NAGPRA negotiations reasserted the position of the SAA's 1986 statement in 1990 (6–7). See also statements by *SAA Bulletin* Editors Dye (1989:1–2, 5) and Plog and Rice (1990:1). On behalf of the SAA, Dye stated in reaction to a nationally mandated piece of legislation that, "The SAA . . . argues that the section of the legislation dealing with repatriation needs revision" (1989:5). William Lovis, Chair of the SAA's Government Affairs Committee, was less than sanguine about the future of archaeological research should the "Inouye" and "McCain/Udall" bills (which eventually became NAGPRA) pass (1990:8–10).

2. See Reid (1992:195) for an unvarnished assessment of archaeological public relations with regard to Native Americans. See also a Harris Poll conducted in 2000 regarding public perceptions of archaeology (http://www.saa.org/pubRel/publiced-poll.html).

3. The Repatriation Committee, like many other committees in the SAA, has the authority to recommend its own members, who are then appointed by the President. The recent appointment reflects some lobbying on the part of the SAA's Native American community.

10

Changing Theoretical Directions in American Archaeology

TIMOTHY R. PAUKETAT *and* LYNN MESKELL

While the 1980s and 1990s were marked by epistemic debates over processual or postprocessual positions, such oppositions have ebbed in the 2000s and are seen by many as irrelevant to ongoing theoretical developments in archaeology as conducted through American institutions (Hegmon 2003; Hodder 2004; Pauketat 2008; VanPool and VanPool 2003). These older divisions were often constituted around a set of bifurcations including objectivity:subjectivity, data:theory, or science:humanism. Since then, debate has given way to a new openness, with theoretical diversity seen to hold the potential for productive cross-fertilizations of thought (Hodder 2001). Such reframing of division into opportunity has occurred in tandem with developments in approach and fieldwork, in turn inextricably linked to cultural heritage concerns at a global scale.

This chapter examines the changing theoretical directions in American archaeology, and underscores the point that data collection, theory building, and heritage development are no longer discrete practices. Rather, their permeable nature has given rise to an exciting and innovative time in archaeology. American archaeologists now routinely venture into other social domains, in part because of geopolitics, not incidentally the particular North and South American histories of colonization, genocide, and indigenous movements (Colwell-Chanthaphonh and Ferguson 2004, 2008; Ferguson and Colwell-Chanthaphonh 2006; Stoffle et al. 2001).

These developments have spurred on new and compelling field projects and insights that are, in turn, producing more rigorous accounts and generating innovative interpretations that move the discipline forward (Edgar et al. 2007; Fine-Dare 2002, 2005; Preucel 2002; Watkins 2001). This positions American archaeology somewhat differently to our British colleagues who have not negotiated such histories and indigenous communities at home. However, recent developments in English Heritage strongly suggest a desire to emulate American practices of repatriation and collaboration, even though theirs are not indigenous claimants but pagan ones (Blain and Wallis 2007; Thackery and Payne 2008). Perhaps the realization of these rich potentials in American archaeology, derived from dialogue and collaboration across a range of communities, mark a real turning point.

To illustrate this directional change, and with the aid of some practical applications, we underline a specific series of interrelated or clustered research foci that connect past and present and theory and practice. For present purposes, we focus on notions of object biography and structured deposition and their links to landscape, phenomenology, materiality, and agency. In the end, we argue that pursuing these and other related foci is producing a more seamless practical, theoretical, and ethical archaeology that is an outgrowth of the disparate alternative archaeologies that exist today.

Theoretical Perspectives

In the 1990s, American archaeology remained entrenched within a social-evolutionary paradigm despite calls to the contrary (Brumfiel 1992; Gronenborn 2006; Pauketat 2007; Paynter and McGuire 1991; Yoffee and Sherratt 1993). Meanwhile, the theoretical innovations that characterized British archaeology, strongly identified with what might be termed postprocessual, contextual, interpretive, or social archaeologies, have continued in the same vein for over a decade now. Topics such as landscape, phenomenology, depositional practice, agency, and embodiment, to name a selection, remain central in British archaeological theory (Bender 2001; Bradley 2000; Brück 2007; Jones 2005; Pollard 2001; Robb 2007; Thomas 1996).

Increasingly, American archaeologists have become engaged with these same issues and have applied a broad swath of theoretical approaches to complex data sets in both preliterate and historical domains (Ashmore and Knapp 1999; Dillehay 2004; Joyce 2001; Kuijt 2008; Loren 2001; Meskell and Joyce 2003; Nakamura 2005; Nassaney 2004; Pauketat 2007; Preucel

2002; Van Dyke and Alcock 2003). As recent research underscores, it is no longer the case that single-issue themes such as gender, landscape, or ethnicity are sufficient (Meskell 2002a), a shift that has prompted archaeologists to adopt multiple lines of enquiry (see chapters in Meskell and Preucel 2004). American archaeologists are increasingly undertaking studies that combine theories about, for example, gender, practice, spatiality, and households (Hendon 2009) or ritual, place, memory, and exchange (Mills 2004). One might say that this growing theoretical awareness has been well matched by the rich and sophisticated materials of the Americas and abroad, which often makes for different projects than, say, our British colleagues.

Here, the importance of cultural resource management cannot be overestimated (Moss 2005), especially as performed by university-based programs or large private firms that place history and heritage ahead of profit (e.g., Walthall et al. 1997). The extensive multilayered data sets that such programs and firms produce, coupled with the contemporary resonances and implications of fieldwork and interpretation, make for a rather different and evocative American research trajectory.

Still, if there is one thing that might be said to underlie this trajectory, linking past and present or the archaeologies of yesterday and today, it is the essential "materiality" of social life and cultural practice (see Miller 2005). Inspired by the rise of material culture studies in Britain, these current directions were shaped by scholars at University College London (e.g., Buchli 2002; Gell 1998; Miller 1987, 1998, 2001; Tilley 1990), many of whom received archaeological training, but were also informed by classic ethnographies from American anthropology (Munn 1986; Myers 2001; Weiner 1992). Another trend in material culture studies has American roots in studies of technology and modernism (Schiffer 1999; Schiffer et al. 2003). Materiality, not materialism or materialization (e.g., DeMarrais et al. 1996), is a powerful concept that views the cultural world as necessarily composed of matter in space and similarly that our practices and experiences have a material dimension. Materiality takes as its remit the exploration of the situated experiences of material life, the constitution of the object world, and concomitantly its shaping of human experience (Meskell 2004:2). Because of this material dimensionality, individual beings are not isolated or removed from social networks, since *being* itself entails multiple interconnected agents within larger historical settings. Moreover, because experiences engage bodies, things, and other phenomena spatially, as parts of landscapes, they are contingent on the beings and happenings of that outside world. Materiality implies historicity, and thus materiality makes life happen. People, places, and things are truly active (a la Hodder 1982, 1986).

Yet not so long ago, many archaeologists would have described material culture as the *subject matter* of archaeology, a static sort of detritus in need of a theoretical approach to infuse it with meaning (Binford 1980). But nothing is further from the truth. In fact, in the last decade, the elaboration of phenomenologically inspired, practice-theoretic, agent-centered, and otherwise historicized efforts in archaeology make such theory:data distinctions moot. It is not the case that theories are separate from the material dimension of theorizing, including fieldwork; our so-called subject matter is continuously infused with theory from the beginning (see Hodder 2001; Johnson 2006; Pauketat 2001). One always enters the archaeological process midstream just as one theorizes through one's body with things in spaces.

Histories and Landscapes

As a discipline, archaeology is well placed to demonstrate that being a human, experiencing the world as a human, or even thinking as a human has a materiality that is not inert. Being, experiencing, and thinking necessitate bodies engaging landscapes of spaces and objects through sensory encounters where thought and action, as well as object and subject, are not usefully separated (Merleau-Ponty 1962). Thus, to understand the implications of materiality in these terms, one must understand it historically. The biographies, genealogies, and histories of people, places, and things—from the palimpsests of urban centers down to the growth patterns in one's bones—are not simply the residuals of cultural processes; they are cultural processes (Pauketat 2001). That is, they are accumulations that inform the now as much as they record the then. Their materiality, especially considering the relative durations of things, continues to construct the experience of the present (Kubler 1962; Nakamura 2004; Olivier 2001).

There may be no better example of this than the spate of studies that highlight the biographies of things and the chains of micro-events (Dobres 2000; Gosden and Marshall 1999; Kopytoff 1986; Meskell 2004; Mills and Walker, eds. 2008). Inspired by Marcel Mauss (1990) and, later, Annette Weiner (1985), archaeologists beginning in the 1980s recognized that the ways or sequences in which people moved and did things (e.g., cooked food, manufactured tools, built houses) possessed a sort of habituated style. Along with the cultural objects associated with such bodily movements and practices, certain things implicated places and identities (and vice versa), at least as these were genealogically configured (Bradley 2000; Costin and Wright 1998; Lemonnier 1993; Mills 2004). This is not to say that every object was endowed with special qualities or agency, or indeed that every space was sacred. Rather archaeologists have become critically attuned, whether through depositional analyses or ethnohistoric evidence, to the contexts where subjects, objects, places, and people might share a suite of salient qualities. In particular societies (such as those in the American Southwest, below) and at particular times, people, places, and things—and the practices that define them all—were understood to have inalienable qualities, with matter and meaning enchained together in larger, complex, and historically contingent webs of social experience or lifeworlds.

Even the ways in which domestic garbage is discarded, once rendered into a near biomechanical science by the original Behavioral Archaeology (Schiffer 1987), are now recognized to be recursively connected to other cultural practices and identities (Pollard 2001). In fact, the older behavioral school is actively being folded into what began as a postprocessual concern for "structured deposition" (LaMotta and Schiffer 2001; Mills and Walker 2008). From this perspective, object life histories and depositional genealogies do not merely reflect some behavioral or mental processes disconnected from depositional practices. Through repetitive depositional encounters, places and memories are instantiated and relationships of the people, places, and things within those places, or larger fields of experience, are entangled, if only momentarily. Things, it seems, make other things happen.

Such emphasis might seem diametrically opposed to other contemporary structural, evolutionary, or macrohistorical approaches in American archaeology (e.g., Beck et al. 2007; Bintliff 2004; see also Fogelin 2007; Shennan 2008). This need not be (and may not long remain) the case, especially given the common concern for understanding the importance of practical diversity, genealogies of cultural productions, and the complexity of the relational fields wherein agents derive their causal powers (see especially Ingold 2000b). Indeed, at the time of writing, intellectual differences, which sometimes boil down to a variable emphasis on fields or long-term trends versus agents or events, *characterize all camps.* There are those evolutionary, structural, and macrohistorical approaches that elevate agents and others that do not (contrast Beck et al. 2007; Bettinger 1991; Brown 2006; Kohler and

Gumerman 2000). The same is true of phenomenologically inspired or practice-theoretic approaches (contrast Bender et al. 1997; Joyce 2001).

So are various alternative approaches in archaeology moving toward an ever-greater productive juxtapositioning of theoretical approaches (sensu Hodder 2001)? Possibly, but one clear obstacle remains. Following various European philosophers, a few archaeologists have underlined the need to minimize Cartesian dualistic thinking (Meskell 1996; Thomas 1996). Much of this work was directed toward breaking down unhelpful bifurcations such as mind:body, structure:agency and subject:object as we have already mentioned and to craft a more nuanced understanding of human intentionality and sociality in the past. Debates raged around how archaeologists might access the culturally contextual understandings of the individual and personhood, emotion, experience of landscapes and monuments, and the nature of society in a host of ancient and recent settings. In the 1990s such debates were framed by the potentials or pitfalls of applying the work of social theorists such as Bourdieu (1977, 1980) and Giddens (1984) on structuration and agency to archaeological studies or Merleau-Ponty (1962) and Heidegger (1996) on embodiment, experience, and being-in-the-world. After a decade or more of debate, many archaeologists would argue that the analytical separation of mind and body, structure and agency, or theory and practice, obscures the simultaneity of practice or experience.

However, avoiding such analytical dualisms in archaeological practice remains difficult, and notions such as materialization, while intended to transcend the problem, often end up recapitulating it by prioritizing mind over matter (DeMarrais 2004; Malafouris 2004; Renfrew 2004). For example, if flintknapping stimulates neural activity in ways that alter skill generally, predisposing the knapper in other ways, then the brain is not separate from the hand or eye, and flintknapping itself is a practice with profound historical and biocultural consequences (Renfrew 2004; see also Dobres 2000). Likewise, if the sensuous experience of bodies in spaces or the manufacture, use, and deposition of cultural objects or sediments in places, disposes those bodies, things, or places in ways that alter the futures of others, then the processes of culture change and the relational fields of experience are one and the same (see case studies, below). To understand the connectivities between them, some scholars have employed theories of the "extended mind," "distributed person," or the "extended artifact" to recognize the blurred boundaries between people, places, and things (e.g., Gell 1998; Gosden 2001; Ingold 2000a; Lazzari 2005; Robb 2004; Strathern 1988).

The evocative potentials of these new theoretical approaches are not necessarily applicable to all data sets across all time and space. Nor do they eliminate the need to understand cause and effect in history (contra O'Brien and Lyman 2004). Rather, they insist on the careful and proximate delineations of contingency. Cause and effect can only be understood historically, and then only as a potentially trans-scalar and trans-dimensional relationship. That is, we must understand the biographies, genealogies, and histories of fields in the most complex of terms. For this reason, an archaeologist's pottery sequences, technological styles, and settlement palimpsests might take on whole new theoretical meaning, primarily as they are parts of such fields or landscapes. Archaeologists must be careful, however, not to treat landscapes as either places where meanings or memories have been fixed, ready to structure the minds of passersby alike (see Carmichael et al. 1994) or as impossible to fathom save as one's own experience (cf. Fleming 2006; Tilley 2004). Rather, landscapes are relational fields always in the process of becoming (Ashmore 2004; Ashmore and Knapp 1999; Thomas 2001). People do not merely interact with them, or move through them. They are part and parcel of them (Ingold 2000b).

Agents and Identities

One might also describe a landscape or a field as a "network" in Latour's (1991, 2000) words or a "causal milieu" in Gell's (1998) terms. Both thinkers understand networks to be comprised of various nodes or agents from whence change derives. To a large extent, such dynamism is a function of the materiality of networks. Following Marx (1992) and Hegel (1977), the real power and potential of the world of things is their capacity to capture so many qualities, associations, and potentials that transgress any perceived convenient boundary between material and immaterial characteristics. Such qualities, associations, and potentials are always and necessarily "bundled together" in ways that "will shift in their relative salience, value, utility, and relevance across contexts" (Keane 2005:188).

Importantly, many archaeologists today see little need to limit causal powers to human individuals. Within the larger relational fields of human experience, objects, images, substances, places, and a host of other sensory experiences (some ostensibly immaterial) have the capacity to affect that which people do, if not also the agency of other nonhuman entities, what Latour would include as "actants" (e.g., Joyce 2008; Kirk 2006; Walker 2008). Depending on the variously bundled or fragmented configurations of such nodes or agents within networks, they may exert more or less influence on, or "afford" a certain kind or direction of change within, the larger fields of concern (Gibson 1979; Ingold 2000a; Knappett 2004).

Given this inherent relationality, archaeologists might analyze the qualities of aspects or agents of landscapes much like one appreciates the power of a topographic feature. A mountain might evoke a memory, an identity, or a narrative (e.g., Basso 1996), but it also directly and differentially engages the senses in ways that alter perceptions and actions, depending on the moment and the configuration of the rest of the field. It brings thunder and rain, alters the play of light and shadow, and bars movement.

Rather than a focus on individual nodes or classes of objects, archaeologists are increasingly considering wider assemblages of technologies, objects, and places in the mesh of time-space (Gosden 2005; Lazzari 2005; Pauketat and Alt 2005). In some measure this has been inspired by new modes of theorizing archaeological science (Jones 2002) that are also receptive to an integrated theorizing of personhood, place making, aesthetics, and agency (Jones 2005; Lazzari 2003). From such modes of theorizing, it has been argued that nonhuman entities have an undertow, or a pull effect on fields. They afford certain human actions and perceptions. But they also can be politically mobilized, brought to bear on social fields through coordinated action and manifested as the theatricality of smoke and mirrors (Inomata and Coben 2006). The latter might be considered not simply in terms of affordance, and the "gathering" effects of some things or contexts, but also in terms of the dispersed and fragmented aspects of fields and their relationships to social identities.

As anticipated by the very idea of materiality, and stemming from earliest of ethnographic studies in anthropology, researchers have long recognized that human agency and identity are not located solely within the body or the body politic (Tylor 1977). They are extended into and thoroughly entangled with the larger relational fields of experience. Comparative ethnographic and historic studies underscore this point, as many peoples recognize putatively inorganic or inanimate objects and unseen forces as living or spiritual entities equal to people, erasing all distinctions between cultural, natural, and supernatural worlds (Bird-David 1999; Byrne 2007; Meskell 2005; Mills and Walker, eds. 2008). Moreover, that which constitutes a person or a community is contingent on the historical configurations of agents within its respective field. Personhood may not always be isomorphic with human bodies. It may be fragmented and dispersed across a landscape of beings, things, and places almost to the point of non-existence outside situated performances. It might be embodied in a monument, a bundle, or a building (Brück 2006; Joyce 2008; Kirk 2006; Zedeño 2008). And it might be virtually coterminous with community (e.g., Pauketat 2008).

The point is, whatever and wherever it is located, the construction of persons or communities can only be understood through the analysis of the complex relational webs and the specific and contingent qualities, associations, and potentials of the nodes, aspects, or agents of those networks. Fields, networks, and webs are enacted, embodied, and experienced in places and moments such that, depending on the juxtapositioning of encounters (sometimes described using concepts such as hybridity or alterity), great change can emerge (Alt 2006; Hall 2000; Loren 2000; Silliman 2005). Such encounters have been productively explored by a new generation of scholars writing on colonialism, indigenous identity, and embodied agency in ways that will, we contend, absorb or historicize more traditional, social-evolutionary concerns with technology, urbanism, complexity, agricultural origins, and so on.

For example, examining lithic and faunal assemblages, Stephen Silliman (2001) suggests individuals staked a claim on their material and social worlds, casting traditional technologies into new social orders. Rather than adopt simplistic models of acculturation, he asserts such objects were materially constitutive in the active forging of native identity, rather than simply the passive vestiges. In pluralistic communities like those at the frontiers of culture contact, heterodox and orthodox practices and choices are materially revealed. Such studies necessarily move across studies of landscapes, settlements, objects, practices, bodies, and persons (Silliman 2006). Similarly, Diana Loren's work (2001) takes agency and intimacy to this embodied level, examining status, race, and gender as it intersects with political, social, and sexual interactions in colonial Louisiana. By focusing on clothing, masculinity, indigenous agency, and colonial desire we move toward hybrid alterities, desirous states, and embodied aesthetics rather than a unidirectional acculturation.

Practical Applications

Such innovative directions, multilayered data sets, and contemporary resonances of American archaeology may be no better exemplified than in the Ancestral Puebloan Southwest (Kantner 2004; Lekson 2009). This is particularly true of the enigmatic Chacoan phenomenon and its historical and contemporary Puebloan descendant communities (Lekson 2006; Mills 2002; Noble 2004; Van Dyke 2007). Beginning in the ninth century A.D., and centered in the semi-arid San Juan Basin of northwestern New Mexico, sedentary maize agriculturalists living in clustered "unit pueblos" constructed, in a series of major coordinated efforts, a network of "Great Houses" in the 20-km-long Chaco Canyon (Lekson 2007; Neitzel 2003). These were monumental constructions in a desolate landscape that, in their horizontal orientations, vertical layerings, and radiating roads actively cited celestial forces (Farmer 2003; Sofaer 2008). In so doing, the sky was emplaced on earth if not also, and literally, in the hands of some Chacoans. Presumably, the roads were formal processional avenues connecting, among other things, ancestral places. Movement along them was a walk through history as well as landscape (Van Dyke 2007).

Chacoan governance, which remains an open and debated issue, was probably inseparable from the multiscaled performances of heritage, identity, religion, and community. In a series of studies, Van Dyke (2003, 2004, 2007) has argued that, in essence, great constructions—as social performances—continuously created pan-regional Chacoan community. Rejecting Cartesian bifurcations, we might assert that community did not exist apart from the great, coordinated projects (Pauketat 2003). Such projects might also be directed toward commemoration, the flipside of which are acts of "forgetting" or memory suppression. As Mills (2008) shows, these practices pervade daily life and rituality at Chaco. Bodies were clothed in cosmic referents and surrounded by animate beings and inalienable things. In great spaces and processions, or in migrations to new homelands, bodies wove together personhood, community, and landscape so tightly as to be indissociable.

Movement, in fact, is part and parcel of contemporary Puebloan heritage, where "each physical movement" is "the construction of a new community" and a renewed sense of the "fluidity of life" (Naranjo 2008:261). In the ancient past, that sense was emplaced and embodied. The heritage of Chaco was remembered through the experience of Great House ruins (Begay 2004; Kuwanwisiwma 2004; Ryan 2008; Snead 2008b). It was personified in its prominent descendants, such as one elderly craftsman killed in an attack on his home pueblo more than a century after Chaco's demise (Kuckelman 2008). And such emplacements, embodiments, and movements inverted and transmogrified cultural spaces and networks. Depending on what happened where, people avoided, and continue to avoid, some ruins (Snead 2008a). Ghosts of the past inhabit the land still and shape the present (Walker 2008). Considered in the terms of cultural fields, an inclusive archaeology of the Southwest is now explaining the large-scale historical consequences of seemingly momentary moves.

Similar arguments focusing on landscape, depositional practices, and identity have been made for other parts of the world, including most recently Mesoamerica, the American Southeast, and Amazonia. Of these, Mesoamerican archaeologists, with their traditional focus on complexity, governance, and ideology, have turned to engage theories emphasizing the recursive material relationships of performance, personhood, and the body politic during the Formative and Classic periods of circa 1500 cal B.C.–A.D. 900 (e.g., Clark 2004; Gillespie 2001; A. Joyce 2004; R. A. Joyce 2000, 2008; Lucero 2008). For instance, after reanalyzing its many foundational sediments, Gillespie (Gillespie 2008:134–135) now concludes that the great Olmec site of La Venta was "a landscape built from generations of depositional practices" that resulted from "[p]erformance and the interplay of remembering and forgetting among multiple groups with both coordinated and competing agendas." Moving earth was a particular sort of commemorative practice that simultaneously, if unintentionally, shaped the contours of Mesoamerica for millennia (see also R. A. Joyce 2004; Pauketat 2000).

Similar theorizing in the later Archaic and Woodland period Southeast (3500 cal B.C.–A.D. 600) and in the late precolumbian mounded landscapes of Amazonia also point out that people "inhabiting" landscapes generated long-term historical change (following Barrett 1999; Heckenberger 2005; Sassaman 2004, 2005; Wallis 2008). In both cases, such theorizing is virtually synonymous with intensive fieldwork, as archaeologists seek lived histories in ways that reveal the recursivity of identity and place in the past and present. The Amazonian research in particular reveals the "critical importance of collaborative research strategies, including archaeological and ethnographic fieldwork, remote-sensed data analysis and geographic information systems, and most important, indigenous participation, to understand the complex interplay of ecological, historical, and political conditions" (Heckenberger et al. 2003:1713). Such research fundamentally relocates the questions archaeologists ask from evolutionary ones, where some process is assumed to have been restricted to a distant time or type of society, to historical ones, where the processes of concern are relationships between identities, experiences, and practices as relevant today as they were yesterday (Pauketat 2007:60).

That fundamental theoretical move is not distinct from archaeological practice: indeed all of our interpretations are indelibly shaped by our fieldwork strategies, international commitments, politics, ethical concerns, and subjectivities. It is simply not true, as often stated in the past, that processual archaeology was concerned with scientific field practice whereas postprocessual archaeology sought only multiple interpretations of material with marginal regard for archaeological science (see also the discussion by Zeder, Buikstra and van der Leeuw, this volume). For instance, excavations at Çatalhöyük, in Turkey, testify that such a bifurcation is both untenable and unhelpful (see Hodder 2005, 2006, 2007). At the same time, the work at Çatalhöyük reveals how political and religious differences are being negotiated through archaeological practices around excavation, reburial, and representation of the past to the public (Hodder 2009). Archaeologists may once have seen such tensions or dialogues as a nuisance that detracted from the real business of fieldwork, yet nowadays are considered a necessary and valuable ethical check or corrective on our practices and interpretations.

Future Directions

As the above examples reveal, American archaeology is being recast in theoretical and practical ways around global-historical issues, cultural resource management, heritage interests, and indigenous concerns (see chapters by Franklin and Paynter, Silliman and Ferguson, and Little and Zimmerman this volume). Such developments have been bolstered by the exigencies of globalization and realized through international field projects and practice. This makes sense; it would be fair to say that there are more American projects overseas than any other nationality and, with such a presence comes greater responsibilities to multiple theoretical and practical matters (Bernbeck and Pollock 2004; MacEachern 2007; McGuire 2008; Meskell 2002b; Meskell, ed. 2009; Scham 1998; Scham and Yahya 2003; Schmidt 1995, 1996; Schrire 1995).

Our present examination of recent research directions is made with the awareness of these responsibilities as well as the recognition of a host of other new directions that we have not discussed here: critical conservation (Hayashida 2005; Matero 2000; Meskell 2009), geographic methods (Kantner 2008), semiotics (Bauer 2002; Lele 2006; Preucel 2008), cultural property (Kersel et al. 2008; Messenger 1999) and even human rights (Schmidt 1996; Silverman and Fairchild Ruggles 2008). Regardless, American archaeology's closest intellectual interlocutors probably still remain our anthropological colleagues, underscored by current research (Geismar 2005; Hasinoff 2006; Lafrenz Samuels 2008) and a sustained sociocultural interest in material culture and material worlds (Edwards et al. 2006; Hoskins 1998; Keane 2003; Spyer 1998; Stoler 2008). Clearly, dialogue between subfields continues (e.g., Joyce and Gillespie 2000; Meskell, ed. 2009; Mortensen and Hollowell 2009) and archaeological studies have affected ethnographic fieldwork (Benavides 2005; Breglia 2006; van der Spek 2008; Wynn 2008). Indeed more ethnographic work is being undertaken by a younger generation of archaeologists, suggesting a more self-confident discipline and one more open to both incorporating and contributing to other fields.

In any case, since the 1990s there has been a growing trend toward social issues in American archaeology, whether one studies materiality in the past or works with descendent and other local communities on the intellectual and ethical challenges of the present. These developments can be tracked across our field research, writings, and public presentations (Meskell 2002a:281–282). In the foregoing we suggested that old dichotomous ways of thinking are being replaced by more integrated, reflexive, and hybrid epistemologies and modes of research. Transforming the classifications of material culture and space to the more active considerations of materiality and spatiality has radically altered the ways in which we approach and theorize much of the archaeological record, and not only objects and monuments, but depositions, practices, and networks of things together. Even the separations of fieldwork and interpretation have been entangled in productive ways, alongside archaeological science and archaeological theory.

In fact, American archaeology is moving from our previous single-issue focus (e.g., gender, landscape, ethnicity, etc.) to consider more numerous, porous and mutually constitutive data sets. Likewise, questions of agency in archaeology have moved from identifying domination and resistance to interrogating places, things, beings, and people that might, in many contexts, be bearers of efficacy and causality.

Not all archaeologists will agree with such moves, and a diversity of approaches will remain into the foreseeable future. But there are signs of rapprochement between camps. In the end, more productive than the current collage of alternate archaeological approaches will be the moves to cross-cut theoretical and disciplinary lines by generating diverse and hybrid research agendas at home and abroad. American archaeology is particularly well suited to pursue these new agendas by focusing on the encounters and experiences of various kinds in the past as well as the present. The result might not be a simple re-inscription of the theoretical dividing lines as they are currently drawn, but a new kind of sensuous or radical empiricism (Jackson 1996). Certainly, the underpinning philosophies of past cultures are now being evocatively revealed by replacing some of our older positivistic models and taxonomies with more dynamic and culturally attuned ones. American archaeology is changing directions and, in so doing, opening up new fields of inquiry into the human experience.

References

Alt, Susan M.
   2006 The Power of Diversity: The Roles of Migration and Hybridity in Culture Change. In *Leadership and Polity in Mississippian Society*, edited by Brian M. Butler and Paul D. Welch, pp. 289–308. Center for Archaeological Investigations, Occasional Paper No. 33. Southern Illinois University, Carbondale.

Ashmore, Wendy
   2004 Social Archaeologies of Landscape. In *A Companion to Social Archaeology*, edited by Lynn M. Meskell and Robert W. Preucel, pp. 255–271. Blackwell, Oxford.

Ashmore, Wendy, and A. Bernard Knapp (editors)
   1999 *Archaeologies of Landscape: Contemporary Perspectives*. Blackwell, London.

Barrett, John C.
   1999 The Mythical Landscapes of the British Iron Age. In *Archaeologies of Landscape: Contemporary Perspectives*, edited by Wendy Ashmore and A. Bernard Knapp, pp. 253–265. Blackwell, Oxford.

Basso, Keith H.
   1996 *Wisdom Sits in Places: Landscape and Language among the Western Apache*. University of New Mexico Press, Albuquerque.

Bauer, Alexander A.
   2002   Is What You See All You Get? Recognizing Meaning in Archaeology. *Journal of Social Archaeology* 2:37–52.
Beck, Robin A., Douglas J. Bolender, James A. Brown, and Timothy K. Earle
   2007   Eventful Archaeology: The Place of Space in Structural Transformation. *Current Anthropology* 48:833–860.
Begay, Richard M.
   2004   Tsé Bíyah 'Anii'áhí: Chaco Canyon and Its Place in Navajo History. In In *Search of Chaco: New Approaches to an Archaeological Enigma,* edited by Davud G. Noble, pp. 54–60. SAR Press, Santa Fe.
Benavides, O. Hugo
   2005   *Making Ecuadorian Histories: Four Centuries of Defining Power.* University of Texas Press, Austin.
Bender, Barbara
   2001   Landscapes on the Move. *Journal of Social Archaeology* 1:75–89.
Bender, Barbara, Sue Hamilton, and Christopher Tilley
   1997   Leskernick: Stone Worlds; Alternative Narratives; Nested Landscapes. *Proceedings of the Prehistoric Society* 63:147–178.
Bernbeck, Reinhard, and Susan Pollock
   2004   The Political Economy of Archaeological Practice and the Production of Heritage in the Middle East. In *A Companion to Social Archaeology,* edited by Lynn M. Meskell and Robert W. Preucel, pp. 335–352. Blackwell, Oxford.
Bettinger, Robert L.
   1991   *Hunter-Gatherers: Archaeological and Evolutionary Theory.* Plenum Press, New York.
Binford, Lewis R.
   1980   Willow Smoke and Dog's Tails: Hunter-Gatherer Settlement Systems and Archaeological Site Formation. *American Antiquity* 45:4–20.
Bintliff, John
   2004   Time, Structure, and Agency: The Annales, Emergent Complexity, and Archaeology. In *A Companion to Archaeology*, edited by John Bintliff, pp. 174–194. Blackwell, Oxford.
Bird-David, Nurit
   1999   'Animism' Revisited: Personhood, Environment, and Relational Epistemology. *Current Anthropology* 40(supplement):67–91.
Blain, Jenny, and Robert Wallis
   2007   *Sacred Sites—Contested Rites/Rights.* Sussex Academic Press, Brighton.
Bourdieu, Pierre
   1977   *Outline of a Theory of Practice.* Translated by Richard Nice. Cambridge University Press, Cambridge.
   1980   *The Logic of Practice.* Stanford University Press, Stanford.
Bradley, Richard
   2000   *An Archaeology of Natural Places.* Routledge, London.
Breglia, Lisa C.
   2006   *Monumental Ambivalence: The Politics of Heritage.* University of Texas Press, Austin.

Brown, James A.
  2006 Where's the Power in Mound Building? An Eastern Woodlands Perspective. In *Leadership and Polity in Mississippian Society*, edited by Brian M. Butler and Paul D. Welch, pp. 197–213. Center for Archaeological Investigations, Occasional Paper No. 33. Southern Illinois University, Carbondale.

Brück, Joanna
  2006 Fragmentation, Personhood and the Social Construction of Technology in Middle and Late Bronze Age Britain. *Cambridge Archaeological Journal* 16:297–315.
  2007 Landscape Politics and Colonial Identities: Sir Richard Colt Hoare's Tour of Ireland, 1806. *Journal of Social Archaeology* 7:224–249.

Brumfiel, Elizabeth M.
  1992 Distinguished Lecture in Archaeology: Breaking and Entering the Ecosystem—Gender, Class, and Faction Steal the Show. *American Anthropologist* 94:551–567.

Buchli, Victor (editor)
  2002 *The Material Culture Reader.* Berg, Oxford.

Byrne, D.
  2007 *Surface Collection: Archaeological Travels in Southeast Asia.* AltaMira, Walnut Creek, California.

Carmichael, David L., Jane Hubert, Brian Reeves, and Audhild Schanche (editors)
  1994 *Sacred Sites, Sacred Places.* Routledge, London.

Clark, John E.
  2004 The Birth of Mesoamerican Metaphysics: Sedentism, Engagement, and Moral Superiority. In *Rethinking Materiality: The Engagement of Mind with the Material World*, edited by Elizabeth DeMarrais, Chris Gosden, and A. Colin Renfrew, pp. 205–224. MacDonald Institute for Archaeological Research, Cambridge.

Colwell-Chanthaphonh, Chip, and T. J. Ferguson
  2004 Virtue Ethics and the Practice of History: Native Americans and Archaeologists Along the San Pedro Valley of Arizona. *Journal of Social Archaeology* 4:5–27.

Colwell-Chanthaphonh, Chip, and T. J. Ferguson (editors)
  2008 *Collaboration in Archaeological Practice: Engaging Descendant Communities.* AltaMira Press, Lanham, Maryland.

Costin, Cathy Lynne, and Rita P. Wright (editors)
  1998 *Craft and Social Identity.* Archeological Papers of the American Anthropological Association, No. 8. Arlington, Virginia.

DeMarrais, Elizabeth
  2004 The Materialization of Culture. In *Rethinking Materiality: The Engagement of Mind with the Material World*, edited by Elizabeth DeMarrais, Chris Gosden, and A. Colin Renfrew, pp. 53–62. MacDonald Institute for Archaeological Research, Cambridge.

DeMarrais, Elizabeth, Louis J. Castillo, and Timothy K. Earle
  1996 Ideology, Materialization, and Power Strategies. *Current Anthropology* 37:15–32.

Dillehay, Thomas D.
   2004 Social Landscape and Ritual Pause: Uncertainty and Integration in Formative Peru. *Journal of Social Archaeology* 4:239–268.

Dobres, Marcia-Anne
   2000 *Technology and Social Agency: Outlining a Practice Framework for Archaeology.* Blackwell Publishers, Oxford.

Edgar, Heather J. H., Edward A. Jolie, Joseph F. Powell, and Joe E. Watkins
   2007 Contextual Issues in Paleoindian Repatriation: Spirit Cave Man as a Case Study. *Journal of Social Archaeology* 7:101–122.

Edwards, Elizabeth, Chris Gosden, and Ruth Phillips (editors)
   2006 *Sensible Objects: Colonialism, Museums and Material Culture.* Berg, Oxford.

Farmer, James D.
   2003 Astronomy and Ritual in Chaco Canyon. In *Pueblo Bonito: Center of the Chacoan World,* edited by Jill E. Neitzel, pp. 61–71. Smithsonian Books, Washington, D.C.

Ferguson, T.J., and Chip Colwell-Chanthaphonh
   2006 *History Is in the Land: Multivocal Tribal Traditions in Arizona's San Pedro Valley.* University of Arizona Press, Tucson.

Fine-Dare, Kathleen S.
   2002 *Grave Injustice: The American Indian Repatriation Movement and NAGPRA.* University of Oklahoma Press, Norman.
   2005 Anthropological Suspicion, Public Interest and NAGPRA. *Journal of Social Archaeology* 5:171–192.

Fleming, Andrew
   2006 Post-Processual Landscape Archaeology: A Critique. *Cambridge Archaeological Journal* 16:267–280.

Fogelin, Lars
   2007 The Archaeology of Religious Ritual. *Annual Review of Anthropology* 36:55–71.

Geismar, Haidy
   2005 Reproduction, Creativity, Restriction: Material Culture and Copyright in Vanuatu. *Journal of Social Archaeology* 5:25–51.

Gell, Alfred
   1998 *Art and Agency: An Anthropological Theory.* Oxford University Press, Oxford.

Gibson, James John
   1979 *The Ecological Approach to Visual Perception.* Houghton Mifflin, Boston.

Giddens, Anthony
   1984 *The Constitution of Society: Outline of a Theory of Structuration.* Polity Press, Cambridge.

Gillespie, Susan D.
   2001 Personhood, Agency, and Mortuary Ritual: A Case Study from the Ancient Maya. *Journal of Anthropological Archaeology* 20:73–112.
   2008 History in Practice: Ritual Deposition at La Venta Complex A. In *Memory Work: Archaeologies of Material Practices,* edited by Barbara J. Mills and William H. Walker, pp. 109–136. SAR Press, Santa Fe.

Gosden, Chris
　2001　Making Sense: Archaeology and Aesthetics. *World Archaeology* 33:163–167.
　2005　What Do Objects Want? *Journal of Archaeological Method and Theory* 12:193–211.
Gosden, Chris, and Yvonne Marshall
　1999　The Cultural Biography of Objects. *World Archaeology* 31:169–178.
Gronenborn, Detlef
　2006　Ancestors and Chiefs: Comparing Social Archaeologies in Eastern North America and Temperate Europe. In *Leadership and Polity in Mississippian Society*, edited by Brian M. Butler and Paul D. Welch, pp. 365–397. Center for Archaeological Investigations, Occasional Paper No. 33. Southern Illinois University, Carbondale.
Hall, Martin
　2000　*Archaeology and the Modern World: Colonial Transcripts in South Africa and the Chesapeake.* Routledge, London.
Hasinoff, Erin L.
　2006　Christian Trophies or Asmat Ethnografica?: Fr. Zegwaard and the American Museum of Natural History Asmat Collection, 1958–9. *Journal of Social Archaeology* 6:147–174.
Hayashida, Frances M.
　2005　Archaeology, Ecological History, and Conservation. *Annual Review of Anthropology* 34:43–65.
Heckenberger, Michael J.
　2005　*The Ecology of Power: Culture, Place, and Personhood in the Southern Amazon, A.D. 1000–2000.* Routledge, New York.
Heckenberger, Michael J., Afukaka Kuikuro, U.T. Kuikuro, J. Christian Russell, Morgan J. Schmidt, Carlos Fausto, and Bruna Franchetto
　2003　Amazonia 1492: Pristine Forest or Cultural Parkland? *Science* 301:1710–1714.
Hegel, Georg W. F
　1977　*Phenomenology of Spirit.* Oxford University Press, Oxford.
Hegmon, Michelle
　2003　Setting Theoretical Egos Aside: Issues and Theory in North American Archaeology. *American Antiquity* 68:213–243.
Heidegger, Martin
　1996　*Basic Writings.* Routledge, London.
Hendon, Julia A.
　2009　*Houses in a Landscape: Memory and Everyday Life in Ancient Mesoamerica.* Duke University Press, Durham, North Carolina.
Hodder, Ian
　1982　*Symbols in Action.* Cambridge University Press, Cambridge.
　1986　*Reading the Past.* Cambridge University Press, Cambridge.
　2001　Introduction: A Review of Contemporary Theoretical Debates in Archaeology. In *Archaeological Theory Today*, edited by Ian Hodder, pp. 3–13. Polity Press, Cambridge.

2009 Mavili's Voice. In *Cosmopolitan Archaeologies*, edited by Lynn M. Meskell, pp. 184–204. Duke University Press, Durham.

Hodder, Ian (editor)
2004 *Archaeological Theory Today.* Cambridge, Polity Press.
2005 *Inhabiting Çatalhöyük: Reports from the 1995–1999 Seasons.* McDonald Institute for Archaeological Research, Cambridge.
2006 *Changing Materialities at Çatalhöyük: Reports from the 1995–99 Seasons.* McDonald Institute for Archaeological Research, Cambridge.
2007 *Excavating Çatalhöyük: South, North and KOPAL Area Reports from the 1995–1999 Seasons.* McDonald Institute for Archaeological Research, Cambridge.

Hoskins, Janet
1998 *Biographical Objects: How Things Tell the Stories of People's Lives.* Routledge, London and New York.

Ingold, Tim
2000a *The Perception of the Environment: Essays in Livelihood, Dwelling and Skill.* Routledge, London.
2000b Making Culture and Weaving the World. In *Matter, Materiality and Modern Culture,* edited by Paul Graves-Brown, pp. 50–71. Routledge, London.

Inomata, Takeshi, and Lawrence S. Coben (editors)
2006 *Archaeology of Performance: Theaters of Power, Community, and Politics.* AltaMira Press, Walnut Creek, California.

Jackson, Michael
1996 Introduction: Phenomenology, Radical Empiricism, and Anthropological Critique. In *Things as They Are: New Directions in Phenomenological Anthropology,* pp. 1–50. University of Indiana Press, Bloomington.

Johnson, Mathew H.
2006 On the Nature of Theoretical Archaeology and Archaeological Theory. *Archaeological Dialogues* 13:117–132.

Jones, Andy
2002 *Archaeological Theory and Scientific Practice.* Cambridge University Press, Cambridge.
2005 Lives in Fragments? Personhood and the European Neolithic. *Journal of Social Archaeology* 5:193–224.

Joyce, Arthur A.
2004 Sacred Space and Social Relations in the Valley of Oaxaca. In *Mesoamerican Archaeology: Theory and Practice,* edited by Julia A. Hendon and Rosemary A. Joyce, pp. 192–216. Blackwell, Oxford.

Joyce, Rosemary A.
2000 Girling the Girl and Boying the Boy: The Production of Adulthood in Ancient Mesoamerica. *World Archaeology* 31(3):473–485.
2001 *Gender and Power in Prehispanic Mesoamerica.* University of Texas Press, Austin.
2004 Unintended Consequences? Monumentality as a Novel Experience in Formative Mesoamerica. *Journal of Archaeological Method and Theory* 11:5–29.
2008 Practice in and as Deposition. In *Memory Work: Archaeologies of Material Prac-*

tices, edited by Barbara J. Mills and William H. Walker, pp. 25–39. SAR Press, Santa Fe.

Joyce, Rosemary A., and Susan D. Gillespie (editors)
  2000 *Beyond Kinship: Social and Material Reproduction in House Societies.* University of Pennsylvania Press, Philadelphia.

Kantner, John
  2004 *Ancient Puebloan Southwest.* Cambridge University Press, Cambridge.
  2008 The Archaeology of Regions: From Discrete Analytical Toolkit to Ubiquitous Spatial Perspective. *Journal of Archaeological Research* 16:37–81.

Keane, Webb
  2003 Self-Interpretation, Agency, and the Objects of Anthropology: Reflections on a Genealogy. *Comparative Studies in Society and History* 45:222–248.
  2005 Signs Are Not the Garb of Meaning: On the Social Analysis of Material Things. In *Materiality,* edited by Daniel Miller, pp. 182–205. Duke University Press, Durham, North Carolina.

Kersel, Morag M., Christina Luke, and Christopher H. Roosevelt
  2008 Valuing the Past: Perceptions of Archaeological Practice in Lydia and the Levant. *Journal of Social Archaeology* 8:298–319.

Kirk, Trevor
  2006 Materiality, Personhood and Monumentality in Early Neolithic Britain. *Cambridge Archaeological Journal* 16:333–347.

Knappett, Carl
  2004 The Affordances of Things: A Post-Gibsonian Perspective on the Relationality of Mind and Matter. In *Rethinking Materiality: The Engagement of Mind with the Material World,* edited by Elizabeth DeMarrais, Chris Gosden, and A. Colin Renfrew, pp. 43–52. MacDonald Institute for Archaeological Research, Cambridge.

Kohler, Timothy A., and George J. Gumerman
  2000 *Dynamics in Human and Primate Societies: Agent-Based Modeling of Social and Spatial Processes.* Oxford University Press, New York.

Kopytoff, Igor
  1986 The Cultural Biography of Things: Commoditization as Process. In *The Social Life of Things: Commodities in Cultural Perspective*, edited by Arjun Appadurai, pp. 64–91. Cambridge University Press, Cambridge.

Kubler, George
  1962 *The Shape of Time: Remarks on the History of Things.* Yale University Press, New Haven.

Kuckelman, Kristin A.
  2008 An Agent-Centered Case Study of the Depopulation of Sand Canyon Pueblo. In *The Social Construction of Communities: Agency, Structure, and Identity in the Prehispanic Southwest*, edited by Mark D. Varien and James M. Potter, pp. 109–121. AltaMira Press, Walnut Creek, California.

Kuijt, Ian
  2008 The Regeneration of Life: Neolithic Structures of Symbolic Remembering and Forgetting. *Current Anthropology* 49:171–197.

Kuwanwisiwma, Leigh J.
  2004 Yupköyvi: The Hopi Story of Chaco Canyon. In *In Search of Chaco: New Approaches to an Archaeological Enigma,* edited by David G. Noble, pp. 41–47. SAR Press, Santa Fe.
Lafrenz Samuels, K.
  2008 Value and Significance in Archaeology. *Archaeological Dialogues* 15:71–97.
LaMotta, Vincent M., and Michael B. Schiffer
  2001 Behavioral Archaeology: Toward a New Synthesis. In *Archaeological Theory Today,* edited by Ian Hodder, pp. 14–64. Cambridge, Polity Press.
Latour, Bruno
  1991 *We Have Never Been Modern.* Translated by C Porter. Harvard University Press, Cambridge.
  2000 When Things Strike Back: A Possible Contribution of 'Science Studies' to the Social Sciences. *British Journal of Sociology* 51:107–123.
Lazzari, Marrisa
  2003 Archaeological Visions: Gender, Landscape and Optic Knowledge. *Journal of Social Archaeology* 3:194–222.
  2005 The Texture of Things: Objects, People, and Social Spaces in Argentine Prehistory. In *Archaeologies of Materiality,* edited by Lynn M. Meskell, pp. 126–161. Blackwell, Oxford.
Lekson, Stephen H.
  2009 *A History of the Ancient Southwest.* SAR Press, Santa Fe.
Lekson, Stephen H. (editor)
  2006 *The Archaeology of Chaco Canyon: An Eleventh-Century Pueblo Regional Center.* SAR Press, Santa Fe.
  2007 *The Architecture of Chaco Canyon, New Mexico.* University of Utah Press, Salt Lake City.
Lele, Veerendra P.
  2006 Material Habits, Identity, Semeiotic. *Journal of Social Archaeology* 6:48–70.
Lemonnier, Pierre (editor)
  1993 *Technological Choices: Transformation in Material Cultures since the Neolithic.* Routledge, London.
Loren, Diana DiPaolo
  2000 The Intersections of Colonial Policy and Colonial Practice: Creolization on the Eighteenth-Century Louisiana/Texas Frontier. *Historical Archaeology* 34(3):85–98.
  2001 Social Skins: Orthodoxies and Practices of Dressing in the Early Colonial Lower Mississippi Valley. *Journal of Social Archaeology* 1:172–189.
Lucero, Lisa J.
  2008 Memorializing Place among Classic Maya Commoners. In *Memory Work: Archaeologies of Material Practices,* edited by Barbara J. Mills and William H. Walker, pp. 187–206. SAR Press, Santa Fe.
MacEachern, Scott
  2007 Where in Africa Does Africa Start?: Identity, Genetics and African Studies

from the Sahara to Darfur. *Journal of Social Archaeology* 7:393–412.
McGuire, Randall H.
   2008   *Archaeology as Political Action.* University of California Press, Berkeley.
Malafouris, Lambros
   2004   The Cognitive Basis of Material Engagement: Where Brain, Body and Culture Conflate. In *Rethinking Materiality: The Engagement of Mind with the Material World,* edited by Elizabeth DeMarrais, Chris Gosden, and A. Colin Renfrew, pp. 53–62. MacDonald Institute for Archaeological Research, Cambridge.
Marx, Karl
   1992 [1887]   *Capital: A Critique of Political Economy.* International Publishers, New York.
Matero, Frank
   2000   Ethics and Policy in Conservation. *Conservation: The GCI Newsletter* 15(1):5–9.
Mauss, Marcel
   1990   *The Gift: The Form and Reason for Exchange in Archaic Societies.* Translated by W. D. Halls. W. W. Norton, New York.
Merleau-Ponty, Maurice
   1962   T*he Phenomenology of Perception.* Translated by Colin Smith. Routledge and Kegan Paul, London.
Meskell, Lynn M.
   1996   The Somatisation of Archaeology: Institutions, Discourses, Corporeality. *Norwegian Archaeological Review* 29:1–16.
   2002a The Intersection of Identity and Politics in Archaeology. *Annual Review of Anthropology* 31:279–301.
   2002b Negative Heritage and Past Mastering in Archaeology. *Anthropological Quarterly* 75(3):557–574.
   2004   *Object Worlds in Ancient Egypt: Material Biographies Past and Present.* Berg, London.
   2009   The Nature of Culture in Kruger National Park. In *Cosmopolitan Archaeologies,* edited by Lynn M. Meskell, pp. 89–112. Duke University Press, Durham, North Carolina.
Meskell, Lynn M. (editor)
   2005   *Archaeologies of Materiality.* Blackwell, Oxford.
   2009   Cos*mopolitan Archaeologies.* Duke University Press, Durham.
Meskell, Lynn M., and Rosemary A. Joyce
   2003   *Embodied Lives: Figuring Ancient Maya and Egyptian Experience.* Routledge, London.
Meskell, Lynn M., and Robert W. Preucel (editors)
   2004   *Companion to Social Archaeology.* Blackwell, Oxford.
Messenger, Phyllis Mauch (editor)
   1999   *The Ethics of Collecting Cultural Property.* University of New Mexico Press, Albuquerque.
Miller, Daniel
   1987   *Material Culture and Mass Consumption.* Blackwell, Oxford.

2001 *The Dialectics of Shopping*. University of Chicago, Chicago.
Miller, Daniel (editor)
  1998 *Material Cultures: Why Some Things Matter*. University of Chicago Press, Chicago.
  2005 *Materiality*. Duke University Press, Durham, North Carolina.
Mills, Barbara J.
  2002 Recent Research on Chaco: Changing Views on Economy, Ritual, and Society. *Journal of Archaeological Research* 10:65–117.
  2004 The Establishment and Defeat of Hierarchy: Inalienable Possessions and the History of Collective Prestige Structures in the Pueblo Southwest. *American Anthropologist* 106:238–251.
  2008 Remembering While Forgetting: Depositional Practices and Social Memory at Chaco. In *Memory Work: Archaeologies of Material Practices*, edited by Barbara J. Mills and William H. Walker, pp. 81–108. School for Advanced Research Press, Santa Fe.
Mills, Barbara J., and William H. Walker (editors)
  2008 *Memory Work: Archaeologies of Material Practices*. School for Advanced Research Press, Santa Fe.
Mills, Barbara J., and William H. Walker
  2008 Memory, Materiality, and Depositional Practice. In *Memory Work: Archaeologies of Material Practices,* edited by Barbara J. Mills and Wiiliam H. Walker, pp. 3–24. School for Advanced Research Press, Santa Fe.
Mortensen, Lena, and Julie Hollowell (editors)
  2009 *Ethnographies and Archaeologies: Iterations of the Past*. University Press of Florida, Gainesville.
Moss, Madonna L.
  2005 Rifts in the Theoretical Landscapes of Archaeology in the United States: A Comment on Hegmon and Watkins. *American Antiquity* 70:581–587.
Munn, Nancy D.
  1986 *The Fame of Gawa: A Symbolic Study of Value Transformation in a Massim (Papua New Guinea) Society*. Duke University Press, Durham, North Carolina.
Myers, Fred (editor)
  2001 *The Empire of Things*. SAR Press, Santa Fe.
Nakamura, Carolyn
  2004 Dedicating Magic: Neo-Assyrian Apotropaic Figurines and the Protection of Assur. *World Archaeology* 36:11–25.
  2005 Mastering Matters: Magical Sense and Apotropaic Figurine Worlds of Neo-Assyria. In *Archaeologies of Materiality*, edited by Lynn M. Meskell, pp. 18–45. Blackwell, Oxford.
Naranjo, Theresa
  2008 Life as Movement: A Tewa View of Community and Identity. In *The Social Construction of Communities: Agency, Structure, and Identity in the Prehispanic Southwest,* edited by Mark D. Varien and James M. Potter, pp. 251–262. AltaMira Press, Walnut Creek, California.

Nassaney, Michael S.
　2004　Native American Gender Politics and Material Culture in Seventeenth-Century Southeastern New England. *Journal of Social Archaeology* 4:334–367.
Neitzel, Jill E. (editor)
　2003　*Pueblo Bonito: Center of the Chacoan World*. Smithsonian Books, Washington, D.C.
Noble, David G. (editor)
　2004　*In Search of Chaco: New Approaches to an Archaeological Enigma*. SAR Press, Santa Fe.
O'Brien, Michael R., and Lee R. Lyman
　2004　History and Explanation in Archaeology. *Anthropological Theory* 4:173-197.
Olivier, Laurent
　2001　Duration, Memory and the Nature of the Archaeological Record. In *It's About Time: The Concept of Time in Archaeology*, edited by H. Karlsson, pp. 61–70. Bricoleur Press, Goteberg.
Pauketat, Timothy R.
　2000　The Tragedy of the Commoners. In *Agency in Archaeology*, edited by Marcia-Anne Dobres and John Robb, pp. 113–129. Routlege, London.
　2001　Practice and History in Archaeology: An Emerging Paradigm. *Anthropological Theory* 1:73–98.
　2003　Materiality and the Immaterial in Historical-Processual Archaeology. In *Essential Tensions in Archaeological Method and Theory*, edited by Todd L. VanPool and Christine S. VanPool, pp. 41–53. The University of Utah Press, Salt Lake City.
　2007　*Chiefdoms and Other Archaeological Delusions*. Altamira, Walnut Creek, California.
　2008　The Grounds for Agency in Southwestern Archaeology. In *The Social Construction of Communities: Agency, Structure, and Identity in the Prehispanic Southwest*, edited by Mark D. Varien and James M. Potter, pp. 233–249. AltaMira Press, Walnut Creek, California.
Pauketat, Timothy R., and Susan M. Alt
　2005　Agency in a Postmold? Physicality and the Archaeology of Culture-Making. *Journal of Archaeological Method and Theory* 12:213–236.
Paynter, Robert, and Randall H. McGuire
　1991　The Archaeology of Inequality: Material Culture, Domination, and Resistance. In *The Archaeology of Inequality*, edited by Randall H. McGuire and Robert Paynter, pp. 1–27. Blackwell, Oxford.
Pollard, Joshua
　2001　The Aesthetics of Depositional Practice. *World Archaeology* 33:315–333.
Preucel, Robert W.
　2008　*Archaeological Semiotics*. Blackwell, Oxford.
Preucel, Robert W. (editor)
　2002　*Archaeologies of the Pueblo Revolt: Identity, Meaning and Renewal in the Pueblo World*. University of New Mexico Press, Albuquerque.
Renfrew, Colin
　2004　Towards a Theory of Material Engagement. In *Rethinking Materiality: The Engagement of Mind with the Material World*, edited by Elizabeth DeMarrais, Chris

Gosden, and A. Colin Renfrew, pp. 23–32. MacDonald Institute for Archaeological Research, Cambridge.

Robb, John

    2004   The Extended Artefact and the Monumental Economy: A Methodology for Material Agency. In *Rethinking Materiality: The Engagement of Mind with the Material World,* edited by Elizabeth DeMarrais, Chris Gosden, and A. Colin Renfrew, pp. 131–140. MacDonald Institute for Archaeological Research, Cambridge.

    2007   *The Early Mediterranean Village: Agency, Material Culture, and Social Change in Neolithic Italy.* Cambridge University Press, Cambridge.

Ryan, Susan C.

    2008   Constructing Community and Transforming Identity at Albert Porter Pueblo. In *The Social Construction of Communities: Agency, Structure, and Identity in the Prehispanic Southwest,* edited by Mark D. Varien and James M. Potter, pp. 69–86. AltaMira Press, Walnut Creek, California.

Sassaman, Kenneth E.

    2004   Complex Hunter-Gatherers in Evolution and History: A North American Perspective. *Journal of Archaeological Research* 12:227–280.

    2005   Poverty Point as Structure, Event, Process. *Journal of Archaeological Method and Theory* 12:335–364.

Scham, Sandra Arnold

    1998   Mediating Nationalism and Archaeology: A Matter of Trust? *American Anthropologist* 100:301–308.

Scham, Sandra Arnold, and Adel Yahya

    2003   Heritage and Reconciliation. *Journal of Social Archaeology* 3:399–416.

Schiffer, Michael B.

    1987   *Formation Processes of the Archaeological Record.* University of New Mexico Press, Albuquerque.

    1999   *The Material Life of Human Beings.* Routledge, London.

Schiffer, Michael B., Kacy L. Hollenback, and Carrie L. Bell

    2003   *Draw the Lightning Down: Benjamin Franklin and Electrical Technology in the Age of Enlightenment.* University of California Press, Berkeley.

Schmidt, Peter R.

    1995   Using Archaeology to Remake History in Africa. In *Making Alternative Histories: The Practice of Archaeology and History in Non-Western Settings,* edited by Peter R. Schmidt and Thomas C. Patterson, pp. 119–147. SAR Press, Santa Fe.

    1996   The Human Right to a Cultural Heritage: African Applications. In *Plundering Africa's Past,* edited by Peter R. Schmidt and Roderick McIntosh, pp. 18–28. University of Indiana Press, Bloomington.

Schrire, Carmel

    1995   *Digging through Darkness: Chronicles of an Archaeologist.* University Press of Virginia, Charlottesville.

Shennan, Stephen

    2008   Evolution in Archaeology. *Annual Review of Anthropology* 37:75–91.

Silliman, Stephen
  2001 Agency, Practical Politics and the Archaeology of Culture Contact. *Journal of Social Archaeology* 1:190–209.
  2005 Culture Contact or Colonialism? Challenges in the Archaeology of Native North America. *American Antiquity* 70:55–74.
  2006 Struggling with Labor, Working on Identities. In *Historical Archaeology*, edited by Martin Hall and Stephen Silliman, pp. 147–166. Blackwell, Oxford.
Silverman, Helaine, and D. Fairchild Ruggles (editors)
  2008 *Cultural Heritage and Human Rights*. Springer, New York.
Snead, James E.
  2008a *Ancestral Landscapes of the Pueblo World*. University of Arizona Press, Tucson.
  2008b History, Place, and Social Power in the Galisteo Basin, A.D. 1250–1325. In *The Social Construction of Communities: Agency, Structure, and Identity in the Prehispanic Southwest*, edited by Mark D. Varien and James M. Potter, pp. 155–167. AltaMira Press, Walnut Creek, California.
Sofaer, Anna
  2008 *Chaco Astronomy: An Ancient American Cosmology*. Ocean Tree Books, Santa Fe.
Spyer, P. (editor)
  1998 *Border Fetishisms: Material Objects in Unstable Places*. Routledge, New York.
Stoffle, Richard W., María Nieves Zedeño, and David B. Halmo (editors)
  2001 *American Indians and the Nevada Test Site: A Model of Research and Consultation*. US Government Printing Office, Washington.
Stoler, Ann L.
  2008 Imperial Debris. *Cultural Anthropology* 23:191–219.
Strathern, Marilyn
  1988 *The Gender of the Gift: Problems with Women and Problems with Society in Melanesia*. University of California Press, Berkeley.
Thackery, D., and S. Payne
  2008 Draft Report on the Request for Reburial of Human Remains from the Alexander Keiller Museum at Avebury. http://www.english-heritage.org.uk/server/show/nav.19819.
Thomas, Julian
  1996 *Time, Culture and Identity*. Routledge, London.
  2001 Archaeologies of Place and Landscape. In *Archaeological Theory Today*, edited by Ian Hodder, pp. 163–186. Polity Press, Cambridge.
Tilley, Christopher
  2004 *The Materiality of Stone: Explorations in Landscape Phenomenology*. Berg, Oxford.
Tilley, Christopher (editor)
  1990 *Reading Material Culture*. Blackwell.
Tylor, Edward B.
  1977 *Primitive Culture: Researches into the Development of Mythology, Philosophy, Religion, Language, Art and Custom*. Volume 1. Gordon Press, New York.

van der Spek, Kees
   2008   Faked Antikas and 'Modern Antiques': The Production and Marketing of Tourist Art in the Theban Necropolis. *Journal of Social Archaeology* 8:163–189.

Van Dyke, Ruth M.
   2003   Memory and the Construction of Chacoan Society. In *Archaeologies of Memory,* edited by Ruth M. Van Dyke and Susan E. Alcock, pp. 180–200. Blackwell, Oxford.
   2004   Memory, Meaning, and Masonry: The Late Bonito Chacoan Landscape. *American Antiquity* 69:413–431.
   2007   *The Chaco Experience: Landscape and Ideology at the Center Place.* SAR Press, Santa Fe.

Van Dyke, Ruth M., and Susan E. Alcock (editors)
   2003   *Archaeologies of Memory.* Blackwell, Oxford.

VanPool, Todd L., and Christine S. VanPool
   2003   Method, Theory, and the Essential Tension. In *Essential Tensions in Archaeological Method and Theory,* edited by Todd L. VanPool and Christine S. VanPool, pp. 1–4. University of Utah Press, Salt Lake City.

Walker, William H.
   2008   Practice and Nonhuman Social Actors: The Afterlife Histories of Witches and Dogs in the American Southwest. In *Memory Work: Archaeologies of Material Practices,* edited by Barbara J. Mills and William H. Walker, pp. 137–158. SAR Press, Santa Fe.

Wallis, Neil J.
   2008   Networks of History and Memory: Creating a Nexus of Social Identities in Woodland Period Mounds on the Lower St. Johns River, Florida. *Journal of Social Archaeology* 8:236–271.

Walthall, John, Kenneth Farnsworth, and Thomas E. Emerson
   1997   Constructing (on) the Past. *Common Ground* 2:26–33.

Watkins, Joe
   2001   *Indigenous Archaeology.* Altamira, Walnut Creek, California.

Weiner, Annette
   1985   Inalienable Wealth. *American Ethnologist* 12:210–227.
   1992   *Inalienable Possessions: The Paradox of Keeping-While-Giving.* University of California Press, Berkeley.

Wynn, L. L.
   2008   Shape Shifting Lizard People, Israelite Slaves, and Other Theories of Pyramid Building: Notes on Labor, Nationalism, and Archaeology in Egypt. *Journal of Social Archaeology* 8:272–295.

Yoffee, Norman, and Andrew Sherratt (editors)
   1993   *Archaeological Theory: Who Sets the Agenda?* Cambridge University Press, Cambridge.

Zedeño, María Nieves
   2008   Bundled Worlds: The Roles and Interactions of Complex Objects from the North American Plains. *Journal of Archaeological Method and Theory* 15:362–378.

11

Interdisciplinary Studies in Archaeology

MELINDA ZEDER, JANE BUIKSTRA,
and SANDER VAN DER LEEUW

Archaeology is inherently interdisciplinary. Reconstructing the human past from material remains, the fundamental objective of the field, naturally requires that archaeologists draw upon a wide range of different disciplines in their research. Archaeologists utilize geophysics, remote sensing, geomorphology, and soil science to locate and excavate archaeological sites. They appeal to principles based in the life and physical sciences in their analyses of the materials recovered from these sites, and they use ethnographic knowledge to help them interpret these materials. This is why, from the earliest antiquarian days, archaeologists have always collaborated with scholars trained in other disciplines—anatomists, botanists, chemists, geologists, and zoologists and researchers drawn from humanistic fields, such as history, art history, and ethnohistory. Originally the contributions of cross-disciplinary collaborators were only very loosely appended to archaeological reports. The job of synthesizing these "technical" studies and explaining their relevance to the study of the human past was generally left to the archaeologist who might have only a very limited understanding of the practice and potential of these various fields. In recent years, however, archaeologists themselves have sought training in these complementary disciplines. As a result, the methods and interpretative applications of cross-disciplinary perspectives tend to be more tightly integrated into both research plans and products.

Not only are archaeologists increasingly expanding the power and scope of interdisciplinary methods in archaeology, they are also discovering that these methods allow them to profitably address high-impact questions that lie well beyond the traditional boundaries of archaeological inquiry. Advances in the application of interdisciplinary methods to archaeology are, in effect, transforming the kinds of problems archaeologists are trying to tackle and opening up whole new frontiers of archaeological inquiry. In so doing they are improving archaeology's potential for addressing important interdisciplinary questions, and inventing new ways to do so.

The Society for American Archaeology has been at the forefront of championing interdisciplinary approaches to archaeological practice. In the late 1970s the SAA established the Fryxell Award for Interdisciplinary Research to highlight the "crucial role of multidisciplinary cooperation in archaeology." Since 1978 this award has been given to researchers who have made significant contributions to high-caliber research in interdisciplinary archaeology, following a five-year cycle of awards in zoological sciences, botanical sciences, earth sciences, physical sciences, and general interdisciplinary studies. The Fryxell Award remains one of the most coveted awards the Society bestows. It is only fitting that in this celebratory 75th anniversary volume the SAA has chosen to spotlight the contributions of interdisciplinary studies to archaeology.

The authors of this paper have all been active in the practice and promotion of interdisciplinary approaches in archaeological research. Here, we explore the trajectory of interdisciplinary studies in archaeology over the past 25 years—since the Society's 50th anniversary. We first evaluate trends in archaeological publication, practice, and job recruitment that underscore the increasingly important role of interdisciplinary studies in archaeology. Next we highlight major topics and promising future directions in interdisciplinary research in the general areas of archaeobiology (the study of plant and animal remains from archaeological sites) and bioarchaeology (the study of human remains and funerary sites) as illustrative of the kinds of questions open to interdisciplinary research in archaeology. While not an emphasis of the chapter, we also touch on advances in other interdisciplinary areas, including archaeological chemistry and chronometry. Finally, we look at the impact of these advances in interdisciplinary research on the future of archaeology and outline how these perspectives are helping reshape the nature of archaeological research and training, as well as the relationship of our discipline to the broader scholarly community.

MELINDA ZEDER, JANE BUIKSTRA, *and* SANDER VAN DER LEEUW

Trends in Interdisciplinary Archaeological Research

We examined three different indices to trace the trajectory of interdisciplinary research in archaeology over the past 25 years: publications, practice, and job postings. Our goal in doing so was to measure the overall impact of interdisciplinary research on American archaeology and to examine trends in the practice of different interdisciplinary applications to archaeological research.

Our assessment of trends in publications is based on a survey of all articles and reports published in *American Antiquity* between January 1983 and July 2008 that featured one or more interdisciplinary topics in a significant way (Table 1). Looking at the distribution of these different topics over the 25-year period (Table 2), we see that with some exceptions (notably the 1988–1992 five-year interval that included an anomalously high number of bioarchaeology articles and reports) the representation of the disciplines is relatively constant over time. Studies that feature archaeobiological research generally constitute between 36 and 45 percent of the interdisciplinary articles published, articles emphasizing bioarchaeology between 14 and 17 percent, and those presenting work grounded in the general category of earth and physical sciences between 40 and 45 percent. Within the earth and physical sciences, the proportion of articles with a focus on geophysical testing, remote sensing, and, especially, GIS applications increased substantially in more recent issues published between 2003 and 2008, reflecting rapid technological and computational developments in these two areas in the last few years. The overall representation of interdisciplinary articles within the total number of articles and reports published in *American Antiquity* (Table 3) has increased considerably over the past 25 years—with articles featuring interdisciplinary research growing from 24 percent in issues published between 1983 and 1987, to 44 percent in issues published between 2003 and 2008. Once again, the most growth is seen in the earth and planetary sciences, and is almost entirely due to the increased number of articles that feature geophysical testing, remote sensing, and GIS applications.

We assessed trends in the practice of these interdisciplinary fields among archaeologists by tallying the number of archaeologists who listed one or more of these fields in their entries in the American Anthropological Association's *Guide to Departments of Anthropology*, comparing the listings for the same 131 different academic departments in the 1983 and the 2007

Table 1. Numbers of Articles in *American Antiquity* with a Major Focus on Interdisciplinary Research.

Five Year Intervals	1983-1987	1988-1992	1993-1997	1998-2002	2003-2008	Total
Archaeobiology						
Archaeobotany	7	8	16	8	14	53
Archaeozoology	15	8	12	17	17	69
Bio-archaeology	8	16	9	12	14	59
Earth and Physical Sciences						
Geoarchaeology	3	4	4	5	2	18
Chemical Analysis	12	9	11	10	10	52
Dating	5	6	7	8	6	32
Remote Sensing	3	4	3	3	7	20
GIS	1	1	0	5	12	19
Total Interdisciplinary Articles	54	56	62	68	82	322
Total Articles & Reports	224	181	163	169	187	924

Table 2. Proportional Representation of Broader Disciplinary Categories among *American Antiquity* Articles with a Major Focus on Interdisciplinary Research.

Five Year Intervals	Archaeobiology	Bioarchaeology	Earth & Physical Sciences
1983–1987	40.7%	14.8%	44.4%
1988–1992	28.6%	28.6%	42.8%
1993–1997	45.2%	14.5%	40.3%
1998–2002	36.8%	17.6%	45.6%
2003–2008	37.8%	17.1%	45.3%
Total	37.9%	18.3%	31.7%

Table 3. Proportional Representation of Articles Emphasizing Interdisciplinary Research among the Total Sample of Articles and Reports Published in *American Antiquity*.

Five Year Intervals	Archaeobiology	Bioarchaeology	Earth & Physical Sciences	Total Interdisciplinary
1983–1987	9.8%	3.6%	10.7%	24.1%
1988–1992	8.8%	8.8%	13.3%	30.9%
1993–1997	17.2%	5.5%	15.3%	38.0%
1998–2002	14.8%	7.1%	18.3%	40.2%
2003–2008	16.6%	7.5%	19.8%	43.9%
Total	13.2%	6.4%	15.2%	34.8%

Table 4. Number of Archaeology Faculty Involved in Interdisciplinary Research in 131 University Departments.

Year	1983	2007
Archaeobotany	13	19
Archaeozoology	17	60
Bioarchaeology	3	36
Geo/Chemical Analysis	19	30
Dating Methods	0	13
Remote Sensing & GIS	2	35
Total Interdisciplinary	54	193

Table 5. Proportional Representation of Archaeology Faculty Involved in Interdisciplinary Research in 131 University Departments.

Year	Archaeobiology	Bioarchaeology	Earth & Physical Sciences	Total Interdisciplinary
1983	5.4%	0.5%	3.8%	9.7%
2007	12.1%	5.5%	11.9%	29.5%

departmental guides. The number of archaeologists working within different interdisciplinary fields examined has increased dramatically over the past 25 years (Table 4). With the exception of archaeobotany, there are now at least twice as many archaeologists who cite expertise in each of these different fields in 2007 as there were in 1983. Archaeozoology is now the most commonly represented interdisciplinary field; archaeologists conducting archaeozoological research outnumber those engaged in other interdisciplinary fields by at least two to one. Overall, the representation of archaeologists in academic departments actively working in one or more of these interdisciplinary sciences has risen from just below 10 percent in 1983 to nearly 30 percent in 2007, with substantial gains seen in all of the fields considered here (Table 5).

Trends in hiring interdisciplinary archaeologists were measured by surveying the job placement listings published in the AAA Anthropology Newsletter in 1983 and in 2006 (Table 6). Mirroring the increased interdisciplinary expertise among archaeologists within academic departments, there has also been a marked increase over the past 25 years in job listings that call for this expertise—from 14 percent in 1983 to 37 percent in 2006 (Table 7). Interestingly, the proportion of listings calling for expertise in archaeobiology has decreased over this time, while the proportion of those specifying expertise

Table 6. Number of Advertised Archaeology Jobs Specifying Expertise in Interdisciplinary Sciences*

Year	1983	2007
Archaeobotany	1	0
Archaeozoology	3	2
Bioarchaeology	0	3
Geo/Chemical Analysis	2	6
Dating Methods	0	1
Remote Sensing & GIS	0	3
Total Interdisciplinary	6	15
Total Archaeology	42	41

*Includes all tenure-track and short term positions in academic departments, museums, private firms, and foundations. Does not include postdoctoral fellowships or administrative positions.

Table 7. Proportional Representation of Advertised Archaeology Jobs Specifying Expertise in Interdisciplinary Sciences.

Year	Archaeobiology	Bioarchaeology	Earth & Physical Sciences	Total Interdisciplinary Sciences
1983	9.5%	0%	4.8%	14.3%
2006	4.9%	7.3%	24.3%	36.6%

in bioarchaeology and, especially, earth and physical sciences has increased. This shift in orientation may be related to the strong representation of archaeobiology (i.e., archaeozoology) among current faculty discussed above (Table 4). New hires may in this period have been oriented toward interdisciplinary sciences that were not as well represented in departments' faculty and staff, with expertise in the area of geo/chemical analysis seeing the most growth over this period.

Major Topics in Interdisciplinary Studies

The growth of interdisciplinary archaeological research documented in these trends has been accompanied by a dramatic increase in the scope and impact of the questions addressed through interdisciplinary methods. This next section explores major research topics in the general areas of archaeobiology and bioarchaeology, the two disciplinary areas most familiar to us. These admittedly broad-brush treatments represent an effort to identify, from our own personal perspectives, enduring research directions that hold special opportunities for future work. In each discussion we trace the development of interdisciplinary research over the past 25 years, highlighting recent work, especially that of younger researchers, which we feel represents exciting new directions in interdisciplinary archaeology. Our focus is on the questions addressed in these interdisciplinary domains, emphasizing how advances in interdisciplinary research methods have transformed the scope and impact of the questions archaeologists are now capable of exploring.

While we do not present a detailed perspective here on key developments in the interdisciplinary physical sciences, we would like to call the reader's attention to several authoritative statements published within the past quarter century. Included are general handbooks on archaeological science (Brothwell and Pollard 2001; Maschner and Chippindale 2005) and those that center on specialized topics, such as chronometry (Aitkin 1990), materials science and archaeology (Henderson 2000), geoarchaeology (Goldberg and MacPhail 2006), and analytical chemistry in archaeology (Pollard et al. 2007).

Archaeobiology

Archaeobiology, as we are defining it here, encompasses all research directed at understanding the history of human interaction with plants and animals through the study of archaeobotanical and archaeofaunal remains. Archaeobotany and archaeozoology (more commonly known as zooarchaeology in the U.S.) have not always been as closely linked as this term implies. Indeed, early practitioners of these disciplines were primarily grounded in botany, zoology, veterinary medicine (in Central Europe), or paleontology, and were not necessarily well versed in archaeological problems or practice. Instead, they engaged in the study of archaeological remains either as a sideline or as a means of obtaining data to apply to more purely biological questions, i.e., paleo-environmental and bio-geographical reconstruction or tracing the phylogeny of specific plant and animal taxa (for an excellent summary of the history of archaeozoology see Reitz and Wing 2008).

From the mid-twentieth century on, studies of plant and animal remains from archaeological sites have increasingly focused on anthropological issues, especially the nature of human-environment interactions and the reconstruction of ancient subsistence economies. Integration of these fields within archaeology became even tighter when, in the 1970s, students based in anthropology graduate programs sought training in either zoology or botany with the explicit aim of applying the study of plant and animal remains to archaeological questions. These questions have grown over the years to include the social and ideological dimensions of the human past in addition to the environmental and economic aspects. The potential for integrating archaeobotanical and archaeozoological data in the address of overarching questions is only now beginning to be realized (see for example the special edition of *Current Anthropology* dedicated to case studies that bring archaeofaunal and archaeobotanical data together in synthetic studies of culture change [Smith and Miller 2009]). But as we begin to work past the methodological barriers that have blocked more synthetic interaction between archeobotanists and archaeozoologists, we are witnessing the transformation of archaeobiology from a holding category for various methodological approaches to the study of nonhuman biological remains, into an exciting and expanding research domain whose centrifugal forces are now capturing the energy of new interdisciplinary domains.

Here we highlight four major research topics in archaeobiology: (1) Foraging Strategies and Human Evolution, (2) Domestication and Agricultural Origins, (3) The Archaeobiology of Social Complexity, and (4) New Directions in Historical Ecology. We recognize that these are well-traveled areas of archaeobiological research. But we believe that each of these enduring research topics have been reinvigorated in recent years thanks to a combination of enhanced analytical methods and the maturation of our understanding of the problems encompassed by these general topics.

(1) Foraging Strategies and Human Evolution. The work of the late Glynn Isaac in the 1970s crystallized attention on the importance of food transport, processing, and sharing in early hominin social evolution (Isaac 1978). The role of meat acquisition and distribution in shaping human evolution has been especially emphasized (Hill 1982; Washburn and Lancaster 1968), although the exploitation of plant resources, especially plants with underground storage organs, has also figured in discussions of engines of evolutionary change in humans (Hartley and Kappelman 1980; Laden and Wrangham 2005).

There have, however, been methodological impediments that limited the archaeobiological study of the interesting connections between food and human evolution. In archaeozoology, questions about the role of humans in the accumulation of archaeofaunal assemblages, the impact of various taphonomic forces on these assemblages, and the optimal quantitative methods for assessing human behaviors through the study of bones had to be addressed before these broader linkages could be explored (e.g., Behrensmeyer and Hill 1980; Grayson 1984, 1989; Lyman 1985, 1992, 1994; Marean and Spencer 1991; Noe-Nygaard 1988). Archaeobotanists, on the other hand, have not had the luxury of worrying about questions of taphonomic bias or quantification of archaeobotanical remains, but instead have had to contend with the almost complete absence of plant remains from early sites.

While questions about taphonomy and quantification appropriately remain at the forefront, archaeozoologists working in this area are increasingly applying the lessons learned from these important middle-range studies to more substantive questions about the linkage between foraging and human evolution. New techniques for the recovery of plant remains, especially for the recovery of plant microfossils (phytoliths and starches) from sediments, human teeth, and tools (i.e., Piperno 2006a; Piperno and Pearsall 1998), are making the archaeobotanial study of the relationship between food and human evolution more feasible.

The other major advance over the past 25 years has been the increasing sophistication of the application of foraging models to archaeobiological research. Moving beyond the now widespread (and sometimes overly simplistic and mechanical) application of optimal foraging theory to the study of archaeobiological remains, researchers are beginning to draw more broadly and with more nuance from the general conceptual framework of Human Behavioral Ecology (HBE) to study the role of foraging in human evolution (see Lupo 2007 for a comprehensive summary of the application of evolutionary foraging models in archaeozoology). Early hominin scavenging, for example, has been portrayed as an example of costly signaling in which the acquisition of meat, directed more toward competitive male displays rather than meeting nutritional needs, is seen as an important element in the sexual division of labor in early humans (Hawkes and Bliege Bird 2002; O'Connell et al. 2002). Considerations of the effects of resource depression on foraging efficiency (Nagaoka 2002, 2005; Ugan 2005), refined applications of prey and patch choice in the construction of diet breadth models (Broughton 2002; Burger et al. 2005), and the use of central place foraging models to understand transport decisions (Lupo 2006) all represent creative uses of HBE as a conceptual context in archaeozoological studies of foraging.

Some of the most interesting research in this area focuses on the behavioral complexity of Neanderthals and anatomically modern humans. Especially noteworthy is the growing body of work that combines sophisticated applications of foraging theory with innovative archaeozoological analysis to examine the behavioral repertoires of early humans (e.g., Assefa 2006; Assefa et al. 2008; Bar-Oz et al. 2002; Burke 2000; Faith 2008; Grayson and Delpech 2006; Hoffacker and Cleghorn 2000; Marean et al. 2007; Morin 2008; Stringer et al. 2008; Yeshurun et al. 2007). The utilization of plants by archaic and early modern humans is less well understood. Recent isotopic studies of Neanderthal remains from more northern parts of their range, in fact, suggest a heavy, apparently almost exclusive, Inuit-like reliance on meat (Bocherens et al. 2005; Richards et al. 2000; Richards et al.2008). There is, however, mounting evidence that plants played an important role in the diets and foraging strategies of Neanderthals located in more temperate parts of the Neanderthal range (Albert et al. 2003; Lev et al. 2005). Recovery of plant microfossils, especially starches and phytoliths recovered from tools and teeth, holds special promise for adding fiber to the diets of archaic humans, and in so doing expands our understanding of Neanderthal diet and foraging behaviors and how these behaviors contributed to their late survival in some places and their earlier replacement by modern humans in others.

Archaeobotanical applications of HBE to transitional foraging societies on the cusp of agriculture are becoming more common (see examples in Kennett and Winterhalder 2006). The work of Gremillion (2002, 2006) in eastern North America and Denham and Barton (2006) in Highland New Guinea provide particularly strong examples of the use of HBE as a heuristic device in the evaluation of the archaeobotanical record of transitional foraging groups. Faunal analogs can be found in Munro's attempts to measure the impact of hunting pressure and occupation intensity in the Epipaleolithic Levant through the study of a variety of faunal indices elegantly embedded in a general context of diet breadth and prey-ranking models (Munro 2004; Munro and Bar-Oz 2005; Stiner and Munro 2002; see also Bar-Oz 2004).

(2) Domestication and Agricultural Origins. Plant and animal domestication and the origin of agriculture have been foundational research areas in archaeobiology for at least 100 years (Pumpelly 1908), but the work of Robert Braidwood (Braidwood and Howe 1960; Braidwood et al. 1983) in the Near East and of Richard MacNeish (Byers 1967) in Central Mexico in

the 1950s and 1960s (both recipients of the SAA Fryxell Award in Interdisciplinary Research) can be credited with setting standards for the interdisciplinary research that continues to shape the study of domestication and agricultural origins today. Recent years have seen a virtual explosion of research in this enduring area of inquiry, due in large measure to methodological advances in the study of plant and animal remains growing out of archaeology, biology, and chemistry (see Zeder et al., eds. 2006; Zeder et al. 2006).

Enhanced methods for the recovery of archaeobotanical remains are providing an increasingly rich empirical record of plant domestication around the world (Smith 2006). Especially impressive are the breakthrough advances in the recovery and analysis of plant micro-fossils that have transformed our understanding of agricultural origins and dispersal in both tropical and temperate areas around the world (e.g., Mbida et al. 2006; Messner et al. 2008; Perry et al. 2006; Perry et al. 2007; Piperno 2006a; Piperno and Pearsall 1998). Recent reappraisal of archaeozoological methods for documenting animal domestication in the archaeological record (see Vigne et al. 2005; Zeder 2006) is weaning archaeozoologists from their reliance on a single, one-size-fits-all marker of animal domestication and, in so doing, opening up new avenues for tracing the process of animal domestication (e.g., Albarella et al. 2006; Mengoni Gonalons and Yacobaccio 2006; Munro 2010; Olsen 2006; Rossel et al. 2008).

From the time of Mendel, domesticates have been a primary research focus in genetics, but genetics and archaeology have come together in the study of domestication in especially powerful ways in the past decade (see Zeder et al., eds. 2006; Zeder et al. 2006). Increasing success in extracting ancient DNA from archaeological plant and animal remains and the close collaboration of archaeologists and geneticists in these studies have resulted in a number of high-impact publications that provide a close-grained picture of domestication in action (Erickson et al. 2005; Jaenicke-Despré et al. 2003; Larson et al. 2007; Snyder and Leonard 2010). Isotopic studies of archaeological animal bones are adding important new dimensions to our understanding of both the climatic parameters and the changing management regimes (Ervnyck et al. 2001; Makarewicz and Tuross 2008; Mashkour et al. 2005) that accompanied the transition from hunting to herding.

Methodological advances in documenting domestication have, in turn, caused a reappraisal of the process of domestication and the emergence of agricultural economies based on domesticates. Growing recognition that morphological markers of domestication may only be manifest relatively late in the domestication process (Tanno and Wilcox 2006; Weiss et al. 2006; Zeder 2009) has focused attention on the long run-up to morphological change during which humans and certain plant and animal species followed an often winding co-evolutionary pathway toward increasing mutual interdependence. The concept of niche construction (Smith 2007a, 2007b) provides a context to this process, casting humans as eco-system engineers manipulating environments to encourage economically useful plants and animals. In some cases that process led to domestic partnerships. Recognition of this deep transitional process also opens up for study a broad middle ground between foragers and farmers, which encompasses a wide range of different low-level food-producing behaviors based on various mixes of wild, managed, and in some cases fully domesticated resources (Smith 2001). This paradigmatic shift in our understanding of domestication and its relationship to agricultural origins sets the stage for the next decade of work in this area, as archaeobiologists' apply an enhanced suite of analytical methods to the documentation of the deep history of human manipulation of environments and biota, and the diverse pathways to domestication and agriculture followed by humans around the world.

(3) The Archaeobiology of Complexity. The 1980s and early 1990s witnessed the first serious attempts to tackle issues of social complexity through the study of archaeological plant and animal remains, with initial archaeobiological studies directed at the study of complexity in economy (Wattenmaker 1998; Wright et al. 1981; Zeder 1991); status (Jackson and Scott 1995; Welch and Scarry 1995); gender (Hastorf 1996); ritual (Wapnish and Hesse 1991); and ethnicity (see Crabtree 1990). Interest in these issues has intensified over the intervening quarter century and there is now a new generation of archaeobiologists taking on the difficult task of teasing out social complexity through the study of plant and animal remains.

Highlights of this recent work include studies of the role of food in the creation and the maintenance of status and ethnic identity in both Old and New World proto- and historic societies (Emery 2003; Ervynck 2004; Ervynck et al. 2003; Jackson and Scott 2003; Lapham 2004; Lev-Tov 2000, 2004; Linseele 2004; Potter 2004; Thomas 2007; Twiss 2007; van der Veen 2007). A particularly interesting subset of this work on food and status examines the varied roles of feasting in reinforcing community cohesion and in creating social distinctions within communities (Fritz and Lopinot 2007;

Kansa and Campbell 2004; Kelly 2001; Lev-Tov and McGeough 2007). The ceremonial use of plants and animals in ritual, especially as it relates to the reification of both secular and religious power, has also been a growth area (Emery 2003; Hastorf 2003; Jing and Flad 2005; Kelly and Kelly 2007; Muir and Driver 2004; Rofes 2004; Russell and McGowan 2003). The use of archaeobiological data to monitor the partitioning of subsistence tasks—especially the gendered separation of labor in procuring and preparing food—often conducted within the framework of household archaeology, is a particularly challenging and promising new direction in the archaeobiology of social complexity (Atalay and Hastorf 2006; Jones 2009; Twiss et al. 2009; VanDerwarker and Detwiler 2002; see also Miller, Morehart and Helmke, and Pankonien in a special volume dedicated to gender and household archaeology, Robin and Brumfiel 2008). And while the marriage between high concepts and hard data is not always complete in this research, this exciting new corpus of work research points the way to further advances in the archaeobiology of complexity.

(4) New Directions in Historical Ecology. A theme that runs throughout all these topical areas is the interplay between humans, plant, and animal exploitation, and environment, which falls under the general category of historical ecology. Archaeobiological research currently being conducted in this area bears little resemblance to earlier work embedded in a one-dimensional framework of environmental determinism (i.e., the environment made them do it) or in simplistic axioms about human impacts on environments (i.e., seeing all human impact as bad, or none of it bad before Columbus). Instead, recent archaeobiological work in this area increasingly uses the multiple and increasing new tools at our disposal to conduct careful, diachronic studies of human interaction with the environments and responses to environmental change, providing a unique and essential historical perspective on the long-term interplay between humans and environments (Hayashida 2005; Kirch 2005).

This body of work includes studies that revisit the thorny issue of sorting the respective role of humans and climate change in animal extinctions (e.g., Fisher in a volume on North American mega-faunal extinctions edited by Haynes 2008). It includes a growing number of longitudinal studies seeking to trace both anthropogenic and natural factors on a variety of different ecological systems from arid regions (Coltrain and Leavitt 2002; Smith and Munro 2009) to the tropics (Emery and Thornton 2008; Piperno 2006b;

Stahl 2006), to temperate zones (Hallett et al. 2003; Kerig and Lechterbeck 2004), to marine coastal regions (see the edited volume by Rick and Erlandson 2008; also Braje et al. 2007; Darwent 2004). Growing recognition of the broad middle ground between foraging and farming and the degree to which humans were engaged in eco-system engineering prior to agricultural emergence has produced impressive new work that seeks to detect the nature and degree of human ecological management, as elegantly exemplified by Lepofsky and Lertzman's (2008) recent paper on detecting ancient plant management in northwestern North America (see also Denham et al. 2003; Fish and Fish 1990; Smith 2010; and various articles in the edited volume by Deur and Turner 2005). The southwestern U.S. has proven to be particularly fertile region for the archaeobiological examination of long-term human/environmental interaction (e.g., Varien et al. 2007). The potential contribution of this work to conservation biology is a particularly exciting new direction that is recently finding special traction in archaeozoology (see Frazier 2007; Grayson 2005; Grayson and Delpech 2005; Lyman and Cannon 2004; Peacock and Mistak 2008).

Bioarchaeology

As with archaeobiology, bioarchaeology began with practitioners from other fields, drawn principally from anatomy and the medical (including dental) sciences, who applied their knowledge to archaeological materials, in this case, human remains. Developing as a serious, scientific study during the nineteenth and twentieth centuries, such research became increasingly anthropological in the Western Hemisphere and archaeological in the U.K., with practitioners currently lodged in social and biomedical departments in universities, museums, and private contracting firms across the globe. The purview of bioarchaeology has also expanded to consider full funerary contexts, both archaeological and historical, drawing upon theories and methodologies from the social, physical, and life sciences.

Bioarchaeology, originally defined as the study of faunal remains (Clark 1972), was quickly generalized to the study of all archaeobiological materials for researchers in the U.K. and most of Europe. In the U.S., bioarchaeology was described independently as the problem-oriented investigation of human remains and funerary sites to investigate diverse topics, including social organization, division of labor, demography, population structure, diet, health, and disease (Buikstra 1977; Buikstra and Beck 2006; Larsen

1987, 1997). Also prominent within the past quarter century is Frank Saul's osteobiographic approach, which focuses first upon single lives and then turns to population characterizations (Saul 1972; Saul and Saul 1989).

In the following section we briefly consider key developments within bioarchaeology during the previous quarter century, focusing upon the following topics: (1) health, diet, and food production; (2) the human lifespan; (3) host-pathogen co-evolution: Homo sapiens and infectious diseases; (4) interpersonal violence, warfare, and cannibalism; (5) communicating with descendent communities; (6) residential histories, mobility, and migration; and (7) bioarchaeology and identity.

(1) Health, Diet, and Food Production. Influenced by the New Archaeology's emphasis upon human ecology and adaptation, a cluster of bioarchaeological investigations of health, diet, and demography have focused upon exploring alternative explanatory models for changes in food production, especially agricultural intensification. Such research requires comparative study of human histories across time and space. Two approaches have assumed prominence.

Beginning with the 1984 publication of a landmark volume in comparative studies of health over time, *On the Origins of Agriculture* (Cohen and Armelagos 1984), interest in exploring the mechanisms that stimulated agricultural intensification (Cohen 1977) was combined with temporally sequential, regionally derived skeletal series that represented periods of agricultural intensification. Additional publications (Cohen 1989; Cohen and Crane-Kramer 2007) have reaffirmed the 1984 conclusions and expanded the earlier database of primarily European and Western Hemisphere sequences to include samples from Africa and Southeast Asia. The main propositions considered in 1984 were (1) that the adoption of agriculture resulted from "need and stress, not invention and choice"; and (2) that health generally declined with the adoption of agriculture. The 1984 data were said to confirm the second proposition and by inference, the first (Cohen and Crane-Kramer 2007:2). And while the demographic model for agricultural origins is open to critique (see Zeder 2006, 2009; Zeder and Smith 2009) this study represents the first use of bioarchaeological data in a global test of theoretical models for the intensification of food production.

A second notable effort at global comparisons, influenced by Cohen and Armelagos (1984), was the Western Hemisphere Health and Nutrition Project (Steckel and Rose 2002). In this case an economic historian (Steckel) and numerous bioarchaeologists joined forces to evaluate the quality of human life through the study of skeletal attributes, which were combined into a quantitative "health index." The results of the Western Hemisphere study, too, argue that throughout the history of the human condition, health has declined. This study is currently being extended globally (Steckel 2002).

Both approaches have elicited critiques. One significant response was from Wood and colleagues (1992) whose "osteological paradox" argued that there could be a positive correlation between observed skeletal pathology and good health, given that one must live sufficiently long to register a bony insult rather than dying precipitously and thus providing the bioarchaeologists with a seemingly "healthy" skeleton (see also Ortner 1992). Arguments over the relationship between skeletal stress markers and community health will undoubtedly continue well into the next quarter century, their results strengthening our science.

A further methodological advance that complements developments in paleopathology has been the resolution afforded by bone chemistry in the study of paleodiets (see reviews in Katzenberg 2008; Schoeninger and Moore 1992; Schwarcz and Schoeninger 1991; Tykot 2006). Isotopic research, pioneered by DeNiro (DeNiro and Epstein 1981) and Vogel and van der Merwe (Vogel and van der Merwe 1977; van der Merwe and Vogel 1978) has been especially effective at addressing regional temporal trends, along with issues of gender and other social differences in ancient diets. For example, bioarchaeologists, working at a regional level and considering evidence both from paleodiet and health studies, have contributed significantly to the debate concerning the mechanisms that led to the Classic Maya collapse, specifically a test of ecological models, which were found wanting (see Wright and White 1996 for a summary).

(2) The Human Lifespan. During the past quarter century, paleodemographers have debated the degree to which the human lifespan and related mortality profiles were significantly different in the past than they are today. A marked critique of paleodemographic methods developed in the early 1980s (Bocquet-Appel and Masset 1982) and encouraged researchers to further address both methodological and theoretical issues (Bocquet-Appel and Masset 1996; Buikstra and Konigsberg 1985; Buikstra et al. 1986; Frankenberg and Konigsberg 2006; Hoppa and Vaupel 2002; Jackes 1985, 2000; Konigsberg and Frankenberg 1992; Sattenspiel and Harpending 1983). Notable among the responses has been the attempt to develop age indicators

useful beyond the sixth decade of life. One such (non-invasive) approach is Transition Analysis (Boldsen et al. 2002; Milner et al. 2000) that combines new observational techniques with Bayesian methods. Transition analysis has performed well in both historical and archaeological records (Boldsen et al. 2002; Buikstra et al. 2005, 2006).

(3) Host-pathogen Co-evolution: Homo sapiens and Infectious Diseases. The study of specific disease histories, especially the infectious diseases that produce diagnostic bone changes such as leprosy and the treponematoses (yaws, nonvenereal syphilis, and tuberculosis), continue to be the focus of considerable bioarchaeological attention. All three of these diseases have received comparative treatments at global scales (Dutour et al. 1994; Palfi et al. 1999; Roberts 2010; Roberts and Buikstra 2005; Roberts et al. 2002). A North American synthesis of information upon the treponematoses (Powell and Cook 2005), for example, provides compelling evidence against the Columbian origins argument, which specifies that Columbus and his crew brought a venereal pathogen back to Europe from the New World. This perspective is not, however, shared by all (Harper et al. 2008).

Remarkable advances in understanding the evolutionary history of two mycobacterial diseases, tuberculosis and leprosy, have been made through the study of human remains, archival materials, and molecular evidence of both contemporary variation in the pathogens and in ancient remnants of the mycobacterial genome. While the only apparently successful attempt to extract and amplify treponemal aDNA (Kolman et al. 2000) has been seriously questioned (Bouwman and Brown 2005), recovery of *M. tuberculosis* complex and *M. leprae* aDNA has increased our ability to confidently diagnose ancient disease and to bioarchaeologically "ground truth" in phylogenetic models based upon investigations of contemporary molecular variability in mycobacterial pathogens, especially tuberculosis (Brosch et al. 2002; Fletcher et al. 2003; Gagneux et al. 2006; Gutierrez et al. 2005; Hughes et al. 2002; Taylor and Mays 2003). A spectacular recent development has been the generation of phylogenetic models that push the origins of *M. tuberclulosis* into deep time, perhaps 35,000 to 2.5-30 mya (Gutierrez et al. 2005; Hughes et al. 2002; Pfister et al. 2008), with the human pathogen being older than *M. bovis.* Prevailing wisdom had been that the zoonotic, bovine form served as the foundation for transfer to humans in the course of intensified animal husbandry in the Eastern Mediterranean approximately 10,000 years ago (Cockburn 1963; Rich 1944).

(4) Interpersonal Violence, Warfare, and Cannibalism. During the past quarter century, bioarchaeologists have contributed significantly to issues surrounding violence in the past. While many earlier archaeologists and bioarchaeologists had accepted prevailing wisdom concerning the lack of violent behaviors among earlier Native Americans, perhaps introduced or at least encouraged by Europeans, recent years have witnessed both archaeological and bioarchaeological evidence for warfare and other forms of interpersonal violence well before the European *entrada* (Haas 1990; Haas and Creamer 1997; Keeley 1996; Milner 1995, 1999; Milner et al. 1991; Willey 1990). Bioarchaeological evidence has, for example, been used to support inferences of cannibalism in the American Southwest (Billman et al. 2000; Turner and Turner 1999; T. White 1992), although archaeologists and bioarchaeologists have proposed alternative interpretations (Darling 1999; Ogilvie and Hilton 2000; Walker 1998). Coprolite evidence does support the notion that a human being consumed human flesh at least once in southwestern antiquity (Marlar et al. 2000).

Other recent studies have focused upon gender-specific violence. Martin and Akins (2001) infer a female underclass between A.D. 1000 and 1300 in SW Colorado, while extreme peri-mortem violence has been conjectured as evidence for political intimidation within the same region (Lekson 2002). In fact, a recent review has concluded that there is bioarchaeological evidence for violence throughout human history, extending in North America from the dart or spear point lodged in Kennewick Man (Chatters 2000) throughout the precontact period and beyond (Walker 2001).

(5) Communicating with Descendent Communities. One of the most profound effects upon bioarchaeology in the United States has been the passage of the Native American Graves Protection and Repatriation Act (NAGPRA; Public Law No: 101-601: http://www.nps.gov/history/nagpra/MANDATES/25USC3001etseq.htm) in 1990 (see also chapters by Sebastian, Wilcox, this volume). This well-known legislation required institutions from across the country to inventory their collections of human remains and funerary objects and to notify potential descendents of federally recognized tribal groups. The 1989 National Museum of the American Indian Act was essentially parallel legislation affecting the Smithsonian Institution. NAGPRA requires consultation and in some cases permission from tribes before human remains are excavated on federal or tribal lands. While this required bioarchaeologists to change their modus operandi, such communication has

productively directed research to topics of interest to living descendents, and it has also enriched our interpretations of past funerary sequences. Contact with living communities, rare but not unknown for United States archaeologists prior to 1990, has, for example, encouraged consultation of ethnohistoric sources when evaluating funerary behavior (e.g., Beck 2005).

Consultation with descendent communities has also stimulated new research trajectories (see also Silliman and Ferguson this volume). Bioarchaeologist Karl Reinhard, for example, has undertaken comparisons of lifestyle features for ancestral and contemporary groups of Omaha Indians as part of a project to investigate causal factors for the observed high prevalence of Type II diabetes (~70 percent) today. He is also developing new methods for observing coprolites, mummies, and skeletal remains as part of his collaborative research on paleoecology and Indian diseases of Indians (Reinhard 2000; Reinhard et al. 1994, http://snr.unl.edu/aboutus/who/people/faculty/reinhard-karl.asp). One aspect of his research is an example of the rapidly growing field of mummy science (Aufderheide 2003).

While most American Indian and First Nations groups that encourage scientific study prefer nondestructive methods (Anyon and Thornton 2002; Brownlee and Syms 1999), the Champagne and Aishihik First Nations (CAFN) agreement between the CAFN and the provincial government specified state-of-the-art scientific study for the remains of a young man who had been recovered in the mountains of northwestern British Columbia. These studies, including paleodietary stable isotope analyses, determined that this youth had lived near the sea for much of his life (Dickson et al. 2004).

Although not covered by NAGPRA, the remains of people of other ethnicities are also frequently of keen interest to descendent communities. One such example is the New York African Burial Ground Project. In the course of discussions between scientists, government representatives, and descendent constituents, major research topics emerged focusing on the cultural background and origins of the population, the cultural and biological transformation from African to African-American identities, the quality of life of enslaved African-Americans, and their modes of resistance to slavery (Blakey 2004; http://www.africanburialTground.gov/FinalReports/HUsbrABG_Ch3_Rvsd.pdf). The last three of these topics were addressed with a combination of standard osteological observations, and archival data, in frequently innovative ways. The investigation of ancestry, however, led to two new forms of interdisciplinary study. In the first, molecular genetic information—specifically ancient mitochondrial DNA—supplemented craniometric and dental comparisons. This aDNA data provide tantalizing evidence of origins in west and central Africa, with a few individuals being more precisely linked to specific geographic areas (Jackson et al. 2004; http://www.africanburialground.gov/FinalReports/HUsbrABG_Ch3_Rvsd.pdf). The second method for evaluating origins is described in the following section (see also Franklin and Paynter, this volume; Silliman and Ferguson, this volume; and Little and Zimmerman, this volume).

(6) Residential Histories, Mobility, and Migration. As with the study of paleodiet, research on human residential mobility has been markedly enhanced through the study of bone chemistry. Isotope ratios such as those of strontium, lead, and oxygen provide clues to residence, as signatures are literally crystallized in bone and teeth as dental tissues form and bones remodel (Ericson 1985; Katzenberg 2008). Reflecting isotopic ratios of bedrock (Sr, Pb) and climate (O), carried up the food web without fractionation, these signatures have been used to address issues such as the origins and route taken by slaves entering North America (Goodman et al. 2004; Thttp://www.africanburialground.gov/TfinalReports/HUsbrABG_Ch3_Rvsd.pdf), gender and residence in the American Southwest (Price et al. 1994), genetic vs. symbolic origins of ancient Maya elite (Buikstra et al. 2006; Price et al. 2006), colonization and migration as forces shaping ancient Andean polities (Knudson et al. 2004; Knudson and Price 2007), immigrants into Teotihuacan (Price et al. 2000), intensity of interaction and mobility for migrants from Oaxaca to Teotihuacan (White et al. 2004), and the physical spread of late Neolithic and early Bronze Bell Beaker people across Europe (Price et al. 1998).

Residential histories have also been estimated through analyses of dental and skeletal morphology, as well as ancient DNA (for reviews see Konigsberg 2006; Stone 2008). Morphological analyses are multiscalar, ranging from postmarital residence and other implications of intra-cemetery variation (Schillaci and Stojanowski 2003; Sutter and Verano 2007; see Stojanowski and Schillaci 2006 for a review), to regional approaches (Konigsberg and Buikstra 1995; Steadman 1998, 2001), and continental and global processes (Blom et al. 1998; González-José et al. 2008; Hallgrímmson et al. 2004; Powell and Neves 1999; Schillaci 2008). Ancient DNA applications have faced technical challenges posed by incomplete recovery, contamination, and related matters (Stone 2008). Cold environments are the best contexts for preservation as, for example, Keyser-Tracqui and colleagues' (Keyser-Tracqui et al. 2003) study of a Mongolian cemetery wherein both mitochondrial and nuclear DNA were preserved. Intra-cemetery and regional studies of ancient mtDNA variation have also proved enlightening (Lewis et al. 2007; Stone and Stoneking 1993, 1996), as have those of single individuals, including Neanderthal remains (Krings et al. 1997) and ancient American Paleoindians, including examples wherein both genetic affinity and sex were estimated (Stone and Stoneking 1996; see also Stone et al. 1996 for additional discussion of sex estimations using aDNA).

(7) The Bioarchaeology of Identity. While many recent advances have engaged bioarchaeologists in theories and/or methods drawn from the natural or physical sciences (see also Larsen 2006), recently bioarchaeologists have also been stimulated by theories developed in the social sciences. Both U.K. and U.S. bioarchaeologists, for example, have tended to approach issues of agency, embodiment, materiality, personhood, and selfhood from slightly different perspectives. Scholars in the U.K. have been apt to focus upon single dimensions of religion, status, ethnicity, gender, age (especially childhood), and disability, or the interaction of gender with one of the other aspects (e.g., Gowland and Knüsel 1997; Sofaer Derevenski 1997). U.S. workers, by contrast, have tended to emphasize the study of multiple identities, drawn from the same menu, in individuals and in groups (Knudson and Stojanowski 2009; Stodder and Palkovich 2009).

Recent studies of identity have used traditional (skeletal and dental observations of morphology and measurements) methods for estimating genetic relatedness, for example, with new theoretical perspectives and models drawn from population genetics, addressing such thorny topics as ethnicity and ethnogenesis (Nystrom 2005, 2009; Stojanowski 2005a, 2005b, 2009). Studies of identity have also examined the manner in which physical modifications, either inscribed in infancy (Lozada and Buikstra 2002; Tiesler Blos 1998; Torres-Rouff 2008) or during later life (Buikstra et al. 2004; Geller 2006; Tiesler Blos 2001; Torres-Rouff 2009) have embodied social, gender, age, or other distinctions. Such visible physical signals are shaped by society and influence the social relations that form the fabric of human existence.

Envisioning the Future of Interdisciplinary Archaeology

As we have emphasized here, the past 25 years have witnessed increasing integration of interdisciplinary research within archaeology. Our discussion of topical research in two interdisciplinary areas, archaeobiology and bioarchaeology, underscores the breadth and reach of work of scholars trained in these fields. They are employing interdisciplinary perspectives and analytical tools to tackle diverse and complex issues including the long-term histories of human-landscape interactions, host-pathogen co-evolution, the complex processes involved in plant and animal domestication, the impact of agriculture on human health, and the framing of cultural identity both in ancient populations and their modern-day descendents.

Our departmental and publication surveys lead us to anticipate increased representation of today's interdisciplinary scholars within archaeology during the next quarter century. However, we also imagine that many of these "specialties" will be fully integrated within the core of archaeology by 2035. As we amply document in this chapter, today's interdisciplinary archaeologists are increasingly addressing in vital new ways questions of traditional interest to archaeologists, including foraging strategies and human evolution, domestication and agricultural origins, social complexity, migration and residential histories, warfare, and diet. In addition, the current generation of interdisciplinary scholars is approaching many topics more recently visible within archaeology, such as gender, identity, ethnicity, and ethnogenesis. We therefore anticipate that the "us-them" distinctions between scholars of stones, ceramics, settlement organization, household organization and those of bones, seeds, and soils will have disappeared over the next quarter century.

This does not mean, however, that such centripetal tendencies will diminish archaeology's interdisciplinarity. In fact, we anticipate increased intellectual fusion with scholars who are either nascent partners with archaeologists or those who are not yet drawn into such collaborations. We further predict that these collaborations will markedly increase in magnitude, including large-scale "transdisciplinary" projects that are designed to address issues of contemporary significance.

Developed earlier in Europe than in North America, archaeological transdisciplinary projects have most commonly organized the collaborative efforts of large numbers of scientists to study long-term human-environment interactions. For example, the ARCHAEOMEDES Research Program

(1992–2002), centered in southern Europe, integrated the efforts of 65 researchers from 7 countries. Focused upon desertification, land degradation, and land abandonment, the research team included mathematicians, physicists, modelers, geologists, geochemists, soil scientists, and life scientists (van der Leeuw 1994, 2005; van der Leeuw, ed. 1998; van der Leeuw and Redman 2002). Within the Vera Basin, one of the ARCHAEOMEDES study areas, researchers clearly illustrated that twentieth-century perspectives are insufficient for exploring the factors causing desertification and designing appropriate methods for remediation. Only the eighth- to fifteenth-centuries Moorish regime of irrigation and arboriculture was sustainable, ensuring future regional vitality. By contrast, externally driven economic initiatives, e.g., the Roman exploitation of minerals and today's tourism and monocropping, have markedly degraded the environment. ARCHAEOMEDES advocated a return to traditional methods of terracing and irrigation that would raise the fresh-water table and avoid the imminent saltwater incursion (Castro et al. 2000).

A similar long-term, transdisciplinary research program has been initiated by Carole Crumley and colleagues, focused upon the rich archaeological and historical record of France, especially that of the Burgundy region. Working with data reflecting the past 6,000 years of agrarian lifeways and 2,000 years of industrialization, Crumley and colleagues address issues of sustainability, moving deftly from small to large temporal and spatial scales. By integrating social and environmental information, this interdisciplinary program underscores the need to integrate local and regional knowledge in long-term planning and policy construction (Crumley 1984, 2006, 2007; http://anthropology.unc.edu/people/faculty/ccrumley).

Recent transdisciplinary studies have centered upon the North American Southwest. The Central Arizona-Phoenix Long-Term Ecological Research project was designed by Charles Redman to monitor the effects of urban development in the vulnerable southwestern environment (Grimm et al. 2000; van der Leeuw and Redman 2002). The fragile nature of the desert Southwest is underscored by the long-term impacts of Hohokam (A.D. 800–1200) wet and dry farming. Only a century of Hohokam dry farming in a Phoenix Basin context has left an imprint measurable today (Briggs et al. 2006).

Modelers represent another disciplinary specialty increasingly integrated with archaeology. With twenty-first century computer technology, modelers can address, for example, the complex interactions that characterize long-term changes in human biological and cultural systems and the manner in which humans and the environment have coevolved as socio-natural systems (Kohler and van der Leeuw 2007). Modeling socio-natural complexity is relatively new to archaeology, but it is now being applied on a global scale, and we predict significant advances over the course of the next quarter-century.

As we noted in our *American Antiquity* survey, very recent years have seen a marked increase in geophysical testing and remote sensing publications, with even more visibility for GIS. These are ingredients that, we believe, can transform the nature of twenty-first century archaeology. Both in the context of cultural resource management and in research contexts, the systematic use of non-invasive methods with limited ground truthing can predict site structural detail. For cultural resource managers, today's non-invasive activities, such as new highway corridors, can be located where there is minimal impact on the archaeological record. Similarly, for research archaeologists, sampling can occur in the context of known subsurface site structure. In both cases the expenditure of scarce archaeological resources is maximized and the impact on the archaeological record is minimized, as are curation needs (e.g., Kvamme 2005).

Finally, we predict increasing interdisciplinary engagement of scholars representing the humanities. While such collaborations are not unknown—for example, Amy Oakland Rodman's interpretations of Peruvian textiles (Rodman 1992; Rodman and Fernandez 2005)—today, however, archaeological scholars more commonly read and interpret published ethnohistories or accounts of oral narratives (e.g., Stojanowski 2009). Even more active collaboration between archaeologists, historians, and ethnohistorians would, of course, be preferable and is a likely outcome of the ongoing permeability of disciplinary barriers that seems a hallmark of twenty-first century scholarship. An impressive example of such a collaboration is the reinterpretation of Eastern Woodland material culture in the light of ethnohistorical data by Reilly and colleagues, recently published under the title *Ancient Objects and Sacred Realms* (Reilly and Garber 2007).

A comparison of recent developments in archaeological science in the U.S. and the U.K. by David Killick (2007) ranks the U.K. far ahead of the U.S. in developing innovative methodologies, in the archaeological application of such methodologies, and in archaeological infrastructure. Killick maintains that technological studies of materials tend to be more advanced in the U.K., including optical petrography, micromorphological applications in geoarchaeology, chronometric methods, including tephrochronology and especially organic chemistry. Funding levels for training and research in archaeological science are also superseded abroad, and national infrastructure planning in the U.S. is lacking, with funding levels and institutional support tending to be driven by individual initiatives rather than sustained commitments to research centers. These discrepancies in long-term infrastructural support for interdisciplinary archeology are matters of some concern, a pattern that may be underscored by the difficulty a number of once prominent programs in archaeological life and physical sciences have faced in trying to sustain themselves after the retirement of their original founders.

The National Science Foundation's Integrative Graduate Education and Research Traineeship (IGERT) program, however, represents a very promising step toward the creation of transdisciplinary graduate-level training programs and a special hope for the future of interdisciplinary archaeology in the U.S. To date, a number of universities have taken advantage of this forward-looking program to promote training in interdisciplinary research in archaeology. The University of Arizona, for example, established an IGERT funded program in Archaeological Sciences that emphasizes human uses of ancient landscapes and cross-cuts the University's Departments of Anthropology, Chemistry, Geosciences, and Materials Science and Engineering, the Arizona State Museum's Laboratory for Tree Ring Research, Center for Applied Spatial Analysis, and Accelerator Mass Spectrometry Laboratory, as well as two local private companies—Desert Archaeology Inc. and Statistical Research Inc. An IGERT-supported program in GIS at the University at Buffalo (State University of New York) draws resources from the Departments of Anthropology, Geography, Geology, Philosophy, Civil, Structural and Environmental Engineering, Computer Science and Engineering, and Industrial Engineering. In the Washington, D.C. area the cross-institutional IGERT supported Dynamics of Behavioral Shifts in Human Evolution Program brings together anthropology, molecular, and organismal biology, earth and environmental sciences, chemistry, physics, materials science, and engineering programs based in the George Washington University, the Smithsonian Institution, Howard University, and Johns Hopkins University. Another innovative IGERT program is the Evolutionary Modeling (IPEM) collaboration between Washington State University and the University of Washington http://ipem.anth.wsu.edu/. IPEM integrates biological and anthropological perspectives through a shared curriculum that emphasizes adaptation and diversification in genomic, behavioral, and cultural domains and training in models for studying evolutionary processes across these domains. Studying with a diverse faculty drawn from the fields of evolutionary biology, biological anthropology, archaeology, and cultural anthropology, students in anthropology and in the biological sciences incorporate archaeological, biological, or contemporary cultural data in interdisciplinary study.

Arizona State University's (ASU) IGERT in Urban Ecology represents another transdisciplinary graduate-level training program that seeks to integrate perspectives and expertise from the social, life, and physical sciences to better understand human-environmental relationships, past and present, in urban contexts. The ASU IGERT program is based in ASU's Global Institute for Sustainability, which is itself one of several cross-cut institutes within the newly created School of Human Evolution and Social Change (SHESC). ASU's restructured anthropology department represents one of the most significant outcomes of this movement toward "transdisciplinary" scholarship, one that may well be transforming the discipline of anthropology itself. While anthropology remains the core of this enterprise, traditional disciplinary boundaries have become permeable and additional anthropologists with interdisciplinary research interests have joined the initiative. Selected non-anthropological scholars have also been added, including geographers, modelers, sociologists, economists, mathematicians, and political scientists. Thus restructured, SHESC is serving as a centroid for significant transdisciplinary research at ASU and beyond. Another high-performing example of a restructured anthropology program built on an interdisciplinary model can be found at the SUNY Stony Brook, which has a well established cross-disciplinary graduate program and a nascent undergraduate program in evolutionary anthropology that reach across traditional disciplinary boundaries in anthropology, anatomy, and biological sciences. These restructured anthropology departments, and others like them, represent, in our minds, a promising path away from the internecine squabbling that troubles so many anthropology departments today toward a revitalized discipline that stands to make substantive contributions to twenty-first century scholarship and society.

In sum, we argue that when the SAA's centennial occurs in 2035, interdisciplinary archaeology will continue to be a vital, even transformative, force within the field. The players will have changed, however, as the current interdisciplinarians become part of the core, which will continue to engage an ever-widening range of scholars from across the humanities and the social, life, and physical sciences in research that addresses the complex nature of past human interactions with each other and with their environment, while also providing models for addressing issues whose resolution is essential for ensuring humankinds' future.

Acknowledgments. The authors would like to thank the following for their comments on trends in interdisciplinary archaeology: Kitty Emery, Gayle Fritz, Don Grayson, Kristen Gremillion, John Hart, Christine Hastorf, Karen Lupo, Fiona Marshall, Deborah Pearsall, Dolores Piperno, Elizabeth Reitz, Bruce Smith, John Speth, and Mary Stiner. Stephanie McBride and Zelalem Assefa contributed hours of greatly appreciated effort collecting statistics on the publication, practice, and job trends in interdisciplinary research and compiling the bibliography of this paper.

References Cited

Aitken, Martin J.
   1990 *Science-Based Dating in Archaeology.* Longman, London.

Albarella, Umberto, Keith Dobney, and Peter Rowley-Conwy
   2006 The Domestication of the Pig (Sus scrofa): New Challenges and Approaches. In *Documenting Domestication: New Genetic and Archaeological Paradigms,* edited by Melinda A. Zeder, Eve Emshwiller, Bruce D. Smith, and Daniel G. Bradley, pp. 209–227. University of California Press, Berkeley.

Albert, Rosa, Ofer Bar-Yosef, Liliane Meignen, and Steve Weiner
   2003 Quantitative Phytolith Study of Hearths from the Natufian and Middle Paleolithic Levels of Hayonim Cave (Galilee, Israel). *Journal of Archaeological Science* 30:461–480.

Anyon, Roger, and Russell Thornton
   2002 Implementing Repatriation in the United States: Issues Raised and Lessons Learned. In *The Dead and Their Possessions: Repatriation in Principle, Policy and Practice,* edited by Cressida Fforde, Jane Hubert, and Paul Turnbull, pp. 190–198. Routledge, New York.

Assefa, Zelalem
   2006 Faunal Remains from Porc-Epic: Paleoecological and Zooarchaeological Investigations from a Middle Stone Age Site in Southeastern Ethiopia. *Journal of Human Evolution* 51:50–75.

Assefa Zelalem, Yin Lam, and H. K. Mienis
   2008 Evidence of Symbolic Use of Terrestrial Snail Opercula from the Middle Stone Age Contexts of Porc-Epic Cave, Ethiopia. *Current Anthropology* 49:746–756.

Atalay, Sonya, and Christine Hastorf
   2006 Food, Meals, and Daily Activities: Food Habitus at Neolithic Çatalhöyük. *American Antiquity* 71:283–319.

Aufderheide, Arthur C.
   2003 *The Scientific Study of Mummies*. Cambridge University Press, Cambridge.

Bar-Oz, Guy
   2004 *Epipalaeolithic Subsistence Strategies in the Levant: A Zooarchaeological Perspective*. The American School of Prehistoric Research (ASPR) Monograph Series. Brill Academic Publishers Inc, Boston.

Bar-Oz, Guy, Daniel S. Adler, T. Meshveliani, N. Tushabramishvili, Anna Belfer-Cohen, and Ofer Bar-Yosef
   2002 Middle and Upper Palaeolithic Foragers of the Southwest Caucasus: New Faunal Evidence from Western Georgia. *Archaeology, Ethnology & Anthropology of Eurasia* 4(12):45–52.

Beck, Lane A.
   2005 Secondary Burial Practices in Hohokam Cremations. In *Interacting with the Dead: Perspectives on Mortuary Archaeology for the New Millennium*, edited by Gordon F. M. Rakita, Lane Beck, Sloan Williams, and Jane Buikstra, pp. 150–154. University Press of Florida, Gainesville.

Behrensmeyer, Anna K., and Andrew Hill
   1980 Taphonomic and Ecological Information from Bone Weathering. *Paleobiology* 4(2):150–162.

Billman, Brian R., Patricia M. Lambert, and Banks L. Leonard
   2000 Cannibalism, Warfare, and Drought in the Mesa Verde Region during the Twelfth Century A.D. *American Antiquity* 65:145–178.

Blakey, Michael L.
   2004 Theory: An Ethical Epistemology of Publicly Engaged Biocultural Research. In *The New York African Burial Ground Skeletal Biology Final Report*, vol. 1, edited by Michael L. Blakey and Lesley M. Rankin-Hill, pp. 98–115. Prepared by Howard University for the U.S. General Services Administration, Northeastern and Caribbean Region.

Blom, Deborah E., Benedikt Hallgrímsson, Linda Keng, Maria C. Lozada C., and Jane E. Buikstra
   1998 Tiwanaku 'Colonization': Bioarchaeological Implications for Migration in the Moquegua Valley, Perú. *World Archaeology* 30:238–261.

Bocherens, Hervé, Dorothée G. Drucker, Daniel Billiou, Marylène Patou-Mathis, and Bernard Vandermeersch
   2005 Isotopic Evidence for Diet and Subsistence Pattern of the Saint-Cesaire I Neanderthal: Review and Use of a Multi-Source Mixing Model. *Journal of Human Evolution* 49:71–87.

Bocquet-Appel, Jean-Pierre, and Claude L. Masset
   1982 Farewell to Paleodemography. *Journal of Human Evolution* 11:321–333.
   1996 Paleodemography: Expectancy and False Hope. *American Journal of Physical Anthropology* 99:571–583.

Boldsen, Jesper L., George R. Milner, Lyle W. Konigsberg, and James W. Wood
  2002 Transition Analyses: A New Method for Estimating Age from Skeletons. In *Paleodemography. I. Age Distributions from Skeletal Samples*, edited by Robert D. Hoppa and James W. Vaupel, pp. 73–106. Cambridge University Press, Cambridge.
Bouwman, Abigail S., and Terence A. Brown
  2005 The Limits of Biomolecular Palaeopathology: Ancient DNA Cannot Be Used to Study Venereal Syphilis. *Journal of Archaeological Science* 32:691–702.
Braidwood, Linda R., Robert J. Braidwood, Bruce Howe, Charles A. Reed, and Patty Jo Watson
  1983 *Prehistoric Archaeology Along the Zagros Flanks*. The Oriental Institute of the University of Chicago Studies in Ancient Oriental Civilization, No. 105. University of Chicago Press, Chicago.
Braidwood, Robert J., and Bruce Howe
  1960 *Prehistoric Investigations in Iraqi Kurdistan*. The Oriental Institute of the University of Chicago Studies in Ancient Oriental Civilization, No. 31. University of Chicago Press, Chicago.
Braje, Todd J., Douglas J. Kennett, Jon M. Erlandson, and Brendan J. Culleton
  2007 Human Impact on Nearshore Shellfish Taxa: A 7,000 Year Record from Santa Rosa Island, California. *American Antiquity* 72:735–756.
Briggs, John M., Katherine A. Spielmann, Hoski Schaafsma, Keith Kintigh, Melissa Kruse, Kari Morehouse, and Karen Schollmeyer
  2006 Why Ecology Needs Archaeologists and Archaeology Needs Ecologists. *Frontiers in Ecology and the Environment* 4:180–188.
Brosch, R., S. V. Gordon, M. Marmiesse, P. Brodin, C. Buchrieser, K. Eiglmeier, T. Garnier, C. Gutierrez, G. Hewinson, K. Kremer, L. M. Parsons, A. S. Pym, S. Samper, D. van Soolingen, and S. T. Cole
  2002 A New Evolutionary Scenario for the Mycobacterium Tuberculosis Complex. *Proceedings of the National Academy of Sciences, USA* 99:3684–3689.
Brothwell, Donald R., and A. Mark Pollard
  2001 *Handbook of Archaeological Sciences*. John Wiley and Sons, Chichester.
Broughton, Jack M.
  2002 Prey Spatial Structure and Behavior Affect Archaeological Tests of Optimal Foraging Models: Examples from the Emeryville Shellmound Vertebrate Fauna. *World Archaeology* 34:60–83.
Brownlee, Kevin, and E. Leigh Syms
  1999 *Kayasochi Kikawenow. Our Mother from Long Ago. An Early Cree Woman and Her Personal Belongings from Nagami Bay, Southern Indian Lake*. The Manitoba Museum of Man and Nature, Winnipeg.
Buikstra, Jane E.
  1977 Biocultural Dimensions of Archaeological Study: A Regional Perspective. In *Biocultural Adaptation in Prehistoric America*, edited by Robert L. Blakely, pp. 57–84. Proceedings of the Southern Anthropological Society, No. 11. University of Georgia Press, Athens.
Buikstra, Jane E., and Lane A. Beck (editors)
  2006 *Bioarchaeology: The Contextual Analysis of Human Remains*. Elsevier, New York.

Buikstra, Jane E., and Lyle W. Konigsberg
   1985 Paleodemography: Critiques and Controversies. *American Anthropologist* 87:316–333.

Buikstra, Jane E., Lyle W. Konigsberg, and Jill Bullington
   1986 Fertility and the Development of Agriculture in the Prehistoric Midwest. *American Antiquity* 51:528–546.

Buikstra, Jane E., George R. Milner, and Jesper L. Boldsen
   2005 Janaab' Pakal: La Controversia de la Edad Cronológica Revisitada. In *Janaab' Pakal of Palenque: Reconstructing the Life and Death of a Maya Ruler*, edited by Vera Tiesler and Andrea Cucina, pp. 103–122. UNAM/UADY, México, D.F.
   2006 The Age-at-death Controversy Re-revisited. In *Janaab' Pakal of Palenque: Reconstructing the Life and Death of a Maya Ruler*, edited by Vera Tiesler and Andrea Cucina, pp. 48–59. University of Arizona Press, Tucson.

Buikstra, Jane E., T. Douglas Price, James H. Price, and Lori E. Wright
   2004 Tombs from Copan's Acropolis: A Life History Approach. In *Understanding Early Classic Copan,* edited by Ellen E. Bell, Marcello A. Canuto, and Robert J. Sharer, pp. 191–212. University of Pennsylvania Museum of Archaeology and Anthropology, Philadelphia.

Burger, Oskar, Marcus J. Hamilton, and Robert Walker
   2005 The Prey as Patch Model: Optimal Handling of Resources with Diminishing Returns. *Journal of Archaeological Science* 32:1147–1158

Burke, Ariane
   2000 Hunting in the Middle Paleolithic. *International Journal of Osteoarchaeology* 10:281–285.

Byers, Douglas S.
   1967 The *Prehistory of the Tehuacan Valley. 1. Environment of Subsistence*. University of Texas Press, Austin.

Castro, Pedro, Sylvia Gili, Vicente Lull, Rafael Micó, Cristina Rihuete, Roberto Risch, Ma. Encarna Sanahuja YII, and Robert Chapman
   2000 Archaeology and Desertification in the Vera Basin (Almería, South-East Spain). *European Journal of Archaeology* 3:147–166.

Chatters, James
   2000 The Recovery and First Analysis of an Early Holocene Human Skeleton from Kennewick, Washington. *American Antiquity* 65:291–316.

Clark, John Grahame Douglas
   1972 *Star Carr: A Case Study in Bioarchaeology.* Modular Publications 10. Addison-Wesley, London.

Cockburn, T. Aidan
   1963 *The Evolution and Eradication of Infectious Diseases*. Johns Hopkins Press, Baltimore.

Cohen, Mark Nathan
   1977 *The Food Crisis in Prehistory: Overpopulation and the Origins of Agriculture*. Yale University Press, New Haven.
   1989 *Health and the Rise of Civilization*. Yale University Press, New Haven.

Cohen, Mark Nathan, and George J. Armelagos (editors)
　1984　*Paleopathology at the Origins of Agriculture.* Academic Press, New York.
Cohen, Mark Nathan, and Gillian M. Crane-Kramer
　2007　*Ancient Health: Skeletal Indication of Agricultural and Economic Interpretations of the Human Past: Local, Regional, and Global Perspectives.* University of Florida Press, Gainesville.
Coltrain, Joan Brenner, and Stephen W. Leavitt
　2002　Climate and Diet in Fremont Prehistory: Economic Variability and Abandonment of Maize Agriculture in the Great Salt Lake Basin. *American Antiquity* 67:453–485.
Crabtree, Pamela
　1990　Zooarchaeology and Complex Societies: Some Uses of Faunal Analysis for the Study of Trade, Status, and Ethnicity. In *Advances in Archaeological Method and Theory*, Vol. 2, edited by Michael B. Schiffer, pp. 155–205. University of Arizona Press, Tucson.
Crumley, Carole
　1984　A Diachronic Model for Settlement and Land Use in Southern Burgundy. In *Archaeological Approaches to Medieval Europe,* edited by Kathleen Biddic, pp. 239–243, The Medieval Institute, Kalamazoo.
　2006　Archaeology in the New World Order: What We Can Offer the Planet. In *Space and Spatial Analysis in Archaeology,* edited by Elizabeth C. Robertson, Jeffery D. Seibert, Deepika C. Fernandez, and Marc U. Zender, pp. 383–395. University of New Mexico Press, Tucson.
　2007　Historical Ecology: Integrated Thinking at Multiple Temporal and Spatial Scales. In *The World System and The Earth System: Global Socio-Environmental Change and Sustainability Since the Neolithic,* edited by Alf Hornborg and Carole Crumley, pp. 15–28. Left Coast Press, Walnut Creek, California.
Darling, J. Andrew
　1999　From Hobbes to Rousseau and Back Again. *Science* 285:537.
Darwent, Christyann M.
　2004　The Highs and Lows of High Arctic Mammals: Temporal Change and Regional Variability in Paleoeskimo Subsistence. In *Colonisation, Migration, and Marginal Areas: A Zooarchaeological Approach*, edited by Mariana Mondini, Sebastián Muñoz, and Stephen Wickler, pp. 62–73. Oxbow Books, Oxford.
Denham, Tim, and Huw Barton
　2006　The Emergence of Agriculture in New Guinea: A Model of Continuity from Pre-existing Foraging Practices. In: *Behavioral Ecology and the Transition to Agriculture,* edited by Douglas Kennett and Bruce Winterhalder, pp. 237–264. University of California Press, Berkeley.
Denham, T., S. G. Haberle, C. Lentfer, R. Fullagar, J. Field, M. Therin, N. Porch, and B. Winsborough
　2003　Origins of Agriculture at Kuk Swamp in the Highlands of New Guinea. *Science* 301:189–193.
DeNiro, Michael J., and Samuel Epstein
　1981　Influence of Diet on the Distribution of Nitrogen Isotopes in Animals. *Geochimica et Cosmochimica Acta* 45:341–351.

Deur, Douglas, and Nancy Turner (editors)
  2005 *Keeping It Living: Traditions of Plant Use and Cultivation on the Northwest Coast.* University of Washington Press, Seattle.
Dickson, James H., Michael P. Richards, Richard J. Hebda, Petra J. Mudie, Owen Beattie, Susan Ramsay, Nancy J. Turner, Bruce J. Leighton, John M. Webster, Niki R. Hobischak, Gail S. Anderson, Peter M. Troffe, and Rebecca J. Wigen
  2004 Kwaday Dan Tsinchi, the First Ancient Body of a Man from a North American Glacier: Reconstructing His Last Days by Intestinal and Biomolecular Analyses. *The Holocene* 14:481–486.
Dutour, Olivier, Gyorgy Palfi, Jacques Berano, and Jean-Pierre Brun (editors)
  1994 L'Origine de la Syphilis en Europe: Avant ou Après 1493? *Proceedings of an International Colloquia in Toulon, France, 25–28 November 1993.* Centre Archeologique du Var, Paris.
Emery, Kitty F.
  2003 The Noble Beast: Status and Differential Access to Animals in the Maya World. *World Archaeology* 34:498–515.
Emery, Kitty F., and Erin Thornton
  2008 Zooarchaeological Habitat Analysis of Ancient Maya Landscape Changes. *Journal of Ethnobiology*, in press.
Erickson, David, Bruce D. Smith, Andrew Clarke, Daniel H. Sandweiss, and Noreen Tuross
  2005 An Asian Origin for a 10,000-year-old Domesticated Plant in the Americas. *Proceedings of the National Academy of Sciences, USA* 102:18315–18320.
Ericson, Jonathan E.
  1985 Strontium Isotope Characterization in the Study of Prehistoric Human Ecology. *Journal of Human Evolution* 14:503–514.
Ervynck, Anton
  2004 Orant, Pugnant, Laborant. The Diet of the Three Orders in the Feudal Society of Medieval North-western Europe. In *Behaviour Behind Bones: The Zooarchaeology of Ritual, Religion, Status, and Identity*, edited by Sharyn Jones O'Day, Wim van Neer, and Anton Ervynck, pp. 215–223. Oxbow Books, Oxford.
Ervynck, Anton, Keith Dobney, Hitomi Hongo, and Richard H. Meadow
  2001 Born Free!: New Evidence for the Status of Pigs from Çayönü Tepesi, Eastern Anatolia. *Paléorient* 27(2):47–73.
Ervynck, Anton, Wim van Neer, Heide Hüster-Plogmann, and Jorge Schibler
  2003 Beyond Affluence: The Zooarchaeology of Luxury. *World Archaeology* 34:428–441.
Faith, John Tyler
  2008 Eland, Buffalo, and Wild Pigs: Were Middle Stone Age Humans Ineffective Hunters? *Journal of Human Evolution* 55:24–36.
Fish, Suzanne, and Paul Fish
  1990 An Archaeological Assessment of Ecosystems in the Tucson Basin of Southern Arizona. In *The Ecosystem Approach in Anthropology*, edited by Emilio Moran, pp. 159–187. University of Michigan Press, Ann Arbor.

Fisher, D. C.
  2008 Paleobiology and Extinction of Proboscideans in the Great Lakes Region of North America. In *American Megafaunal Extinctions at the End of the Pleistocene*, edited by Gary Haynes, pp. 55–76. Springer Science and Business Media B.V., New York.
Fletcher, H. A., Helen D. Donoghue, J. Holton, I. Pap, and Mark Spiegelman
  2003 Widespread Occurrence of Mycobacterium Tuberculosis DNA from 18th–19th Century Hungarians. *American Journal of Physical Anthropology* 120:144–152.
Frankenberg, Susan R., and Lyle W. Konigsberg
  2006 A Brief History of Paleodemography from Hooton to Hazards Analysis. In B*ioarchaeology: The Contextual Analysis of Human Remains*, edited by Jane E. Buikstra and Lane A. Beck, pp. 227–261. Elsevier, New York.
Frazier, Jack
  2007 Sustainable Use of Wildlife: The View from Archaeozoology. *Journal of Nature Conservation* 15:163–173.
Fritz, Gayle, and Neal H. Lopinot
  2007 Native Crops at Early Cahokia: Comparing Domestic and Ceremonial Contexts. *Illinois Archaeology* 15/16:90–111.
Gagneux, S., K. DeRiemer, T. Van, M. Kato-Maeda, B. C. de Jong, S. Naryanan, M. Nicol, S. Niemann, K. Kremer, M. C. Gutierrez, M. Hilty, P. C. Hopewell, and P. M. Small.
  2006 Variable Host-Pathogen Compatibility in Mycobacterium Tuberculosis. *Proceedings of the National Academies of Science, USA* 103:2869–2873.
Geller, Pamela
  2006 Conceiving Sex: Fomenting a Feminist Bioarchaeology. *Journal of Social Archaeology* 8:113–138.
Goldberg, Paul, and Richard I. MacPhail
  2006 *Practical and Theoretical Geoarchaeology.* Blackwell, Malden, Massachusetts.
González-José, Rolando, Maria Catira Bortolini, Fabrício R. Santos, and Sandro L. Bonatto
  2008 The Peopling of America: Craniofacial Shape Variation on a Continental Scale and its Interpretation from an Interdiscplonary View. *American Journal of Physical Anthropology* 187:175–187.
Goodman, Alan, J. Jones, J. Reid, M. E. Mack, M. L. Blakey, D. Amarasiriwardena, P. Burton, and D. Coleman
  2004 Isotopic and Elemental Chemistry of Teeth: Implications for Places of Birth, Forced Migration Patterns, Nutritional Status, and Pollution. In *The New York African Burial Ground Skeletal Biology Final Report*. Vol. 1, edited by Michael L. Blakey and Lesley M. Rankin-Hill, pp. 216–265. Prepared by Howard University for the U.S. General Services Administration, Northeastern and Caribbean Region.
Gowland, Rebecca, and Christopher Knüsel
  1997 *The Social Archaeology of Human Remains.* Oxbow, Oxford.
Grayson, Donald K.
  1984 Quantitative *Zoorchaeology: Topics in the Analysis of Archaeological Faunas.* Academic Press, Orlando, Florida.

    1989 Bone Transport, Bone Destruction, and Reverse Utility Curves. *Journal of Archaeological Science* 16:643–652.
    2005 A Brief History of Great Basin Pikas. *Journal of Biogeography* 32:2101–2111.
Grayson, Donald K., and F. Delpech
    2005 Pleistocene Reindeer and Global Warming. *Conservation Biology* 19:557–562.
    2006 Was there Increasing Dietary Specialization Across the Middle-to-Upper Paleolithic Transition in France? In *When Neanderthals and Modern Humans Met*, edited by N. J. Conard, pp. 377–417. Tübingen Publications in Prehistory. Kerns Verlag, Tübingen, Germany.
Gremillion, Kristen
    2002 Foraging Theory and Hypothesis Testing in Archaeology: An Exploration of Methodological Problems and Solutions. *Journal of Anthropological Archaeology* 21:142–164.
    2006 Central Place Foraging and Food Production on the Cumberland Plateau, Eastern Kentucky. In *Behavioral Ecology and the Transition to Agriculture*, edited by Douglas Kennett and Bruce Winterhalder, pp. 41–62. University of California Press, Berkeley.
Grimm, N. B., J. M. Grove, S. T. A. Picket, and C. L. Redman
    2000 Integrated Approaches to Long-Term Studies of Urban Ecological Systems. *BioScience* 70:571–584.
Gutierrez, M. C., S. Brisse, R. Brosch, M. Fabre, B. Omais, M. Marmiesse, P. Supply, and V. Vincent
    2005 Ancient Origin and Gene Mosaicism of the Progenitor of Mycobacterium Tuberculosis. *PLOS Pathogens* 1: e5 DOI: 10.1371/journal.ppat.0010005
Haas, Jonathan (editor)
    1990 *The Anthropology of War*. Cambridge University Press, Cambridge.
Haas, Jonathan, and Winifred Creamer
    1997 Warfare among the Pueblos: Myth, History, and Ethnography. *Ethnohistory* 44:235–261.
Hallett, D. J., D. Lepofsky, R. W. Mathewes, and K. P. Lertzman
    2003 11,000 Years of Fire History and Climate in the Mountain Hemlock Rainforests of Southwestern British Columbia Based on Sedimentary Charcoal. *Canadian Journal of Forestry Research* 33:292–312.
Hallgrímsson, Benedikt, Barra Ó Donnabháin, G. Bragi Walters, David M. L. Cooper, Daniel Guðbjartsson, and Kari Stefánsson
    2004 Composition of the Founding Population in Iceland: Biological Distance and Morphological Variation in Early Historic Atlantic Europe. *American Journal of Physical Anthropology* 124:257–274.
Harper, K. N., P. S. Ocampo, B. M. Steiner, R. W. George, and M. S. Silverman
    2008 On the Origin of the Treponematoses: A Phylogenetic Approach. *PLoS Neglected Tropical Diseases* 2(1): e148. doi:10.1371/journal.pntd.0000148.
Hartley T., and John Kappelman
    1980 Bears, Pigs, and Plio-Pleistocene Hominids: A Case for the Exploitation of Belowground Food Resources. *Human Ecology* 8:371–387.

Hastorf, Christine
   1996 Gender, Space and Food in Prehistory. In *Contemporary Archaeology in Theory*, edited by Robert W. Preucel and Ian Hodder, pp. 460–484. Blackwell Press, Oxford.
   2003 Andean Luxury Foods: Special Food for the Ancestors, Deities, and the Élite. *Antiquity* 77:545–554.

Hawkes, Kristen, and Rebbeca Bliege Bird
   2002 Showing Off, Handicap Signaling, and the Evolution of Men's Work. *Evolutionary Anthropology* 11:58–67.

Hayashida, Frances M.
   2005 Archaeology, Ecology and Historical Conservation. *Annual Review of Anthropology* 34:43–65.

Haynes, Gary (editor)
   2008 *American Megafaunal Extinctions at the End of the Pleistocene*. Springer Science and Business Media B.V., New York.

Henderson, Julian
   2000 *The Science and Archaeology of Materials*. Routledge, London.

Hill, Kim
   1982 Hunting and Hominid Evolution. *Journal of Human Evolution* 11:521–544.

Hoffacker, John, and Naomi Cleghorn
   2000 Mousterian Hunting Patterns in the Northwestern Caucasus and the Ecology of the Neanderthals. *International Journal of Osteoarchaeology* 10:368–378.

Hoppa, Robert D., and James W. Vaupel (editors)
   2002 *Paleodemography: Age Distributions from Skeletal Samples*. Cambridge University Press, Cambridge.

Hughes, A. L., R. Friedman, and M. Murray
   2002 Genome Wide Pattern of Synonymous Nucleotide Substitution in Two Complete Genomes of Mycobacterium Tuberculosis. *Emerging Infectious Diseases* 8:1342–1346.

Isaac, Glynn
   1978 The Food-Sharing Behavior of Proto-Human Hominids. *Scientific American* 238(xx):90–108.

Jackes, Mary K.
   1985 Pubic Symphysis Age Distributions. *American Journal of Physical Anthropology* 68:281–299.
   2000 Building the Bases for Paleodemographic Analysis: Adult Age Estimation. In *Biological Anthropology of the Human Skeleton*, edited by Ann M. Katzenberg and Shelley R. Saunders, pp. 417–466. Wiley-Liss, New York.

Jackson, F. L. C., A. Mayes, M. E. Mack, A. Froment, S. O. Y. Keita, R. Kittles, M. George, K. Shujaa, M. L. Blakey, and L. M. Rankin-Hill
   2004 Origins of the New York African Burial Ground Population: Biological Evidence of Lineage and Population Affiliation Using Genetics, Craniometrics, and Dental Morphology. In *The New York African Burial Ground Skeletal Biology Final Report*. Vol. 1, edited by Michael L. Blakey and Lesley M. Rankin-Hill,

pp.150–215. Prepared by Howard University for the U.S. General Services Administration, Northeastern and Caribbean Region.

Jackson, H. Edwin, and Susan L. Scott
  1995 The Faunal Record of the Southeastern Elite: The Implications of Economy, Social Relations, and Ideology. *Southeastern Archaeology* 14:103–119.
  2003 Patterns of Elite Faunal Utilization at Moundville, Alabama. *American Antiquity* 68:552–572.

Jaenicke-Despré, Viviane, Ed Buckler, Bruce D. Smith, M. Thomas, P. Gilbert, Ala Cooper, John Doebley, and Svante Pääbo.
  2003 Early Allelic Selection in Maize as Revealed by Ancient DNA. *Science* 302:1206–1208.

Jing, Yuan, and Rowan Flad
  2005 New Zooarchaeological Evidence for Changes in Shang Dynasty Animal Sacrifice. *Journal of Anthropological Archaeology* 24:252–270.

Jones, Sharyn
  2009 *Food and Gender in Fiji: Ethnoarchaeological Explorations.* Lexington Books/Rowman & Littlefield.

Kansa, Sarah W., and Stuart Campbell
  2004 Feasting with the Dead?—A Ritual Bone Deposit at Domuztepe, Southeastern Turkey (c. 5550 cal BC). In *Behaviour Behind Bones: The Zooarchaeology of Ritual, Religion, Status, and Identity,* edited by Sharyn Jones O'Day, Wim van Neer, and Anton Ervynck, pp. 2–13. Oxbow Books, Oxford.

Katzenberg, Anne M.
  2008 Stable Isotope Analysis: A Tool for Studying Past Diet, Demography, and Life History. In *Biological Anthropology of the Human Skeleton,* edited by Anne M. Katzenberg and Shelley R. Saunders, pp. 413–440. Wiley-Liss, New York.

Keeley, Lawrence
  1996 *War Before Civilization.* Oxford University Press, Oxford.

Kelly, Lucretia. S.
  2001 A Case of Ritual Feasting at the Cahokia Site. In: *Feasts: Archaeological and Ethnographic Perspectives on Food, Politics, and Power,* edited by Michael Dietler and Brian Hayden, pp. 334–367. Smithsonian Institution Press, Washington, DC.

Kelly, Lucretia S., and John E. Kelly
  2007 Swans in the American Bottom during the Emergent Mississippian and Mississippian. *Illinois Archaeology* 15/16:112–141.

Kennett, Douglas J., and Bruce Winterhalder (editors)
  2006 *Behavioral Ecology and the Transition to Agriculture.* University of California Press, Berkeley.

Kerig, Tim, and Jutta Lechterbeck
  2004 Laminated Sediments, Hunting Impact, and a Multivariate Approach: A Case Study in Linking Palynology and Archaeology. *Quaternary International* 113:19–39.

Keyser-Tracqui, Christine, Eric Crubézy, and Bertrand Ludes
  2003 Nuclear and Mitochondrial DNA Analysis of a 2,000-Year-Old Necropolis in the Egyin Gol Valley of Mongolia. *American Journal of Human Genetics* 73(2):247–260.

Killick, David
   2007 Archaeological Science in America and Britain. In *Archaeological Concepts for the Study of the Cultural Past,* edited by Alan Sullivan, pp. 40–64. University of Utah Press, Salt Lake City.

Kirch, Patrick
   2005 Archaeology and Global Change: The Holocene Record. *Annual Review of Environment and Resources* 30:409–440.

Knudson, Kelly J., and T. Douglas Price
   2007 Utility of Multiple Chemical Techniques in Archaeological Residential Mobility Studies: Case Studies from Tiwanaku- and Chiribaya-Affiliated Sites in the Andes. *American Journal of Physical Anthropology* 132: 25–39.

Knudson, Kelly J., T. Douglas Price, Jane E. Buikstra, and Deborah E. Blom
   2004 The Use of Strontium Isotope Analysis to Investigate Tiwanaku Migration and Mortuary Ritual in Bolivia and Peru. *Archaeometry* 46:5–18.

Knudson, Kelly J., and Christopher Stojanowski (editors)
   2009 *Bioarchaeology and Identity in the Americas.* University of Florida Press, Gainesville.

Kohler, Timothy A., and Sander E. van der Leeuw
   2007 Introduction: Historical Socionatural Systema and Models. In *The Model-Based Archaeology of Socionatural Systems,* edited by Timothy A. Kohler and Sander E. van der Leeuw, pp. 1–12. School for Advanced Research Press, Santa Fe.

Kolman, Connie J., Arturo Centurion-Lara, Sheila A. Lukehart, Douglas W. Owsley, and Noreen Tuross
   2000 Identification of *Treponema pallidum* Subspecies *pallidum* in a 200-year-old Skeletal Specimen. *The Journal of Infectious Diseases,* 180:2060–2063.

Konigsberg, Lyle W.
   2006 A Post-Neumann History of Biological and Genetic Distance Studies in Bioarchaeology. In *Bioarchaeology: The Contextual Analysis of Human Remains,* edited by Jane E. Buikstra and Lane A. Beck, pp. 263–279. Academic Press, New York.

Konigsberg, Lyle W., and Jane E. Buikstra
   1995 Regional Approaches to the Investigation of Past Human Biocultural Structure. In *Regional Approaches to Mortuary Analysis,* edited by Lane A. Beck, pp. 191–219. Plenum Press, New York.

Konigsberg, Lyle W., and Susan R. Frankenberg
   1992 Estimation of Age Structure in Anthropological Demography. *American Journal of Physical Anthropology* 89:235–256.

Krings, Matthias, Anne C. Stone, Ralf W. Schmitz, Heike Krainitzki, Mark Stoneking, and Svante Pääbo
   1997 Neandertal DNA Sequences and the Origin of Modern Humans. *Cell* 90(1):19–30.

Kvamme, Kenneth
   2005 Terrestrial Remote Sensing in Archaeology, In *Handbook of Archaeological Methods,* edited by Herbert D. G. Maschner and Christopher Chippindale, pp. 423–477. AltaMira Press, Lanham, Maryland.

Laden, Greg, and Richard Wrangham
  2005 The Rise of the Hominids as an Adaptive Shift in Fallback Foods: Plant Underground Storage Organs (USOs) and Australopith Origins. *Journal of Human Evolution* 49:482–498.
Lapham, Heather
  2004 Zooarchaeological Evidence for Changing Socioeconomic Status within Early Historic Native American Communities in Mid-Atlantic North America. In *Behaviour Behind Bones: The Zooarchaeology of Ritual, Religion, Status, and Identity*, edited by Sharyn Jones O'Day, Wim van Neer, and Anton Ervynck, pp. 293–303. Oxbow Books, Oxford.
Larsen, Clark Spencer
  1987 Bioarchaeological Interpretation of Subsistence Economy and Behavior from Human Skeletal Remains. *Advances in Archaeological Method and Theory* 10:339–445.
  1997 *Bioarchaeology: Interpreting Behavior from the Human Skeleton*. Cambridge University Press, Cambridge.
  2006 The Changing Face of Bioarchaeology: An Emerging Interdisciplinary Science. In *Bioarchaeology: The Contextual Study of Human Remains,* edited by Jane E. Buikstra and Lane A. Beck, pp. 365–384. Elsevier, New York.
Larson, Greger, Umberto Albarella, Keith Dobney, Peter Rowley-Conwy, Jörg Schibler, Anne Tresset, Jean-Denis Vigne, Ceiridwen J. Edwards, Angela Schlumbaum, Alexandru Dinu, Adrian Bălăçsescu, Gaynor Dolman, Antonio Tagliacozzo, Ninna Manaseryan, Preston Miracle, Louise Van Wijngaarden-Bakker, Marco Masseti, Daniel G. Bradley, and Alan Cooper
  2007 Ancient DNA, Pig Domestication, and the Spread of the Neolithic into Europe. *Proceedings of the National Academy of Sciences USA* 104:15276–15281.
Lekson, Stephen H.
  2002 War in the Southwest, War in the World. *American Antiquity* 67:607–624.
Lepofsky, Dana, and Kenneth Lertzman
  2008 Documenting Ancient Plant Management in the Northwest of North America. *Botany* 86:129–145.
Lev, Efraim, Mordechai E. Kislev, Ofer Bar-Yosef
  2005 Mousterian Vegetal Food in Kebara Cave, Mt. Carmel. *Journal of Archaeological Science* 32:475–484.
Lev-Tov, Justin S.
  2000 The Influences of Religion, Social Structure, and Ethnicity on Diet: An Example from Frankish Corinth. In *Paleodietary Studies in the Aegean: Contributions from the Wiener Laboratory, American School of Classical Studies, Athens, Greece,* edited by Sarah Vaughan and W.D.E. Coulson, pp. 85–98. Oxbow Books, Oxford.
  2004 Implications of Risk Theory for Understanding Nineteenth Century Slave Diets in the Southern United States. In *Behaviour Behind Bones: The Zooarchaeology of Ritual, Religion, Status, and Identity*, edited by Sharyn Jones O'Day, Wim van Neer, and Anton Ervynck, pp. 304–317. Oxbow Books, Oxford.

Lev-Tov, Justin S. E., and K. McGeough
  2007 Examining Feasting in Late Bronze Age Syro-Palestine through Ancient Texts and Bones. In *The Archaeology of Food and Identity*, edited by Katheryn C. Twiss, pp. 85–111. Occasional Papers 34, Southern Illinois University Press, Carbondale.

Lewis, Cecil M., Jane E. Buikstra, and Anne C. Stone
  2007 Ancient DNA and Genetic Continuity in the South Central Andes. *Latin American Antiquity* 18(2):145–160.

Linseele, Veerle
  2004 Cultural Identity and the Consumption of Dogs in Western Africa. In *Behaviour Behind Bones: The Zooarchaeology of Ritual, Religion, Status, and Identity*, edited by Sharyn Jones O'Day, Wim van Neer, and Anton Ervynck, pp. 318–326. Oxbow Books, Oxford.

Lozada, Maria C., and Jane E. Buikstra
  2002 *El Señorío de Chiribaya en la Costa Sur del Perú*. Instituto de Estudios Peruanos, Lima-Peru.

Lupo, Karen D.
  2006 What Explains the Carcass Field Processing and Transport Decisions of Contemporary Hunter-Gatherers? Measures of Economic Anatomy and Zooarchaeological Skeletal Part Representation. *Journal of Archaeological Method and Theory* 13:19–66.
  2007 Evolutionary Foraging Models in Zooarchaeological Analysis: Recent Applications and Future Challenges. *Journal of Archaeological Research* 15:143–189.

Lyman, R. Lee
  1985 Bone Frequencies: Differential Transport, In Situ Destruction, and the MGUI. *Journal of Archaeological Science* 12:221–236.
  1992 Anatomical Considerations of Utility Curves in Zooarchaeology. *Journal of Archaeological Science* 19:7–22.
  1994 *Vertebrate Taphonomy*. Cambridge University Press, Cambridge, UK.

Lyman, R. Lee, and Kenneth P. Cannon (editors)
  2004 *Zooarchaeology and Conservation Biology*. University of Utah Press, Salt Lake City.

Makarewicz, Cheryl, and Noreen Tuross
  2008 Mechanisms of Early Goat Domestication Processes in the Near East Revealed in Stable Carbon, Nitrogen, and Oxygen Isotopes, submitted *Proceedings of the National Academy of Sciences USA*.

Marean, Curtis W., and L. M. Spencer
  1991 Impact of Carnivore Ravaging on Zooarchaeological Measures of Element Abundance. *American Antiquity* 56:645–658.

Marean, Curtis W., Miryam Bar-Matthews, Jocelyn Bernatches, Erich Fisher, Paul Goldberg, Andy I. R. Herries, Zenobia Jacobs, Antonieta Jerardino, Panagiotis Karkanas, Tom Minichillo, Peter J. Milssen, Erin Thompson, Ian Watts, and Hope M. Williams
  2007 Early Human Use of Marine Resources and Pigment in South Africa during the Middle Pleistocene. *Nature* 449:905–908.

Marlar, Richard A., Banks L. Leonard, Brian R. Billman, Patricia M. Lambert, and Jennifer E. Marlar
   2000 Biochemical Evidence of Cannibalism at a Prehistoric Puebloan Site in Southwestern Colorado. *Nature* 407:74–78.

Martin, Debra L., and Nancy J. Akins
   2001 Unequal Treatment in Life as in Death: Trauma and Mortuary Behavior at La Plata (A.D. 1000–1300). In *Ancient Burial Practices in the American Southwest: Archaeology, Physical Anthropology, and Native American Perspectives*, edited by Douglas R. Mitchell and Judy L. Brunson-Hadley, pp. 223–248. University of New Mexico Press, Albuquerque.

Maschner, Herbert D. G., and Christopher Chippindale (editors)
   2005 *Handbook of Archaeological Methods, Vol. I and II*. AltaMira Press, Lanham, Maryland.

Mashkour, M. H. Bocherens, and I. Moussa
   2005 Long Distance Movement of Sheep and Goats of Bakhtiari Nomads Tracked with Intra-Tooth Variation of Stable Isotopes (^{13}C and ^{18}O). In *Diet and Health in Past Animal Populations: Current Research and Future Directions*, edited by J. Davies, M. Fabis, I. Mainland, M. Richards, and R. Thomas, pp. 113–124, Oxbow, Oxford.

Mbida, Charles, E. DeLanghe, Luc Vrydaghs, Henri Doutrelepont, Robert Swennen, Wim Van Neer, and Pierre de Maret
   2006 Phytolith Evidence for the Early Presence of Domesticated Banana (Musa) in Africa. In *Documenting Domestication: New Genetic and Archaeological Paradigms*, edited by Melinda A. Zeder, Eve Emshwiller, Bruce D. Smith, and Daniel G. Bradley, pp. 68–81. University of California Press, Berkeley.

Mengoni Goñalons, Guillermo, and Hugo Yacobaccio
   2006 The Domestication of South American Camelids: A View from the South-Central Andes. In *Documenting Domestication: New Genetic and Archaeological Paradigms*, edited by Melinda A. Zeder, Eve Emshwiller, Bruce D. Smith, and Daniel G. Bradley, pp. 228–244. University of California Press, Berkeley.

Messner, Timothy, Ruth Dickau, and Jeff Harbison
   2008 Starch Grain Analysis: Methodology and Applications in the Northeast. In *Current Northeast Paleoethnobotany II,* edited by John P. Hart, New York State Museum Bulletin 512. The University of the State of New York, Albany.

Miller, Alexandra
   2008 Changing Responsibilities and Collective Action: Examining Early North African Pastoralism. In *Gender, Households, and Society: Unraveling the Threads of the Past and the Present*, edited by Cynthia Robin and Elizabeth M. Brumfiel, pp. 76–86. Archeological Papers of the American Anthropological Association, No. 18. American Anthropological Association, Arlington, Virginia.

Milner, George R.
   1995 Osteological Evidence for Prehistory Warfare. In *Regional Approaches to Mortuary Analysis,* edited by Lane A. Beck, pp. 221–244. Plenum Press, New York.
   1999 Warfare in Prehistoric and Early Historic Eastern North America. *Journal of Archaeological Research* 7:105–151.

Milner, George R., Eve Anderson, and Virginia G. Smith
  1991 Warfare in Late Prehistoric West-Central Illinois. *American Antiquity* 56:581–603.
Milner, George R., James W. Wood, and Jesper L. Boldsen
  2000 Paleodemography. In *Biological Anthropology of the Human Skeleton*, edited by Anne M. Katzenberg and Shelley R. Saunders, pp. 467–497. Wiley–Liss, New York.
Morehart, Christopher T., and Christophe G. B. Helmke
  2008 Situating Power and Locating Knowledge A Paleoethnobotanical Perspective on Late Classic Maya Gender and Social Relations. In *Gender, Households, and Society: Unraveling the Threads of the Past and the Present*, edited by Cynthia Robin and Elizabeth M. Brumfiel, pp. 60–75. Archeological Papers of the American Anthropological Association, No. 18. American Anthropological Association, Arlington, Virginia.
Morin, Eugène
  2008 Evidence for Declines in Human Population Densities During the Early Upper Paleolithic in Western Europe. *Proceedings of the National Academy of Sciences, USA* 105:48–53.
Muir, Robert J., and Jonathan C. Driver
  2004 Identifying Ritual Use of Animals in the Northern American Southwest. In *Behaviour Behind Bones: The Zooarchaeology of Ritual, Religion, Status, and Identity*, edited by Sharyn Jones O'Day, Wim van Neer, and Anton Ervynck, pp. 128–143. Oxbow Books, Oxford.
Munro, Natalie D.
  2004 Zooarchaeological Measures of Hunting Pressure and Occupation Intensity in the Natufian: Implications for Agricultural Origins. *Current Anthropology* 45(Supplement):S5–S33.
  2010 Domestication of the Turkey in the American Southwest. In *The Subsistence Economies of Indigenous North American Societies*, edited by Bruce D. Smith, Smithsonian Institution Scholarly Press, Washington D.C., in press.
Munro, Natalie D., and Guy Bar-Oz
  2005 Gazelle Bone Fat Processing in the Levantine Epipalaeolithic. *Journal of Archaeological Science* 32:223–239.
Nagaoka, Lisa
  2002 The Effects of Resource Depression on Foraging Efficiency, Diet Breadth, and Patch Use in Southern New Zealand. *Journal of Anthropological Archaeology* 21:419–442.
  2005 Declining Foraging Efficiency and Moa Carcass Exploitation in Southern New Zealand. *Journal of Archaeological Science* 32:1328–1338.
Noe-Nygaard, Nanna
  1988 Taphonomy in Archaeology with Special Emphasis on Man as a Biasing Factor. *Journal of Danish Archaeology* 6:7–52.
Nystrom, Kenneth
  2005 The Biological and Social Consequences of Inka Conquest of the Chachapoya Regions of Peru. Ph.D. Dissertation. University of New Mexico, Albuquerque.

2009 The Reconstruction of Identity: A Case Study from Chachapoya, Peru. In *Bioarchaeology and Identity in the Americas,* edited by Kelly J. Knudson and Christopher Stojanowski, pp. 82–102. University of Florida Press, Gainesville.

O'Connell, J. F., K. Hawkes, K. D. Lupo, and N. G. Blurton Jones
2002 Male Strategies and Plio-Pleistocene Archaeology. *Journal of Human Evolution* 43:831–872.

Ogilvie, M., and Charles Hilton
2000 Ritualized Violence in the Prehistoric American Southwest. *International Journal of Osteoarchaeology* 10:23–48.

Olsen, Sandra
2006 Early Horse Domestication on the Eurasian Steppe. In *Documenting Domestication: New Genetic and Archaeological Paradigms,* edited by Melinda A. Zeder, Eve Emshwiller, Bruce D. Smith, and Daniel G. Bradley, pp. 245–269. University of California Press, Berkeley.

Ortner, Donald J.
1992 Skeletal Pathology: Probabilities, Possibilities and Impossibilities. In *Disease and Demography in the Americas,* edited by John W. Verano and Douglas H. Ubelaker, pp. 5–14. Smithsonian Institution, Washington, D.C.

Palfi, Gyorgy, Olivier Dutour, Judity Deak, and Imre Hutas (editors)
1999 *Tuberculosis: Past and Present.* Golden Book/Tuberculosis Foundation, Szeged.

Pankonien, Dawn
2008 She Sells Seashells: Women and Mollusks in Huatulco, Oaxaca, Mexico. In *Gender, Households, and Society: Unraveling the Threads of the Past and the Present*, edited by Cynthia Robin and Elizabeth M. Brumfiel, pp. 102–114. Archeological Papers of the American Anthropological Association, No. 18. American Anthropological Association, Arlington, Virginia.

Peacock, Evan, and Sarah Mistak
2008 Freshwater Mussel Remains from the Bilbo Site, Mississippi, U.S.: Archaeological Considerations and Resource Management Implications. *Archaeofauna* 17:9–20.

Perry, Linda, Ruth Dickau, Sonia Zarrillo, Irene Holst, Deborah M. Pearsall, Dolores R. Piperno, Mary Jane Berman, Richard G. Cooke, Kurt Rademaker, Anthony J. Ranere, J. Scott Raymond, Daniel H. Sandweiss, Franz Scaramelli, Kay Tarble, and James A. Zeidler
2007 Starch Fossils and the Domestication and Dispersal of Chili Peppers (*Capsicum* spp. L.) in the Americas. *Science* 315: 986–988.

Perry, Linda, Daniel H. Sandweiss, Dolores R. Piperno, Kurt Rademaker, Michael A. Malpass, Adán Umire, and Pablo de la Vera
2006 Early Maize Agriculture and Interzonal Interaction in Southern Peru. *Nature* 440:76–79.

Pfister, Luz A., Michael S. Rosenberg, and Anne C. Stone
2008 Full Genome Comparison of Mycobacterium: Insight into the Origin of Tuberculosis and Leprosy. *American Journal of Physical Anthropology* 135 (S46): 171.

Piperno, Dolores R.
  2006a *Phytolith Analysis in Archaeology and Environmental History*. AltaMira Press, Walnut Creek, California.
  2006b Quaternary Environmental History and Agricultural Impact on Vegetation in Central America. *Annales of the Missouri Botanical Garden* 93:274–296.
Piperno, Dolores R., and Deborah M. Pearsall
  1998 *The Origins of Agriculture in the Lowland Neotropics*. Academic Press, San Diego.
Pollard, A. Mark, Cathy Batt, Ben Stern, and S. M. M. Young
  2007 *Analytical Chemistry in Archaeology*. Cambridge University Press, Cambridge.
Potter, James M.
  2004 Hunting and Social Differentiation in the Late Prehispanic American Southwest. In *Behaviour Behind Bones: The Zooarchaeology of Ritual, Religion, Status, and Identity*, edited by Sharyn Jones O'Day, Wim van Neer, and Anton Ervynck, pp. 285–292. Oxbow Books, Oxford.
Powell, Joseph, and Walter A. Neves
  1999 Craniofacial Morphology of the First Americans: Pattern and Process in the Peopling of the Americas. *Yearbook of Physical Anthropology* 42:153–188.
Powell, Mary Lucas, and Della Collins Cook
  2005 *The Myth of Syphilis: The Natural History of Treponematosis in North America*. University Press of Florida, Gainesville.
Price, T. Douglas, James H. Burton, Vera Tiesler, S. Martin, and Jane Buikstra
  2006 Geographic Origin of Janaab' Pakal and the Red Queen: Evidence from Strontium Isotopes. In *Janaab' Pakal of Palenque: Reconstructing the Life and Death of a Maya Ruler*, edited by V. Tiesler and A. Cucina, pp. 91–101. University of Arizona Press, Tucson
Price, T. Douglas, Gisela Grupe, and P. Schröter
  1998 Migration and Mobility in the Bell Beaker Period in Central Europe. *Antiquity* 72:405–411.
Price, T. Douglas, C. M. Johnson, Joseph A. Ezzo, J. Ericson, and James Burton
  1994 Residential Mobility in the Prehistoric Southwest United States: A Preliminary Study Using Strontium Isotope Analysis. *Journal of Archaeological Science* 21:315–330.
Price, T. Douglas, Linda Manzanilla, and William D. Middleton
  2000 Immigration and the Ancient City of Teotihuacan in Mexico: A Study Using Strontium Isotope Ratios in Human Bone and Teeth. *Journal of Archaeological Science* 27:903–913.
Pumpelly, Raphael
  1908 *Explorations in Turkestan with an Account of the Basin of Eastern Persia and Sistan; Expedition of 1903 under Raphael Pumpelly*. Carnegie Institute of Washington, Washington.
Reilly, F. Kent, III, and James Garber
  2007 *Ancient Objects and Sacred Realms: Interpretations of Mississippian Iconography*. University of Texas Press, Austin.

Reinhard, Karl
  2000 Reburial, International Perspectives. In *Archaeological Method and Theory: An Encyclopedia*, edited by L. Ellis, pp. 512–518. Garland Publishing, New York and London.
Reinhard, Karl J., Larry L. Tieszen, Karin L. Sandness, Lynea M. Beiningen, Elizabeth Miller, A. Mohammed Ghazi, Christiana El Miewald, and Sandra V. Barnum
  1994 Trade, Contact, and Female Health in Northeast Nebraska. In *In the Wake of Contact: Biological Responses to Conquest*, edited by Clark S. Larsen and George R. Milner, pp. 63–74. Wiley-Liss, New York.
Reitz, Elizabeth J., and Elizabeth S. Wing
  2008 *Zooarchaeology*. Second Edition. Manuals in Archaeology. University of Cambridge Press, Cambridge, UK.
Rich, A. R.
  1944 *The Pathogenesis of Tuberculosis*. Charles C. Thomas, Springfield, Illinois.
Richards, Michael P., Paul B. Pettitt, Erik Trinkaus, Fred H. Smith, Maja Paunovic, and Igor Karavanic
  2000 Neanderthal Diet at Vindija and Neanderthal Predation: The Evidence from Stable Isotopes *Proceedings of the National Academy of Sciences, USA* 97:7663–7666.
Richards, M. P., G. Taylor, T. Steele, S. P. McPherron, M. Soressi, J. Jaubert, J. Orschiedt, J. B. Mallye, W. Rendu, and J. J. Hublin
  2008 Isotopic Dietary Analysis of a Neanderthal and Associated Fauna from the Site of Jonzac (Charente-Maritime), France. *Journal of Human Evolution* 55:179–185.
Rick, Torben C., and Jon M. Erlandson (editors)
  2008 *Human Impacts on Ancient Marine Ecosystems: A Global Perspective*. University of California Press, Berkeley.
Roberts, Charlotte A.
  2010 *The Bioarchaeology of Leprosy: A Global Perspective on a Declining Disease*. University Press of Florida, Gainesville, in press.
Roberts, Charlotte A., and Jane E. Buikstra
  2005 *The Bioarchaeology of Tuberculosis: A Global View on a Reemerging Disease*. University of Florida Press, Gainesville.
Roberts, Charlotte A., Mary E. Lewis, and Keith Manchester
  2002 *The Past and Present of Leprosy: Archaeological, Historical, Palaeopathological and Clinical Approaches*, British Archaeological Reports, International Series 1054. ArchaeoPress, Oxford.
Robin, Cynthia, and Elizabeth M. Brumfiel (editors)
  2008 *Gender, Households, and Society: Unraveling the Threads of the Past and the Present*. Archaeological Papers of the American Anthropological Association, No. 18. American Anthropological Association, Arlington, Virginia.
Rodman, Amy Oakland
  1992 Textiles and Ethnicity: Tiwanaku in San Pedro de Atacama, North Chile. *Latin American Antiquity* 3:326–340.
Rodman, Amy Oakland, and Giaconda Arabel Fernandez Lopez
  2005 North Coast Style after Moche: Clothing and Identity at El Brujo, Chicama Valley, Peru. In *Us and Them: Archaeology and Ethnicity in the Andes*, edited by

Richard Martin Reycraft, pp. 115–133. Monograph 53, The Cotsen Institute of Archaeology, University of California, Los Angeles.

Rofes, Juan
  2004 Prehispanic Guinea Pig Sacrifices in Southern Perù, the Case of el Yaral. In *Behaviour Behind Bones: The Zooarchaeology of Ritual, Religion, Status, and Identity*, edited by Sharyn Jones O'Day, Wim van Neer, and Anton Ervynck, pp. 95–100. Oxbow Books, Oxford.

Rossel, Stine, Fiona Marshall, Joris Peters, Tom Pilgram, Matthew D. Adams, and David O'Connor
  2008 Domestication of the Donkey: Timing, Processes, and Indicators. *Proceedings of the National Academy of Sciences* 105:3715–3720.

Russell, Narissa, and K. J. McGowan
  2003 Dance of the Cranes: Crane Symbolism at Çatalhöyük and Beyond. *Antiquity* 77:445–455.

Sattenspiel, Lisa, and Henry C. Harpending
  1983 Stable Populations and Skeletal Age. *American Antiquity* 48:489–498.

Saul, Frank P.
  1972 *The Human Skeletal Remains of Altar de Sacrificios: An Osteobiographic Analysis*. Papers of the Peabody Museum of Archaeology and Ethnology, Vol. 63, No. 2. Peabody Museum of Archaeology and Ethnology, Harvard University, Cambridge.

Saul, Frank P., and Julie M. Saul
  1989 Osteobiography: A Maya Example. In *Reconstruction of Life from the Skeleton*, edited by Mehmet Yasar Iscan and Kenneth A. R. Kennedy, pp. 287–302. Alan R. Liss, New York.

Schillaci, Michael A.
  2008 Human Cranial Diversity and Evidence for an Ancient Lineage of Modern Humans. *Journal of Human Evolution* 54:814–826.

Schillaci, Michael A., and Christopher A. Stojanowski
  2003 Postmarital Residence and Biological Variation at Pueblo Bonito. *American Journal of Physical Anthropology* 120:1–15.

Schoeninger, Margaret J., and Katherine Moore
  1992 Bone Stable Isotope Studies in Archaeology. *Journal of World Prehistory* 6:247–296.

Schwarcz, Henry P., and Margaret J. Schoeninger
  1991 Stable Isotope Analyses in Human Nutritional Ecology. *Yearbook of Physical Anthropology* 34:283–321.

Smith, Alexia, and Naomi F. Miller
  2009 Integrating Plant and Animal Data: Delving Deeper into Subsistence, Introduction to a Special Section. *Current Anthropology* 50:925–936.

Smith, Alexia, and Natalie D. Munro
  2009 A Holistic Approach to Examining Ancient Agriculture: A Case Study from the Bronze and Iron Age Near East. *Current Anthropology* 50:925–936.

Smith, Bruce D.
  2001 Low Level Food Production. *Journal of Archaeological Research* 9:1–43.

    2006 Documenting Plant Domestication in the Archaeological Record. In *Documenting Domestication: New Genetic and Archaeological Paradigms*, edited by Melinda A. Zeder, Eve Emshwiller, Bruce D. Smith, and Daniel G. Bradley, pp. 15–24. University of California Press, Berkeley.

    2007a The Ultimate Ecosystem Engineers. *Science* 315:1797–1798.

    2007b Niche Construction and the Behavioral Context of Plant and Animal Domestication. *Evolutionary Anthropology* 16:189–199.

    2010 Shaping the Natural World: Patterns of Human Niche Construction by Indigenous Small-Scale Societies in North America. In *The Subsistence Economies of Indigenous North American Societies*, edited by Bruce D. Smith, Smithsonian Institution Scholarly Press, Washington D.C., in press.

Snyder, Lynn M., and Jennifer A. Leonard

    2010 The Diversity and Origin of American Dogs. In *The Subsistence Economies of Indigenous North American Societies*, edited by Bruce D. Smith, Smithsonian Institution Scholarly Press, Washington D.C., in press.

Sofaer Derevenski, Johanna

    1997 Age and Gender at the Site of Tiszapolgar-Basatanya, Hungary. *Antiquity* 71:875–889.

Stahl, Peter

    2006 Microvertebrate Synecology and Anthropogenic Footprints in the Forested Neotropics. In *Time and Complexity in Historical Ecology: Studies from the Neotropical Lowlands*, edited by William Balée and Clark Erickson, pp. 127–149. Columbia University Press, New York.

Steadman, Dawnie Wolfe

    1998 The Population Shuffle in the Central Illinois Valley: A Diachronic Model of Mississippian Biocultural Interactions. *World Archaeology* 30:306–326.

    2001 Mississippians in Motion? A Population Genetic Analysis of Interregional Gene Flow in West-Central Illinois. *American Journal of Physical Anthropology* 114:61–73.

Steckel, Richard H.

    2002 A Global History of Health: The Evolution of a Research Agenda. *Physical Anthropology* 3:3–4.

Steckel, Richard H., and Jerome C. Rose (editors)

    2002 *The Backbone of History: Health and Nutrition in the Western Hemisphere*. Cambridge University Press, New York and Cambridge.

Stiner, Mary C., and Natalie D. Munro

    2002 Approaches to Prehistoric Diet Breadth, Demography, and Prey Ranking Systems in Time and Space. *Journal of Archaeological Method and Theory* 9:175–208.

Stodder, Ann, and Ann Palkovich (editors)

    2009 *The Bioarchaeology of Individuals*. University Press of Florida, Gainesville.

Stojanowski, Christopher

    2005a *Biocultural Histories in La Florida: A Bioarchaeological Perspective*. University of Alabama Press, Tuscaloosa.

2005b The Bioarchaeology of Identity in Spanish Colonial Florida: Social and Evolutionary Transformation Before, During, and After Demographic Collapse. *American Anthropologist* 107:417–431.

2009 Bridging Histories: The Bioarchaeology of Identity in Postcontact Florida. In *Bioarchaeology and Identity*, edited by Kelly Knudson and Christopher Stojanowski, pp. 59–81. University Press of Florida, Gainesville.

Stojanowski, Christopher A., and Michael A. Schillaci
  2006 Phenotypic Approaches for Understanding Patterns of Intracemetery Biological Variation. *American Journal of Physical Anthropology* 131:S43:49–88.

Stone, Anne C.
  2008 DNA Analysis of Archaeological Remains. In *Biological Anthropology of the Human Skeleton*, Second edition, edited by M. Anne Katzenberg and Shelley R Saunders, pp. 461–483. Wiley Liss, New York.

Stone, Anne C., George R. Milner, Svante Pääbo, and Mark Stoneking
  1996 Sex Determination of Ancient Human Skeletons using DNA. *American Journal of Physical Anthropology* 99:231–238.

Stone, Anne C., and Mark Stoneking
  1993 Ancient DNA from a Pre-Columbian Amerindian Population. *American Journal of Physical Anthropology* 92:463–471.
  1996 Genetic Analyses of an 8000 year-old Native American Skeleton. *Ancient Biomolecules* 1:83–87.

Stringer, C. B., J. C. Finlayson, R. N. E. Barton, Y. Fernández-Jalvo, I. Cáceres, R. C. Sabin, E. J. Rhodes, A. P. Currant, J. Rodriguez-Vidal, F. Giles-Pacheco, and J. A. Riquelme-Cantal
  2008 Neanderthal Exploitation of Marine Mammals in Gibraltar. *Proceedings of the National Academy of Sciences, USA* 105:14319–14324.

Sutter, Richard C., and John W. Verano
  2007 Biodistance Analysis of the Moche Sacrificial Victims from Huaca de la Luna Plaza 3C: Matrix Method Test of their Origins. *American Journal of Physical Anthropology* 132:193–206.

Tanno, Ken-ichi, and George Wilcox
  2006 How Fast was Wild Wheat Domesticated? *Science* 311:1886.

Taylor, G. Michael, and Simon Mays
  2003 A First Prehistoric Case of Tuberculosis from Britain. *International Journal of Osteoarchaeology* 13:189–196.

Thomas, Richard M.
  2007 Food and the Maintenance of Social Boundaries in Medieval England. In *The Archaeology of Food and Identity*, edited by Katheryn C. Twiss, pp. 130–151. Occasional Papers 34, Southern Illinois University Press, Carbondale.

Tiesler Blos, Vera
  1998 *La Costumbre de la Deformación Cefálica entre los Antiguos Maya*. Colección Científica, INAH, México, D. F.
  2001 *Decoraciones Dentales entre los ntiguos Mayas*. Ediciones Euroamericanas/INAH, México, D.F.

Torres-Rouff, Christina
   2008   The Influence of Tiwanaku on Life in the Chilean Atacama: Mortuary and Bodily Perspectives. *American Anthropologist* 110:325–337.
   2009   The Bodily Expression of Ethnic Identity: Head Shaping in the Chilean Atacama. *Bioarchaeology and Identity in the Americas*, edited by Kelly J. Knudson and Christopher Stojanowski, pp. 212–227. University of Florida Press, Gainesville.

Turner, Christy G., II, and Jacqueline A. Turner
   1999   *Man Corn: Cannibalism and Violence in the Prehistoric American Southwest*. University of Utah Press, Salt Lake City.

Twiss, Katheryn C. (editor)
   2007   *The Archaeology of Food and Identity*. Occasional Papers 34, Southern Illinois University Press, Carbondale.

Twiss, Katheryn C., Amy Bogaard, Mike Charles, Jennifer Henecke, Nerissa Russell, Louise Martin, and Glynis Jones
   2009   Plants and Animals Together: Interpreting Organic Remains from Building 52 at Çatalhöyük. *Current Anthropology* 50:885–895.

Tykot, Robert H.
   2006   Isotope Analyses and the Histories of Maize. In *Histories of Maize: Multidisciplinary Approaches to the Prehistory, Linguistics, Biogeography, Domestication, and Evolution of Maize*, edited by John E. Staller, Robert H. Tykot, and Bruce F. Benz, pp. 131–142. Academic Press, New York.

Ugan, A.
   2005   Climate, Bone Density, and Resource Depression: What is Driving Variation in Larger and Small Game in Fremont Archaeofaunas? *Journal of Anthropological Archaeology* 24:227–251.

van der Leeuw, Sander E.
   1994   Whispers from the Context of Real life: Towards Pluriformity in Archaeology. *Archaeological Dialogues* 1:132–164.
   2005   Climate, Hydrology, Land use, and Environmental Degradation in the Lower Rhone Valley during the Roman Period. C.R. *Geoscience* 337:9–27.

van der Leeuw, Sander E. (editor)
   1998   *The Archaeomedes project: Understanding the Natural and Anthropogenic Causes of Land Degradation and Desertification in the Mediterranean Basin*. Luxembourg: Office for Official Publication of the European Communities.

van der Leeuw, Sander E., and Charles Redman
   2002   Placing Archaeology at the Center of Socio-Natural Studies. *American Antiquity* 67:597–605.

van der Merwe, Nikolaas J., and John. C. Vogel
   1978 ^{13}C Content of Human Collagen as a Measure of Prehistoric Diet in Woodland North America. *Nature* 276:815–816.

van der Veen, M.
   2007   Food as an Instrument of Social Change: Feasting in Iron Age and Early Roman Southern Britain. In *The Archaeology of Food and Identity*, edited by Katheryn C. Twiss, pp. 112–129. Occasional Papers 34, Southern Illinois University Press, Carbondale.

VanDerwarker, Amber M., and Kandace R. Detwiler
  2002 Gendered Practice in Cherokee Foodways: A Spatial Analysis of Plant Remains from the Coweeta Creek Site. *Southeastern Archaeology* 21:21–28.
Varien, Mark D., Scott G. Ortman, Timothy A. Kohler, Donna M. Glowacki, and C. David Johnson
  2007 Historical Ecology in the Mesa Verde Region: Results from the Village Ecodynamics Project. *American Antiquity* 72:273–300.
Vigne, Jean-Denis, Joris Peters, and Daniel Helmer
  2005 New Archaeozoological Approaches to Trace the First Steps of Animal Domestication. In *The First Steps of Animal Domestication*, edited by Jean-Denis Vigne, Joris Peters, and Daniel Helmer, pp. 1–16. Oxbow Books, Oxford.
Vogel, John C., and Nikolaas J. van der Merwe
  1977 Isotopic Evidence for Early Maize Cultivation in New York State. *American Antiquity* 42:238–242.
Walker, Philip
  2001 Bioarchaeological Perspective on the History of Violence. *Annual Review of Anthropology* 30:573–596.
Walker, William H.
  1998 Where are the Witches of Prehistory? *Journal of Archaeological Method and Theory* 5:245–308.
Wapnish, Paula, and Brian Hesse
  1991 Faunal Remains from Tel Dan: Perspectives on Animal Production at a Village, Urban, and Ritual Center. *ArchaeoZoologia* 4:9–86.
Washburn, Sherwood, and Jane Lancaster
  1968 The Evolution of Hunting. In *Man the Hunter*, edited by Richard Lee and Irvin DeVore, pp. 293–303. Aldine, Chicago.
Wattenmaker, Patricia
  1998 *Household and State in Upper Mesopotamia: Specialized Economy and the Social Uses of Goods in an Early Complex Society*. Smithsonian Institution Press, Washington, D.C.
Weiss, Ehud, Mordechai E. Kislev, and Anat Hartmann
  2006 Autonomous Cultivation before Domestication. *Science* 312:1608–1610.
Welch, Paul D., and C. Margaret Scarry
  1995 Status-related Variation in Foodways in the Moundville Chiefdom. *American Antiquity* 60:397–419.
White, Christine D., Michael W. Spence, and Fred J. Longstaffe
  2004 Demography and Ethnic Continuity in the Tlailotlacan Enclave of Teotihuacan: The Evidence from Stable Oxygen Isotopes. *Journal of Anthropological Archaeology* 23:385–403.
White, Tim D.
  1992 *Prehistoric Cannibalism at Mancos 5MTUMR–2346*. Princeton University Press, Princeton.
Willey, Patrick S.
  1990 *Prehistoric Warfare on the Great Plains*. Garland Publishing, New York.

Wood, James W., George R. Milner, Henry C. Harpending, and Kenneth M. Weiss
   1992 The Osteological Paradox: Problems of Inferring Prehistoric Health from Skeletal Samples. *Current Anthropology* 33:343–370.
Wright, Henry T., Naomi F. Miller, and Richard W. Redding
   1981 Time and Process in an Uruk Rural Center. In *L'archéologie de l'Iraq: Perspectives et limites de l'interpretation anthropologique des documents*, pp. 265–282. Colloques internationaux du CNRS 580.
Wright, Lori E., and Christine D. White
   1996 Human Biology in the Classic Maya Collapse: Evidence from Paleopathology and Paleodiet. *Journal of World Prehistory* 10:147–198.
Yeshurun, Reuven, Guy Bar-Oz, Mina Weinstein-Evron
   2007 Modern Hunting Behavior in the Early Middle Paleolithic: Faunal Remains from Misliya Cave, Mount Carmel, Israel. *Journal of Human Evolution* 53:656–677.
Zeder, Melinda A.
   1991 *Feeding Cities: Specialized Animal Economy in the Ancient Near East.* Smithsonian Institution Press, Washington, DC.
   2006 Archaeological Approaches to Documenting Animal Domestication. In *Documenting Domestication: New Genetic and Archaeological Paradigms*, edited by Melinda A. Zeder, Eve Emshwiller, Bruce D. Smith, and Daniel G. Bradley, pp. 171–180. University of California Press, Berkeley.
   2009 The Neolithic Macro-(R)evolution: Macroevolutionary Theory and the Study of Culture Change. *Journal of Archaeological Research* 17:1–64.
Zeder, Melinda A., Daniel G. Bradley, Eve Emshwiller, and Bruce D. Smith (editors)
   2006 *Documenting Domestication: New Genetic and Archaeological Paradigms*, University of California Press, Berkeley.
Zeder, Melinda A., Eve Emshwiller, Bruce D. Smith, and Daniel G. Bradley
   2006 Documenting Domestication, the Intersection of Genetics and Archaeology. *Trends in Genetics* 22:139–155.
Zeder, Melinda A. and Bruce D. Smith
   2009 A Conversation on Agricultural Origins: Talking Past Each Other in a Crowded Room. *Current Anthropology* 50:681–691.

12

Communicating Archaeology in the 21st Century

MITCHELL ALLEN *and* ROSEMARY A. JOYCE

You're riffling through the weekly mail. Amid the DSL ads, snarky notes from your department chair, and bookstore requests for a list of your spring course titles, there is a slick postcard from HarperCollins or Bloomsbury announcing a revolutionary new archaeology book about the research topic you've labored over for the past 20 years. The author? No, it's not you, but some hack science writer who once called you and asked a couple of inane questions.

You put a "public education" component into the bid for that big Department of Transportation contract. You'd provide some kind of interpretive report for the community to help explain to them the heritage of their neighborhood. At the time, you figured you'd give the local community association a discount on multiple copies of the final CRM report you're submitting. The report has ballooned to 650 pages with eight technical appendixes. Now you're close to the end of the contract, it's time to do something concrete. How do you think the community association will respond to your offer?

There's an exciting new website, full of glitz and glamour, www.gonzoarchaeology.net, just waiting for you to send the pieces of your latest project. They've begged you for it. They can include the 200 color images, the webcam set up in the dig house, the 3-D reconstructions of the site architecture. But your department chair has hinted strongly that your best course of action would be to submit an article to American Antiquity *instead.*

Welcome to archaeological communication in the twenty-first century. The twentieth-century world of multivolume site reports, finely ground monographs, kitchen sink collections of conference papers, even 16-chapter textbooks with student exercises, seems old and quaint less than a decade into the new millennium. Archaeologists are busy YouTubeing, self-publishing their ideas, uploading their data into online archives, and offering their findings to the (sometimes illiterate) communities in which they work. The ways archaeologists write are changing faster than the reward systems universities have in place for publication, posing challenges to how we judge good communication.

Has the world left you behind?

Not really. The refereed journal article is still the coin of the academic realm, publishers still produce edited volumes, the mass of gray literature is still a mass and still gray, and most students still buy textbooks in September and sell them in December (even if they are increasingly unlikely to read them in between). So any attempt at describing the future of archaeological communication must both address the problems we have always faced and the new ones that have arisen, the solutions that the Brave New Digital World may provide and the problems that have to be addressed in an old fashioned way. We—a well-published tenured scholar and a well-traveled scholarly publisher—will suggest a few problems and a few solutions, old and new.

We don't always agree on the answers. Where we do emphatically agree is that archaeologists either will take control of their communications in the twenty-first century or risk seeing the public pass us by, substituting mass-market popularization for the pursuit of real and exciting knowledge that keeps every professional and avocational archaeologist engaged.

What's Old

Writing the Ecology of the Discipline

> *The annual meeting is underway, and you're headed for the room where you'll spend your entire day. Your own paper for the session is something you've been waiting to give for months: you finally have enough data to show your colleagues that the proposal NSF funded*

panned out. For a change, you got a text to the discussant ahead of time (stuffing a printout into an envelope and leaving it at the message desk two days ago), so you hope she will single your new work out for comment.

While the organizers haven't talked about an edited volume yet, you're sure they will want to do one: both of them just started tenure-track jobs and need to get something out with their names on the cover. Of course, your advisor is telling you to send the paper in to American Antiquity, *but you really want to be included in the volume if there is one: everyone who writes about this topic in the future will have to cite it, after all. Besides, the two senior people in the session are certainly the reviewers who gave your proposal their support, or else why were you invited to be part of this session? Who knows where this could lead?*

Writing and publishing does more than simply disseminate information. The specific communicative practices of archaeologists actually create and sustain the entire ecology of niches that we recognize as the discipline of archaeology (Joyce 2002, 2006). Long gone is any possibility for archaeology to speak with a single voice. "All archaeologists believe..." is an anachronistic statement. In many corners of the profession, we can find small bands of archaeologists using terms that their listeners understand because they have been present for years of conference presentations, reading the same journals and serving as peer-reviewers for them, enforcing a particular way of writing, and clustering as authors and editors of books from specific presses with known emphases and formats. Multiply these phenomena across national boundaries and specializations, and what you find is that archaeologists speak a variety of specialist languages and so constitute a rich array of separate disciplinary conversations.

Specific terms used as technical language have always been read as signs of ecological difference within archaeology. Long before Lewis Binford gave us ideotechnic, sociotechnic, and technomic as fighting words drawing the line between the New Archaeology of the 1960s and the old (but still with us today) cultural history, the eminent British archaeologist V. Gordon Childe (1926:171) commented on what he took to be excessive Americanisms in a book he was reviewing for the British journal *Man*: "Considering the undoubted points of contact between English and American, the translation of this work is not so easy as might be expected. We may gloss: hypothecation = supposition, provenience = provenance, deposition = act of placing, location = site." For many English-speaking Americanist archaeologists today, talking about the *provenience* of an object serves not just to indicate national origin, but is a positioning move in debates across the lines between anthropological archaeology and art historical archaeology over the utility of objects collected in nonprofessional excavations.

What Childe and Binford each in their own way were doing in their writing of archaeology was as important as what they did in their field practice. Walter Taylor (1948:34–35) and James Deetz (1988:15–20) argued for recognition that even the word "archaeology" has two meanings, one of them "the writing of contexts from the material culture of past actuality" (Deetz 1988:18). It is still the only academic discipline whose name can be correctly spelled in two ways. Truly, we are a tribal society, fractured along many lines of ideology, nationality, academic culture, and language.

Nonetheless, our cultures have some commonalities. Deetz (1998:94) noted that the dominant form of archaeological writing in the U.S. in the late twentieth century seemed "to have been perpetuated by example; if that report is written in this fashion, then mine must be as well." The result has been a general convergence of form in archaeology, toward the now-venerable technical article and monograph.

Recognizable technical reports presenting conclusions in third-person abstraction replaced earlier archaeological reports, often written in the form of first-person narration in letters, by the late nineteenth or early twentieth century (Hodder 1989). These defining genres of contemporary archaeology employ conventions that only insiders understand without explanation. How well are these conventions understood outside our world? Try asking beginning undergraduates to explain some of the figures in any book or article you assign in teaching, and be prepared to be startled by what you learn.

Even within site reports or CRM reports read only by the cognoscenti, we need to rethink our use of language. While the expert is capable of following the dense, passive thread of archaeological reporting, they are still narratives of a field project or a study, a tale you tell of your data. And, while more technical than an *Archaeology Magazine* article, there are basic conventions of narrative writing that bound what we produce.

If its products are so hard to read, how does our archaeological scribal culture reproduce itself? Two words: peer review.

Peer review is, of course, what we all rely on to tell us that other people's findings are good bases for us to build on. "One trusts that making use of a claim to know originated by one of one's fellow scientists will not let one down in a debate" (Harré 1990:83). But to attain that level of trustworthiness, a peer-reviewed publication has to eliminate all that might go beyond the consensus of the community invited to judge the work. Peer-reviewed articles are treated as the most valuable currency in hiring, tenure, and promotion, and we learn to perform what is rewarded.

Space for innovation, in print at any rate, is limited. Edited volumes, especially those fostered by smaller presses, have been one of the last refuges for more edgy work, and for work that is so specialized that only the inhabitants of a very small archaeological niche will be able to read and build on it. But the economics of publication, like everything else in the global economy, have been changing. The ever-dwindling body of built-in buyers represented by large university libraries, and the legions of students in undergraduate courses at all levels, are becoming the last (sometimes only) reliable audiences for books. Those edited volumes, among the least salable for publishers, become the first casualties of the economic realities.

What will preserve this edge, this ability to communicate to our audiences? And what will allow our fractured tribal system to maintain the common banner of "archaeologists," with or without the extra "a?" Among the conditions that may make or break the reception these consumers, both inside and outside the discipline, give to archaeological writing is how engaging they find what we write.

Why Do We Write So Badly?

> *He's in the room. There, by the book case or behind the pile of unread student assignments. As you stare at the blank screen you can feel him lurking over your shoulder. Looking. Thinking. Judging. Professor WNC is there with you whenever you begin to write. He is as old as many of your sites, was critiquing articles for* American Antiquity *when Binford and Flannery were mere whelps. He has a thin mouth, always slightly downturned. When crossed, he thunders. When you timidly hand him your latest paper, the downturned mouth drops a hint lower.*

> He's always there when you're writing, looking over your shoulder with the slightest of disappointed sighs. But, that is enough. When you excitedly type "they were smelting copper at this site! I know it," you add a prefix: "Based upon the data analyzed to date, it might be possible to hypothesize that...." Any further out on the limb, and your Worst Nightmare Critic's sighs will turn to peals of derisive laughter before he rips your argument to shreds.

It's not just archaeologists who suffer the barbs of Professor Worst Nightmare Critic. The victims seem to inhabit all of academia. In defending our work against any possible attacks from Dr. WNC, scholars write defensively, conservatively, passively. No wonder the standard journal article isn't read by anyone! When we want to inhale the enthusiasm for what our colleagues have discovered in the field, we find them droning in monotone. When we want to be challenged by ideas that rock our conventional wisdom, we find them couched inside convoluted language and impenetrable jargon. What if, instead, we were to write that article for our favorite advanced undergraduate, the one who sits in the front row and smiles at all our jokes, whose jaw drops at the brilliant paradox with which we end our lecture? What if it was she (or he) looking over our shoulder while we wrote, waiting anxiously for us to pound out each sentence so she could ask a dozen breathless questions about our argument?

Wouldn't you rather read that journal article?

Our words should be tailored to the audience we're addressing. Precise academic prose is expected in a journal article. Even here, good, active writing is possible, writing that speaks to those outside the niche as well as the insiders to the language circle. A number of archaeologists have given us beautifully written passages that allow us to conjure up in our mind's eye an image of the archaeological data shimmering through the visualized scenes of past actors.

Consider this passage, written by Rebecca Yamin (2002:122–123) immediately following an analysis of distributions at marbles at three historic sites:

> Marbles, like cards, is an internally interesting game, and although it is a game of skill, there is also an element of luck. Sometimes you win and sometimes you don't. Sometimes you're up (with a pocketful of marbles to click the way some men jangle change) and sometimes you're down. Importantly, you are expected to keep playing in marbles,

to stay in the game long enough to give your opponents a chance to win back what they have lost. The excitement of winning and the disappointment of losing are shared experience—players can feel each other's ups and downs (Robin Stevens, personal communication). There is a sense of commonality and solidarity in the game just as there was in the tenements where everyone's troubles, as well as their triumphs, were visible to everyone else, and there was an ebb and flow of good times and bad.

Yamin presents her data using frequency bar graphs, a professional visual format based on conventions that are quite opaque to those outside our discipline. The writing that follows gives instead an image of the marbles in use, teasing out the kinds of implications on which contemporary archaeologists base the claim that the smallest things in context can inform us about society at large.

Yamin (1998:85) wrote about some of her previous experiments in writing professional articles that "the construction of a narrative vignette provides a methodological beginning point. It forces the scholar to go out on a limb—to interpret what it all might mean—and it allows any interested party, either professional or nonprofessional, to question the interpretation and/or add to it. Most importantly, the process of writing a narrative tells you what you don't know thereby providing a reason to keep searching."

But even the clearest academic prose may not work in trying to address a broader audience. There is a relationship between an author and the people he or she imagines reading the text that requires different ways of writing. Ideally, we would speak to big questions, and not just to those stereotypes of archaeological journalism, stories of "origins" and new discoveries. Mark Pluciennik (1999:667) notes that the majority of archaeological writing presents "a sequential story of, rather than in, the past—but also a markedly external or birds-eye view. The story is typically told in the third-person passive."

Some archaeologists have experimented with new formats explicitly to overcome these limitations. One of the most widely cited archaeological experiments with writing new ways to communicate to broader audiences was Janet Spector's *What This Awl Means* (1993). Spector reported that she "wanted to communicate in an easily accessible way" what she had learned about a nineteenth-century Wahpeton Dakota village, especially for the contemporary descendant community (Spector 1993:17).

Two decades earlier, Robert Ascher and Charles Fairbanks experimented with the form of the journal article, providing a compelling interpretation they likened to a film: "Here is an interpretation of what was found in the ruins of a slave cabin.... Our presentation includes a soundtrack and pictures. The soundtrack is composed from eye-witness accounts, slave narratives, and other sources. You are encouraged to sound out the words; the soundtrack selections are based on their auditory value and on their connection with the archaeological findings.... You are invited to reassemble the components to best suit yourself" (Ascher and Fairbanks 1971:3–4).

Experimenting with writing genres has become more common in recent years as archaeologists realize the value of communicating beyond the converted. "Teaching novels" by experienced archaeologists are a more common sight in college courses (Nelson 1999; Praetzellis 2000, 2003). Archaeological comic books have ridden the tail of the youthful passion for Japanese manga (Kantner 2005). And archaeologists are increasingly overcoming their aversion to asking for help. In addition to archaeology's own public intellectuals—Brian Fagan, Paul Bahn and Neil Silberman, among others—books on important archaeological topics are being coauthored with professional science writers (Adovasio et al. 2007; Morwood and Van Oosterzee 2007). CRM companies are also hiring professional writers to make their reports more accessible to the contracting agency or community. Archaeologist Nancy Marie White (2008) has even braved professional hazing by penning *Archaeology for Dummies* in the iconic Dummies series.

Nor do we always need to use only words. Here, we might want to admit that our most effective form of communication is actually still an oral tradition, best seen at professional meetings, where droning through pages of text is a signal to your audience to doze, while the best speakers present lively narratives illustrated by appropriately selected images. This is the form of archaeological publication that gets us our best public response, whether it is the on-site talk during Archaeology Week or the on-air interview cut into a Discovery Channel filler program. New digital media need us to capture that freshness, and to use our fluency in visual communication in ways few publishers today can actually afford to support.

Archaeologists clearly do know how to write, if we want to, in clear and even exciting prose. Most of us actually have a lot more to say than appears in print. Our ability to acceptably reproduce the forms favored within our discipline occupies too much of our attention as writers. It is worth considering why so few of us end up writing for the public, or even just writing beyond the specialized niches we occupy.

Why Do We Write So Little?

An imaginary interview with Brian Fagan, emeritus professor of archaeology, UC Santa Barbara and author of dozens of archaeology textbooks, popular books, reference volumes, articles, critical reviews, and magazine pieces (after Fagan 2005)

Mitch Allen: Brian, how do you write so much? It must be the light load at a research university that gives you the time to produce so much work. Maybe you were assigned half a dozen research assistants.

Brian Fagan: I taught the introductory archaeology course at UCSB for over 30 years, 300 students a year. I don't think it was due to having a light load, just a commitment to writing. And my writing is my own, I rarely had research assistance.

MA: So what is the secret to writing so much.

BF: It is to write, write regularly, write daily. Several hours a day, without my email, without disturbance, with complete focus. As I explain in workshops and my writing book (Fagan 2005), if you can produce 4 pages a day (1,000 words), that's an article each week and a full-length book in 2 months. Once the words are on the page, it is possible to edit, organize, and delete them. But they first need to be on a page.

MA: But this can't apply to research articles, you're writing more popular stuff. Writing research must be much harder.

BF: On the contrary, it is much simpler. Most of what you put in your article is data, theory, interpretation. The format of a research article is standard and known to you since you were an undergrad. When I write textbooks or popular books, I am synthesizing dozens of these articles into a coherent narrative that someone not familiar with archaeology can follow. I tell stories.

MA: And that's the difference between professional writing and popular writing?

BF: Actually no, the researcher is also a story teller. Your article has a beginning, middle, and an end, and should follow the general rules of narrative. Tell a story with your data and you will communicate the data to the reader.

Telling stories with our data is where archaeological writing began, in those nineteenth-century narrative reports. Now there are new ways to tell those compelling stories, and so far, it isn't us using them. Rather, they're told by people whose views of the past and of how we know about the past we are arguing against. It's time for us to change that.

What's New

Marketing Archaeology

There is no lack of interest in archaeology from the general public. Turn on any documentary TV channel and you'll get a steady diet of "Mysteries of the Pyramids," "Secrets of the Bible," or "Lost Temples of the Inca." Coffee-table books are filled with Greek temples, English henges, and Cambodian spires. Indiana Jones rakes in hundreds of millions at the box office and fills our undergraduate classes with wannabes in need of reprogramming. We're hot, but unlike our hip-hop contemporaries, we make little use of it.

Archaeology has never lauded its public intellectuals, labeling them with the derogatory term "popularizer." But others have noticed the public passion for archaeology, even if we haven't. Ever watch a documentary series called *The Naked Archaeologist* (http://www.visiontv.ca/NakedArchaeologist/index2.htm)? He's neither. Or followed Graham Hancock (http://www.grahamhancock.com), the latest in a long line of charlatans using archaeology to justify outlandish claims about the past in such works as *The Sign and the Seal* and *Fingerprints of the Gods*? There is money to be made here, passions to be fueled, knowledge (real or pseudo) to be imparted. In the absence of a commitment of professional archaeologists to fill the gap, it has been co-opted by snake oil salesmen.

Perhaps the worm is turning. Perhaps archaeologists, members of The Cult of Arcane Knowledge of the Past, finally realize that survival is dependent on popular notice, public funding, and contemporary relevance (Sabloff 2008). Those topics are highlighted elsewhere in this volume (see Little and Zimmerman, this volume), and should be a driving force in our communication patterns as well. For each research project published in *Journal of Field Archaeology* or *American Antiquity*, there should be a piece in the local newspaper, a handout at the local historical society, or a YouTube documentary showing our work to the community. There are multiple audiences for our work—we need to pay more attention to the ones so long ignored. Both SAA and the British Archaeological Association now have awards for books for the general public. *Archaeology* magazine online gets between 81,000 and 142,500 page views each week for news and information generated by professional archaeologists (Mark Rose, personal communication 2009). The web-based Archaeology Channel has over 100 videos, most generated by archaeological field projects (www.archaeologychannel.org). Public education components are now routinely built into large cultural resource management contracts.

But even if we compete with Graham Hancock or Simcha Jacobovici for public attention, why should the public listen to us and not them? After all, we are constrained by facts, by the recognition of the limitations of our knowledge. Ethically, we have to tell what we know and, more importantly, what we don't know. Charlatans have no such restrictions. So, in addition to being good storytellers, we have to be able to document how the story is told: What is the basis of our claims about the past and what we cannot claim? Which stories can we tell with some authority and which are just speculation? What makes our narratives different from *The Da Vinci Code*? Our story—the story of the process of doing science, of its triumphs and pitfalls, of the slow accretion of knowledge, the development and overturning of Kuhnian paradigms—does carry authority with all but the least discriminating public. But it is not an easy story to tell and requires us to be *more accomplished* at storytelling than the average pseudoarchaeologist. Our stories must be more nuanced, more ambiguous, more like Pulitzer-quality adult fiction than formulaic romance novels.

Which is difficult to do. Writing good stories is an art, as any serious author of fiction knows. Lu Ann De Cunzo (1998:42–43) writes "telling these stories is far from easy.... The key to good stories, as to good scholarship, is details—an object, an action, a thought, a look. The stories I tell and the images I present here negotiate a difficult path. My imagination should paint in few of the details while allowing the stories to communicate the messages and meanings I intend." Archaeologists who succeed in constructing compelling narratives draw on small details to show, rather than tell (Joyce 2002, following Gass 1970:55–76).

Here, then, is one of the key challenges for the twenty-first century archaeologist—to become that storyteller, that craftsperson of (metaphorical) adult fiction, whether on the web, in an explanatory pamphlet, an op-ed piece, a blog, or a book. It is in marketing these ideas that we will establish our place in the cacophony of voices in the contemporary hypermediated world and become the authoritative voice of interpretation of the past that our training and skill warrant.

The Digital Revolution

Archaeologists have not been laggards in the application of computers to their research. Not surprisingly, we have so much data that adopting computers quickly was a necessary survival mechanism. But communicating these data has never been easy. Databases were hand crafted for each project, data not easily accessed by outsiders nor readily aggregated for comparative studies.

In the twenty-first century world, this guild craft is no longer an option. Researchers, funders, and the public alike expect access to the knowledge we've amassed long before it is ready to be rolled out in a polished final site report. There are often good reasons for delays, including technical analyses in progress and data verification that is part of our responsibility. Still, there probably should be some statute of limitations. One of us was responsible for publishing such a report, Alfred Kroeber's volume about his 1926 field season in Nasca, Peru.... in 1999 (Kroeber 1999)!

There are dozens of unfinished site reports living half digested on someone's hard drive, or buried in the back of a filing cabinet, often lagging decades after the completion of the project. Archaeology is one of the few disciplines in which funders have to beg for reports, giving money just to get the writing done, as has The Shelby White-Leon Levy Program for Archaeological Publications administered by Harvard University (http://www.fas.harvard.edu/~semitic/wl/).

Yet even the most elaborate completed reports sitting proudly on your bookcase contain only a small fraction of the data collected by the research project, carefully filtered through the interpretive lens of the project staff.

The technology is now available to make *all* your data available to colleagues and anyone else interested. Interpretation of data can be broadened to include others not part of the original research team, even the general public.

Digital media should be a natural for archaeologists. In reality, our excavations provide the basis for many different narratives, not a single linear storyline. Relationships exist between excavated materials at multiple scales, from the landscape to micro deposits, and can be established through many different techniques, some linking discontinuously distributed things, others establishing continuous patterns of distribution. In many if not most instances, these multiple radiating connections exist in palimpsests of a series of different moments in time, each of which can have completely different stories to tell.

As many people have noted, digital media allow a closer representation of what the development of knowledge of a site really is like than the static linear form of a paper text (Joyce 2002; Joyce and Tringham 2007; Lopiparo and Joyce 2003). Their capacity to spatially represent relations between things and to associate multiple kinds of representations of data derived from the same point in space make map-indexed databases a more transparent way of recording sites. The ability of digital media to form part of multi-linear (hypertext) webs of associations, and to be amended, added to, and to cumulatively accrue additional commentaries, offers unique potential for multiple authors, including publics, to engage with archaeological data (McDavid 1999; Tringham 2004; Wolle and Tringham 2000).

So why is this potential of digital publication still used so sparingly by archaeologists?

First, populating a website with site data requires the ability to translate it into formats accessible to outsiders. Hand-crafted databases, understood only by the dig director and IT staff, are not easily readable by other researchers, let alone the public or archaeology students. Even when proper instructions can be crafted or the database built in a way that it can be read, it requires continual updating as technology changes, as database programs change, as the data itself changes (Richards 2002, 2006). Such long-term commitment to making data available is hard to sustain after the project has shut down and funding halted.

Additionally, in a world of hand-crafted databases, even the material that can be read by an outsider cannot be matched up with other data from other projects designed with similar boutique databases—the fields/ programs/ values don't translate. Lithics from Site A cannot be readily compared to lithics from Site B; the programs don't match up. Finally, there is the human factor. Publishing site data has always been about "interpretive primogeniture," the ability of a project director to be able to offer the first interpretation of a body of data from a project (Allen 2007). Without this, the foundational interpretation goes to the swift, not the one with the most experience with the data. Thus, data from a project has traditionally been kept sequestered until the project staff can complete their analysis and interpretations. These data are available to outsiders only by the benevolence of the project staff, benevolence that can be withheld. Valuable data may be hidden from the rest of the field for years, sometimes decades. How can we foster a more universal sharing of basic data? Reasonable people can differ in their response.

Mitch's solution: We need to be able to read each other's tables, lists of loci, laboratory analyses, with all their inherent flaws in order to incorporate these data into our own work. More important, we need them before the research team is finished polishing them to a piece of fine art a decade after the data was collected. This requires that they be available electronically, that they be available soon after the completion of the fieldwork, that they be available in a form easily readable to many, and that they be in a form that is standard enough to use in comparative studies. This requires standardization far beyond what archaeologists have traditionally done. A challenge to your academic freedom? Nonsense, it's a way of communicating new data while we're all still alive to do something with it.

This process is taking place in a neighboring universe, the museum world, where the collections management software has narrowed to a few standard programs, where virtual exhibits online are popping up daily, and where standardized nomenclature and best practices for documentation are being developed by the major professional associations. There's no reason that archaeology can't do the same. There have been experiments in this direction, like the Alexandria Archive (http://www.alexandriaarchive.org). More experiments need to follow.

Rosemary's solution: I agree that initiatives like Keith Kintigh's NSF-funded project, The Digital Archaeological Record (http://www.tdar.org/confluence/display/TDAR/Home), which builds on the best practices of the University of York's Archaeology Data Service, and other recent initiatives, many from the Mellon Foundation (http://msc.mellon.org), are critical for archaeology. But none exhausts the potential of digital media for archaeology, and they expose other challenges posed by the real lack of standardization of what constitutes "data."

The illusion that standardization will actually do what we want breaks down, in my view, when we consider the difference between the material phenomena that are traces of people in the past, and the representations of these phenomena that we conventionally call data. We measure, record the color, shape, size (in grams? or ounces? or some other system?), draw, photograph, and otherwise "document" material things. That is, we replace material things with representations. We designed these representations in the first place to answer specific questions. So, what we measure on some object (say, a chipped biface) is based on what we think are the important data for our research question (Fotiadis 1992; Hamilton 2000). They will not necessarily serve for someone else's research question now, nor in the future. And they may not be the kinds of things a member of the public wants to use to group specific observations together for a new interpretive purpose.

We do need to make all our observations (data records) available to others more quickly than we currently do. Digital media are ideal for this purpose. We also need to make it easy for others to identify associated data in different tables or other data constructs, as The Digital Archaeological Record helps us do through its explicit capture of ontologies and rules, not just records and fields.

The practices still dominant in many parts of the discipline, that encourage independent referencing of different materials that obscures the original three-dimensional provenience within sites, could do with standardization: use one form of reference, and keep it transparent. But different archaeologists will continue to ask different kinds of questions, so rather than standardize some ideal record-keeping system, what would pay off far more quickly for us is investing the necessary time in documenting our existing data recording formats. How many projects are prepared today to publish their entire field manual, their data protocols, what any database specialist would demand as their metadata? No one is rewarded (or indeed, allowed the space!) to describe how they measure their lithics (at what points, using what tools, to what tolerances?). But that metadata are critical to allowing me to know if my descriptions are really of things different than yours, or just incommensurate ways of describing the same things.

Going digital should not be delayed waiting for the onset of some standardizing regime. What projects like the The Digital Archaeological Record and The Alexandria Archive are doing that is indispensable are such things as focusing on metadata. We should especially insist on the use of Open Source approaches in these and future projects. I can live with the need to make my own records of the things I locate in other people's digitally published data, because I don't expect that other people will also be noting the observations I need for my own research questions. But I cannot work with other people's data if they end up in proprietary systems that try to limit the circulation of records, in a digital repeat of stories of hoarded artifacts and field notes.

The New Golden Age

> "It's harder to get published now. Site reports won't be picked up by publishers any more. I promised my panel that I'd find a publisher for the papers from our SEAC session, but none are interested. Archaeological publishing is an endangered species."

For the longest time, archaeologists have been decrying the death of the site report, joining the cacophonous chorus throughout the academy over the premature death of the research monograph. And don't forget all that gray literature, lurking beneath the radar screens of even the most library-obsessed archaeologist. The digitization revolution mentioned above has resuscitated all in Lazarus-like fashion. No longer does an archaeological project depend on the publications subsidy to assume the costs of the 10-volume set that looks good on the project staff's shelf and in half a hundred carefully selected libraries, but is generally unavailable anywhere else. Uploading data as they come in, analyses as they are completed, and interpretations as they are finalized can be an ongoing process available to all interested readers in real time.

And that research monograph? In a world of open access publications, Google, inexpensive self publishing through outlets like I-Universe or Lulu, and mega-websites hosted by most major universities, anyone can produce and publish their well-crafted theories at no cost (if hosted by your university) or at a minimal cost (if paid for by you). The same holds true for all those fugitive CRM reports. Look, for example, at Adrian Praetzellis's reports on his work in West Oakland, Sacramento Chinatown, or Los

Vaqueros reservoir (http://www.sonoma.edu/users/p/praetzel/publications.html) online and buck naked for the world to see.

If anything, we are in a *golden age* of archaeological publication.

Got your attention? You know the previous statement to be untrue, despite Richard Pryor's admonition "Are you going to believe me or your lying eyes?" Field reports are still torturously difficult to bring to closure, monographs float through the publishing establishment for years before settling in the dust in the filing cabinet, and the gray literature has rarely been deconstructed into black and white. But the problems here, in our humble opinions, are not ones of publishing, but of the culture of the discipline.

Culture, you say? As in anthropology's pet concept, carefully guarded against art critics, media pundits, and postmodernists alike?

Yes, the very same culture, the "culture of archaeology" and "culture of academia" more broadly. When the publisher half of this authorial pair asked an unnamed major multidisciplinary, multinational, multidecade, multiproblem field project to put all their data online and write a short interpretive book for a much broader audience, the response was one of horror. "Sorry, we have already parceled out the lithics to Dr. Figenbottom, the ceramics to Professor Egorama, and Ms. Penitent is working up the stratigraphy volume as her dissertation. We couldn't disappoint them." Maybe when these volumes (and the rest of the site reports) were completed, they would consider the broader book.

Which assistant professor can self-publish her monograph rather than waiting for the university press of choice, thereby getting the book out quickly but without the imprimatur of peer refereed approval? It would be suicide when she comes up for review of her tenure case.

CRM professionals are generally on to their next contract before finding a way of doing more than submitting their last report to the local State Historic Preservation Officer. A publication is nice, a paycheck is nicer.

None of these problems is insolvable if we were willing and able to change the culture of the professional and academic structure in which we operate. Will the tenure committee weigh equally the article in an open source journal with one in *American Antiquity*? Will a vibrant website explaining Early Classic Maya sculpture to the great unwashed receive the same kudos as a dense tome published by Dumbarton Oaks? Will the CRM firm loading all their site reports onto their website help them get more contracts from Bureau of Land Management? The academic and professional reward systems are glacial in their pace of change needed to meet new conditions. Culture doesn't change easily, and these publication problems will be with us until it does.

Ironically, part of the solution is in the changing nature of the discipline itself. As fewer archaeologists are employed by universities and more end up in the government or private sectors, the tenure and promotion committee becomes less of a factor in shaping how archaeologists write. A discipline full of professionals might have less time than one full of academics to communicate, but they also have fewer cultural restraints on *how* they communicate.

The 10 Step Program

We've demonstrated, to no surprise to most of our readers, what we see as the major problems facing archaeologists in communicating their discipline to each other, to their students, and to the wider world. But we can't leave it here, without some suggestions to help archaeologists become better communicators. So, herewith is the Allen/Joyce 10 Step Program to improve the communication skill of archaeologists.

1. Think Bronte, not Baudrillard or Binford. Learn how to write. Well. While you're struggling through graduate school, add "join a writing group" to the To Do list. If you're a full professor, do the same. Share your writing with non-archaeological friends to see if it makes sense to them.

2. Get more web literate and use the medium to its fullest.

3. Recognize the various publics for archaeological information and appropriately present your message to each. Understand your audience and present information in the medium most comfortable to THEM, not to you.

4. Create spaces for the sharing of innovation, for bridging the niches in the archaeological community. Foster creative ideas, not just those already widely agreed upon.

5. Establish means by which the outside world can identify authoritative, rather than gonzo, archaeological interpretations. Explain what distinguishes real archaeology from the fake kind.

6. If needed, bring in the cavalry—science writers, web designers, videographers—to help communicate to audiences for whom you're not comfortable writing.

7. Look beyond traditional publication sources for ways to present your data and interpretation.

8. Write for the receptive student who wants to hear about your work, not the Worst Nightmare Critic who will pan it no matter how passive the language you use.

9. Show, don't tell.

10. Have fun writing, and your readers will have fun reading what you wrote. But whatever you do, write. The more you do, the easier it gets.

Acknowledgments. We gratefully acknowledge Brian Fagan's permission to use his name in the fictional dialogue included here. We even more gratefully acknowledge his comments on a previous version, encouraging us to foreground even more the importance of writing continuously as a way to be more productive, and questioning our use of the word "popularizer" in the original version. We also thank several anonymous reviewers and the volume editors for their helpful suggestions.

References Cited

Adovasio, James M., Olga Soffer, and Jake Page
   2007 *The Invisible Sex: Uncovering the True Roles of Women in Prehistory.* Smithsonian Institution Press, New York.

Allen, Mitch
   2007 Think Small! *Near Eastern Archaeology* 70:196–197.

Ascher, Robert, and Charles H. Fairbanks
   1971 Excavation of a Slave Cabin: Georgia, U.S.A. *Historical Archaeology* 5:3–17.

Childe, V. Gordon
   1926 Review of *Italic Hut-Urns and Hut-Urn Cemeteries: A Study of the Early Iron Age in Latium,* by W. R. Bryan. *Man* 26:170–171.

De Cunzo, Lu Ann
   1998 A Future after Freedom. *Historical Archaeology* 32:42–54.

Deetz, James
   1988 History and Archaeological Theory: Walter Taylor Revisited. *American Antiquity* 53:13–22.
   1998 Discussion: Archaeologists as Storytellers. *Historical Archaeology* 32:94–96.

Fagan, Brian
   2005 *Writing Archaeology: Telling Stories About the Past.* Left Coast Press, Walnut Creek, California.

Fotiadis, Michael
   1992 Units of Data as Deployment of Disciplinary Codes. In *Representations in Archaeology,* edited by Jean-Claude Gardin and Christopher S. Peebles, pp.

132–148. Indiana University Press, Bloomington.

Gass, William H.
   1970   *Fiction and the Figures of Life*. Knopf, New York.

Hamilton, Naomi
   2000   The Conceptual Archive and the Challenge of Gender. In *Towards a Reflexive Method in Archaeology: The Example at Çatalhöyük*, edited by Ian Hodder, pp. 95–99. British Institute of Archaeology at Ankara Monograph No. 28. McDonald Institute for Archaeological Research, Cambridge.

Harré, Rom
   1990   Some Narrative Conventions of Scientific Discourse. In *Narrative in Culture: The Uses of Storytelling in the Sciences, Philosophy, and Literature*, edited by Christopher Nash, pp. 81–101. Routledge, London.

Hodder, Ian
   1989   Writing Archaeology. *Antiquity* 63:268–274.

Joyce, Rosemary A.
   2002   *The Languages of Archaeology: Dialogue, Narrative, and Writing*. Blackwell, Oxford.
   2006   Writing Historical Archaeology. In *Cambridge Companion for Historical Archaeology*, edited by Dan Hicks and Mary Beaudry, pp. 48–65. Cambridge University Press, Cambridge.

Joyce, Rosemary A., and Ruth E. Tringham
   2007   Feminist Adventures in Hypertext. *Journal of Archaeological Method and Theory* 14:328–358.

Kantner, John (editor)
   2005   Cartoons in Archaeology. Special issue of *The SAA Archaeological Record* 5:9–37.

Kroeber, Alfred, and Donald Collier
   1999   *The Archaeology and Pottery of Nazca, Peru: Alfred Kroeber's 1926 Expedition*, edited by Patrick Carmichael, afterword by Katharina J. Schreiber. AltaMira, Walnut Creek, California.

Lopiparo, Jeanne, and Rosemary A. Joyce
   2003   Crafting Cosmos, Telling Sister Stories, and Exploring Archaeological Knowledge Graphically in Hypertext Environments. In *Ancient Muses: Archaeology and the Arts*, edited by John H. Jameson Jr., Christine Finn, and John E. Ehrenhard, pp. 193–203. University of Alabama Press, Tuscaloosa.

McDavid, Carol
   1999   From Real Space to Cyberspace: Contemporary Conversations About the Archaeology of Slavery and Tenancy. *Internet Archaeology* 6. Electronic document, http://intarch.ac.uk/journal/issue6/mcdavid/toc.html, accessed January 12, 2009.

Morwood, Mike, and Penny van Oosterzee
   2007   *A New Human: The Startling Discovery and Strange Story of the "Hobbits" of Flores, Indonesia*. Smithsonian Institution Press, New York.

Nelson, Sarah Milledge
   1999   *Spirit Bird Journey*. RKLOG Press, Littleton, Colorado.

Pluciennik, Mark
  1999 Archaeological Narratives and Other Ways of Telling. *Current Anthropology* 40:653–678.
Praetzellis, Adrian
  2000 *Death by Theory: A Tale of Mystery and Archaeological Theory.* AltaMira, Walnut Creek, California.
  2003 *Dug to Death: A Tale of Archaeological Method and Mayhem.* AltaMira, Walnut Creek, California.
Richards, Julian
  2002 Digital Preservation and Access. *European Journal of Archaeology* 5:343–367.
  2006 Electronic Publication in Archaeology. In *Digital Archaeology: Bridging Method and Theory*, edited by Thomas L. Evans and Patrick Daly, pp. 213–225. Routledge, London.
Sabloff, Jeremy A.
  2008 *Archaeology Matters: Action Archaeology in the Modern World.* Left Coast Press, Walnut Creek, California.
Spector, Janet
  1993 *What this Awl Means: Feminist Archaeology at a Wahpeton Dakota Village.* Minnesota Historical Society Press, St. Paul.
Tringham, Ruth E.
  2004 Interweaving Digital Narratives with Dynamic Archaeological Databases for the Public Presentation of Cultural Heritage. In *Enter the Past: The E-way into the Four Dimensions of Cultural Heritage: CAA 2003*, edited by Wien Stadtarcheologie, pp. 196–200. Computer Applications and Quantitative Methods in Archaeology: Proceedings of the 31st Conference, Vienna, Austria, April 2003. Archeopress. BAR International Series 1227, Oxford, UK.
Taylor, Walter W.
  1948 *A Study of Archeology.* American Anthropological Association, Menasha, Wisconsin.
White, Nancy Marie
  2008 *Archaeology for Dummies.* Wiley, New York.
Wolle, Anja-C., and Ruth Tringham
  2000 Multiple Çatalhöyüks on the World Wide Web. In *Towards a Reflexive Method in Archaeology: The Example at Çatalhöyük*, edited by Ian Hodder, pp. 207–217. British Institute of Archaeology at Ankara Monograph No. 28. McDonald Institute for Archaeological Research, Cambridge.
Yamin, Rebecca
  1998 Lurid Tales and Homely Stories of New York's Notorious Five Points. *Historical Archaeology* 32:74–85.
  2002 Children's Strikes, Parents' Rights: Paterson and Five Points. *International Journal of Historical Archaeology* 6:113–126.

13

Trends in Employment and Training in American Archaeology

JEFFREY H. ALTSCHUL *and* THOMAS C. PATTERSON

"Can I get a job as an archaeologist?" Professional archaeologists are asked this question all the time, often by students who have taken a class or two and are wavering about whether to commit to what is perceived to be a risky career choice, but also increasingly by early and mid-career individuals who gave up on archaeology because they were told there were no jobs. The traditional answer is that "it's really hard," which reflects the realities of a small, highly competitive academic labor market. In the last four decades, however, academia has been supplanted by cultural resource management (CRM) as the major employer of archaeologists. Numbers of employed archaeologists have swelled at all levels, ranging from field technicians with B.A.s to principals of consulting firms and regulatory agencies with M.A.s and Ph.D.s. The answer to the employment question has changed and with it so have traditional ideas about what archaeologists do and what types of training they need to be successful.

In this chapter we explore the changing face of American archaeology as viewed from the United States. Unlike previous studies (e.g., Snead and Sabloff, this volume; Zeder 1997), we are less concerned with profiling American archaeologists than with projecting trends for the next few decades and offering ideas about the skill sets needed to be successful in this new world (Silliman and Ferguson, this volume). We begin by examining the economics of American archaeology: How much is spent on archaeology? How does this compare with the CRM industry as a whole? Once we have a handle on the economics, we turn to the employment side of the question. How many people are employed in CRM? How many of these are archaeologists? How does this compare to the academy? The answers to these questions lead into a consideration of the types of jobs that will be available to the next generation of archaeologists and the training they will need to be successful.

How Big Is the Breadbox?

For a nation that measures the value of so many things in dollars and cents, it is curious that so few statistics exist about the economics of American archaeology and CRM (see, for contrast, Aitchison and Edwards 2003, 2008 for the U.K.). Here we make a first approximation of CRM expenditures in the United States in 2008. For our purposes, we define CRM as those services and activities that are conducted to comply with legal statutes, mandates, and regulations affecting historical or cultural properties or values. As such, CRM encompasses the disparate fields of historic preservation, archaeology, anthropology, history, historic architecture, architectural history, and landscape architecture. Key federal laws affecting CRM are the National Historic Preservation Act, the National Environmental Policy Act, the Archaeological Resources Protection Act, and the Native American Graves Protection and Repatriation Act (see chapters by Sebastian and by Wilcox, this volume). There are others and many of the laws and their implementing regulations are duplicated or mimicked at state, tribal, and municipal levels. Indeed, the legal landscape of historic preservation has become so complex that one of the emerging fields in CRM is preservation law.

No centralized government figures exist on the aggregate amount spent either on CRM or archaeology in the United States. The Secretary of the Interior is charged with reporting to Congress the impact of federal programs and activities on the nation's archeological heritage. Part of this report is a detailed spreadsheet that presents for each federal agency such items as total numbers of acres inventoried, numbers of sites evaluated, and, of particular interest to this chapter, the amount of money expended. Unfortunately, not all agencies report; the Secretary's reports for 1998 through 2003 (http://www.nps.gov/archeology/src/index.htm) present the funds allocated to all CRM activities for 14 agencies, mostly from the Department of the Interior, the Department of Energy, and the Department of Agriculture. Agencies reporting spending in excess of $1 million in any given year are: the Bureau of Indian Affairs, Bureau

Table 1. Funding on CRM Projects as Reported in the Secretary of the Interior's Report to Congress, 1998–2003.

Year	Total Dollars Allocated by Agencies and Others
1998	$66,679,764
1999	$57,416,044
2000	$62,859,212
2001	$80,100,991
2002	$79,266,413
2003	$75,145,280

of Land Management, Bureau of Reclamation, Forest Service, Fish and Wildlife Service, National Park Service, and the Department of Energy (combined) (Table 1). Funds allocated for CRM activities appear fairly volatile, sometimes increasing or decreasing by as much as 20 percent between years. By and large, however, the trend has been toward increasing funding. Between 1998 and 2001, CRM expenditures increased about 17 percent, followed by a 6 percent decrease in the following two years.

Absent from the Secretary's report are the "Big Spenders" of American CRM: defense and transportation. The Department of Defense (DoD) independently reports to Congress annually on its environmental programs, including cultural resources (https://www.denix.osd.mil/portal/page/portal/denix/environment/ARC/FY2007). Appendix C of the report is a spreadsheet that presents nonrecurring costs of the CRM program. Since 2004, nonrecurring costs have increased from about $50 million to $63 million. Brian Lione (personal communication 2008), the deputy federal preservation officer of DoD, points out that these numbers do not clearly show all costs of the DoD CRM program.[1] Personnel costs of CRM professionals cannot be isolated, because recurring salaries and expenses are combined for all conservation programs.

The DoD report does not include all military-related CRM spending. The Army Corps of Engineers (COE) spends considerable sums on CRM each year, both in support of military missions and for a suite of civil water resource development projects. Although many of the COE's military expenses are presumably captured in DoD's report to Congress, the civil works projects are excluded. The CRM costs of the civil works projects are difficult to gauge, because these are almost always performed in conjunction with a nonfederal sponsor (e.g., a county, city, or state). Which party actually pays for CRM or how the costs are divided differs by project. We will assume that the COE's civil CRM program budget is about 20–25 percent of the total DoD CRM budget, and that annual DoD nonrecurring costs are $60 million with another $5 million for recurring costs Therefore, the COE's annual expenditures should be around $15 million. It is important to point out that the COE also has important regulatory functions, particularly in relation to the Clean Water Act, that require permit applicants to sponsor CRM projects; these are not included in the estimate of the COE's CRM expenditures but are accounted for later when discussing nongovernmental spending on CRM.

DoD annual expenditures for compliance-related CRM services are about $80 million. Missing from this figure are "special" projects, such as the Joint Prisoner's of War Missing in Action Accounting Command (JPAC) or the Mass Graves projects in Iraq or Kosovo. Other federal agencies, particularly the Federal Emergency Management Agency (FEMA), also have special projects (e.g., natural disasters such as hurricanes and forest fires), which are difficult to predict and for which the money is nearly impossible to track. We have allocated $25 million per year for these projects.

The largest consumer of CRM services in the United States is the transportation industry. CRM expenditures are not centralized in Washington. Instead, federal funds are allocated to each state Department of Transportation (DoT), bundled in projects so that identifying exact CRM costs is exceedingly difficult. Terry Klein (personal communication 2008) estimates that annual CRM spending by state DoTs averages between $4 and $5 million. How much of this $200–250 million is spent on archaeology varies tremendously. The Federal Highway Administration's archaeologist Owen Lindauer (personal communication 2008) compiled information about DoT spending on CRM archaeology from 15 states for 2007 (Table 2). Much like DoD, Lindauer's estimates do not include all recurring costs associated with archaeology (staff salaries and benefits).

The average annual expenditure among the 15 states is just under $2 million. Although the variation is great, the percent spent on archaeology in relation to a state's total transportation costs is consistently low. In Table 2 we provide information for eight states obtained from Lindauer. Archaeological expenditures average less than one-fifth of one percent of total spending on transportation.

Rounding out public sector spending on CRM, Congress appropriates approximately $37 million for the Historic Preservation Fund, which is pri-

Table 2. Archaeological Expenditures by 15 State DoTs in 2007.

State	$ Spent on Archaeology	$ Spent on Total Transportation Program	Percent of Total Transportation Program spent on Archaeology
Arizona	$4,400,000		
Connecticut	$600,000	$400,000,000	.15
Illinois	$1,800,000		
Massachusetts	$100,000		
Minnesota	$800,000	$1,100,000,000	.07
Missouri	$1,800,000		
Nebraska	$465,000	$608,540,000	.08
New Mexico	$2,000,000		
New York	$3,700,000	$3,700,000,000	.10
North Dakota	$808,000	$232,000,000	.35
Oregon	$3,000,000		
South Dakota	$343,000		
Texas	$6,000,000	$3,090,000,000	.19
Utah	$800,000	$387,000,000	.21
Wyoming	$750,000	$400,000,000	.19

marily used to assist state and tribal historic preservation efforts (http://www.nps.gov/history/hps/hpf/). In addition to federal CRM programs, state, tribal, and local governments throughout the country expend funds on CRM. Few figures exist on how much is expended at these levels; we estimate 2008 expenditures to be $10 million.

Finally, we need to consider research funding. The National Science Foundation spends about $12.5 million on archaeology (John Yellen, personal communication 2008). About $6.2 million is allocated to the archaeology and archaeometry program, while the rest is spread between a series of multidisciplinary programs. Other sources of research funding include the National Endowment for the Humanities as well as private sources like the National Geographic Society, Wenner-Gren Foundation, Henry T. Luce Foundation, and Andrew K. Mellon Foundation. While the amount they allocate for archaeological research is difficult to ascertain, it is doubtful that the aggregate matches NSF funding. Thus, a generous estimate of annual research funds for archaeology is $25 million, of which no more than $5 million derives from private sources.

The private sector is the other source of CRM funding. Companies buy CRM services to comply with laws affecting historical and archaeological resources. They may need a federal permit—e.g., a Section 404 permit issued by the COE—to comply with the Clean Water Act or a license issued by the

Federal Energy Regulatory Commission to operate a gas pipeline; or they are being assisted by federal funds, such as a cost-share agreement by an irrigation district with the Bureau of Reclamation. At local levels, changes in zoning or rights-of-way across state or tribal land might require CRM compliance.

The regulation of CRM compliance is dispersed among a variety of agencies, none of which collect information on CRM spending. We are mindful that private funding of CRM is volatile, closely following regional development and the national business cycle. In the past, there have been lively discussions on the members-only listserv of the American Cultural Resources Association (ACRA), a trade association of about 140 firms providing CRM services, about the magnitude of private sector CRM expenditures. Estimates have ranged between 50 and 100 percent of government funding, which places private sector expenditures in 2008 between about $225 and 500 million. In comparison, in 2000 private sector funding accounted for 130 percent of public sector funding for archaeology in England (Policy Studies Institute 2002), and in 2003, private sector funding in the United Kingdom was estimated to be £144 (or about 230 million in 2003 U.S. dollars) (Hinton and Jennings 2007).

Table 3 summarizes our estimate of public and private sector spending on CRM in 2008 in the United States. We suspect that at least half this amount was spent on archaeology, with the balance expended on other aspects of historic preservation.[2]

How Many Are There? And, What Do They Do?

Two observations can be made about the economics of archaeology and CRM. First, a lot of money is spent each year in this country on archaeology; and second, a lot more money is spent on CRM services. To put these numbers in perspective, in 2005 the entire environmental industry in the United States had revenues of $264.6 billion, of which the consulting and engineering segment (the best match for CRM) received $22.4 billion, contained 3,650 companies, and employed more than 220,000 people (EBJ 2006:6). Even accounting for the current downturn in the economy, the long-term prospect for environmental services such as CRM is quite good.

CRM expenditures support an industry composed of specialists in many fields including archaeology, anthropology, earth sciences, history, architecture, landscape design, conservation, and collections management as well as

Table 3. Estimates of 2008 Expenditures on CRM Services in the United States.

Source	Organization(s)	Amount ($)
Public	Department of Transportation	$200,000,000–$250,000,000
	Department of Defense (including COE)	$80,000,000
	All other Federal agencies	$80,000,000
	Historic Preservation Fund	$37,000,000
	All other non Federal government agencies	$10,000,000
	Special Federal Projects	$25,000,000
	National Science Foundation and other government research programs	$20,000,000
	Subtotal – Public Sector	$452,000,000–$502,000,000
Private	Compliance related spending	$226,000,000–$502,000,000
	Private research institutions	$5,000,000
	Subtotal – Private Sector	$231,000,000–$507,000,000
Total	CRM Annual Expenditures	$683,000,000–$1,009,000,000

a cadre of supporting positions in contract management, administration, human resources, information technology, and other fields. No one knows how many people are employed in the CRM field. Importantly for this paper, there are no good estimates of how many archaeologists are employed in the CRM field, let alone what they do.

In 2004 and 2005, the Society for American Archaeology (SAA) conducted surveys to estimate the number of professional archaeologists in the United States. A "professional" was defined as "academics at the instructor level or above and nonacademics at the crew chief level or above" (Snow 2006:2). Using 2000 U.S. Census and the U.S. Bureau of Labor Statistics data, the 2004 survey estimated that there were 1,503 academic archaeologists and 3,648 nonacademic archaeologists for a total of 5,150. Because the data reported by nearly half the states and all the territories were incomplete, the SAA membership committee thought that the estimate was low, perhaps underestimating the number of American archaeologists by half (Snow 2006:1). Another SAA survey was conducted at the end of 2005 using a very different methodology. Archaeologists from seven states—Pennsylvania, Virginia, Michigan, Florida, North Carolina, New Mexico, and California—carried out "snapshot" surveys of archaeological employment in their state, with the results generalized to the country as a whole. The 2005 survey estimated that there were 7,000 professional archaeologists in the United States, two-thirds of whom worked in nonacademic settings.

The SAA surveys focused on membership; how many archaeologists were there in the United States who were not members of the SAA? Our purpose is different. We want to know how many jobs there are, how many are filled by archaeologists, and what types of training are needed. We want to know about all archaeologists, not just professionals. To that end, we focus first on employment in CRM and then in academia. As in the previous section, we divide CRM employment between the public and private sector.

Employment in American CRM—Public Sector

We queried representatives of federal agencies that employ the largest numbers of CRM specialists. Mike Kaczor (personal communication 2008), the Federal Preservation Officer of the Forest Service, estimated that his agency employs 340 heritage personnel; Paul Rubenstein (personal communication 2008), who holds the same position with the COE, estimated that the agency employs about 100 CRM specialists. Frank McManamon (personal communication 2008), Chief Archaeologist with the National Park Service, pointed out that in September 2007, the Office of Personnel Management (OPM) reported that 400 archaeologists (GS-193 series) were employed in various agencies in the Department of the Interior (DOI). DOI employs other CRM specialists, such as historians, ethnographers, and architectural historians, which we estimate at 150. Brian Lione (personal communication 2008) estimated that in 2008 DoD employed or contracted for 375 CRM specialists. Finally, we estimate that there are 50 CRM specialists hired in other federal agencies (36 are listed in the AAA guide for JPAC alone).

CRM specialists involved in transportation are primarily hired by state DoTs. Numbers vary from states employing one CRM specialist to California, which employs 120. Nationwide, we estimate that there are 375 transportation-related CRM specialists.

There are 57 State Historic Preservation Offices (SHPOs) (50 states and 7 trust territories). We calculated the number of SHPO staff by visiting 10 SHPO websites of both states and territories that listed staff by name and position. The average was 21 employees excluding clerical and support staff. Multiplying by the number of SHPOs yielded a rough estimate of about 1,200 employees. Few Tribal Historic Preservation Offices (THPOs) have their own websites so this method could not be extended to the 76 THPO offices. Most THPOs have small staffs; we simply assumed an average staff

Table 4. Estimate of Public Sector CRM Professionals.

Agency	Estimate of Full-time CRM specialists
Corps of Engineers	100
Forest Service	340
Department of Defense	375
Department of the Interior	550
Other Federal Agencies	50
State Departments of Transportation	375
State and Tribal Historic Preservation Offices	1,430
All other State and Municipal agencies	1,000
Total	4,220

of 3 employees for an estimate of 230. Our estimate of SHPO and THPO employees is 1,430.

Many CRM professionals work for cities, counties, state, and tribal governments outside of SHPOs and THPOs. Some ensure compliance with state and local laws affecting historic, traditional, and archaeological resources. Others work in state, tribal, and local museums, which are responsible for curating and managing collections, site files, and archives created as part of CRM projects as well as providing public education and outreach, often sponsored through CRM expenditures. We assumed that at least 20 such individuals are present in each state to reach an estimate of 1,000.

We estimate that there are approximately 4,220 individuals employed full-time as CRM specialists in public sector (Table 4). This number does not include part-time or seasonal employees or federal employees trained in other fields (e.g., wildlife biology) whose responsibilities include some aspect of cultural resources. It does include, however, land planners, building specialists, architectural historians, historic architects, public historians, tribal liaisons, etc. employed in CRM.

Employment in American CRM—Private Sector

Few data exist on private sector employment in CRM. Estimates are made difficult by the fluidity of the marketplace. CRM projects are often short term, with field personnel hired on a project basis. The number of employees, particularly in small to medium-sized firms, can fluctuate dramatically throughout the year. It is not only employees, however, that fluctuate. CRM consulting firms also are quite dynamic; at any given time some fail, others relocate, some retract, and some expand.

Table 5. Archaeologists in New Mexico[1] November 18, 2005.

Employment sector	Crew chief and above	Techs, lab workers, etc.	Total	Prehistorians or "generalists"	Historical archaeologists
Federal agencies	119		119	117	2
State and local governments	33		33	31	2
Tribal programs[2]	9	1	10	10	
Universities, colleges3	30		30	28	2
Museums[4]	29		29	no data	no data
Contract firms and consultants	184	107	291	275[5]	16
Other[6]	20		20	no data	no data
Total	424	108	532		

1. The count of employees involved only agencies, firms, tribes, etc., headquartered in New Mexico.
2. This does not include tribal CRM programs, which are counted with Contract Firms and Consultants.
3. This includes adjunct faculty who live in New Mexico and are not employed in one of the other categories; it does not include students.
4. Includes research affiliates who live in New Mexico and are not employed in one of the other categories.
5. These numbers should be considered as an approximation.
6. This includes archaeologists working in nontraditional settings and retired archaeologists who are not adjuncts or museum research affiliates.

To account for these factors, one approach is to develop estimates by state. As part of the 2005 SAA survey, Lynne Sebastian (personal communication 2008) compiled a relatively complete census of archaeologists working in New Mexico (Table 5). Although the survey was restricted to archaeologists, we believe the percentages of public and private sector employment can be generalized to other parts of the CRM field. Of CRM archaeologists in New Mexico, about 32 percent work for the public sector. We believe this percentage is somewhat higher than the national average because of the large amount of federal land and the intense development pressures from oil and gas exploration, military activities, and urban encroachment on those lands.

Assuming that the public sector nationwide employs about 25 to 30 percent of CRM specialists, an estimate of 4,220 public sector archaeologists implies that there are 9,850 to 12,650 private sector CRM specialists. The total number of CRM full-time specialists in the United States in 2008, then, is estimated to be 14,000 to 16,850.

A second approach to estimating the number of employees is to use gross CRM expenditures. Since founding a CRM firm (Statistical Research, Inc.) in 1983, Altschul has noted a strong linear relationship between the number of employees and the firm's gross revenues. For every $100,000 of revenue, one employee is added. This figure was somewhat lower in the first few years of the firm when it was imperative to minimize expenditures on benefits and other overhead costs. However, once a certain economic stability was reached, this relationship became established. A similar trend was noted by Charles Niquette (personal communication 2008), president of Cultural Resources Analysts, Inc. We suspect that the relationship between gross revenue and numbers of employees fluctuates between companies based on profitability and maturity, but that for the CRM industry as a whole the $100,000 figure is a reasonable estimate.

Using the low estimate of $683 million in CRM expenditures, we arrive at a minimum estimate of private sector employment of about 7,000, whereas the higher figure of $1 billion yields an estimate of 10,000. Combined with 4,200 public sector jobs, we reach an estimate of CRM specialists working full time in the United States in 2008 of between 11,200 and 14,200.

The two estimates provide a range of between 11,000 and 17,000 people employed in a CRM technical activity. The estimates converge on a figure of about 14,000, which we will use as the basis of further estimates.

Estimating the Number of American CRM Archaeologists

Of the 14,000 estimated CRM specialists in the United States, we suspect that most are archaeologists by training. The reason is that compared to other CRM services, archaeology is much more labor intensive. Private-sector archaeologists are more likely than their public-sector colleagues to conduct survey and excavation, clean and process artifacts, analyze material culture and faunal remains, perform specialized analyses in geoarchaeology and archaeometry, and write technical reports presenting the results and conclusions of field and analytical efforts. In contrast, the jobs of public-sector CRM archaeologists revolve around the process of compliance—i.e., assessing whether a project may affect cultural resources, identifying the effort needed to find cultural resources, evaluating the importance of those resources, developing plans to treat important resources, developing scopes-of-work and overseeing contractors, managing resources under agency control, making sure that all stakeholders are included in the process, and communicating their efforts with the public.

There is certainly overlap between the descriptions of private and public sector jobs, but the important point is that traditional archaeological training is not as relevant to job activities in the public sector. Consequently, only about 60 percent of public sector CRM specialists (2,500 out of 4,200) are archaeologists. In contrast, the typical CRM firm employs more archaeologists than other specialists, perhaps as high as 75 percent. Our estimate of private sector archaeologists, therefore, is 7,350 and the total number of archaeological FTEs in CRM is about 10,000.

The actual number of individuals working as archaeologists in CRM is substantially higher. Many field and laboratory technicians are project-specific employees hired for a specific project task (e.g., fieldwork) and laid off when that task is complete. According to the 2005 ACRA salary survey, about 30 percent of all employees at CRM firms work part-time (ACRA 2005). Assuming this percentage applies to the entire private sector, of the 7,350 private sector jobs, about 2,200 FTE positions are split among part-time employees.

Education, Gender, and Compensation in CRM Archaeology

Federal agencies as well as SHPOs and many other governmental organizations follow the Secretary of Interior (SOI) Standards and Guidelines projects, which became effective in 1983 (http://www.nps.gov/history/local-law/arch_stnds_0.htm). Among other issues, the standards and guidelines define the minimum education and experience required to perform the basic inventory, evaluation, registration, and treatment functions stipulated in the National Historic Preservation Act. Archaeologists responsible for these functions should have a graduate degree in archaeology, anthropology, or a related field as well as a year of professional experience in archaeological research, administration, or management; four months of supervised field and lab experience in North American archaeology; demonstrated research ability; one year of full-time professional experience at a supervisory level for studies of either prehistoric archaeological resources (for a specialist in prehistory) or historical archaeological resources (for a specialist in historical archaeology).

In the 1980s and early 1990s, many federal agencies went beyond SOI standards, requiring principal investigators of large archaeological projects to hold a Ph.D. or its equivalent. Field and lab directors as well as analysts were required to hold at least an M.A., and qualifications for field and lab crews were a B.A. plus a field school or a year of professional experience. Over time, these standards have been relaxed, partly because the number of Ph.D.s specializing in American archaeology has not kept up with the need for archaeological CRM specialists. When the National Historic Preservation Act was passed in 1966, 27 Ph.D.s in archaeology were granted (Boites et al. 2005:1). That number quadrupled to 110 in 1997, and has remained relatively flat ever since. During the same period, however, expenditures in American archaeology increased more than 100 fold, from about $3 million in 1960 to between a third and half a billion dollars today (Charles R. McGimsey, III personal communication 2006).

The void created by the lack of Ph.D.s was filled by a cadre of professionals holding M.A.s. According to the ACRA salary survey, the professional and management staff of a typical CRM firm is composed of 13 percent Ph.D.s and 55 percent M.A.s. Until recently, the vast majority of M.A.-level archaeologists held degrees in anthropology. In the last few years, there has been a proliferation of degrees in such fields as historic preservation, American Indian studies, geography and GIS, material culture, archaeometry, museum studies, etc. Just as some archaeologists have taken on responsibilities in other fields of CRM, some trained in "related" fields are supervising archaeological projects. Another recent trend is the growth in distance-learning M.A. programs. Although many have voiced concern over the level of training, particularly field training, associated with these programs, graduates of these programs are finding employment in CRM.

Few data exist on age and gender among CRM professionals. Federal agencies in the *AAA Guide* list slightly more men (55 percent) than women. Information from the Register of Professional Archaeologists (RPA) suggest that private-sector CRM is more male-dominated; in a 2006 needs assessment, more than 60 percent of the respondents were male (Association Research, Inc. 2006). These archaeologists were in their late 40s and overwhelmingly white.

Data on current salaries in CRM comes from two surveys: the 2005 SAA/Society of Historical Archaeology (SHA) salary survey and the 2005 ACRA salary survey. Both report great variation in salaries and benefits. The ACRA survey, which is dedicated exclusively to private sector CRM, reports the maximum salary ($224,640) for business owner/principal was more than 10 times greater than the lowest ($20,800). The wide swing makes sense when one considers that a principal's compensation is directly tied to the profitability of the firm, which in some years may be negative and other years quite substantial. Perhaps the most accurate way of interpreting the results is that CRM principals have the potential to earn several times more than their public CRM professional counterparts, but their salaries are also much more vulnerable to changes in market conditions or management practices.

The wide variation in compensation for all positions documented in the ACRA survey suggests a diverse marketplace, with some firms emphasizing price-point bidding and others relying on technical quality. The former have a very flat fee schedule, with principals making about twice what field technicians are paid. We suspect that these firms tend to be small and focused largely on single markets (e.g., oil and gas exploration or real estate development). Larger, more stable firms tend to be diversified into all CRM fields and target clients who want to minimize their risk of litigation or disruption to project schedules. These firms place a heavy reliance on the skills and expertise of their senior staff. Managers and technical staff are paid near the maximum end of the pay scale, with managers in many cases earning more than $100,000 and technical specialists, virtually all of whom have advanced degrees, earning between $50,000 and $90,000. B.A.-level technicians in the private sector make the equivalent of a full-time annual salary of between $20,000 and $30,000. Those technicians who work on federal contracts are subject to provisions of the Service Contract Act, which establishes minimum pay rates and benefits that must be paid on that project. These tend to be substantially higher than non-federal rates.

The SAA/SHA survey suggests that salaries for public sector CRM average around $60,000 per year. However, this is deceiving, because the survey places district, regional, and state archaeologists in one category and park, forest, and field office archaeologist in another. It is not clear that there is any difference in the two categories beyond job titles. A more in-depth analysis that correlates job responsibilities with General Schedule (GS) pay rating for Federal employees and the equivalent for state, tribal, and municipal workers might distinguish patterns in public sector careers.

In short, an advanced degree is critical for advancement in CRM. Without an M.A. or Ph.D., an archaeologist is likely to hit a "hard" ceiling at about $30,000 per year. Careers in the public sector are largely closed to those that do not meet SOI qualifications. In the private sector, a B.A.-level archaeologist might rise to the level of crew chief, but without an advanced degree, such a person would find it difficult to obtain positions of greater responsibility. In contrast, an advanced degree opens the door to a wide range of career paths and opportunities in both the public and private sector.

An archaeologist can choose to specialize in a technical subfield, such as geoarchaeology, bioarchaeology, material culture, geophysics, geographic information systems, project design and supervision, public archaeology, working with tribes and other descendant communities, CRM law and policy, heritage tourism, collections management, conservation, business and project management, etc. The gap between a Ph.D. and an M.A. with regard to responsibility and pay has narrowed, with the recognition that neither provides the entire skill sets necessary to be successful in CRM.

The U.S. Academic Labor Market

Fewer than 100 individuals, mostly men, earned their livelihoods as archaeologists before World War I. Between 1894 and 1942, 39 men and 2 women wrote dissertations concerned with Americanist archaeology—i.e., 21 percent of the 191 Ph.D. degrees awarded by the seven U.S. universities granting doctorates in anthropology. Seven worked in universities and about 20 in museums. This changed dramatically after World War II when the GI Bill of Rights provided 2.1 million men and 65,000 women with tuition and stipends to attend college. Higher education became a growth industry in the United States, and the number of colleges and universities increased from about 1,200 to over 3,000 during the next few decades. The number of anthropology departments grew steadily through the 1950s and 1960s, both as new campuses opened and as already established joint anthropology-sociology programs split. These became major sources of employment for new Ph.D.s. Typically, a new program would hire several cultural anthropologists and then round out its faculty with an archaeologist, linguist, and biological anthropologist (Patterson 1999).

Mass education also witnessed an explosion in the number of archaeologists as well as changes in the composition of the profession as increasing numbers of women and individuals with non-Anglo surnames began to appear on SAA membership lists. The organization, whose membership stood at 976 in 1956, grew at an annual rate of 3 percent in the decade following the war. The growth rate doubled over the next 17 years, and its membership stood at 3,916 in 1973, 23.6 percent of whom were women. From a different standpoint, the number of women increased from 75 (11.3 percent) in 1946 to 923 in 1973. A significant number of men and women became archaeologists in that period. One explanation of how this happened is that the influx of male GIs in the late 1940s temporarily altered the sex ratio of college students in the U.S. from parity before the war to two men for every woman in 1957. The relatively equal ratio of the 1930s was reestablished in the mid-1960s as the children of first-wave, GI Bill recipients entered college. While their fathers may have majored in science, engineering, or business, the post-1964 students chose from a wider array of options. Many enrolled in anthropology courses or even majored in anthropology. The number of baccalaureates awarded in anthropology rose from 4,057 in 1971–72 to 6,324 by the end of the 1970s, declined to less than 4,000 in the early 1990s, and rose steadily to 10,276 in 2006–2007. During the last four decades, a steadily increasing number of men and women entered one of the established or new graduate programs; received advanced degrees; joined professional organizations, like the American Anthropological Association (AAA) or the SAA. A smaller number became tenure-track faculty in colleges and universities as the academy increasingly became the career path of choice.

The shape of the discipline in the academy still reflects demographic trends set in motion in the 1940s. Today, there are more than 2,500 community colleges, colleges, and universities in the United States. The *AAA 2007–2008 Guide* lists 388 anthropology programs in the United States that employ 3,767 anthropologists in full-time, tenure-track faculty positions. This figure should be taken as an absolute minimum and is probably more than 4,000, since community colleges and temporary and part-time faculty typically were not listed in this edition of the guide. The biographical sketches indicate that 875 individuals (23 percent) identify themselves primarily as archaeologists. This minimal number does not include the 195 archaeologists (112 men and 83 women) whose employment is listed as "museums," "anthropologists in other departments," or those who are employed on a temporary or part-time basis. If they were included, then the SAA's 2004 estimate of 1,500 academic archaeologists is reasonable.

Of the 875 individuals, 140 men and 86 women are assistant professors (25 percent of the total); 151 men and 86 women are associate professors (27 percent of the total); and 309 men and 94 women are full professors (48 percent of the total). When gender is considered, 39 percent of the academic archaeologists are women, a figure that corresponds well with the fact that they have written about 35 percent of the doctoral dissertations in archaeology since the mid-1970s, a percentage that rose to 45 percent (48/105) in

2007. When gender and rank are considered together, 38 percent of the assistant professors are women, 36 percent are associate professors, and 23 percent are full professors. Another way of viewing this is that the pipeline is full at the lower ranks but not yet at the full professor level. The higher percentage of men at the full professor level is likely a residue of the demographic composition of the field in the 1960s.

The numbers cited above tell us little about diversity beyond gender. The *1997 AAA Survey of Anthropology Ph.Ds* indicates that most minority doctorates in anthropology were in cultural or applied (Givens et al. 1997:4). Of the 278 Ph.D. recipients in anthropology as a whole in 1972, 4 percent or about 11 individuals were minorities. This number rose to 16 percent or roughly 75 out of the 464 anthropology doctorates awarded in 1995. In 1997–1998, minority professors constituted 11 percent of full-time anthropology faculty in the United States, a figure that has remained virtually unchanged since 1988. In 1994–1995, none of the 75 archaeology doctorates (44 men and 29 women) self-identified as minorities; two years later, in 1996–1997, 16 percent of the 110 (68 men and 42 women)—i.e., 17 or 18 individuals—self-identified as minorities. Lest we get too excited about the rapidly increasing diversity of archaeology, we should keep in mind that roughly 14.4 percent of U.S. residents with doctorates in anthropology are foreign-born immigrants, and it is not clear how they were counted in the *AAA Survey*. As a result, the archaeological professoriate still remains overwhelmingly white and predominantly male.

While this information provides some insights into the structure of academic archaeology today, it tells us nothing about the problems institutions of higher education have confronted in the past 40 years, the issues they are addressing now, or those they will tackle in the future. How they have responded or will respond in the future will shape significantly the structure of academic archaeology and the size of the labor market. It is important to remember that there may be significant differences between public and private institutions, between public institutions in different states and even between different campuses of the same university, between Research 1 universities with doctoral programs and M.A.-granting comprehensive universities, and among 2-year community colleges, 4-year liberal arts colleges, and universities with graduate programs. Four factors come immediately to mind.

First, the cost of higher education to students was largely borne by the federal government for veterans or by states for public institutions from

1945 through the mid-1960s. After that, the federal and various state governments began to cut allocations to both students and institutions. This meant that students increasingly bore the costs of education through loans, and that institutions began to re-allocate how they spent their annual appropriations. These processes were initiated in the late 1960s and early 1970s—i.e., at the same time the costs of the Vietnam War, the OPEC Oil Embargo, and the devaluation of U.S. currency were becoming apparent. The immediate effect was that the rapid growth in the size and number of anthropology programs during the 1960s slowed as universities moved from planning models based on modestly rapid growth to ones stressing slow growth, replacement (zero growth), or negative growth. The changes coincided with rising fees and diminishing financial packages for graduate students, as the concerns of central administrations rather than academic programs consumed expanding percentages of total annual budgets, and as emerging fields, like biochemistry or women's studies, competed for dwindling resources with existing or recently created anthropology departments. These processes continue today.

Second, because of their inability to hire new tenure-track faculty, departments at both public and private institutions have relied increasingly since the mid-1970s on temporary or part-time instructors to teach the growing numbers of students arriving on their campuses. This led to a two-tier faculty: a tenure-track faculty with comparatively good salaries and benefits and a steadily growing number of part-timers with fewer benefits and significantly lower salaries (Shumar 1997). This trend was exacerbated on some campuses where renowned scholars were hired partly to ensure a steady flow of students—"cash cows"—who would do part-time teaching to supplement their loans as they struggled to finance their educations and complete their dissertations. This process also continues to the present day.

Third, public institutions are susceptible to economic cycles and the inability of state governments to raise sufficient revenues to pay for continued growth of higher education. California, for instance, has had two budget crises in the last eight years (ENRON and the stock market decline in the wake of the dotcom crash in the early 2000s, and the sub-prime mortgage scandal, collapse of residential construction, currency devaluation, and rapid increases in the cost of gasoline, steel, and other consumer goods in 2007–present). At UCR, where Patterson works, budget cuts of several percent in the early 2000s entailed the implementation of slow-growth or replacement models of faculty recruitment. After several years of slow growth, there was a two-year hiring spurt that will be followed by another slow-growth period beginning in 2008–2009. The potential impact is complicated by the fact that the number of students arriving on campus, and hence the total size of the allocation based on student enrollment from the university's central administration, may increase in the near future.

Fourth, baccalaureates and increasingly M.A. degrees are seen as necessary credentials for entry-level positions in the economy. This potentially ensures a continuing flow of new students onto campuses in many but not all states, since not all regions or states have the same demographic and economic characteristics. Hence, one campus of a statewide system might be growing while another is in a steady-state mode. At the same time, all institutions engage in various forms of entrepreneurial activity, such as leasing patent or logo rights, and attempt to attract gifts from donors and alumni. Their success at the latter reflects the demographic and economic characteristics of the pool whose gifts they are attempting to attract and depends in significant ways on the skills of their fund-raisers.

We have mentioned four factors that might differentially affect the numbers and kinds of future employment that will be available in the academy to archaeologists. Faculty members who received their doctorates in the 1960s and early 1970s are already retiring or will soon do so. Whether all or only part of them will be replaced with new tenure-track faculty is an open question—one that will not be answered in the same way on every college campus in the United States given present-day conditions, the economic circumstances of the institutions, and the dispositions of their trustees and senior administrators. Nevertheless, with growing numbers of students on many campuses, there is a need for qualified teachers and researchers.

Salaries and benefits received by tenure-track faculty vary widely from public to private institutions, from one state to another, from one campus of the same university to another, and from research universities that award graduate degrees to colleges that award only baccalaureates to community colleges. Moreover, the expectations for tenure and promotion also differ dramatically. Each year, *The Chronicle of Higher Education* publishes salaries and other forms of compensation provided by the colleges and universities. It is safe to say that entry-level positions in research universities and liberal arts colleges require Ph.D. degrees, while M.A. degrees may suffice for community colleges. In California, where salary information is public at least for state institutions, entry-level assistant professors in universities can expect beginning salaries of approximately $60,000; those in community colleges will be comparable or higher depending on previous experience. Salaries for full professors probably start at about $85,000 and range upward toward $200,000.

Trends in Employment

We estimate that there are 11,350 FTE archaeological positions in the United States (Table 6). Roughly two-thirds are professional archaeologists working in the public or private sectors of CRM; about 13 percent hold academic positions. About 20 percent of all positions are held by B.A.-level technicians. An unknown, but substantial, percentage of technician positions are held by part-time employees.

In comparison, the 12 countries participating in the "Discovering the Archaeologists of Europe" project employ more than 16,500 archaeologists (Aitchison 2009).[3] Given that several countries that employ significant numbers of archaeologists were not included in the study (e.g., France), Europe may employ twice the number of archaeologists than the United States. The composition of the archaeological labor force is quite different, however, with the United States relying much more heavily on professional qualifications. For example, we have estimated that archaeological technicians compose 20 percent of all archaeologists in the United States, whereas in the European study this percentage is three times higher (60), with 17 percent of European archaeologists having a high school diploma as their highest degree. It is worth noting that even within Europe qualifications differ greatly, with some countries, such as Germany, Ireland, and Austria, heavily dependent on non-degreed labor and others requiring most, if not all, those working as archaeologists to have at least a B.A. degree.

Since the end of World War II, the number of jobs in American archaeology has grown steadily. Initially, the rate of increase was relatively modest, around 3 percent annually with most of the growth in universities. The rate of employment increased dramatically after the establishment of the CRM field. From a few hundred employed primarily in government service at its birth in the 1960s, CRM has grown to about 14,000 specialists today, of which almost 10,000 are archaeologists. Will this trend continue, or have we reached the apogee of CRM employment? Because there have been so few

Table 6. Number of Archaeologists working in the United States, 2008.

Employment Setting	Number of Archaeologists	Percent
Public	2,500	22.0
Private	5,150	45.4
Academic	1,500	13.2
Total (professionals)	9,150	[80.1]
Technicians (FTE)	2,200	19.4
Total	11,350	100.0

estimates of the number of archaeologists in the United States since the 1960s, and those that have been made use very different methods, it is difficult to do much more than speculate on future employment trends.

CRM is funded through a "polluter pays" principle—i.e., the agent that disturbs an archaeological site assumes the responsibility of mitigating the adverse effect of their action. With respect to the future of archaeological CRM employment, the single-most important question is whether there will be any change to the polluter pays model. Government agencies, particularly those whose core missions have nothing to do with historic preservation, are constantly trying to minimize their CRM costs. Similarly, private corporations and individuals who sponsor CRM have a financial interest in minimizing these costs. Periodically, these interests are given voice through attempts to change or eliminate key pieces of legislation or alter regulations. The CRM community thus far has successfully fought back such attempts. But there is no question that the historic preservation community must be ever vigilant as well as proactive in engaging the general public and specific interested parties (e.g., Native American communities) to demonstrate the importance of protecting and preserving cultural values and resources (see chapters by Sebastian and Wilcox, this volume).

Although it is dangerous to project several decades into the future, we see nothing on the horizon that will fundamentally change the polluter pays approach to CRM. Both in surveys and in action (i.e., visits to historical and archaeological sites), the public supports historic preservation and, for the most part, supports the premise that an entity benefiting from development should bear the cost of mitigating its actions. It is worth noting that the polluter pays principle is not only the cornerstone of CRM in the United

States, but also the touchstone of heritage management law throughout the world, where if anything, it is gaining strength.

If we assume that the polluter pays principle remains and that the historic preservation community is successful in maintaining current CRM laws and regulations, then CRM funding should vary only with the amount of development. Assuming further that development is correlated with the overall national economy, then we see little reason that CRM should not continue to grow. Yet, we do not foresee increases in CRM jobs continuing its historical trend. Instead we project that job growth will slow, eventually becoming in line with the national economy. We suspect that the private sector will be the first part of the CRM industry to flatten out. Already in 2008 as the nation's economy slows, we are witnessing a slowing of job growth in some regions and job loss in others.

While jobs in compliance-related services may trend toward the national growth rate, there is one major area of potential dramatic growth—heritage tourism. We suspect that many jobs in this field will involve improving the tourist's experience, making archaeology fun and interpretable to the public will be key skills. What is less clear is how much archaeological research will be sponsored to support heritage tourism.

Job prospects in the public sector are more difficult to predict. In the short term, we anticipate a spurt in job opportunities as baby boomers retire. Along with replacing existing positions, we see a continued growth in job opportunities at tribal and local government levels. Many large cities and counties have CRM specialists on staff, with this trend expanding to smaller local governments and even agencies within local governments (e.g., city and county departments of transportation, utility companies, and irrigation districts,). As more tribes and tribal communities petition to become THPOs, there will be an increase in job opportunities, particularly for tribal members.

Finally, we suspect during the next several decades that more effort will be placed on the built environment than on the archaeological record. When the SAA reaches its 100th birthday (2037), all structures built in 1987 or before will be of historical vintage. The sheer number of post-World War II homes, buildings, facilities, roads, pipelines, transmission lines, and all types of other structures could easily overwhelm the historic preservation community. We are not suggesting the effort placed on archaeological resources will decrease, only that the time spent by CRM specialists on the built environment will increase at a far greater pace. Archaeologists who are not cross-trained in other fields of historic preservation will be at a great disadvantage.

Assuming no fundamental changes in the U.S. political economy, we think that some sort of slow growth model will hold in the academic labor market in the near future for the following reasons. First, the number of anthropology programs, excluding community colleges, listed in the AAA's annual guides has remained essentially constant at 370–390 from 1994 to 2007. Second, the number of job advertisements in *Anthropology News*, where most academic positions in anthropology are listed, has remained constant at 330–340 per year from the late 1990s through 2007; in addition, the AAA has also listed more than 5,000 positions, including 731 in archaeology (about 14 percent of the total), on the job website it launched in August 2001. Fifty of the 55 archaeology (90 percent) online listings between September 2007 and June 2008 were for tenure-track positions; using this as a sample, we infer that about 650 of the 731 listings since 2001 were for tenure-track positions. Third, during the same period, the AAA's annual guides listed 875 archaeology dissertations, about 715 to 740 of which were completed at U.S. universities; these individuals would presumably constitute an important segment of the labor pool from which U.S. colleges and institutions draw new faculty. There is a gap between number of academic jobs and Ph.D. recipients in 2001–2007; however, whether it is 65 to 90 or smaller is not clear, because an unknown number of those 715–740 individuals did not enter the U.S. academic labor market for reasons other than the availability of tenure-track jobs—e.g., attending law school.

Trends in Education

Over the next 25 years, we can assume that most, if not all, of the 9,150 professional archaeologists will need to be replaced. The production of Ph.D.s and M.A.s in archaeology in U.S. universities has been relatively flat since the mid-1990s—roughly 120 and 300 per year, respectively. If this rate remains steady for the next 25 years, then 3,000 Ph.D.s and 7,500 M.A.s will join the labor market. If, however, we assume a modest 3 percent annual growth rate in the demand for professional archaeologists, then we will need to train at least 19,150 archaeologists during that period. Research I universities account for all of the doctorates (29 percent of the approximately 420 advanced degrees awarded annually), and they and the comprehensive universities account for all of the M.A. degrees. If the 3 percent growth pertains during this period, then these institutions will need to expand their capacity to train graduate students in archaeology, especially at the M.A.-level. The reason for this is that current employment demands for Ph.D. archaeologists is greatest in the academy, whereas the demand for professional archaeologists in CRM is 85 percent M.A. and 15 percent Ph.D. There is no reason to believe that these trends will not continue.

We also recognize that exposure to more than just archaeology will be critical for success in both the academy and CRM. At a time when old disciplinary distinctions are fraying, the ability to think critically in new ways across bodies of information is the surest way of participating meaningfully in debates that will shape the wider society. Thus students pursuing careers in archaeology need to understand the diversity of the field itself in both CRM and the academy. This includes information technology and data management, project and personnel management, and the ability to communicate with and mediate effectively between groups—such as tribes, developers, officials, lawyers, and archaeologists—that have diverse, often opposed interests (see Little and Zimmerman, this volume; Allen and Joyce, this volume). These are as important as if not more so, than traditional archaeological skills as field methods or artifact analysis (see Silliman and Ferguson, this volume).

Acknowledgments. We wish to thank Leslie Aiello, Kenneth Aitchison, Tobi Brimsek, Sarah Herr, Mike Kaczor, Terry Klein, Charles Kolb, Owen Lindauer, Brian Lione, Chuck Niquette, Charles McGimsey III, Frank McManamon, Paul Rubenstein, Lynne Sebastian, Dean Snow, Richard Thomas, Dinah Winick, and John Yellen for providing us with information and comments. Our ideas were also sharpened by comments received from the editors and two anonymous reviewers. Errors are the authors' alone.

References Cited

Aitchison, Kenneth
    2009 Discovering the Archaeologists of Europe: Transnational Report. Institute for Archaeologists, Reading, U.K.

Aitchison, Kenneth, and Rachel Edwards
    2003 *Archaeology Labour Market Intelligence: Profiling the Profession 2002/03*. Cultural Heritage National Training Organisation and the Institute of Field Archaeolo-

gists, Bradford, U.K. (http://www.archaeologists.net/modules/icontent/inPages/docs/prof/LMI_Reports1.pdf.).

2008 *Archaeology Labour Market Intelligence: Profiling the Profession 2007/08*. Institute of Field Archaeologists, Reading U.K. (http://www.archaeologists.net/modules/icontent/inPages/docs/lmi%200708/Archaeology_LMI_report_colour.pdf.).

Association Research, Inc.
  2006 2005 Needs Assessment. Report prepared for the Register of Professional Archaeologists, Baltimore.

Boites, Salvadore Z., Pamela Geller, and Thomas C. Patterson
  2005 The Growth and Changing Composition of Anthropology, 1966–2002. Report of the American Anthropological Association (http://www.aaanet.org/ar/Changing_Composition.pdf)

Environmental Business Journal (EBJ)
  2006 Environmental Industry Tops 5% Growth in 2005. *Environmental Business Journal* 19(9/10):1–7.

Givens, David B., Patsy Evans, and Timothy Jablonski
  1997 1997 Survey of Anthropology PhDs. American Anthropological Association, Arlington. (http://www.aaanet.org/resources/departments/97Survey.cfm)

Givens, David B., and Timothy Jablonski
  1996 1996 Survey of Anthropology PhDs. American Anthropological Association, Arlington. (http://www.aaanet.org/resources/departments/96Survey.cfm)

Hinton, Peter, and David Jennings
  2007 Quality Management of Archaeology in Great Britain: Present Practice and Future Challenges. In *Quality Management in Archaeology*, edited by Willem J. H Willems and Monique H. Van den Dries, pp. 100–112. Oxbow Books, Oxford, England.

Patterson, Thomas C.
  1999 The Political Economy of Archaeology in the United States. *Annual Review of Anthropology* 28:155–174.

Policy Studies Institute
  2002 Private Sector Foots Half the Bill for Today's Archaeology. Policy Studies Institute, London. (http://www.psi.org.uk/news/pressrelease.asp?news_item_id=5).

Shumar, Wesley
  1997 *College for Sale: A Critique of the Commodification of Higher Education*. Falmer Press, Washington, D.C.

Snow, Dean
  2006 Snapshot Survey to Estimate Number of Professional Archaeologists in the United States. Report Submitted to Board of Directors, SAA. Washington, D.C.

Zeder, Melinda A.
  1997 *The American Archaeologist: A Profile*. AltaMira Press, Walnut Creek, California.

Notes

1. Positions noted in this chapter were current as of 2008.

2. The worldwide economic downturn that began late in 2008 and is expected to extend throughout 2009 and perhaps beyond begs the question of whether the analysis presented for 2008 has been superseded by a radically different economic landscape. As of this writing (June 2009), there is little evidence that federal spending on archaeology has changed dramatically in the United States. Some agencies, including the National Park Service, Forest Service, U.S. Army Corps of Engineers, and the National Science Foundation are in line to receive "stimulus" money under the American Recovery and Reinvestment Act, some of which may be spent on programs involving CRM or archaeological investigations. Thus, it is entirely possible that public sector funding for archaeology will increase in 2009 and 2010. Private sector CRM spending is much more difficult to assess. Certain sectors, such as real estate development, have witnessed steep declines in spending, whereas others, notably energy—particularly "green" energy (e.g., wind and solar farms)—have been growing steadily. Although a full analysis of the 2009 archaeological economy will not be possible for several years, at least from our vantage point the American archaeological economy has shown remarkable resilience. We suspect that archaeological spending in the United States for 2009 will fall comfortably within the range estimated for 2008, and we would not be surprised to find 2009 spending actually falling on the "high" side of the range.

3. Countries included are Austria, Belgium, Cyprus, Czech Republic, Germany, Greece, Hungary, Ireland, Netherlands, Slovak Republic, Slovenia, and United Kingdom.

14

Politicae et Publicae: *Aspects of Influence*

JOE E. WATKINS

As we celebrate the 75th anniversary year of the Society for American Archaeology, I wonder what the framers of the SAA would think of it today, and wonder also whether any of the issues we face today would have been anywhere in their minds as they created this Society. In the last 25 years since the Society last examined itself in its reflexive 50th anniversary volume, it has grappled with some major issues. I'm not sure anyone in 1985 would have envisioned the issues facing archaeology today as it has spread out of the academy and into an ever-increasing public realm.

The forcible opening of archaeology to public scrutiny—regardless of who those publics are—has contributed to its growth. Archaeology no longer is the property of the academic, but has been required (sometimes grudgingly) to share joint ownership or stewardship. This has created issues when the more open nature of the discipline has required archaeologists to justify their actions.

A quick comparison between the 50th anniversary volume and this one exemplifies changing issues that confront archaeology today. That volume focused on the "Big Questions" that were facing American archaeology as an academic discipline—the themes, problems, and prospects of the discipline as it was envisioned. The authors wrote about the status of theory and history, and their historiographic discussions of events and aspects of the discipline figured prominently in its growth into the young adult it has become. This volume, however, is a much more philosophical yet pragmatic examination of the issues that are and will be facing archaeologists and the discipline as it enters the last quarter of its first century.

This is not to say that this volume doesn't produce a historical discussion of the discipline as it is viewed today, but the volume goes beyond a mere reporting of that history. James Snead and Jeremy Sabloff give us insight into one of the issues that the Society must face as it has moved forward along the trajectory from primarily an academic endeavor to a more applied profession. They ask an important and perplexing question: "Can the Society become increasingly tilted toward its professional responsibilities without losing all its intellectual roots?" It is a resounding question that can have a major impact on what archaeology will become. While these intellectual roots often get lost in the discussions, they are around which most of our discussions arise in one form or another.

As we hover on the threshold of the last quarter of a century as a professional society, we must come to grips with two primary issues: politics and the public.

Politica

Politics have always been tied up in archaeology, even though many refuse to identify the extent to which it exists. The mere act of "joining" the Society is a political statement as the Society's political voice might often be seen to be at odds with the individual wishes of some of its members; the Society is imbued with a political power that sets it apart from a collection of individual archaeologists.

Politics can be international in scope. In their chapter, authors José Luis Lanata and Robert Drennan look at conflicts between archaeologists created by international politics and boundaries that inhibit face-to-face communication, impediments to the free flow of communication and ideas. Importantly they note "the use of archaeology in the construction of narratives of national identity is a highly exclusionary activity" that can "create one of the most difficult challenges archaeologists must face in attempting to cross boundaries."

Politics also plays a major role in the examination of questions of identity and power as played out in past cultures. Maria Franklin and Robert Paynter's chapter is illuminating when we realize that the questions they seek to answer exist *not only in the study of the past, but within the discipline that proposes to study the past.* They talk about the need to de-center archaeological authority, give equal weight to alternative knowledge claims and epistemologies, multivocality, critical self-reflection, and practicing archaeology in ways that are relevant to destabilizing inequity in contemporary society—basically by placing archaeology within the racial and economic politics that occur in the broader society at large. While the authors point out the influence of the Black Power movement on the establishment of black studies (and a resultant development of interest in African American archaeology), such apparently has not been true with the similar impact of Red Power on Native American Studies classes. There apparently has not been a concomitant positive influence on Native American relationships with the discipline.

Publica

Section 1(b)(1) of the National Historic Preservation Act of 1966 declares that "the spirit and direction of the Nation are founded upon and reflected in its historic heritage"; part 4 of that same section establishes that "the preservation of this irreplaceable heritage is in the public interest." The word "public" appears at the ninety-fourth word, yet nowhere is that word defined. The law does not say that the preservation of America's heritage is in the government's interest or in business's interest, but that it is in the interest of the American public, however defined, to preserve America's heritage. Barbara Little and Larry Zimmerman discuss the difficulty of identifying "the public" as well as the necessity of keeping them interested and involved in the results of our research in order to ensure the survival of the discipline. We must continue to work to demonstrate that archaeology has *relevance* to "people" outside of our profession. This quest for relevance does not necessarily mean we have to answer world questions but only that we present our information in such a way that people understand that what we do has *value* to humanity beyond our own curiosities.

As we continue into and through the age of electronic communication, our need to maintain and foster communication with the people we serve will continue to evolve. Mitchell Allen and Rosemary Joyce remind us of the necessity for archaeology to write stories that matter to those who will read them—our public, however defined. This is perhaps the best way that we can continue to enforce our relevance.

Politica et publica

It is interesting to ruminate about the possible loss of "intellectual roots": how much of the discipline is "academic" and how much of it is "commercial"? Timothy Pauketat and Lynn Meskell discuss the changing theoretical directions in American archaeology. Taking the view that theory frames the archaeologist's interpretation of the materials encountered, they note that "data collection, theory building, and heritage development are no longer discrete practices." They remind us of the growing trend toward examining social issues in American archaeology, whether studying materiality in the past or working with native and local communities on the intellectual and ethical challenges of the present through more integrated, reflexive, and hybrid epistemologies and modes of research.

In some ways, however, this begs the question: Do we need theory to drive our research, or can the end-product be equally viable without it. As Jeffrey Altschul and Thomas Patterson note, much (most?) of the work performed by archaeologists is framed within cultural resource management. Trained practitioners can use a set of techniques to gather data that can be turned into information that answers some questions about the cultural past or past cultures while at the same time turning a profit. How great is the divide between academic archaeology (where one can derive hours of conversation concerning the philosophical underpinnings of the field) and cultural resource management (where rapid fieldwork utilizing a generally transportable set of techniques provides answers)? This is NOT by any means to imply that cultural resources management is without theory or that it does not provide important contributions to the discipline. I merely wish to illustrate the underlying differences between these two subdisciplines as they currently exist in archaeology. Is this a difference between philosophy and application, or something larger? Is the divide between intellectuals and pragmatists, or between epistemology and economics? As we have wrestled with the "evolution" of the Society of Professional Archaeologists into the Register of Professional Archaeologists, a very basic question has remained—is archaeology a science or a set of techniques?

Regardless, as Altschul and Patterson note, students pursuing careers in archaeology must be willing to experience the diversity of the field itself in both the cultural resources management and academic milieus. Their education should include various seemingly non-archaeological skills such as "information technology and data management, project and personnel management, and the ability to communicate with and mediate effectively between groups such as tribes, developers, officials, lawyers, and archaeologists—that have diverse, often opposed interests." These skills, according to the authors, "are as important as if not more so, than traditional archaeological skills as field methods or artifact analysis."

The relationship between archaeologists as members of the SAA and descendant communities is a public issue that has marked political implications. This has been one of the major forward moves that the discipline has taken toward relevancy. "Descendant community" does not necessarily equate to "Native American community," even though many archaeologists initially think of Native Americans when consultation, communication, or collaboration are mentioned. Most often because of federal legislation or other requirements, archaeologists have worked to involve descendant communities in their research.

In their chapter, Stephen Silliman and T. J. Ferguson raise an important point: "While archaeologists consult with communities because of legal and professional requirements, they collaborate *because they want to*" (emphasis added). They note also that both consultation and collaboration require more than merely "public outreach," which "tends to create a one-sided delivery from archaeologists to others." They believe that archaeologists have moved from being primarily concerned about advancing scientific goals to being concerned with social issues.

Even while individual archaeologists move forward within the ethical sphere, the discipline has been greatly impacted by three legislative actions. In their chapters, Lynne Sebastian and Michael Wilcox write about the impact the National Historic Preservation Act, the National Museum of the American Indian Act, and the Native American Graves Protection and Repatriation Act laws have had, and continue to have, on the practice and continuing development of archaeology. While the National Historic Preservation Act created a mechanism for the protection of the public heritage, the 1992 amendments changed and fostered the involvement of individual Native Americans and of Indian tribes in cultural resource management and archaeology and created a growing sense of need by those American Indian groups for an understanding of the archaeological *process* if not the discipline itself.

But perhaps some would argue that the most political action was the passage of repatriation legislation in 1989 and 1990. At the very basic level, these two repatriation laws have relatively small impact on the practice of archaeology. The majority of the laws' impact is felt by bioarchaeologists and museums and the materials recovered from archaeological excavations. But, as Melinda Zeder, Jane Buikstra, and Sander van der Leeuw point out, repatriation legislation has not destroyed bioarchaeology. It "required bioarchaeologists to change their modus operandi, ... productively directed research to topics of interest to living descendents, and it has also enriched our interpretations of past funerary sequences."

The contributors to this volume have presented their ideas and thoughts on the discipline as it stands today and the directions it may be headed over the course of the next 25 years. The pathway is not necessarily rosy, but neither is it fraught with potholes or pitfalls. It is interesting to note that the discussion of most of the authors in this volume is not centered on issues related to theory or "Big Questions," but focus mostly on archaeology's relationships with the broader world outside of the academic thrust of the profession. All these authors write about boundaries—social, disciplinary, ethnic, geographical, and political boundaries—and question how the Society for American Archaeology will or might work to make those boundaries less rigid and more permeable.

Looking backward on the 40 years I've been an archaeologist, I am awestruck by the political direction the discipline seems to have taken. The involvement of American Indian tribes in the cultural resource management process has created a more educated and savvy group of consumers. As of April 15, 2008, there were 76 National Park Service-recognized Tribal Historic Preservation Officers who have assumed the responsibilities of the State Historic Preservation Officers for their tribal lands on a land base exceeding 34 million acres and spanning 24 states. These groups have chosen to use existing processes to integrate (at least to some extent) archaeology with their own heritage needs. Whether this use of archaeology is merely to maintain compliance with federal funding requirements or based on some other reason, these groups have taken an active role in protecting their heritage rather than relying on outside archaeologists to do so. Yet, as American Indian tribes are political creations and political bodies, their actions are viewed primarily as political action rather than as social action.

Repatriation also has created a situation where politics has taken center stage, effectively muting conversation in many instances. In the Kennewick/Ancient One situation, for example, the "Big Question" concerning the initial habitation of the "New World" gets lost in the political implications such answers (or even the asking of the question) seem to bring to bear on contemporary societies. But repatriation is merely another movement through which archaeology will pass, though not necessarily unscathed. The setbacks and struggles we face, perhaps more than the questions and discussions we initiate, create the strength of character that helps the discipline continue to evolve.

We must find better ways of making archaeology relevant to those populations that we need. We must understand the various perspectives we take into the field with us, and the need to place our ideas and thoughts into the social milieu of which we are a part, without drowning in our own ethnocentrism or plagued by the uncertainty of too much subjectivism. We need to communicate more clearly so that no one needs to translate our convoluted phrasings into the language of those who should be using the ideas we expound.

Now is the time for us to set goals that will establish our legacy for the Society's 100th anniversary. We must work toward creating a better understanding of "the past" however defined, constructed, or delineated. We must step beyond the paradigms that bind us to our own perspectives and blind us to other explanatory models. We must learn to explain the discovered and reconstructed past in ways that gives meaning to the lives of the people who lived in that past. We must meld the interests of the professional and avocational archaeologists while reintegrating academic and cultural resource archaeologies. We must learn to understand the politics and strengthen our relationships with outside entities so that we can continue to strengthen our own discipline.

Today's archaeology is built on a sturdy framework, but we must continue to strive to ensure that archaeology's future grows more *inclusive* rather than *exclusive*.

About the Contributors

Mitchell Allen is Publisher of Left Coast Press, Inc., an academic press specializing in archaeology and related topics. He is also Adjunct Professor of Anthropology at Mills College. Allen has a Ph.D in archaeology from UCLA and is a specialist on the Ancient Near East and premodern world systems as well as issues of scholarly publishing.

Jeffrey H. Altschul is founder and Chairman of Statistical Research, Inc. and Nexus Heritage-SRI, Ltd, comprehensive cultural resource management firms based in the United States and the United Kingdom, respectively. He is also president of the SRI Foundation, whose mission is to advance historic preservation through education, training, and research.

Wendy Ashmore is Professor of Anthropology at the University of California, Riverside. Since the 1970s, she has conducted archaeological research about ancient Maya and neighboring societies, in Guatemala, Honduras, and Belize. Her publications focus on understanding social meanings of space.

Jane E. Buikstra is a Regents' Professor and Director of the Center for Bioarchaeological Research at Arizona State University. She also directs the Center for American Archaeology in Kampsville, IL. Author of numerous books and articles, her research interest include forensic anthropology and bioarchaeology. She has active research projects in the North American Midwest and Latin America.

Margaret W. Conkey is the Class of 1960 Professor of Anthropology at UC Berkeley and she is currently the President of the Society for American Archaeology. She received her advanced degrees in Anthropology from the University of Chicago. She is currently carrying out a landscape archaeology field project in the French Pyrènèes, and has contributed to feminist archaeology.

Robert Drennan researches early chiefdom development in global comparative perspective. He has carried out fieldwork aimed at documenting patterns of social, political, and economic organization in chiefdoms in Mexico, Colombia, and China. He is a Distinguished Professor of Anthropology at the University of Pittsburgh.

T. J. Ferguson owns Anthropological Research, LLC, a small research company in Tucson, Arizona, where he is also a Professor of Practice in the School of Anthropology at the University of Arizona. He works extensively with tribes in the southwestern United States, researching issues related to land and water rights, repatriation, and traditional cultural properties.

Maria Franklin is an Associate Professor in the Department of Anthropology and the African and African Diaspora Studies Department at the University of Texas–Austin. She is a historical archaeologist whose interests include African diaspora studies, theories of race, gender, and culture, and the politics of archaeology.

Rosemary A. Joyce, Professor of Anthropology at the University of California, Berkeley, has conducted archaeological fieldwork in Honduras since 1977. Co-author of a pioneer digital work and co-editor of a series of edited volumes for use in teaching, she addresses topics from identity and materiality in the past to the place of archaeology in the contemporary world in numerous articles and books, most recently *The Languages of Archaeology* and *Ancient Bodies, Ancient Lives*. She received her Ph.D in anthropology from the University of Illinois, Urbana-Champaign.

José Luis Lanata. Director of the Instituto de Investigaciones en Diversidad Cultural y Procesos de Cambio (IIDyPCa), Universidad de Río Negro, Bariloche, Argentina and Simón Bolivar Professor at the University of Cambridge, UK. Member of the CONICET, Argentina.

ABOUT THE CONTRIBUTORS

Dorothy Lippert is Case Officer for the southeast and Alaska regions, Repatriation Office, National Museum of Natural History, Smithsonian Institution.

Barbara J. Little is an Adjunct Professor of Anthropology and affiliate of the Center for Heritage Resource Studies at the University of Maryland, College Park and an archaeologist for the National Park Service in Washington, DC.

Lynn Meskell is Professor of Anthropology at Stanford University and Honorary Professor at the University of the Witwatersrand in South Africa. Her most recent books include *Cosmopolitan Archaeologies* (ed. Duke, 2009), *Archaeologies of Materiality* (ed. Blackwell, 2005) and *Object Worlds in Ancient Egypt: Material Biographies Past and Present* (Berg, 2004). She is founding editor of the *Journal of Social Archaeology* (Sage) and of the Material Worlds Series (Duke). Her current research projects include the constructs of natural and cultural heritage in post-apartheid South Africa, and the social constitution of figurine worlds at Neolithic Çatalhöyük, Turkey.

Barbara J. Mills is Professor of Anthropology and Director of the School of Anthropology at the University of Arizona, where she also holds appointments in the Arizona State Museum and the American Indian Studies Program. She has worked throughout the Southwest U.S. with a focus on ceramics and the use of material culture to interpret issues of identity, migration, inequality, and social memory. Her most recent book is *Memory Work: Archaeologies of Material Practices* (co-editor, SAR Press, 2008).

Thomas C. Patterson is Distinguished Professor and Chair of Anthropology, University of California, Riverside. His works include: *Karl Marx, Anthropologist* (2009); *Marx's Ghost: Conversations with Archaeologists* (2003); *A Social History of Anthropology in the United States* (2001); *Toward a Social History of Archaeology in the United States* (1994); *Inventing Western Civilization* (1997); *Foundations of Social Archaeology: Selected Writings of V. Gordon Childe* (2004 with Charles E. Orser, Jr); and *Making Alternative Histories: The Practice of Archaeology and History in Non-Western Settings* (1996 with Peter Schmidt).

Timothy Pauketat is an archaeologist and Professor of Anthropology at the University of Illinois in Urbana-Champaign, having previously taught at the University of Oklahoma and the State University of New York, Buffalo. He advocates practice-theoretical, phenomenological, and historical approaches in archaeology and focuses on pre-Columbian eastern North Americas, specifically the relationship between religion, materiality, identity, and political formations in the Midwest, Midsouth and eastern Plains. His ongoing field project seeks to understand an ancient instance of colonization and religious conversion in Wisconsin.

Robert Paynter is Professor of Anthropology at the University of Massachusetts Amherst. An historical archaeologist, Paynter's research concerns archaeological approaches to the study of inequality, with a focus on the materiality of race, class, gender, and state processes in the creation of the modern world.

Jeremy A. Sabloff is the President of the Santa Fe Institute. He is a former President of the SAA and a former editor of *American Antiquity*, as well as a member of the National Academy of Sciences, American Academy of Arts and Sciences, and the American Philosophical Society. His most recent book is *Archaeology Matters: Action Archaeology in the Modern World* (Left Coast Press, 2008).

Lynne Sebastian received her Ph.D. from the University of New Mexico and carried out fieldwork as a contract archaeologist throughout the Four Corners region of the American Southwest. After serving as the New Mexico State Archaeologist and State Historic Preservation Officer for eleven years, she became a private consultant with the SRI Foundation, where she is Director of Historic Preservation Programs. Dr. Sebastian is a former SAA president and holds an Adjunct Associate Professor appointment in the Department of Anthropology at the University of New Mexico.

Stephen W. Silliman received his Ph.D. at UC Berkeley and has been teaching at the University of Massachusetts, Boston, since 2001, where he currently holds the positions of Associate Professor of Anthropology and Graduate Program Director in Historical Archaeology. His publications in numerous journals and edited books cover topics pertaining to colonialism, postcolonialism, collaborative methodologies, Indigenous issues, historical archaeology, heritage politics, and social theories of identity, practice, and materiality. His books include *Collaborating at the Trowel's Edge: Teaching and Learning in Indigenous Archaeology* (editor, 2008, University of Arizona Press), *Historical Archaeology* (co-editor with Martin Hall, 2006, Blackwell Publishing), and *Lost Laborers in Colonial California* (2004, University of Arizona Press).

James E. Snead is Associate Professor of Anthropology at George Mason University and Research Associate at the Cotsen Institute of Archaeology, UCLA. His research interests include the history of archaeology, cultural landscapes, and the archaeological study of conflict and warfare.

Sander van der Leeuw is an archaeologist and historian by training. He taught at the universities of Leyden, Amsterdam, Cambridge (UK), and the Sorbonne. His research interests include archaeological theory, ancient ceramic technologies, regional archaeology, (ancient and modern) man-land relationships, GIS and modeling, and Complex Systems Theory. He did archaeological fieldwork in Syria, Holland and France, and conducted ethno-archaeological studies in the Near East, the Philippines and Mexico. Since 1992 he has coordinated interdisciplinary research projects on socionatural interactions and environmental problems in past and present, and more recently on invention and innovation. He currently is Professor of Anthropology and Director of the School of Human Evolution and Social Change, at Arizona State University. His publications include 16 books and over 120 papers and articles on archaeology, ancient technologies, socio-environmental and sustainability issues, as well as invention and innovation.

Joe E. Watkins is the Director of the Native American Studies program and Associate Professor of Anthropology at the University of Oklahoma. He has been doing archaeology for more than 40 years and has published extensively on his research interests—the ethical practice of anthropology and anthropology's relationships with descendant communities and aboriginal populations.

Michael Wilcox is an Assistant Professor in the Department of Anthropology at Stanford University. He received his Bachelor's Degree in Anthropology from the University of California Santa Barbara in 1993 and his MA (1995) and Ph.D. (2001) from Harvard University. He is interested in ethnicity, DNA, and the rebirth of scientific racism and the use of archaeological narratives in popular and scientific literature. His research interests include collaborative and Indigenous Archaeologies, the relationship between contemporary ethnic groups and the past, colonial and contact period archaeologies and contemporary Pueblo communities. His book *The Pueblo Revolt and the Mythology of Conquest: An Indigenous Archaeology of Contact* (2009, University of California Press) examines these issues in detail.

Melinda A. Zeder holds the position of Senior Scientist in the Archaeobiology Program, National Museum of Natural History, Smithsonian Institution. Her research interests include the plant and animal domestication and the origins of agricultural economies, the development of specialized subsistence economies in early complex societies, and the intersection of archaeology and genetics in documenting the domestication of plant and animal species.

Larry J. Zimmerman is Professor of Anthropology and Museum Studies at Indiana University-Purdue University Indianapolis (IUPUI) and the Eiteljorg Museum where he serves as Public Scholar of Native American Representation.

Index

academic fair trade, 80
action archaeology, 136–37
Advisory Council on Historic Preservation, 162, 174
African Americans: antiracist archaeological investigations of, 104–7; archaeological collaboration with, 59; bioarchaeological study of, 238; early archaeological studies of, 103–4; feminist scholarship and, 110–11; 1960s political mobilization of, 102–3
African Burial Ground Project, 59, 104–5, 115, 238
agency, 12–13, 99, 200, 201
Akademie der Wissenschaft, 17, 20
Akins, Nancy J., 237
Allen, Mitchell, 319
Altschul, Jeffrey H., 320–21
American Anthropological Association, 32–33; *Anthropology News,* 224, 313; Survey of Anthropology Ph.Ds, 307
American Antiquarian Society, 28
American Antiquity, 34; interdisciplinary research in, 222, 223
American Cultural Resources Association (ACRA), 296, 302, 303, 304
American Ethnological Society, 28, 32, 41
American Indian Religious Freedom Act, 167, 184
American Indians. *See* Native Americans
American Journal of Archaeology, 31, 34
American Philosophical Society, 28

Anthropological Society of Washington, The, 32
Antiquities Act of 1906, 31, 41, 53, 160
Anyon, Roger, 148
archaeobiology, major research topics of: bone chemistry, 235, 239; disease, 236; domestication and agricultural origins, 229–31; foraging strategies and human evolution, 227–29; historical ecology, 232–33; human lifespan, 235–36; social complexity, 231–32
Archaeological and Historic Preservation Act, 135
Archaeological Institute of America, 31, 32, 33, 34
Archaeologist, The (The American Archaeologist), 30
archaeologists: amateur, 36; erasing boundaries within anthropology, 15; lack of interaction with descendant communities of, before NAGPRA, 180–81, 182–83; low socioeconomic diversity of, 114; non-archaeological skills needed by, 320–21; number in New Mexico, 300; number of professional, 297; oppositional relationship between science and religion created by, 182; "professional," 297. *See also* education; employment
archaeology: action, 136–37; behavioral, 197; "Big Questions" of, 180, 188, 317; "blind-spots" in, 9; "co-

futures" in, 16; community, 57; contrasted with ethnography, 183; as creator of community, 61, 63; defining, 133; democratizing, 115; effect of neoliberalism on, 99; giving back to community in, 61, 63; as hegemonic institution, 97, 106; of homelessness, 144–46; humanism in, 11–12; issue of new technologies in, 11–13; knowledge in, 10; marketing of, 279–81; Marxist, 58; as middle-class discipline, 99; multivocality of, 19, 57, 111; non-archaeologists use of, 139–40; problems in defining, 133; as public heritage, 135; public interest in, 131–34, 279–80; as public service, 131; reflexivity in, 20, 97; relationship to ethnography of, 205; research funding for, 295; re-visioning, 9–10; as "somewhat marginal," 14; specialization in, 17; unity of, 15; as White Public Space, 114. *See also* collaborative archaeology; communicating archaeology; cultural resource management (CRM); feminist archaeology; historical archaeology; interdisciplinary archaeology; politics; public archaeology
Archaeology Channel, 280
Archaeology in Annapolis, Maryland, 100, 105–6
Archaeology magazine, 11–12, 34, 280
ARCHAEOMEDES Research Program, 241–42
Argentina, 77
Arizona State University: Central Arizona-Phoenix Long-Term Ecological Research project, 242; Long-Term Vulnerability and Transformation Project, 149–50, School of Human Evolution and Social Change, 245
Art and Archaeology, 31, 33, 34
Ascher, Robert, 277

Bandelier, Adolph, 31
Barad, Karen, 8, 10
behavioral archaeology, 197
Bey, George, 147
Binford, Lewis, 272, 273
bioarchaeology, key developments in: bone chemistry, 235; communicating with descendant communities, 237–39; health, diet, and food production, 234–35; host-pathogen co-evolution, 236; human lifespan, 235–36; identity, 240; interpersonal violence, warfare, and cannibalism, 237; residential histories, mobility, and migration, 239–40
Black Power, 102–3
Black Studies movement, 103
Blakey, Michael, 104–5
Boas, Franz, 28, 33
Bolivia, 76–77
boundaries: comparative research made difficult by, 75; crossing physically, 86–88; crossing through inter-institutional collaboration, 88; crossing through curriculum design, 85–86; crossing through information technology, 90–92; crossing through publication, 88–89; inequalities within and between, 77–79; invisible colleges and, 78, 79, 80, 81, 82, 83, 86, 92; linguistic, 80–84; national character of, 76–77; restrict communication, 73; theoretical perspectives and, 75–76, 83–84
boundary organizations, 148–49
Bourdieu, Pierre, 198

Braidwood, Robert, 229–30
Bray, Tamara, 16–17
Briones, Claudia, 30
Brumfiel, Elizabeth, 147
Buchli, Victor, 131
Buikstra, Jane, 322
Bureau of American Ethnology, 29
Burney, Michael, 148
Burton, Antoinette, 9

Canada, 36, 56
Çatalhöyük, 57, 204
cause and effect, 199
Chacoan phenomenon, 202–3
Champagne and Aishihik First Nations agreement, 238
Childe, V. Gordon, 272–73
Chile, 77
China, 77, 82, 83
Chirikure, Shadreck, 81
Clark, Geoffrey A., 15
class, 99, examples in post-Columbian world of, 100–101; lack of archaeological analysis of, 99; use in Latin America of, 100
Cohen, Mark Nathan, 234
collaborative archaeology: in archaeobiology, 237–39; in Canada, 56; coauthorship in, 60–61; consultation as, 49; as continuum, 52–53; definition of, 51; early examples of, 55; increased by NAGPRA, 55; interinstitutional, 88; as multivocal and multicultural practices, 60–62; in museum settings, 55; peer review in, 60, 61; politics in, 58; process as important as results, 61–62; trust as underpinning of, 62; what?, 51–53; when?, 53–56; why?, 56–60, 146–47
Collins, Patricia Hill, 110

Colorado Cliff Dwellings Association (CCDA), 30–31
Colorado Coal Field War Project, 58
Colwell-Chanthaphonh, Chip, 52
Committee on Native American Relations (SAA), 37
Committee on the Americas (SAA), 36–37
Committee on the Status of Women in Archaeology (SAA), 37
communicating archaeology: creates and sustains discipline, 272; experimenting with writing genres in, 277; making data available, 281–85; narrative vignette and, 275–76; need for popularizing, 279–80; New Golden Age in, 285–87; oral communication and, 277; peer review and, 274; perpetuated by example, 273; political implications of, 115; Professor Worst Nightmare Critic and, 274–75; role of technical language in, 272–73; 10 Step Program to improving, 287–88; storytelling and, 280–81; third-person vs. first-person in, 273
community archaeology, 57–58, 147. See also collaboration
Conkey, Margaret W., 58, 108, 109
Council of Affiliated Societies, 36
Crowley, H., 107
Crumley, Carole, 242
cultural resource management (CRM), 135–36; age, gender, and race in, 303; as challenge to academic focus of SAA, 34; civil rights movement and, 102; community archaeology in, 147–48; employment in private sector, 299–301, 302; employment in public sector, 298–99; expenditures in, 292–95, 297; lack of Ph.D.s

in, 303; legal foundations of, 161; low impact of NAGPRA on, 172–73; "polluter pays" principle of, 311–12; salaries in, 303–4; standards for archaeologists in, 302–3; tribal involvement in, 54–55, 148, 173. *See also* Section 106 (NHPA)
Curtis, Cassidy, 143

Daston, Lorraine, 17
Davenport Academy, 30
De Cunzo, Lu Ann, 280–81
Deetz, James, 273
Deloria, Vine, 179
depositional practices, 197, 203
descendant communities: consultation with, 48–49, 54–55, 321; definition of, 50. *See also* African Americans; collaborative archaeology; Native Americans
Diamond, Jared, 139
Digital Archaeological Record, The, 283–84
DNA, 230, 239–40
Drennan, Robert D., 318
Dunnell, Robert, 12, 15
Dye, David H., 191n1

East Asia, 84
education: broad trends in, 313–14; cost of, 307–8; of CRM archaeologists, 302–3; effect of neoliberalism on, 113–14; SAA and, 37–38
Eisler, Riane, 140
employment: academic, 305–7, 308–10; in Europe, 310; hiring of interdisciplinary, 224–25; in private sector, 299–301; in public sector, 298–99; salaries, 303–4, 310; trends in, 310–13
England/United Kingdom, 243–44, 296

English language, 80–82
Epperson, Terrence, 104, 105, 107
ethics: of collaboration, 57; legislated, 49; SAA Code of, 39–40, 48, 131, 132
ethnographic archaeologies, 62–63
ethnography, 183
Europe, 310
Evans Report, 35
Executive Order 11593, 163–64

Fagan, Brian, 11
Fagan, Brian (fictional), 278–79
Fairbanks, Charles, 103, 136, 277
feminist archaeology: challenges of, 111–12; historical context of, 107–9; theory and practice of, 109–10
Ferguson, T. J., 52, 148, 321
Fletcher, Alice, 30, 42
Ford, Richard, 137
Franklin, Maria, 318–19
Fritz, John, 137
Fryxell Award for Interdisciplinary Research, 221

Galison, Peter, 15
Garbage Project, 141
Gell, Alfred, 199
gender: of CRM archaeologists, 303; historical trends in, 305–7; equality and the SAA, 37; parity shift in archaeology of, 113. *See also* feminist archaeology
Gero, Joan, 20
Giddens, Anthony, 198
Gillespie, Susan D., 203
Global Justice Movement, 140
Goodwin, Charles, 10
Gordon, Edmund, 104
Gould, Richard, 141
Graffiti Archaeological Project, 143

Guston, David, 149

Hancock, Graham, 279
Harré, Rom, 274
Harvey, David, 98
Heckenberger, Michael J. et al., 204
Hegel, Georg W. F., 199
Hegmon, Michelle, 19, 149–50
Heidegger, Martin, 198
heritage tourism, 312
historical archaeology, 103; antiracist politics in, 104–6; processualism in, 104; reluctance to address race in, 107
historical ecology, 232–33
Historic Preservation Fund, 162, 163
Historic Sites Act, 160
Hodder, Ian, 57
Hohokam, 149, 242
Holmes, W. H., 33
Holthaus, Gary, 138
homelessness, archaeology of, 144–46
Hopi, 148
human behavioral ecology, 228, 229

identity, 200; bioarchaeology of, 240; national, 76–77; politics, 134
Indian Claims Commission, 55
inequality: definition of, 96; in SAA 50th Anniversary volume, 94–95; within and between national boundaries, 77–79
Indigenous archaeology, 59–60
Indigenous Populations Interest Group (SAA), 186
Inouye, Daniel, 178
Integrated History and Future of People on Earth, 140
intellectual property, archaeological data as, 175

interdisciplinary archaeology, 220–21; hiring in, 224–25; transdisciplinary projects in, 241–46; trends in, 222–25;
Isaac, Glyn, 227

Jelderk, Judge, 187
Jordan, Brigitte, 20
Joyce, Rosemary, 111, 319

Keane, Webb, 199
Kehoe, Alice, 135
Kelly, Robert, 140
Kennewick Man, 52, 187, 237, 322
Keyser-Tracqui, Christine et al., 240
Killick, David, 243–44
King, Tom, 163
Kingsley Plantation, 136
Kleindienst, Maxine R., 137
Knudson, Ruthann, 12
Kuwanwisiwma, Leigh, 62

Lanata, José Luis, 318
landscapes, 148, 196; intensive fieldwork and, 203–4; power of, 200; as relational fields, 199
Latin America: archaeological theory in, 82–84; increased foreign archaeological participation in, 80; linguistic boundaries and, 81–82; SAA and, 36–37, 84; students in North America from, 87; trends in archaeology of, 79–85; university development in, 84
Latin American Antiquity, 36
Latour, Bruno, 199, 200
La Venta, 203
learned societies: function of, 27–28; funding of archaeology by, 29–30; local, as advocates of preservation,

30, 31; regional, 41–42; role of women in, 30
Leone, Mark P., 95, 105–6
Lindauer, Owen, 294
Little, Barbara, 138, 139, 319
Loren, Diana, 201
Lovis, William A., 191n1
Ludlow Collective, 100–101, 132
Lyng v. Northwest Indian Cemetery Protective Association, 168

Mack, Mark E., 105
MacNeish, Richard, 229–30
Manifest Destiny, 134
Martin, Debra L., 237
Marx, Karl, 199
Marxist archaeology, 58
material culture, 195-96
materiality, 195–96, 199
Matthews, Christopher, 59
Mauss, Marcel, 196
Maya, 239
Mazoyer, Marcel, 139
McClurg, Virginia, 30, 31, 42
McDavid, Carol, 57–58, 147, 148
McGhee, Fred L., 147–48
McGimsey, Charles, 135
McGuire, Randall H., 19, 20, 58
McIntosh, Roderick et al., 20
McKern, W. C., 34
Merleau-Ponty, Maurice, 198
Mesa Verde, 31, 149
Meskell, Lynn, 320
Mexico, 76
Mills, Barbara J., 202
Mimbres, 149
Minnis, Paul E., 139
Moundbuilder Myth, 134–35
Mullins, Paul R., 59
Munro, Natalie D., 229

Naranjo, Theresa, 202
National Environmental Policy Act, 161
National Historic Preservation Act (NHPA), 53, 54, 135, 148, 161, 319, 321; public in, 319; Section 110 of, 163. *See also* Section 106 (NHPA)
National Register of Historic Places, 163–64, 168–69
National Science Foundation, 244–45, 295
Native American Graves Protection and Repatriation Act (NAGPRA), 37, 148; ambiguity of, 179; conservatism of SAA regarding, 186–87; culturally unidentifiable remains and, 187; effect on bioarchaeology of, 237–38, 322; as extension of 1960s activism, 184; increased dialogue between museums and Native Americans because of, 55, 181; increase in collaborative research because of, 55; not initiated by the discipline, 180; oppositional relationship created by, 182; perceived as threat to archaeology, 180, 181; questions raised by, 188
Native Americans: as archaeologists, 181–82, 186; as archaeology professors, 186; cultural resource management and, 54, 148, 167–69, 173; issue of identity and, 187; Section 106 and, 167, 168, 169, 171–72
Native American Scholarship Fund (SAA), 37
Neanderthals, 229
neoliberalism, 98–99, 113–14
New Archaeology, 135, 183, 184
niche construction, 231

Orser, Charles, 107

Patel, Samir S., 142, 143
Patterson, Thomas C., 113, 320
Pauketat, Timothy R., 320–21
Paynter, Robert, 318–19
Peabody Museum of Archaeology and Ethnology, 29
personhood, 201
Peru, 76–77, 83
Pikirayi, Innocent, 141
Plog, Fred, 137
Pluciennik, Mark, 276
politics: identity as, 134; in archaeology, 77, 318–19; in collaboration archaeology, 58, 59; racial, in archaeology, 104. *See also* feminist archaeology
post-processual archaeology, 38, 57, 136, 194, 204
Powell, John Wesley, 31
Praetzellis, Adrian, 285–86
processual archaeology, 38, 104, 135, 136, 180, 204
public archaeology, 60, 135; activist politics in, 58–59; community building and civic renewal in, 140; contributions to wisdom by, 138; contribution to ecological issues by, 137–38; gains of archaeology from, 147; issue of public interests in, 58, 131–34; non-archaeological problems in, 141–46; transformative learning and, 151; translational research and, 150–51. *See also* collaborative archaeology
Public Education Committee (SAA), 38
public interest, 132–33, 319
Putnam, Frederic Ward, 29

Quirigua, 32

racism: anti-, in historical archaeology, 103, 104–7; ending, 140; as fundamental challenge, 107; as too sensitive a topic in early archaeological studies, 103–4
Reagan administration, 162
Redman, Charles, 134, 139, 242
Red Power, 319
Register of Professional Archaeologists, 41, 303
Reilly, F. Kent, III, 243
Reinhard, Karl, 238
repatriation, 322–23 *See also* Native American Graves Protection and Repatriation Act (NAGPRA)
Repatriation Committee (SAA), 187, 192n3
Rodman, Amy Oakland, 243
Roudart, Laurence, 139

SAA Archaeological Record, The, 186
Sabloff, Jeremy, 136–37, 318
sacred sites: landscape scale of, 173–74; preserving, 168–69
Saitta, Dean J., 100, 101
Sandlin, Jennifer, 147
sankofa, 139
Sapienza, John Thomas, 21
science: English as language of, 81; mummy, 238; and religion, 182. *See also* theory
Sebastian, Lynne, 321
Section 106 (NHPA): "adverse effects" and, 164–66, 170; eligibility and, 163–64; Native American involvement with, 167, 168, 169, 171–72; 1979 regulation, 161–63, 164, 165, 166; 1986 changes in, 163, 164–66; 1992 changes in, 163, 166–69; 1999 changes in, 170–71, 173; prognostication on, 173–76; sacred sites and, 171–72, 173–74
Shanks, Michael, 19

Shelby White-Leon Levy Program for Archaeological Publication, The, 281
Silliman, Stephen, 201, 321
Singleton, Theresa, 102, 136
Snead, James, 318
Society for American Archaeology (SAA), 31; championing of interdisciplinary approaches by, 221; Code of Ethics, 39–40, 48, 131, 132; conservatism regarding NAGPRA of, 185, 186–88; continuity of issues dealt with, 41; Evans Report, 35; 50th anniversary of, 1, 11, 12, 35, 94–95; growth in membership of, 305; mission statement, 40–41; NAGPRA causes split in direction of, 180–81; Native American involvement in, 186; 1986 Statement Concerning the Treatment of Human Remains of, 180; preservation law and, 160, 163; student constituency of, 37–38; trends in last 25 years of, 35–41. *See also* names of individual committees
Society for Historical Archaeology, 303, 304
Society of Professional Archaeologists, 34
Spector, Janet, 58, 108, 276–77
Stapp, Darby, 148
State Archaeological Association of Ohio, 30
state historic preservation offices (SHPOs), 148, 162
Stoecker, Randy, 146–47
Stoffle, Richard, 148
Stottman, Jay, 142–43
Student Affairs Committee (SAA), 37
Suchman, Lucy, 12–13, 17–18, 20
SUNY Stony Brook, 245

Taylor, Walter W., 273

technology: in archaeology, 11–13; digital revolution in communication, 281–85; non-invasive, 13, 243; as a way of crossing boundaries, 90–92
Teotihuacan, 239
theory, 196, 198; in cultural resource management, 320; dualisms in, 193
Thomas, David Hurst, 63
Titterington, P. F., 34
traditionally associated communities, 50
traditional cultural properties, 169
transformative learning, 151
translational research, 150–51
tribal historic preservation offices/officers, 54, 148, 181–82, 322
Trigger, Bruce G., 94, 95
Tringham, Ruth, 111
tuberculosis, 236

United Mine Workers, 101, 132
United Nations' Millennium Development Goals, 141
University College London, 195
University of Louisville Litter Project, 142
University of Pittsburgh, 87
Upham, Steadman, 184
U. S. Army Corps of Engineers, 293–94
U. S. Department of Defense, 293–94, 298, 299
U. S. Department of the Interior, 298, 299
U. S. Department of Transportation, 294, 298, 299

van der Leeuw, Sander E., 134, 322
Van Dyke, Ruth M., 202
visioning, 109–10

Watkins, Joe E. et al., 48
Watson, Patty Jo, 137

Weiner, Annette, 196
Wen, Jiabao, 74
Western Hemisphere Health and Nutrition Project, 234–35
White, Nancy Marie, 277
Wilcox, Michael, 321
Wilkie, Laurie, 110–11
wisdom, 138–39
Women's Anthropological Society of the United States, 30

Wood, James W. et al., 235
World Archaeological Congress, 85, 141
Wright, Henry T., 94–95
Wylie, M. Alison, 15, 108–10

Yamin, Rebecca, 275–76

Zeder, Melinda, 113, 114, 149, 322
Zimmerman, Larry, 63, 144, 319
Zuni, 148